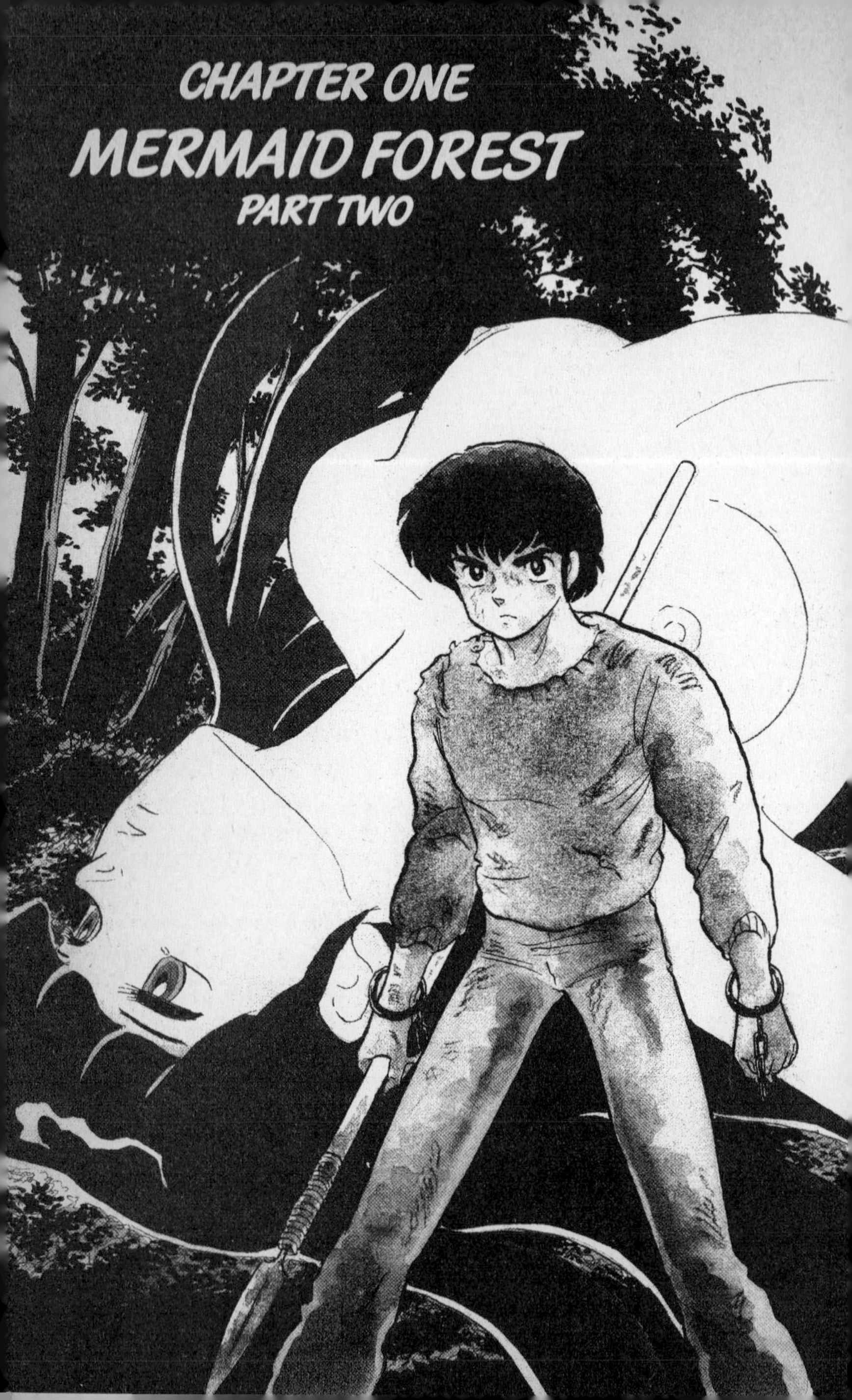
CHAPTER ONE
MERMAID FOREST
PART TWO

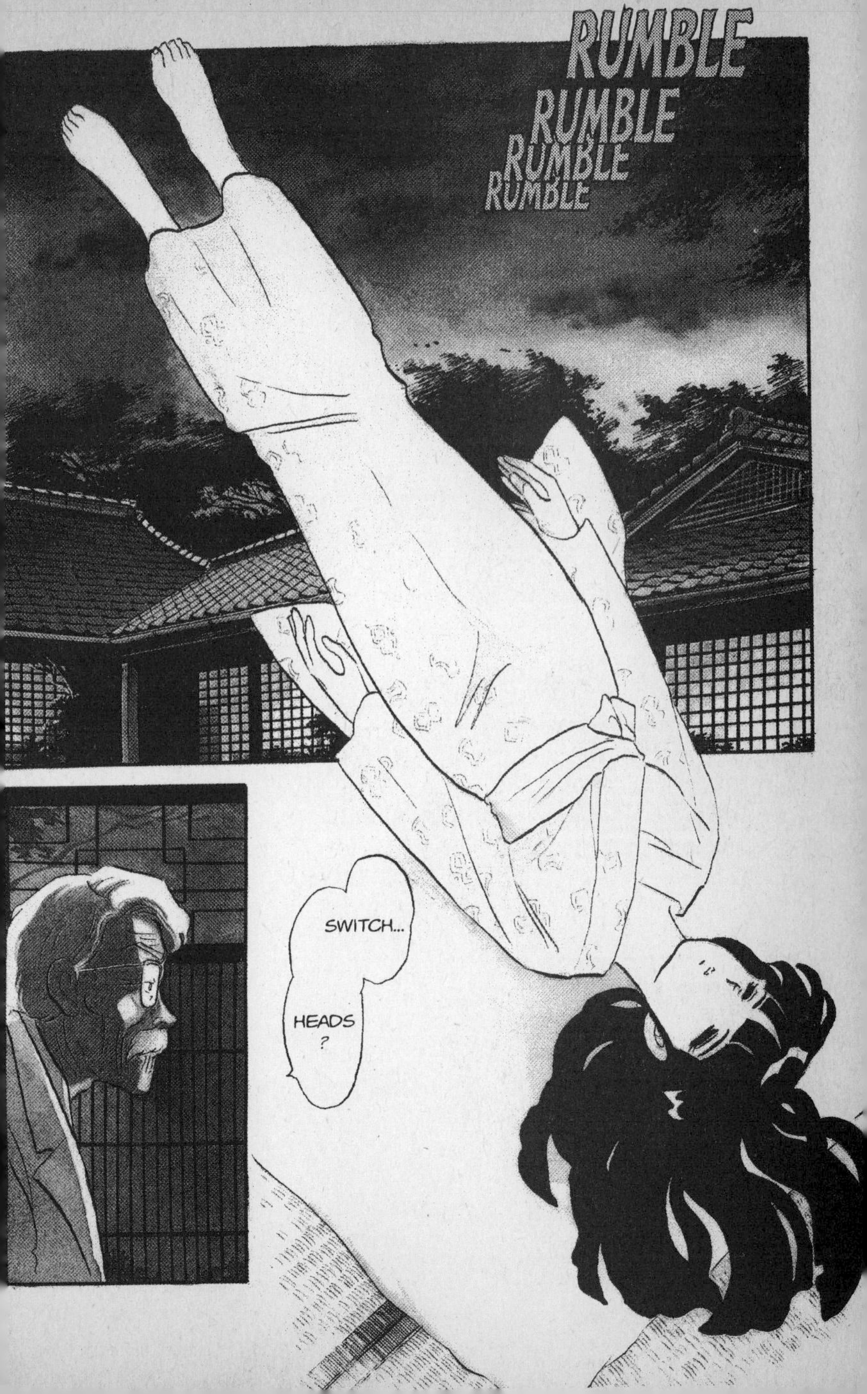
RUMBLE RUMBLE RUMBLE RUMBLE
SWITCH...
HEADS?

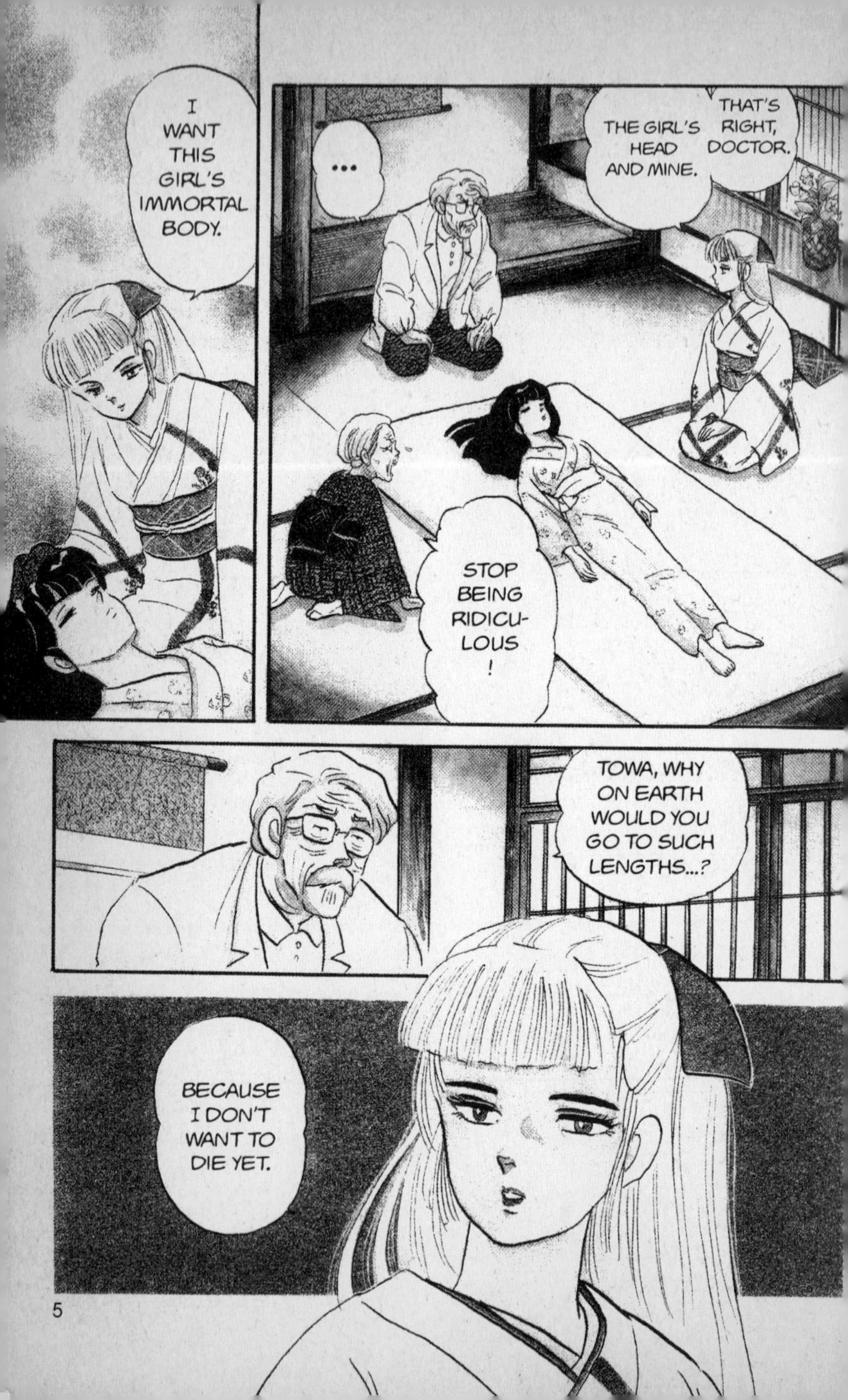
THAT'S RIGHT, DOCTOR.
THE GIRL'S HEAD AND MINE.
...
STOP BEING RIDICU-LOUS!
I WANT THIS GIRL'S IMMORTAL BODY.
TOWA, WHY ON EARTH WOULD YOU GO TO SUCH LENGTHS...?
BECAUSE I DON'T WANT TO DIE YET.

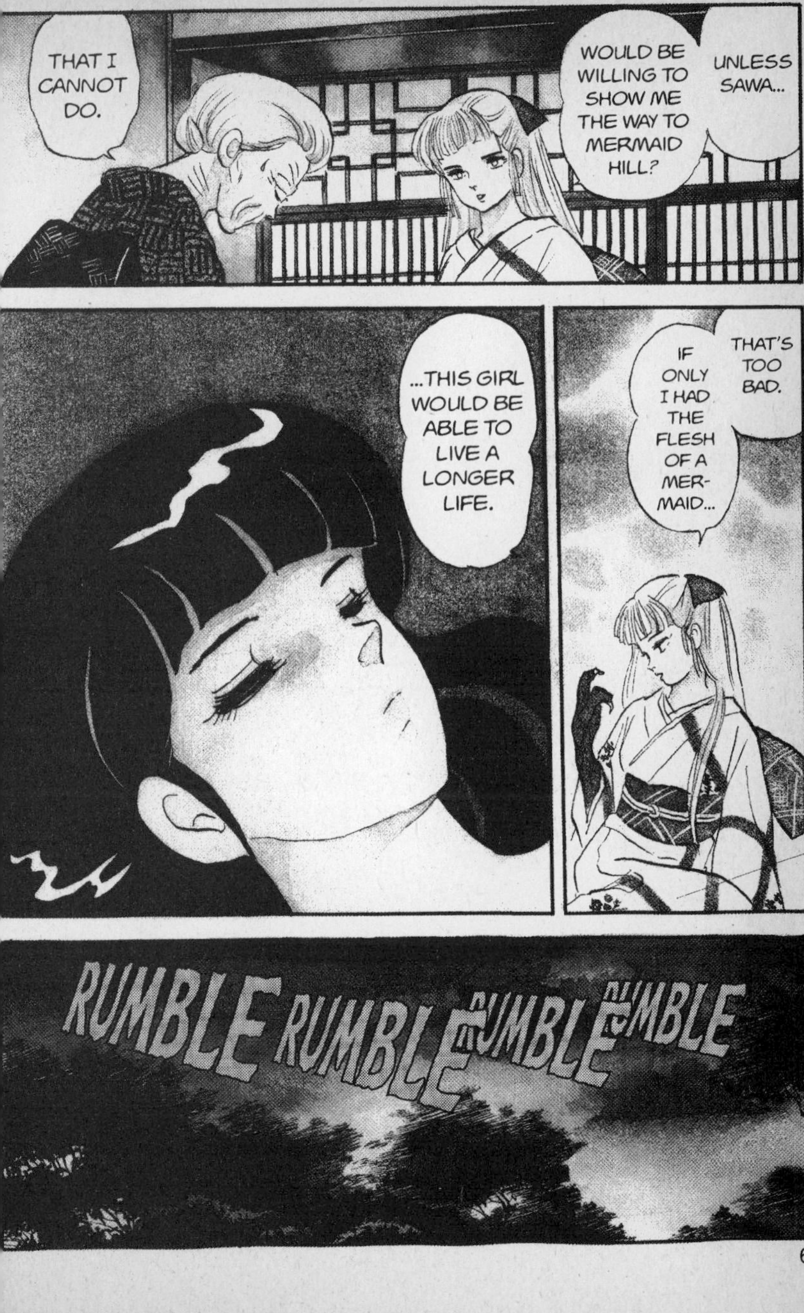
UNLESS SAWA...
WOULD BE WILLING TO SHOW ME THE WAY TO MERMAID HILL?
THAT I CANNOT DO.
THAT'S TOO BAD.
IF ONLY I HAD THE FLESH OF A MER-MAID...
...THIS GIRL WOULD BE ABLE TO LIVE A LONGER LIFE.
RUMBLE RUMBLE RUMBLE RUMBLE

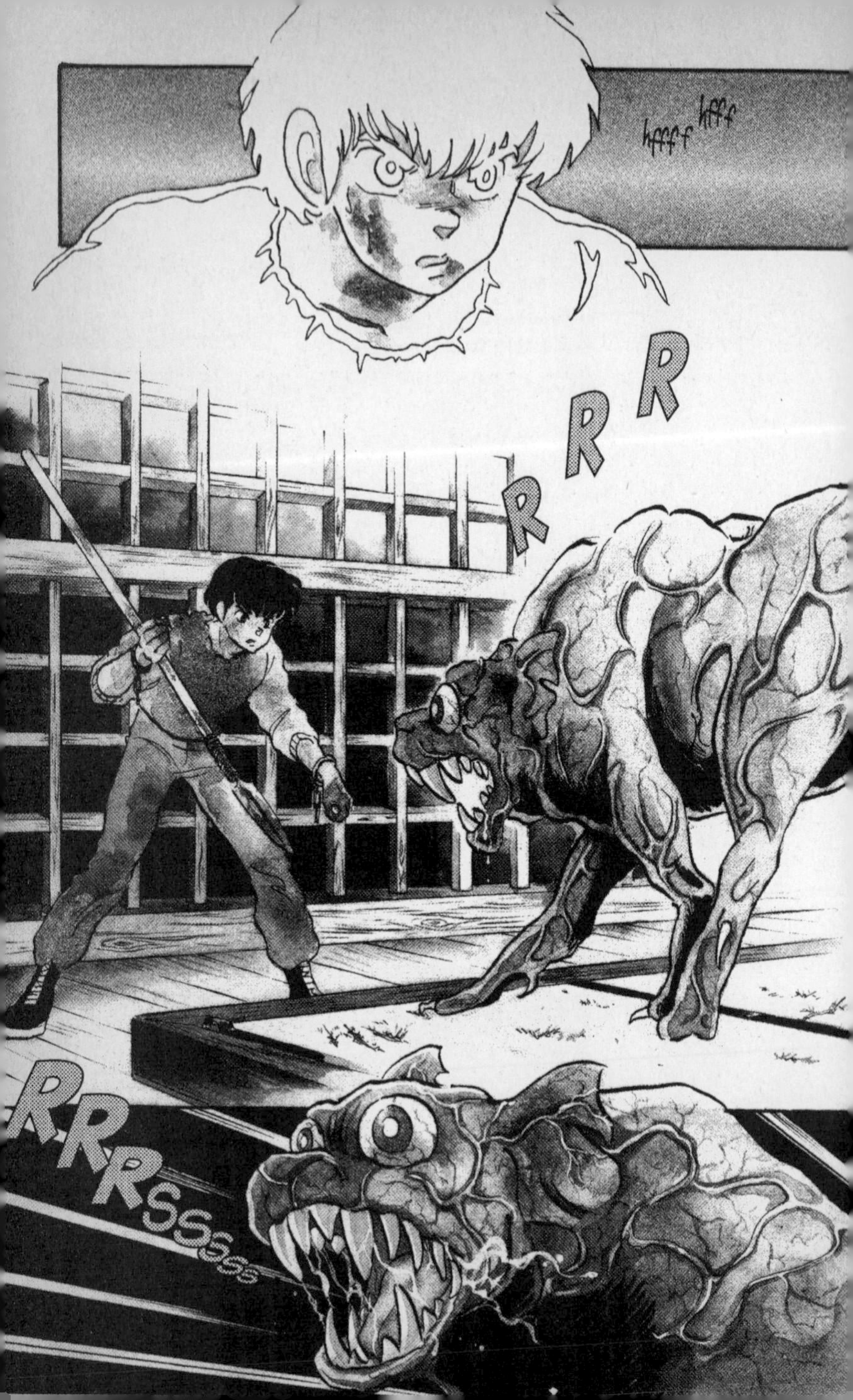
hfff hfff
RRRR
RRRSSSSSS

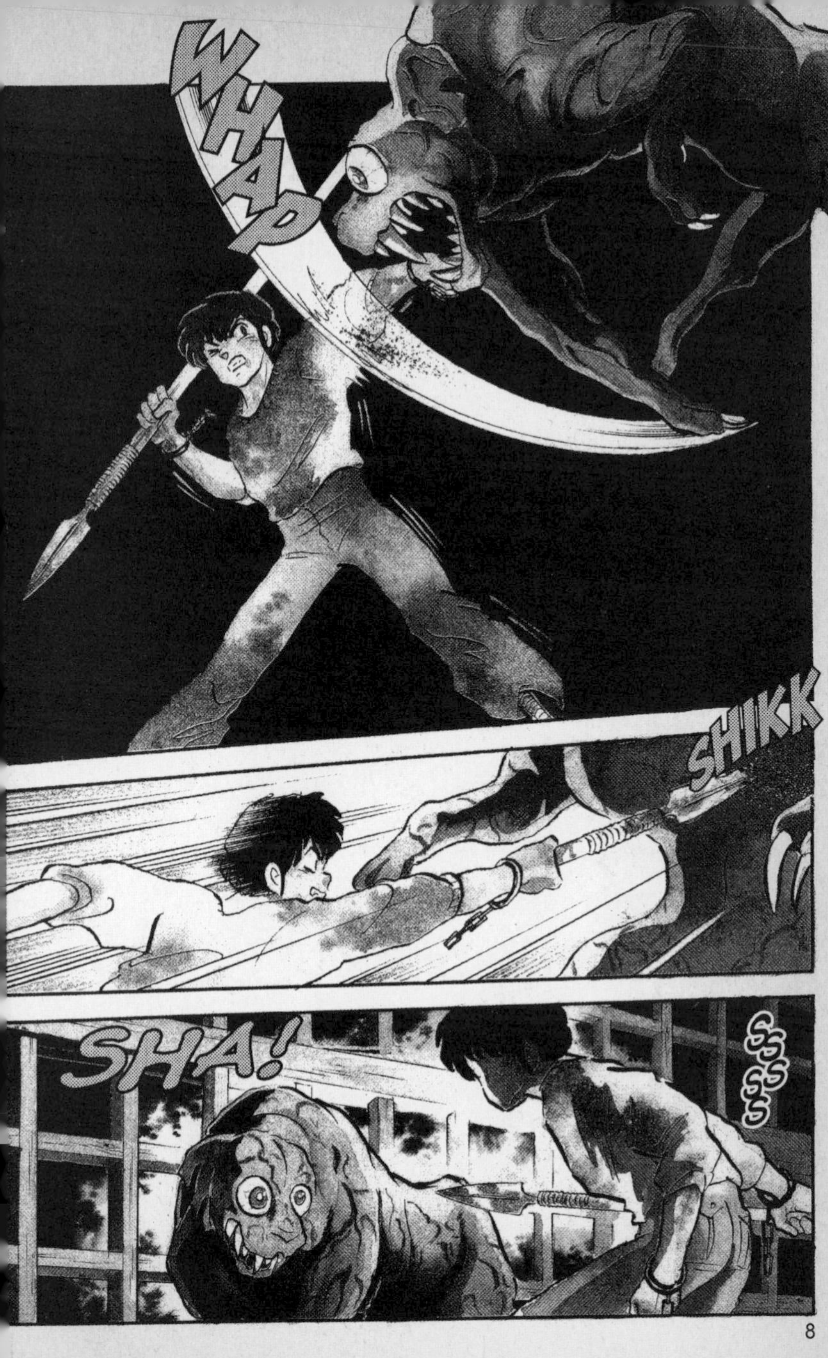

WHAP
SHIKK
SSSSS
SHA!

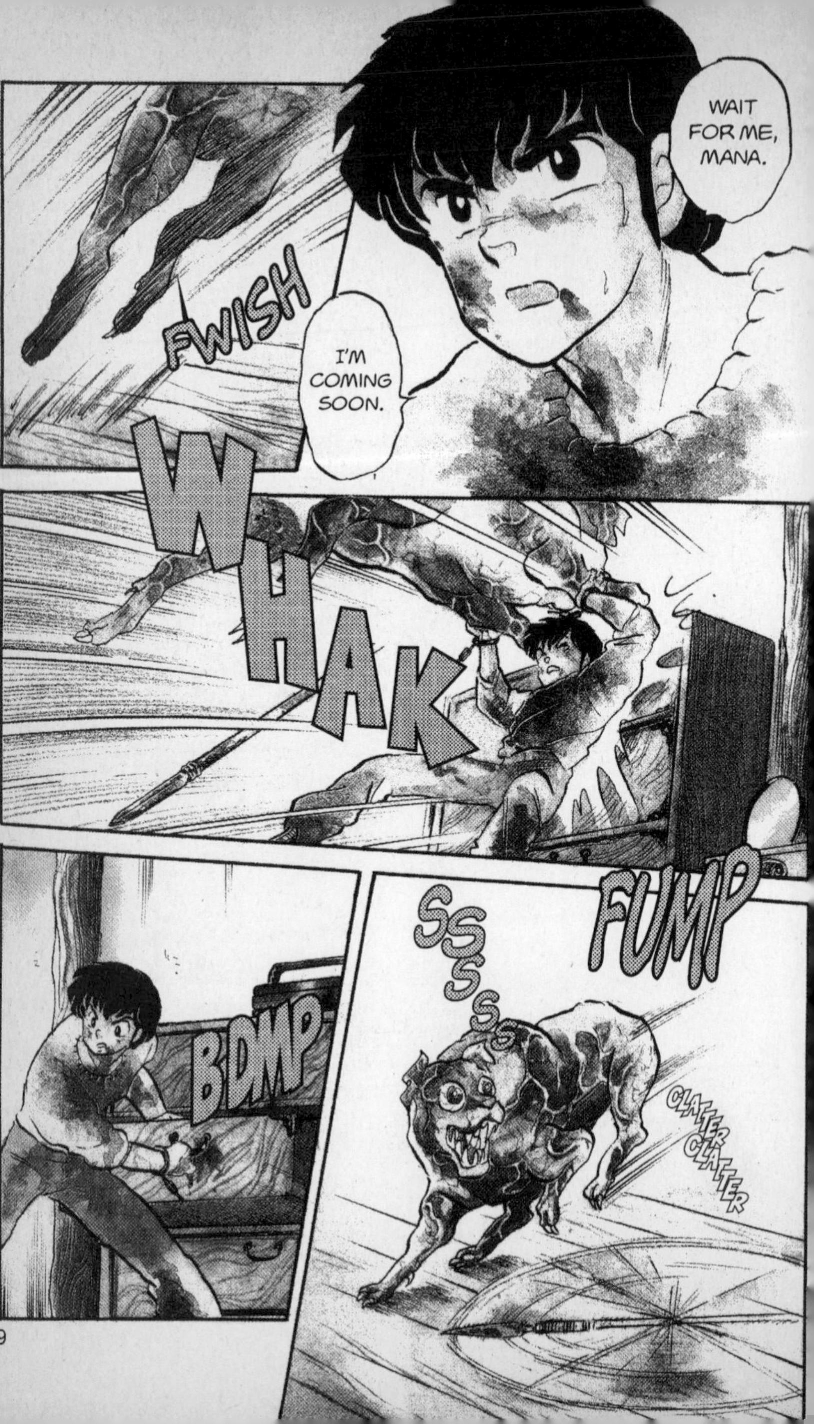
WAIT FOR ME, MANA.
I'M COMING SOON.
FWISH
WHAK
FUMP
SSSSSS
CLATTER CLATTER
BDMP

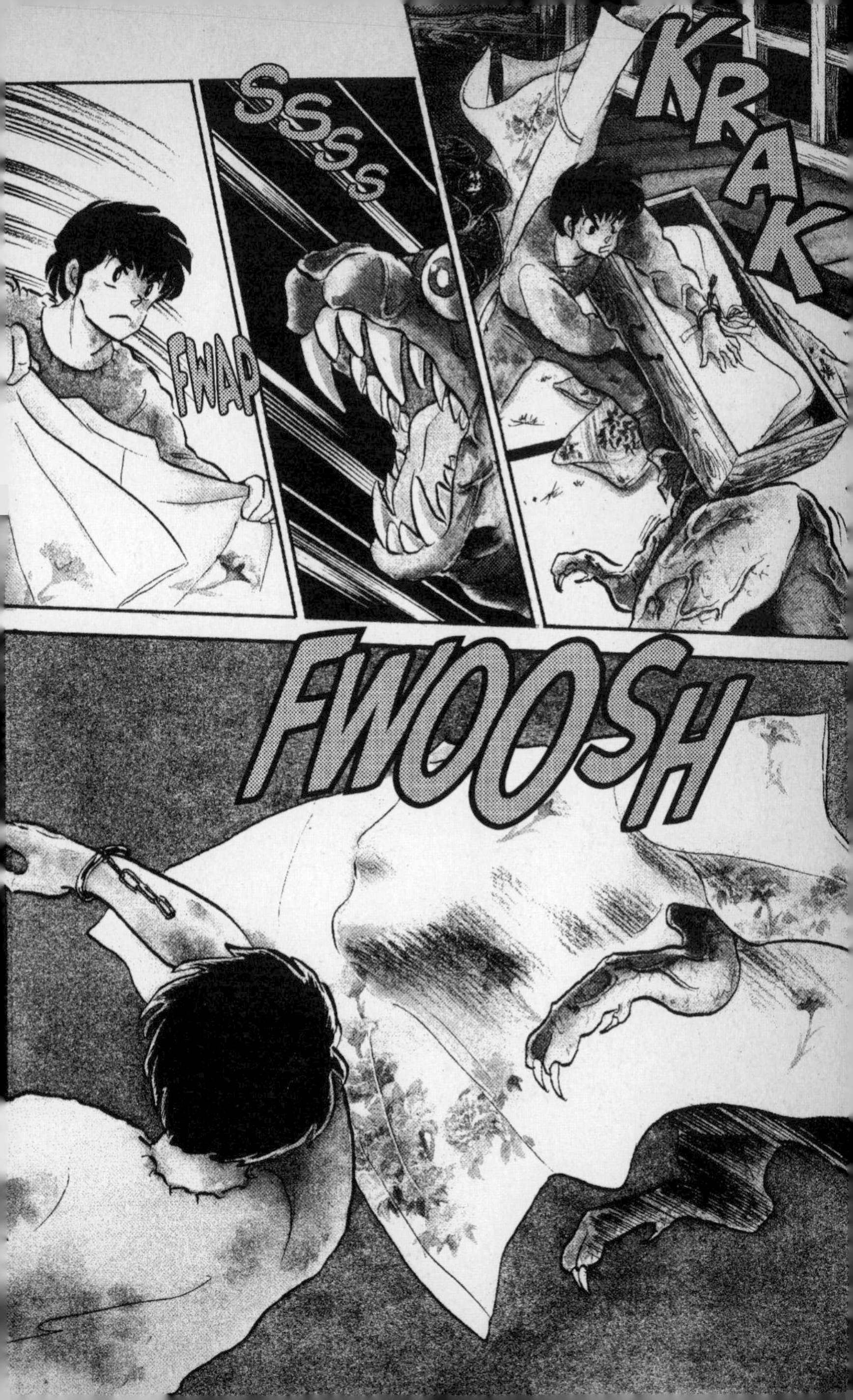
KRAK
SSSS
FWAP
FWOOSH

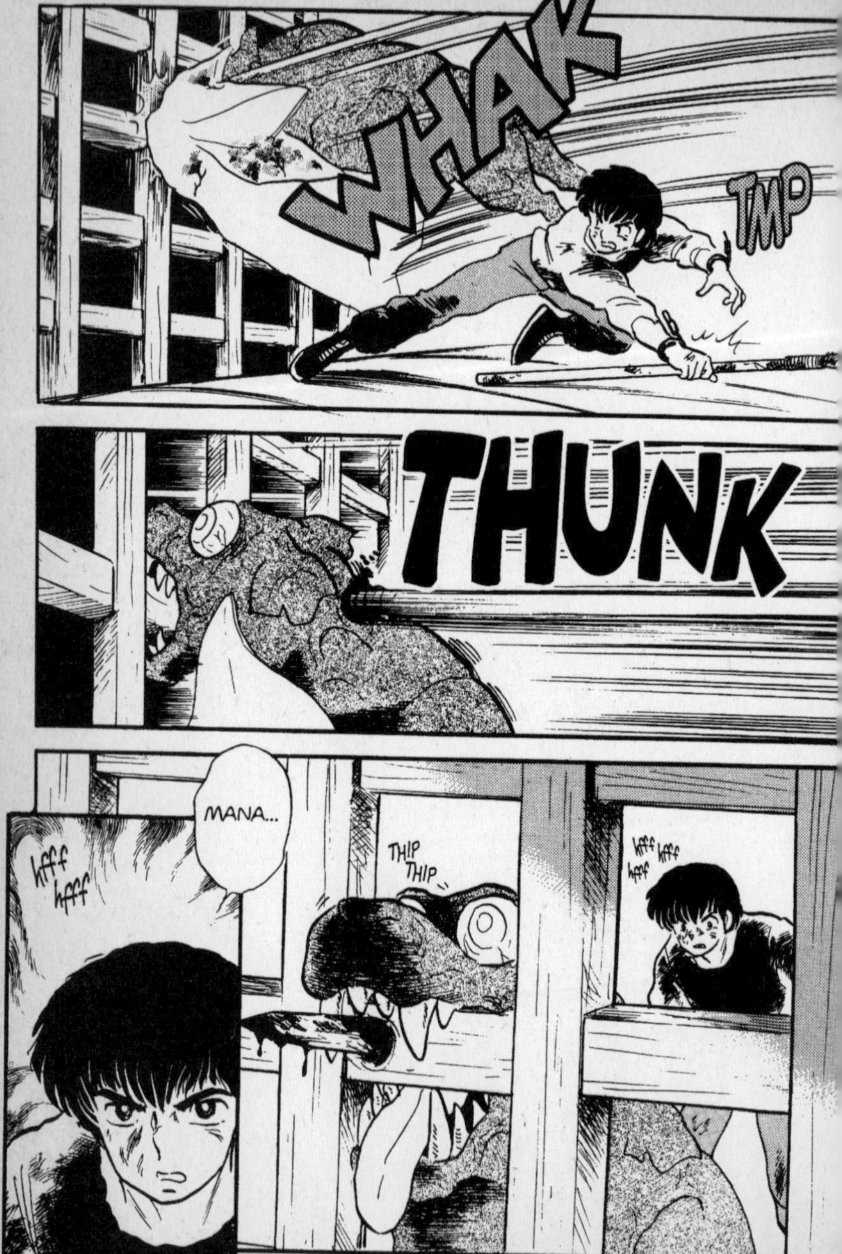
WHAK
TMP
THUNK
hfff hfff hfff
THIP THIP
MANA...
hfff hfff

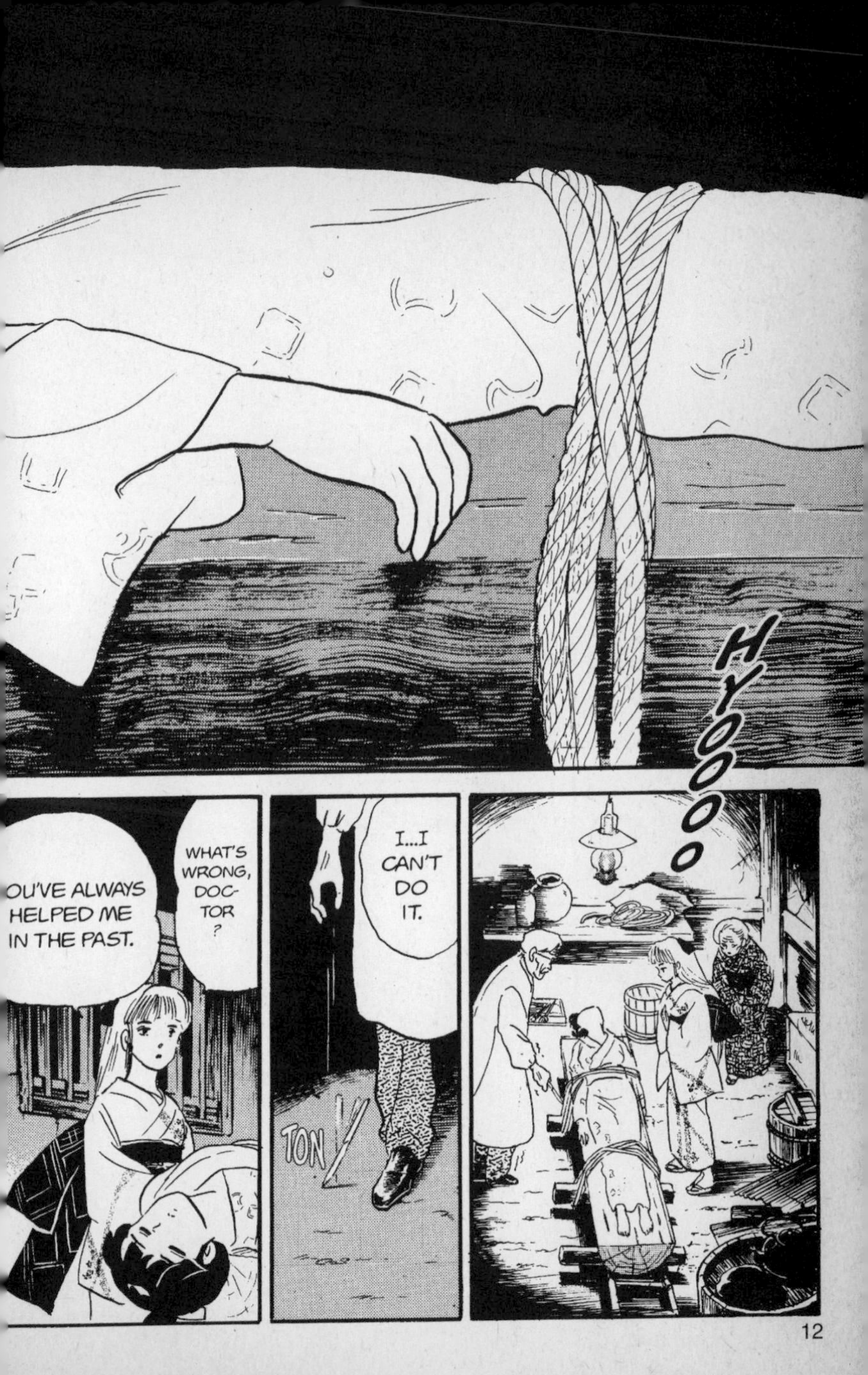
HYOOOOO
I...I CAN'T DO IT.
TON
WHAT'S WRONG, DOCTOR?
OU'VE ALWAYS HELPED ME IN THE PAST.

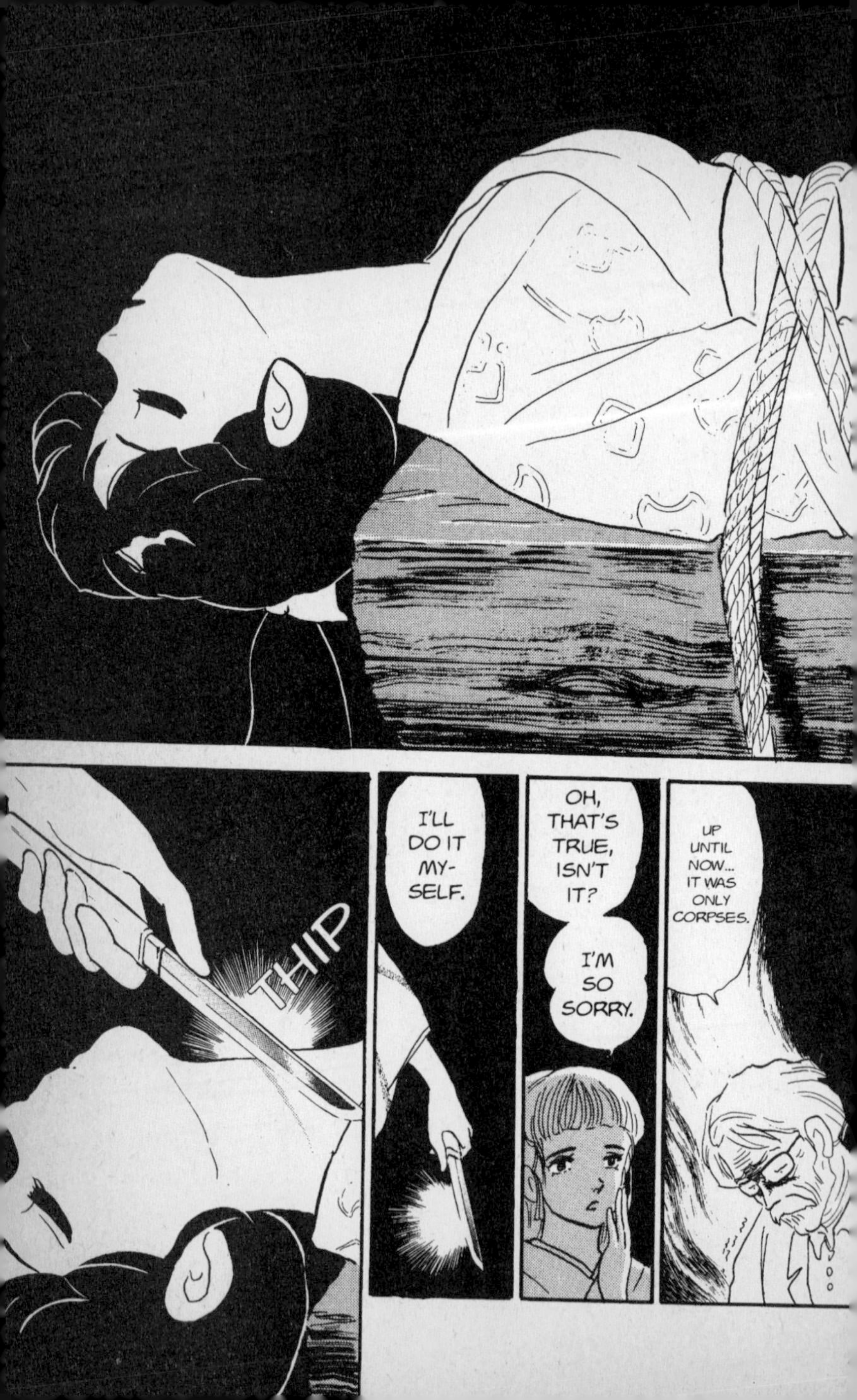
UP UNTIL NOW... IT WAS ONLY CORPSES.
OH, THAT'S TRUE, ISN'T IT?
I'M SO SORRY.
I'LL DO IT MY-SELF.
THIP

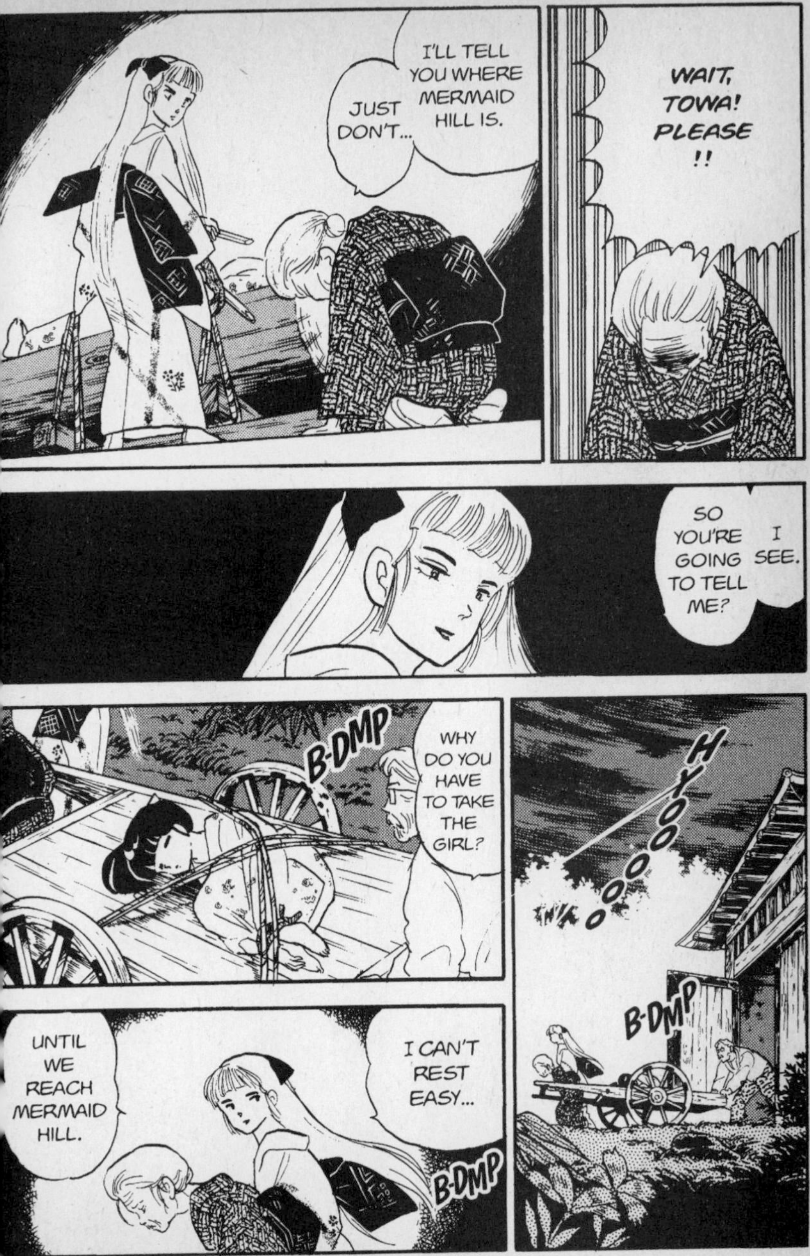
WAIT, TOWA! PLEASE !!
I'LL TELL YOU WHERE MERMAID HILL IS.
JUST DON'T...
I SEE.
SO YOU'RE GOING TO TELL ME?
HYOOOOOO
B-DMP
B-DMP
WHY DO YOU HAVE TO TAKE THE GIRL?
I CAN'T REST EASY...
UNTIL WE REACH MERMAID HILL.
B-DMP

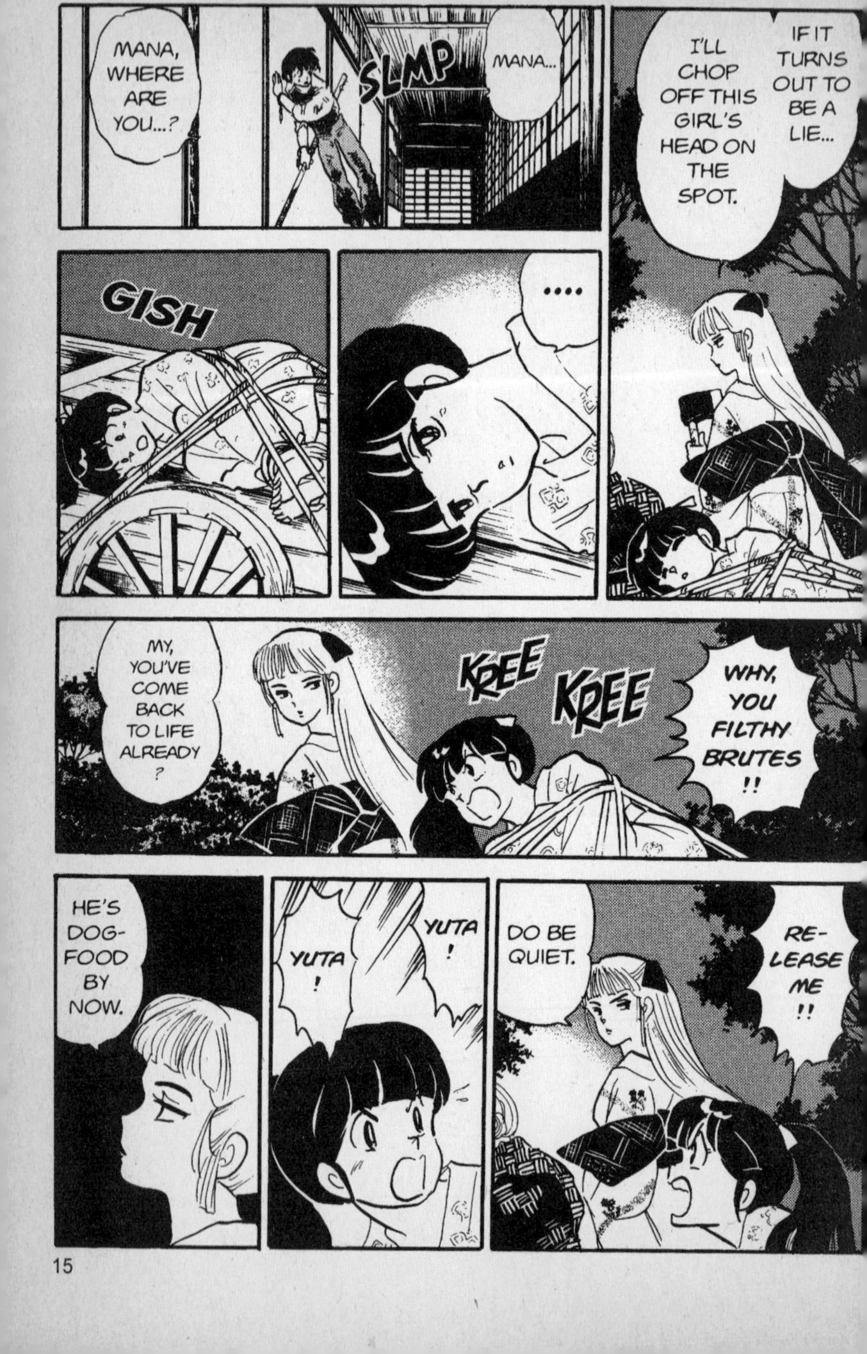
IF IT TURNS OUT TO BE A LIE...
I'LL CHOP OFF THIS GIRL'S HEAD ON THE SPOT.
MANA...
SLMP
MANA, WHERE ARE YOU...?
....
GISH
WHY, YOU FILTHY BRUTES !!
KREE KREE
MY, YOU'VE COME BACK TO LIFE ALREADY ?
RE-LEASE ME !!
DO BE QUIET.
YUTA !
YUTA !
HE'S DOG-FOOD BY NOW.

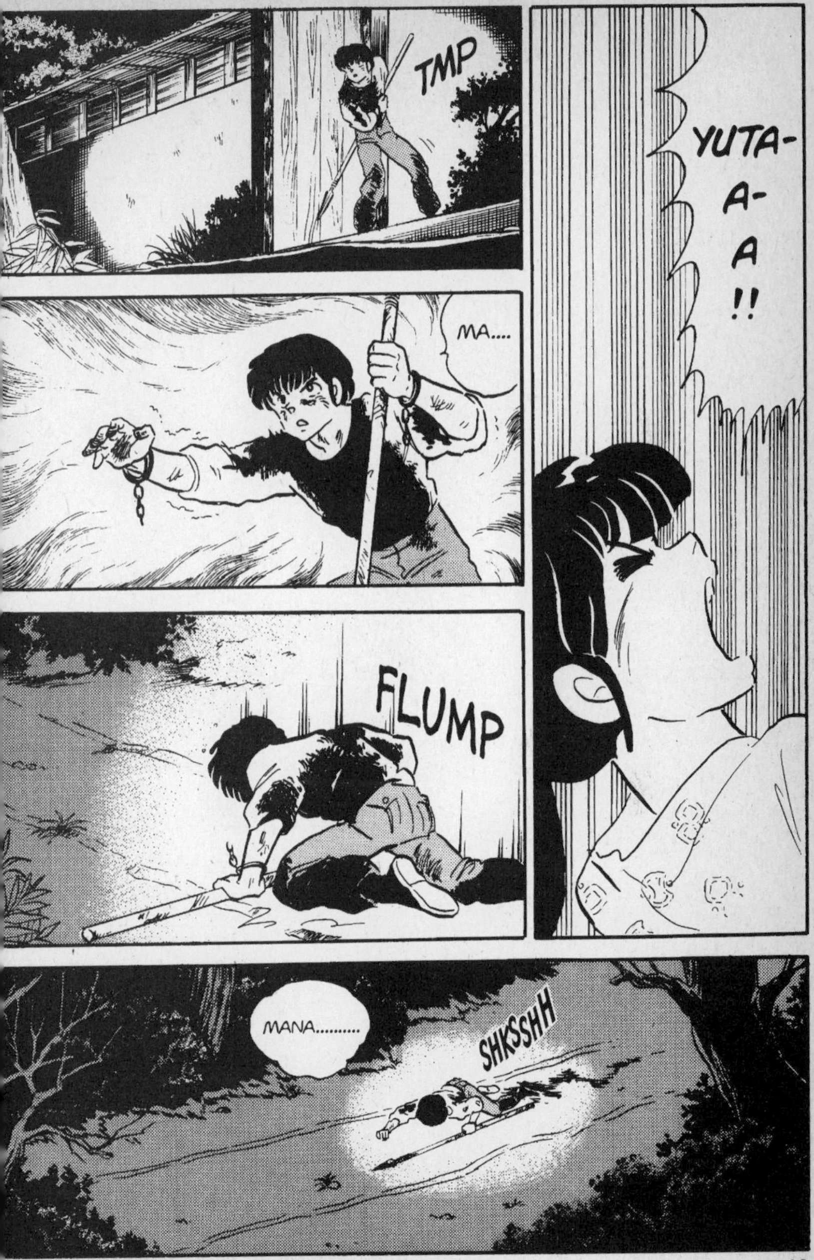
YUTA-A-A!!
TMP
MA....
FLUMP
SHKSSHH
MANA..........

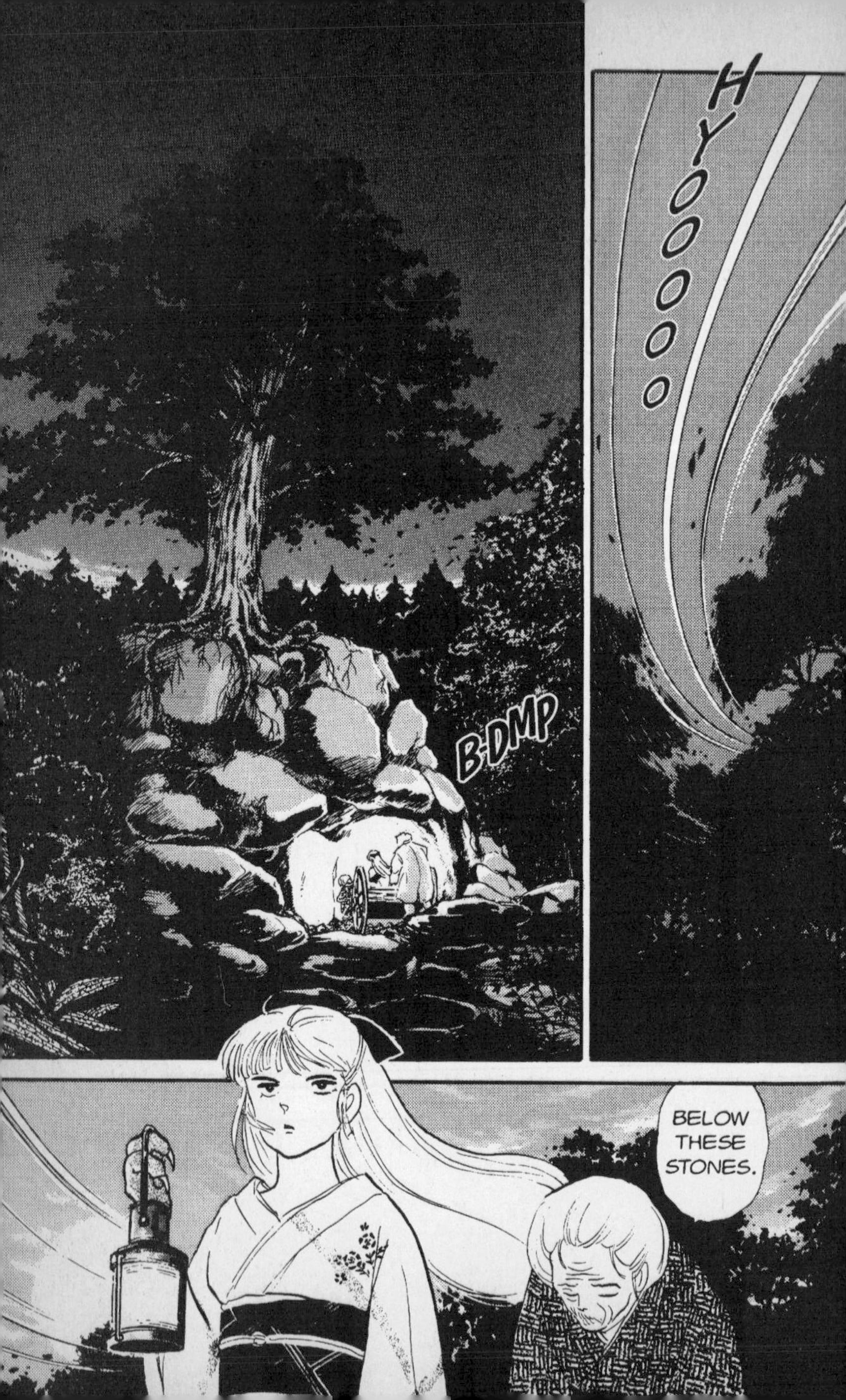
HYOOOOOO
B-DMP
BELOW THESE STONES.

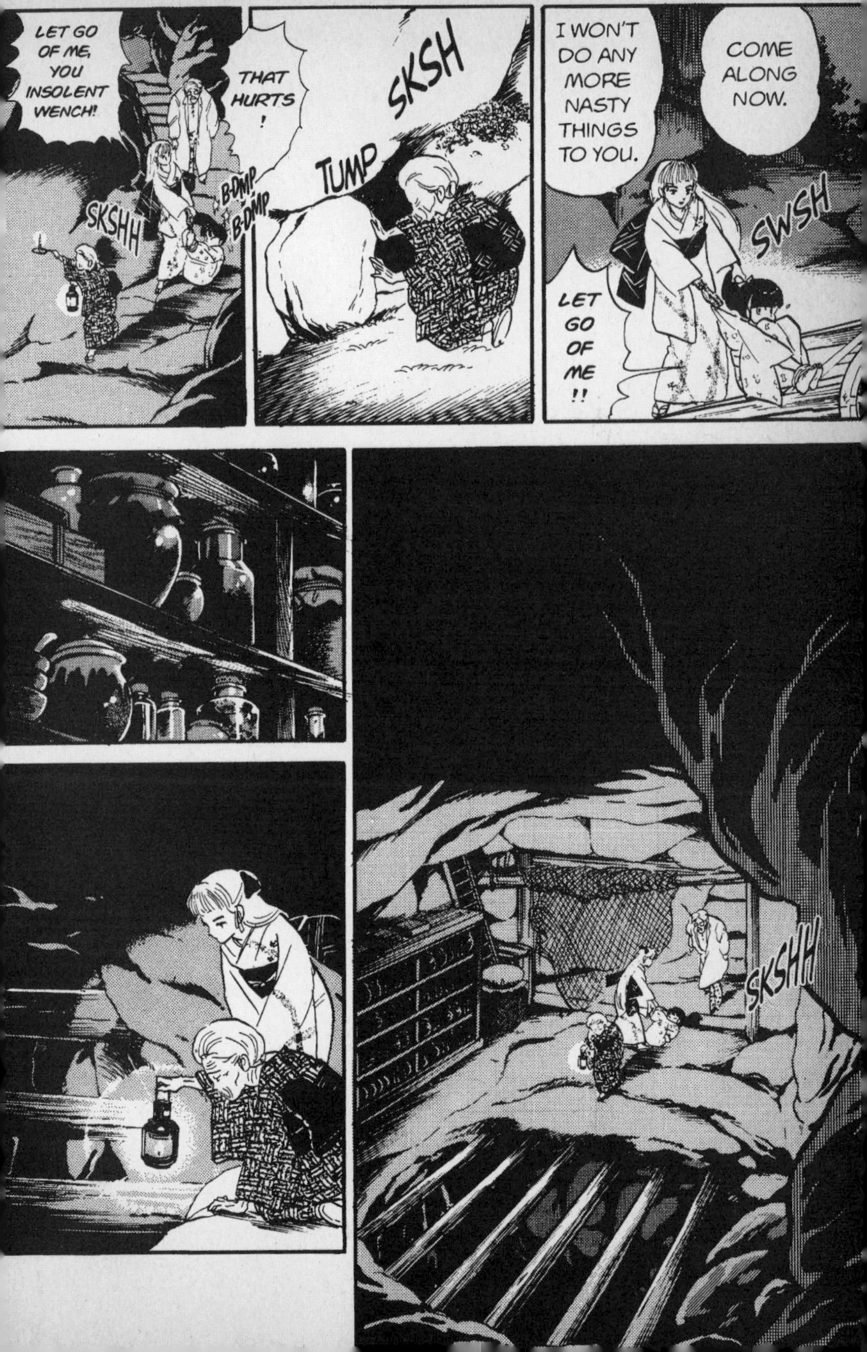
COME ALONG NOW.
I WON'T DO ANY MORE NASTY THINGS TO YOU.
SWSH
LET GO OF ME !!
SKSH
THAT HURTS !
TUMP
B-DMP B-DMP
LET GO OF ME, YOU INSOLENT WENCH!
SKSHH
SKSHH

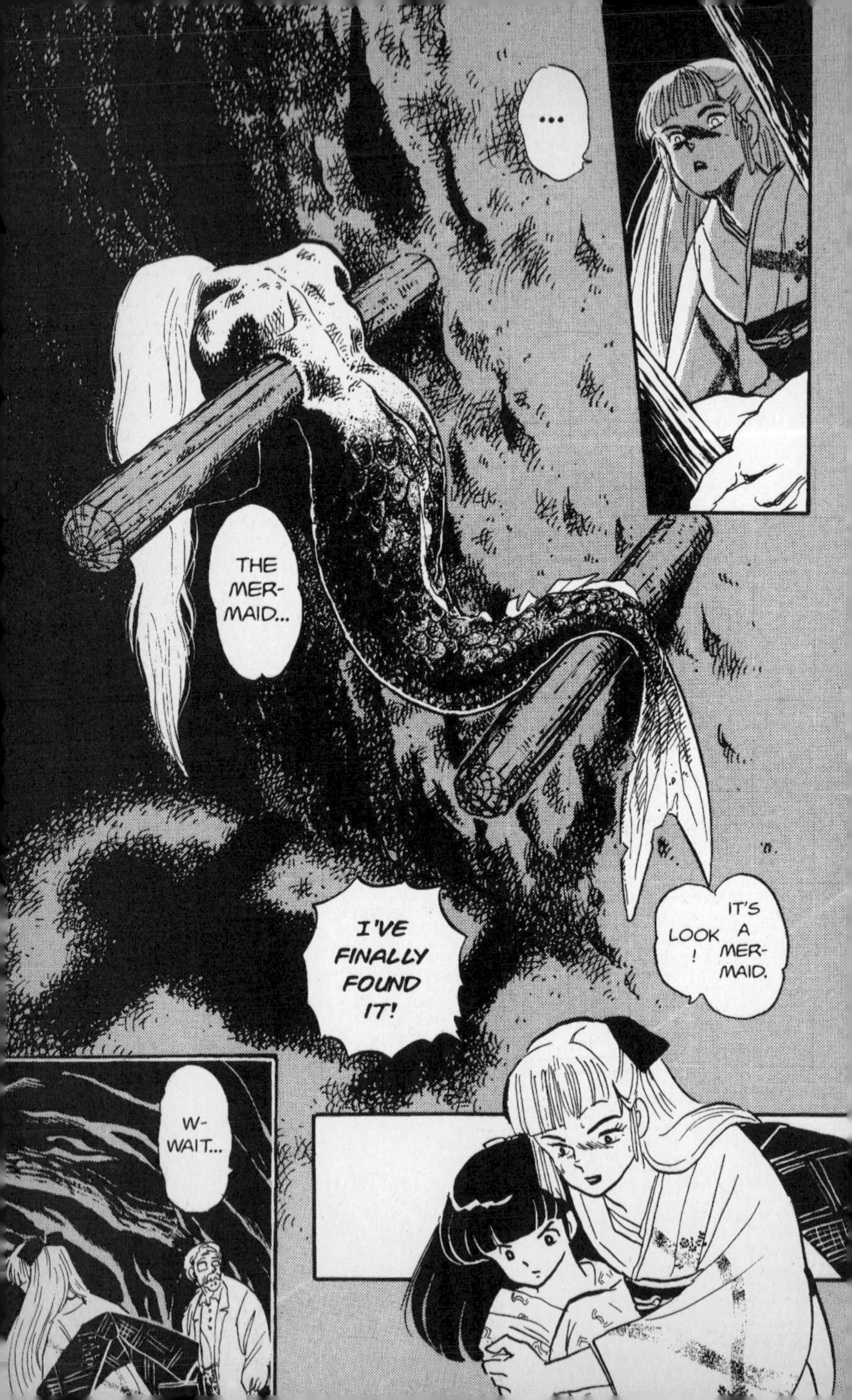
...
THE MER-MAID...
LOOK! IT'S A MER-MAID.
I'VE FINALLY FOUND IT!
W-WAIT...

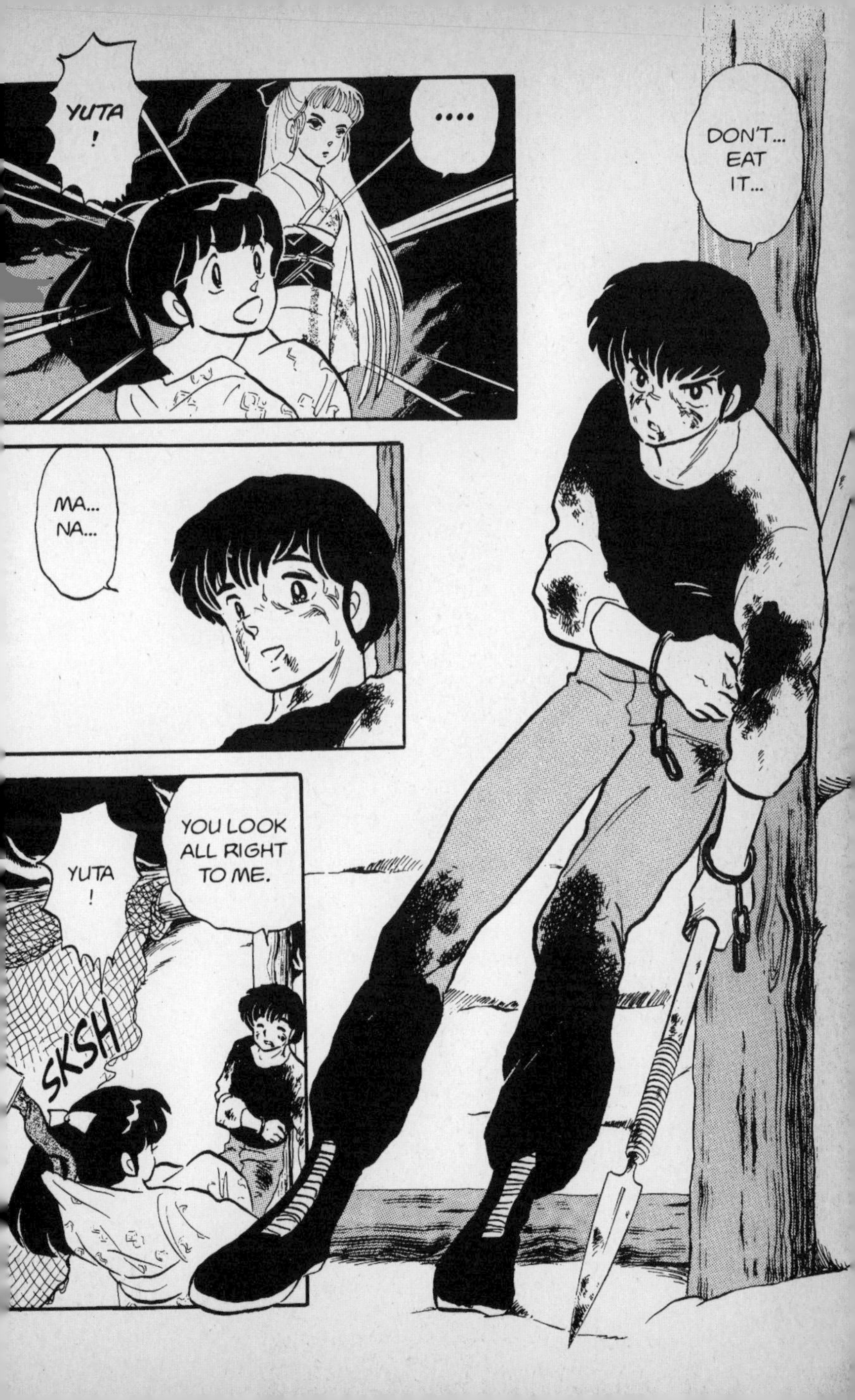
DON'T... EAT IT...
YUTA !
....
MA... NA...
YOU LOOK ALL RIGHT TO ME.
YUTA !
SKSH

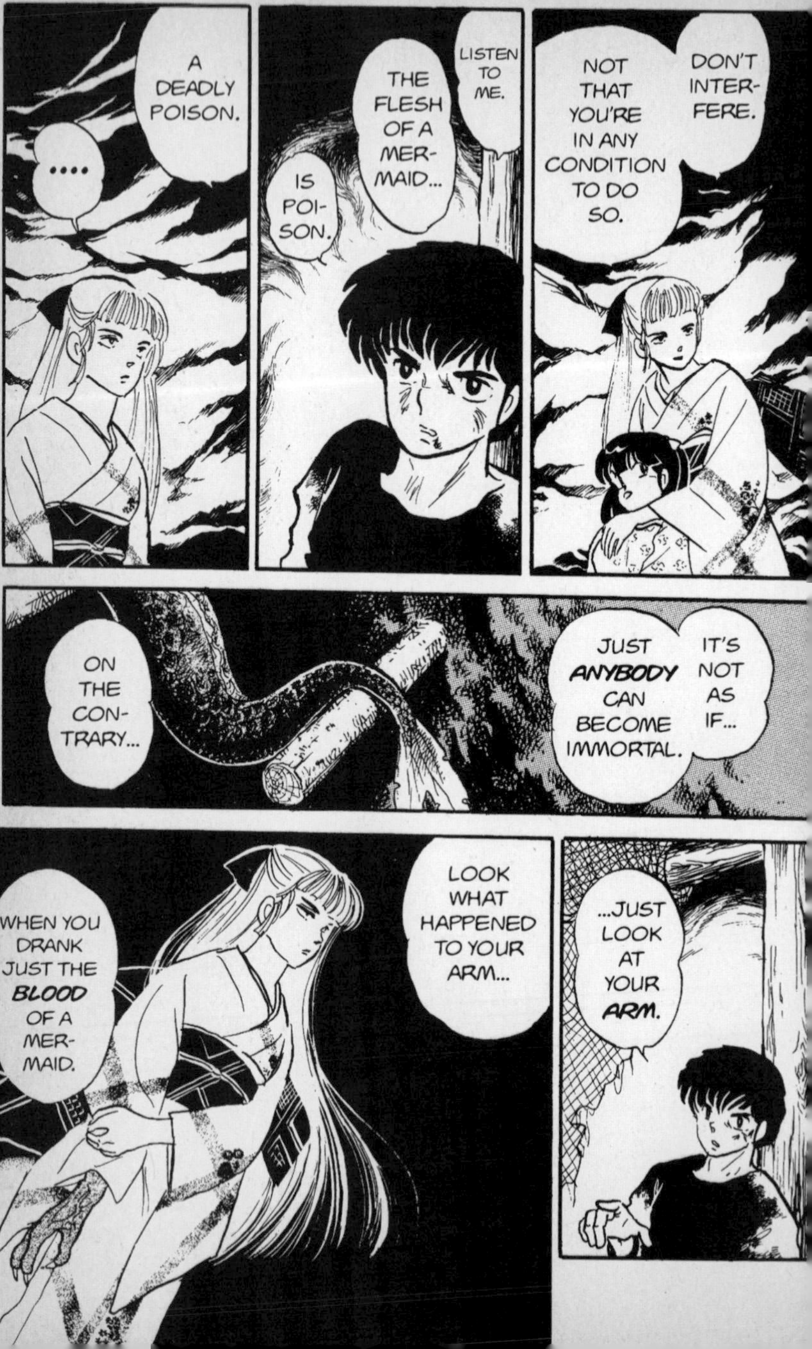
DON'T INTER-FERE.
NOT THAT YOU'RE IN ANY CONDITION TO DO SO.
LISTEN TO ME.
THE FLESH OF A MER-MAID...
IS POI-SON.
A DEADLY POISON.
....
IT'S NOT AS IF...
JUST **ANYBODY** CAN BECOME IMMORTAL.
ON THE CON-TRARY...
...JUST LOOK AT YOUR **ARM**.
LOOK WHAT HAPPENED TO YOUR ARM...
WHEN YOU DRANK JUST THE **BLOOD** OF A MER-MAID.

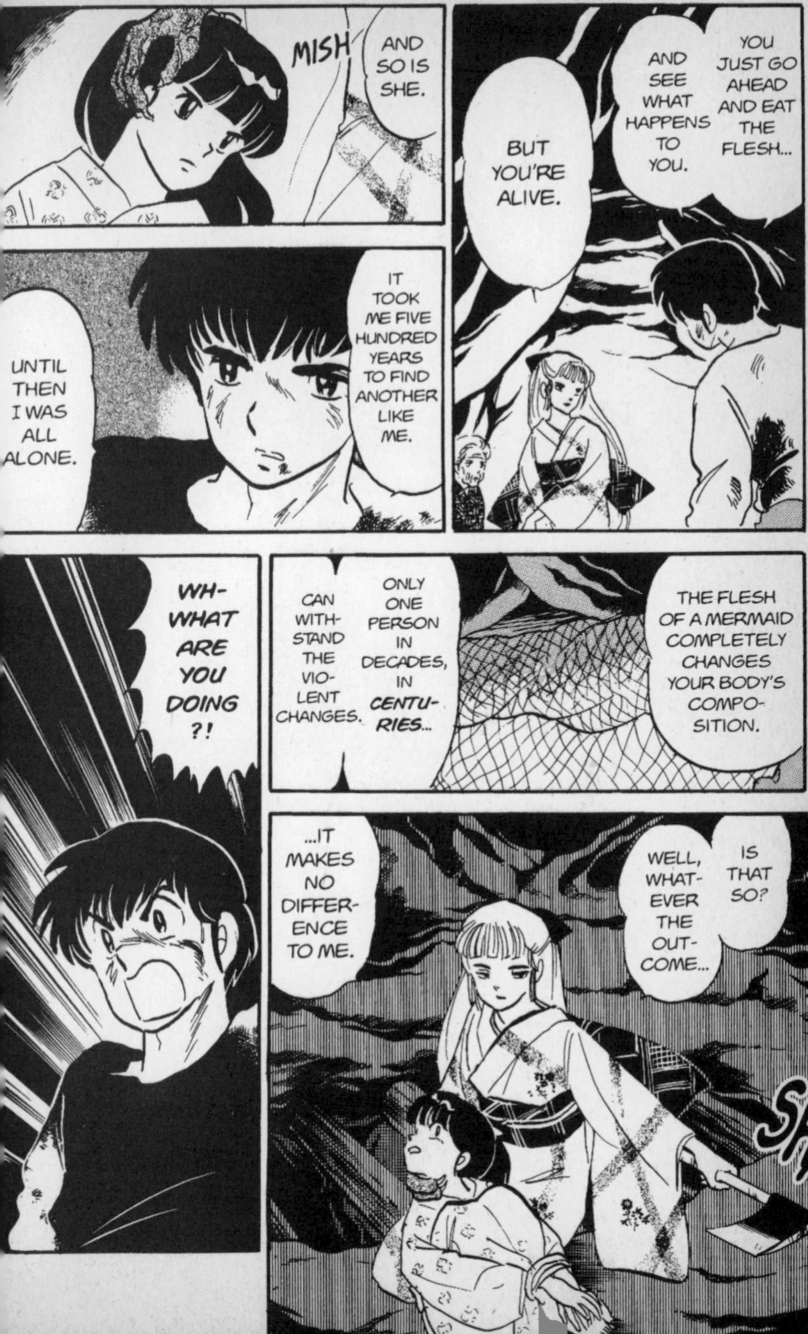
YOU JUST GO AHEAD AND EAT THE FLESH...
AND SEE WHAT HAPPENS TO YOU.
BUT YOU'RE ALIVE.
MISH
AND SO IS SHE.
IT TOOK ME FIVE HUNDRED YEARS TO FIND ANOTHER LIKE ME.
UNTIL THEN I WAS ALL ALONE.
THE FLESH OF A MERMAID COMPLETELY CHANGES YOUR BODY'S COMPO-SITION.
ONLY ONE PERSON IN DECADES, IN *CENTU-RIES*...
CAN WITH-STAND THE VIO-LENT CHANGES.
IS THAT SO?
WELL, WHAT-EVER THE OUT-COME...
...IT MAKES NO DIFFER-ENCE TO ME.
SHA
WH-WHAT ARE YOU DOING?!

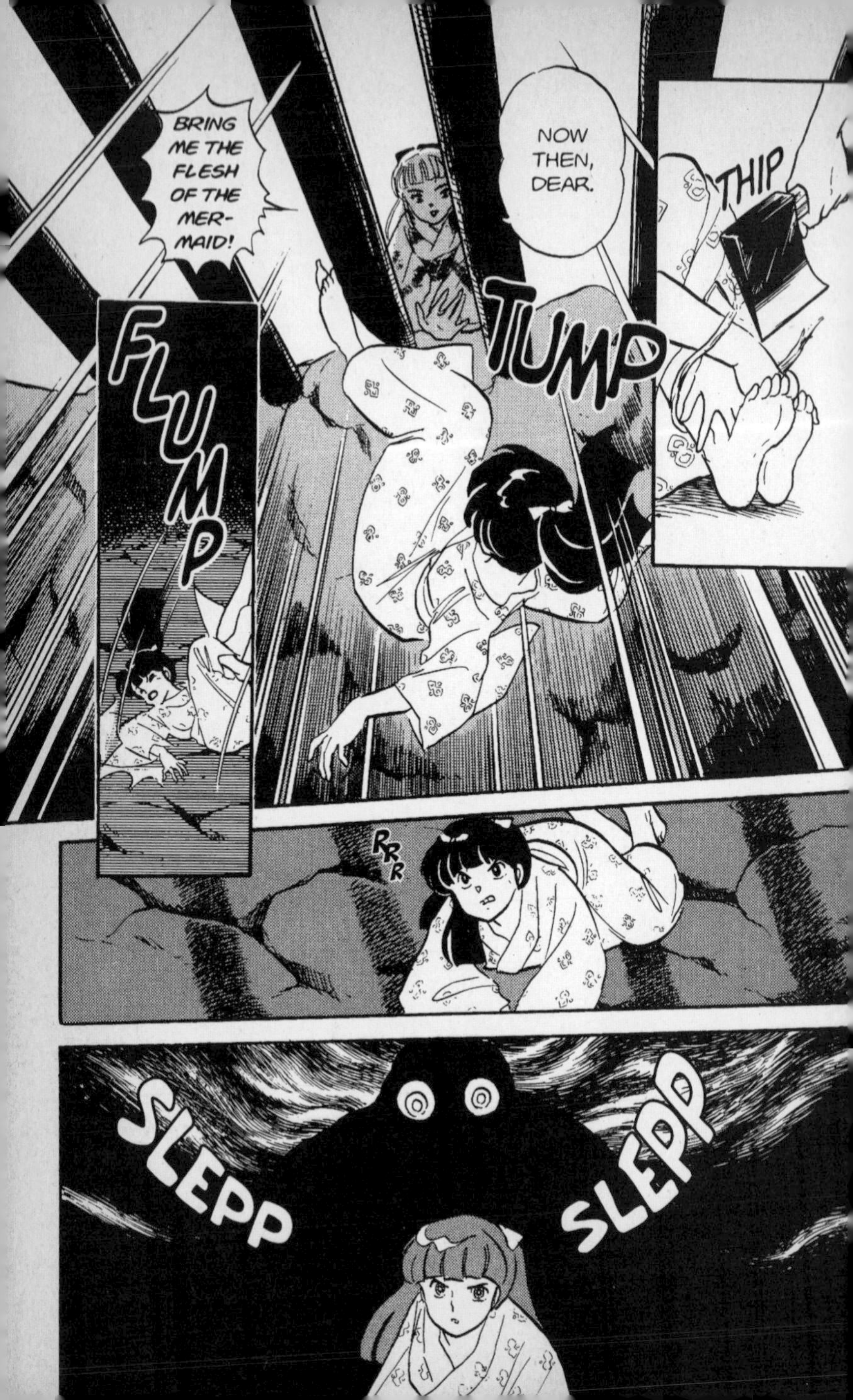
THIP
NOW THEN, DEAR.
TUMP
BRING ME THE FLESH OF THE MERMAID!
FLUMP
RRR
SLEPP
SLEPP

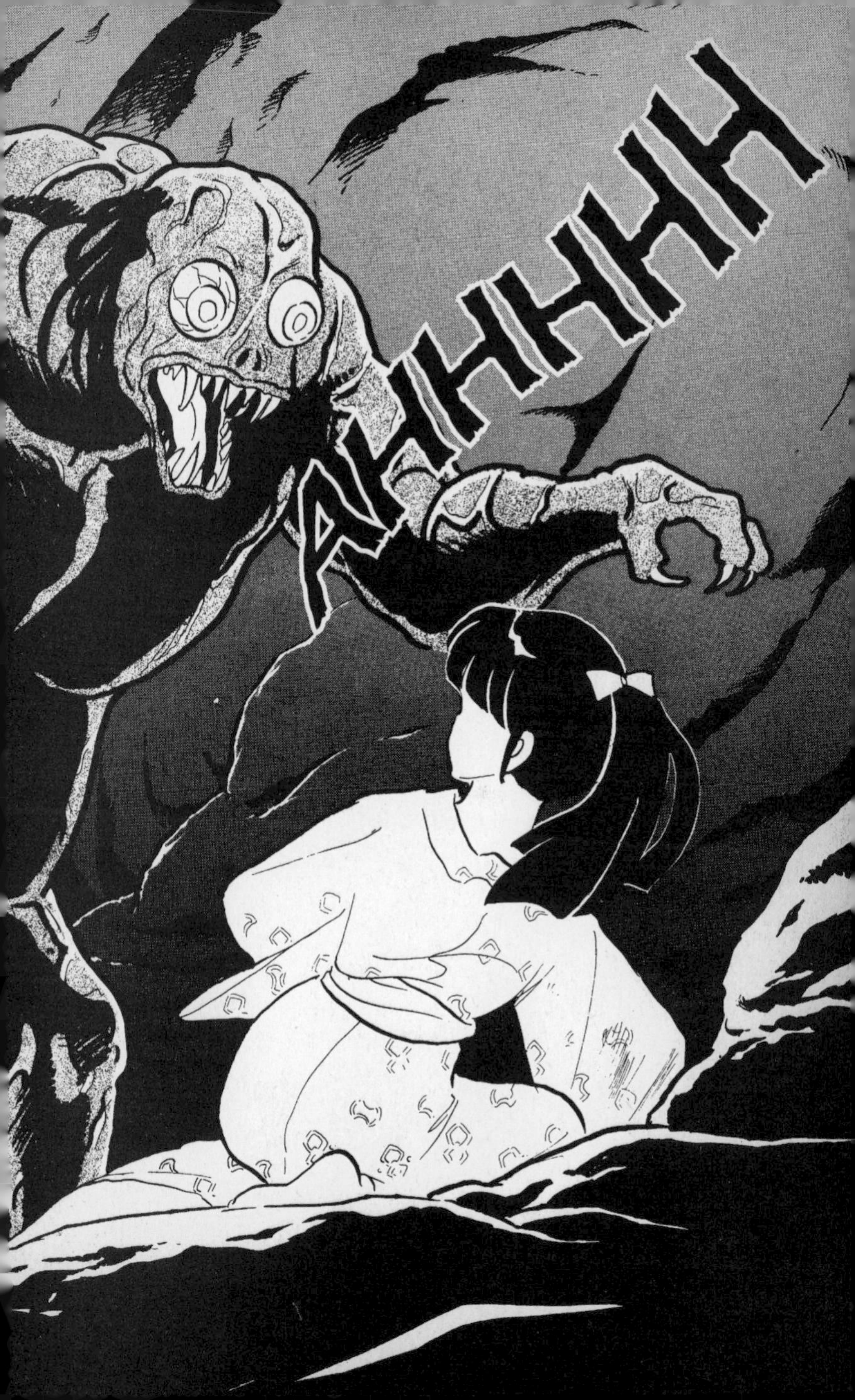
AHHHHHH

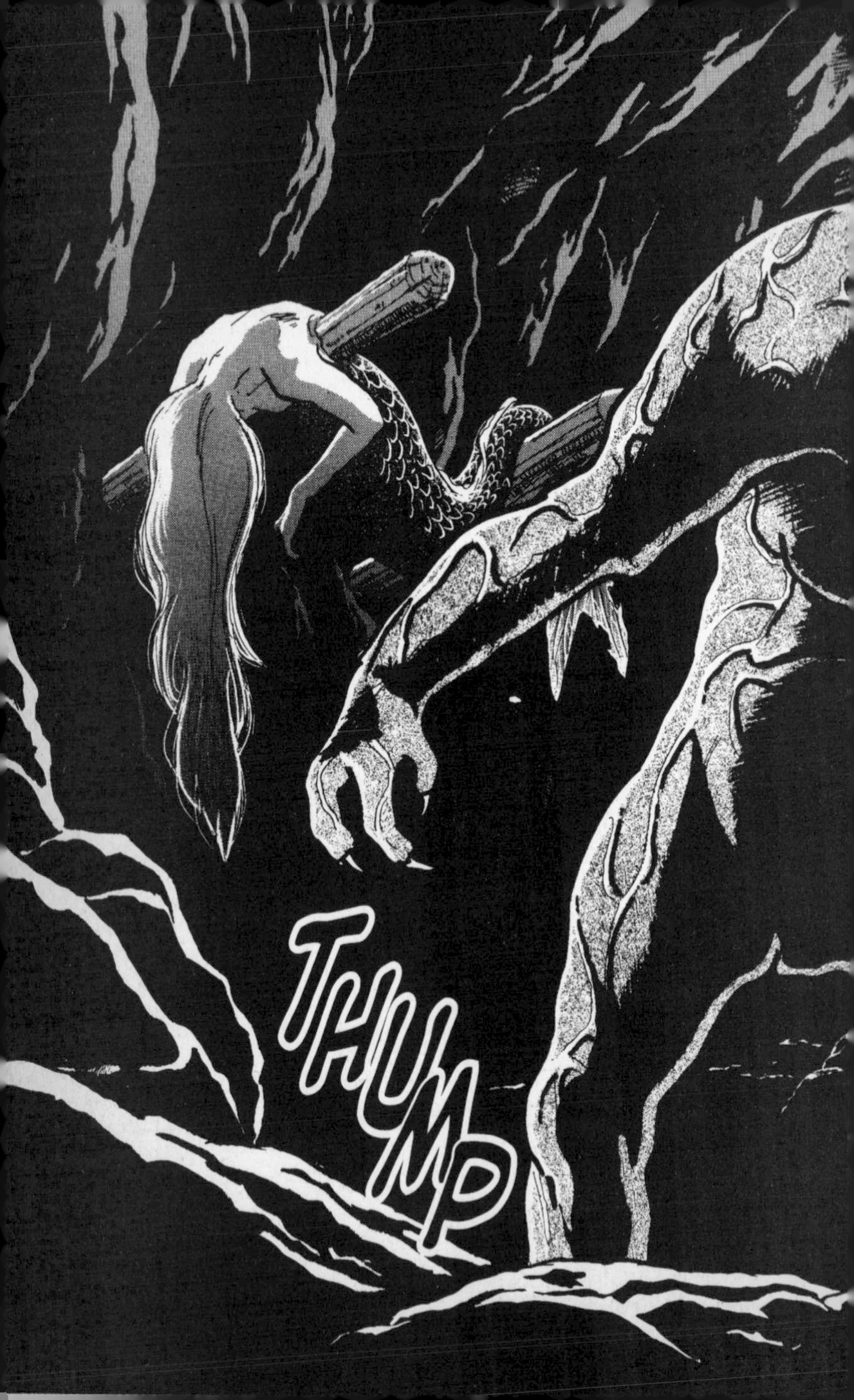
THUMP

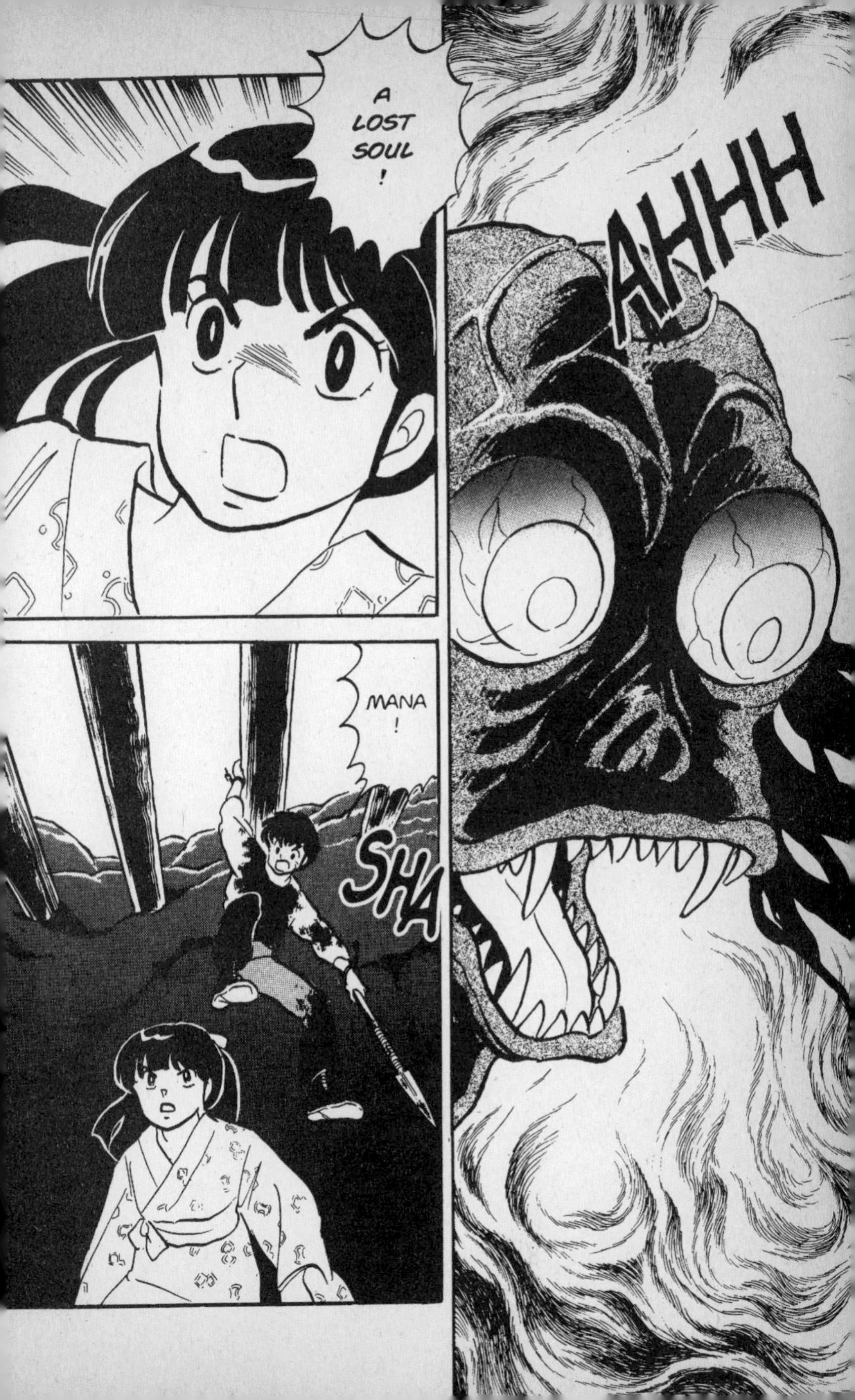
AHHH
A LOST SOUL!
MANA!
SHA

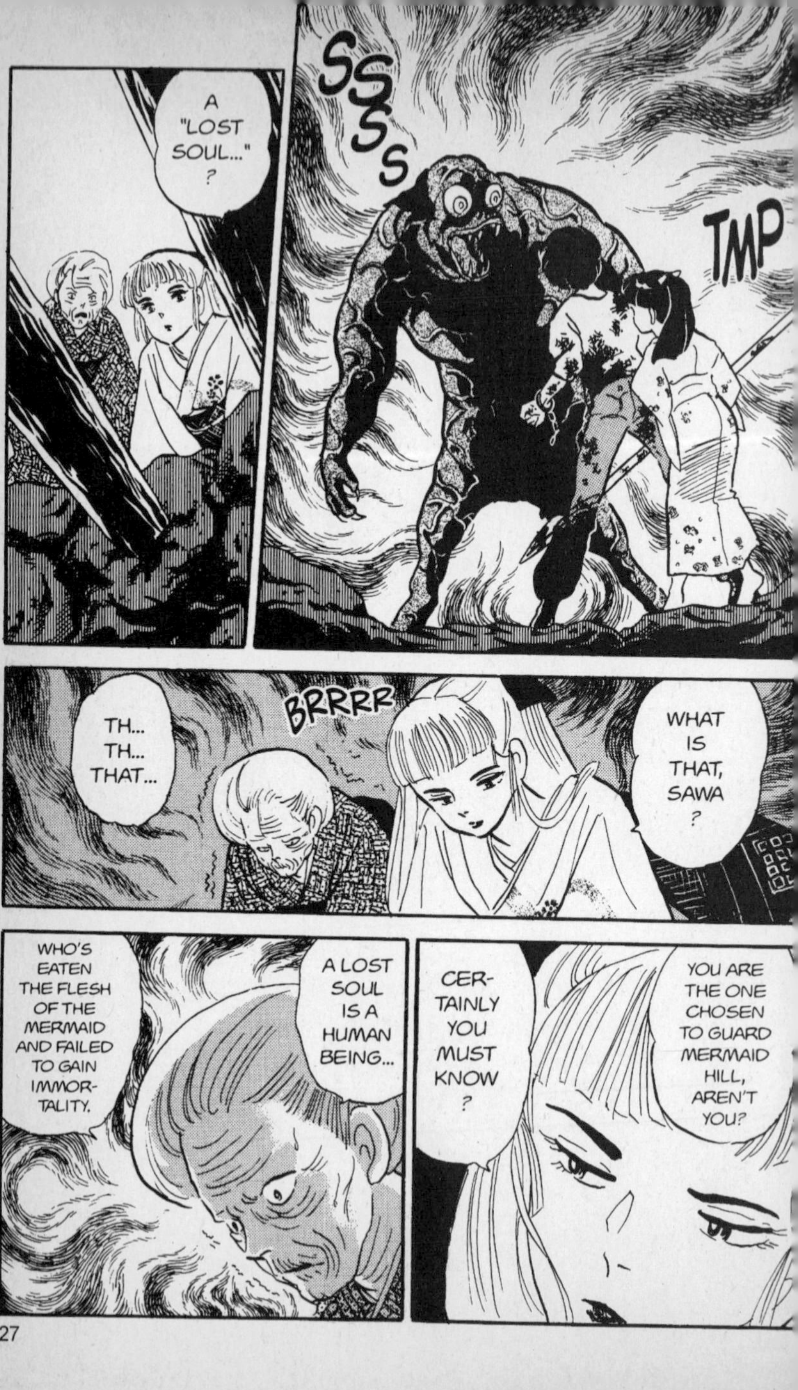
SSSS
TMP
A "LOST SOUL..." ?
WHAT IS THAT, SAWA ?
BRRRR
TH... TH... THAT...
YOU ARE THE ONE CHOSEN TO GUARD MERMAID HILL, AREN'T YOU?
CER-TAINLY YOU MUST KNOW ?
A LOST SOUL IS A HUMAN BEING...
WHO'S EATEN THE FLESH OF THE MERMAID AND FAILED TO GAIN IMMOR-TALITY.

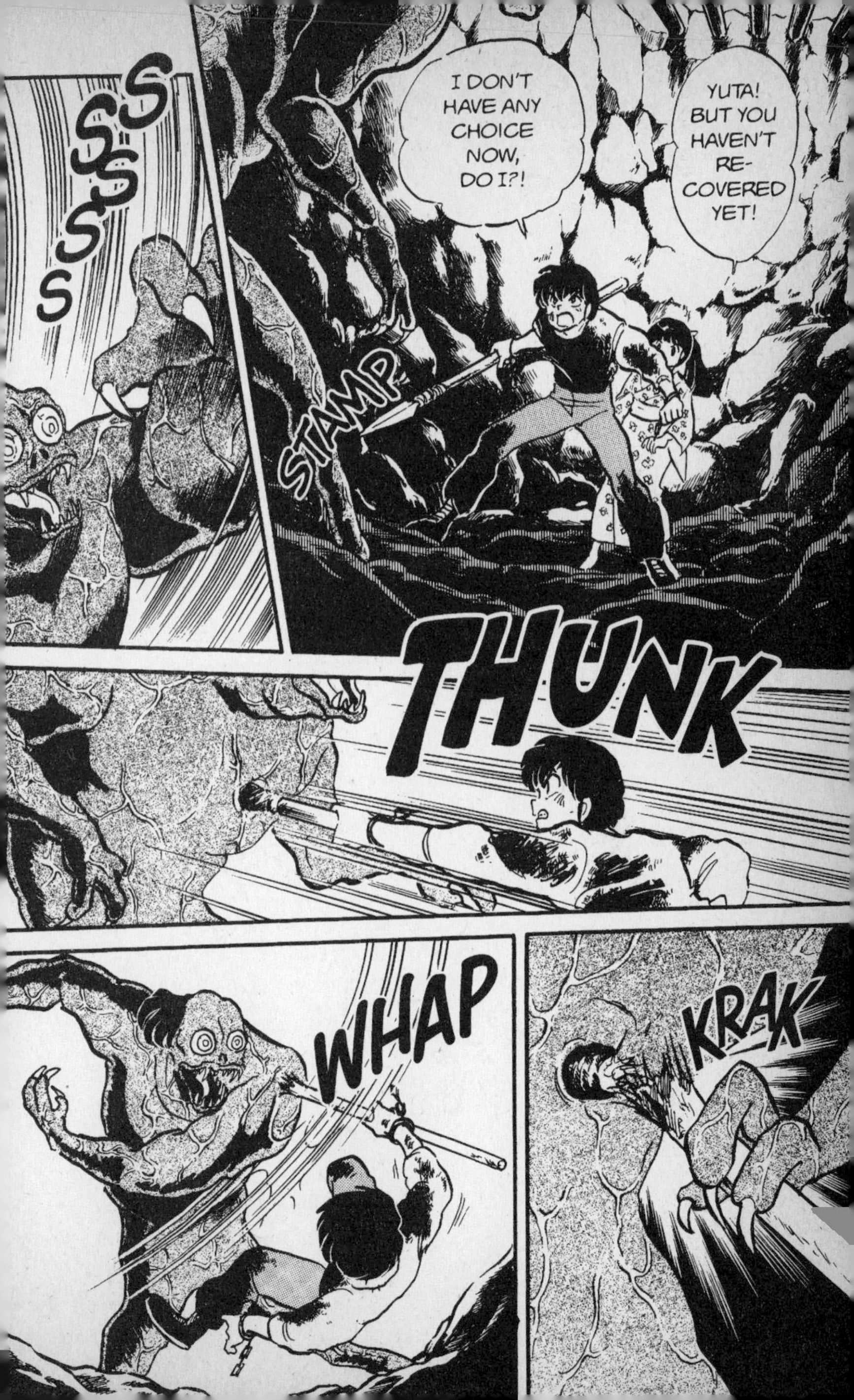
YUTA! BUT YOU HAVEN'T RE-COVERED YET!
I DON'T HAVE ANY CHOICE NOW, DO I?!
STAMP
SSSSS
THUNK
KRAK
WHAP

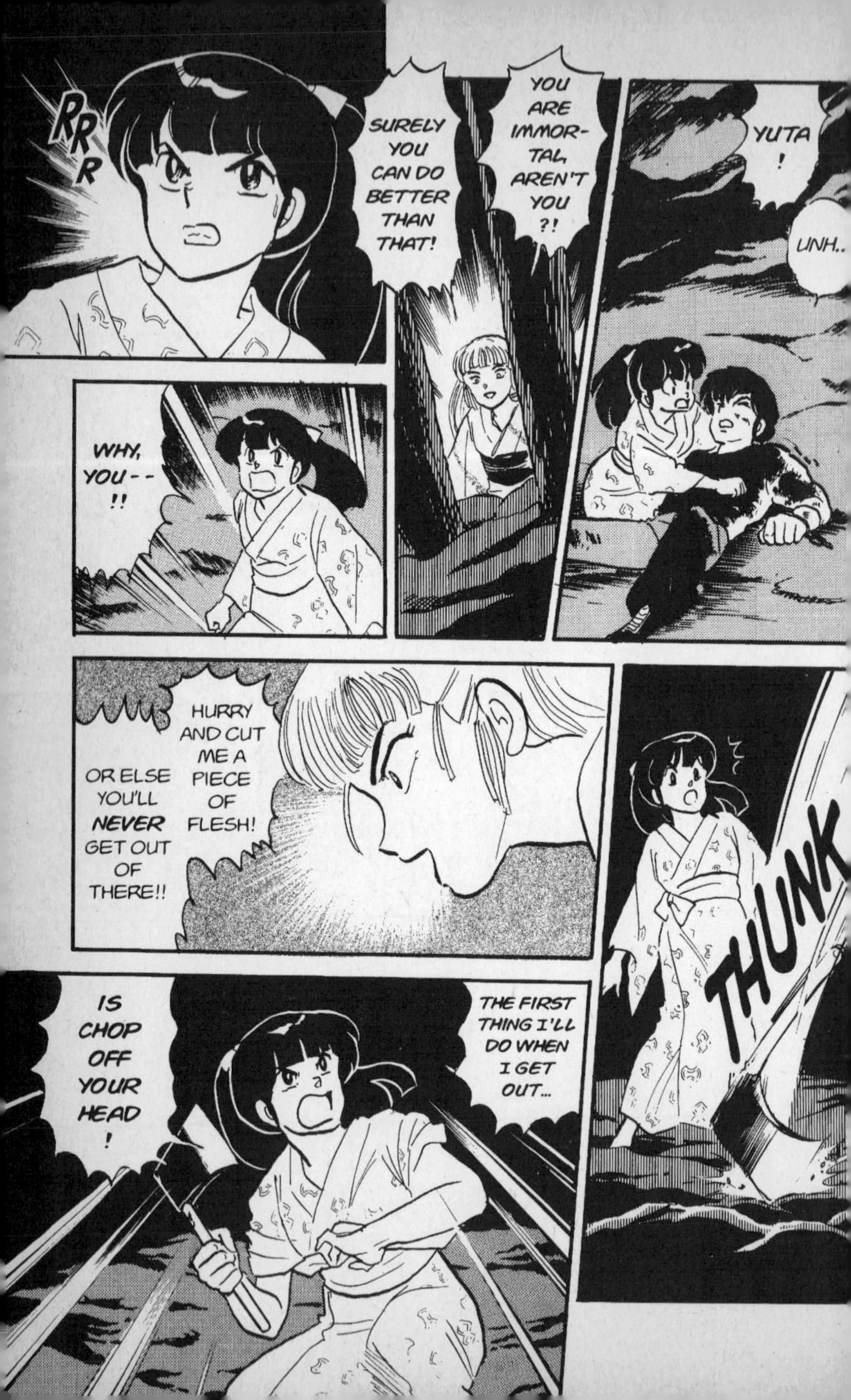

YUTA!
UNH..
YOU ARE IMMORTAL, AREN'T YOU?!
SURELY YOU CAN DO BETTER THAN THAT!
RRR
WHY, YOU--!!
THUNK
HURRY AND CUT ME A PIECE OF FLESH!
OR ELSE YOU'LL NEVER GET OUT OF THERE!!
THE FIRST THING I'LL DO WHEN I GET OUT...
IS CHOP OFF YOUR HEAD!

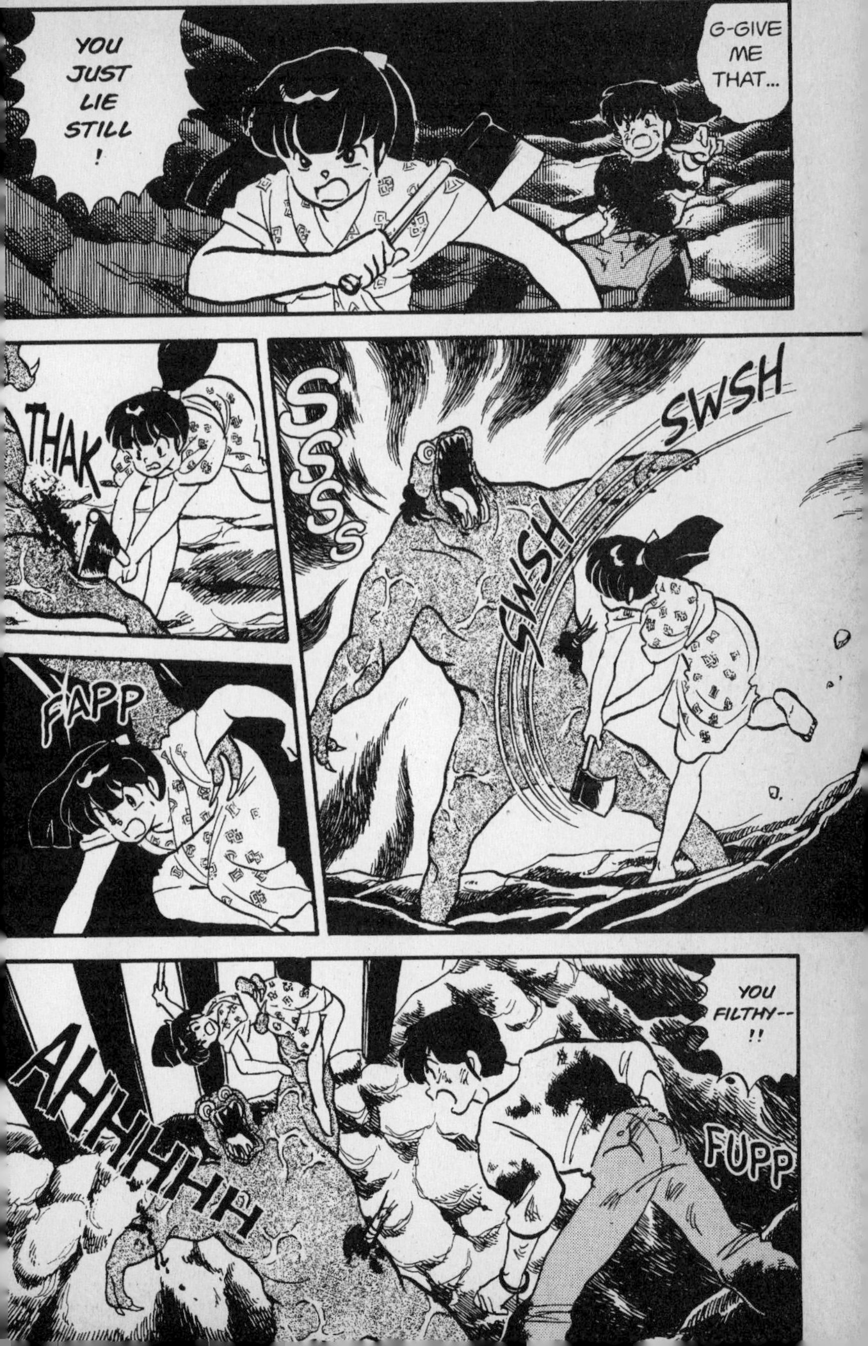
G-GIVE ME THAT...
YOU JUST LIE STILL!
SWSH
SSSSS
SWSH
THAK
FAPP
YOU FILTHY--!!
FUPP
AHHHHHH

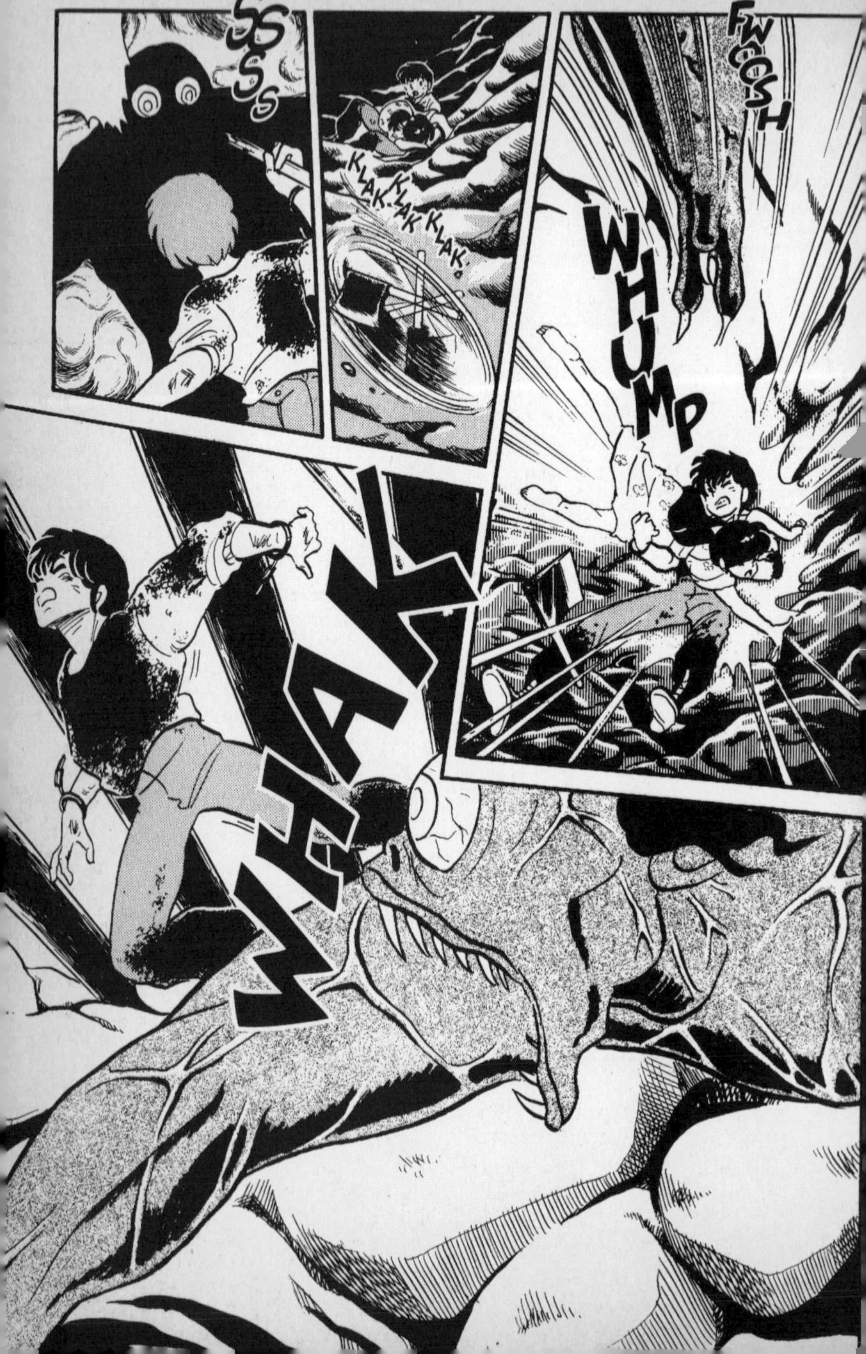
FWOOSH
WHUMP
KLAK KLAK KLAK KLAK
SSSSS
WHAK

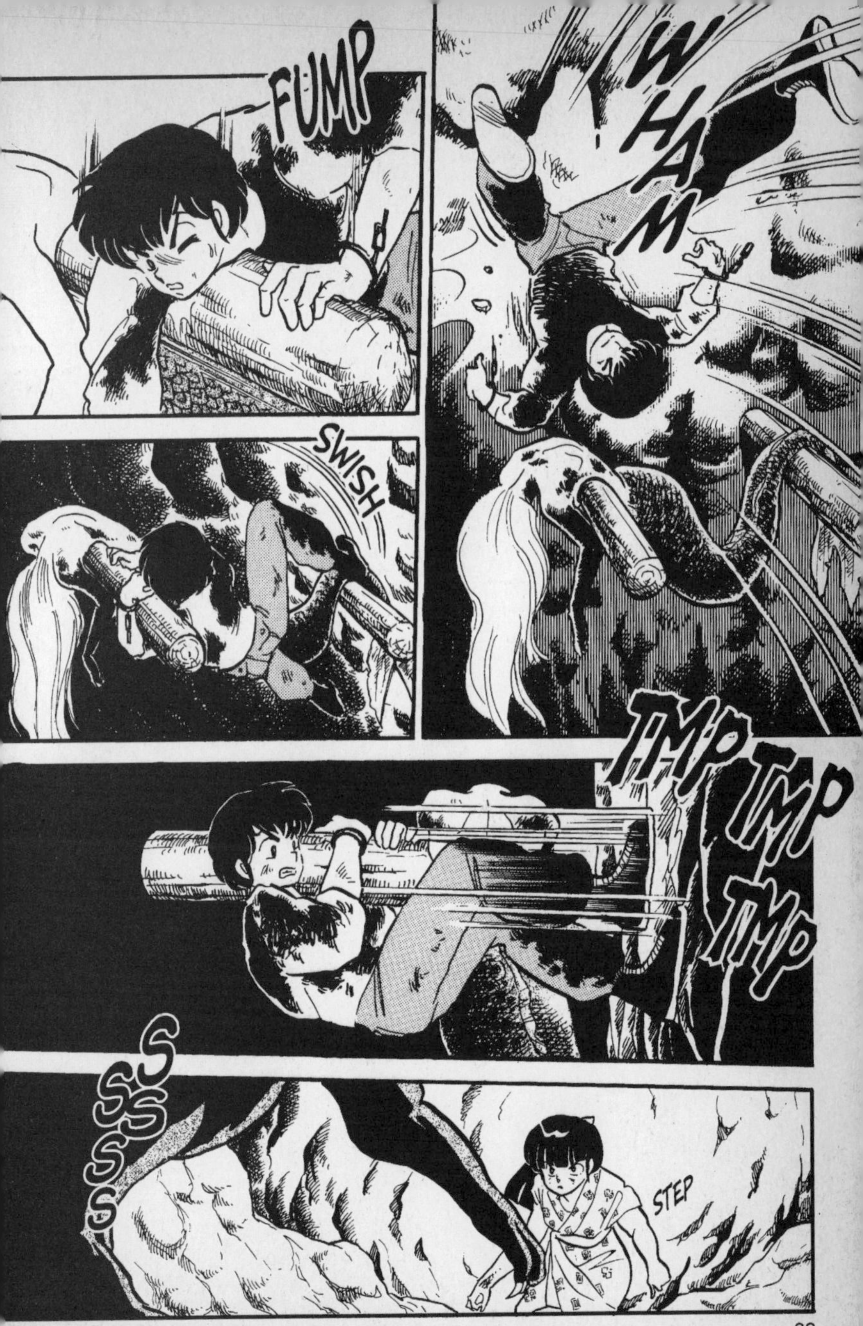
WHAM
FUMP
SWISH
TMP TMP TMP TMP
STEP
SSSSS

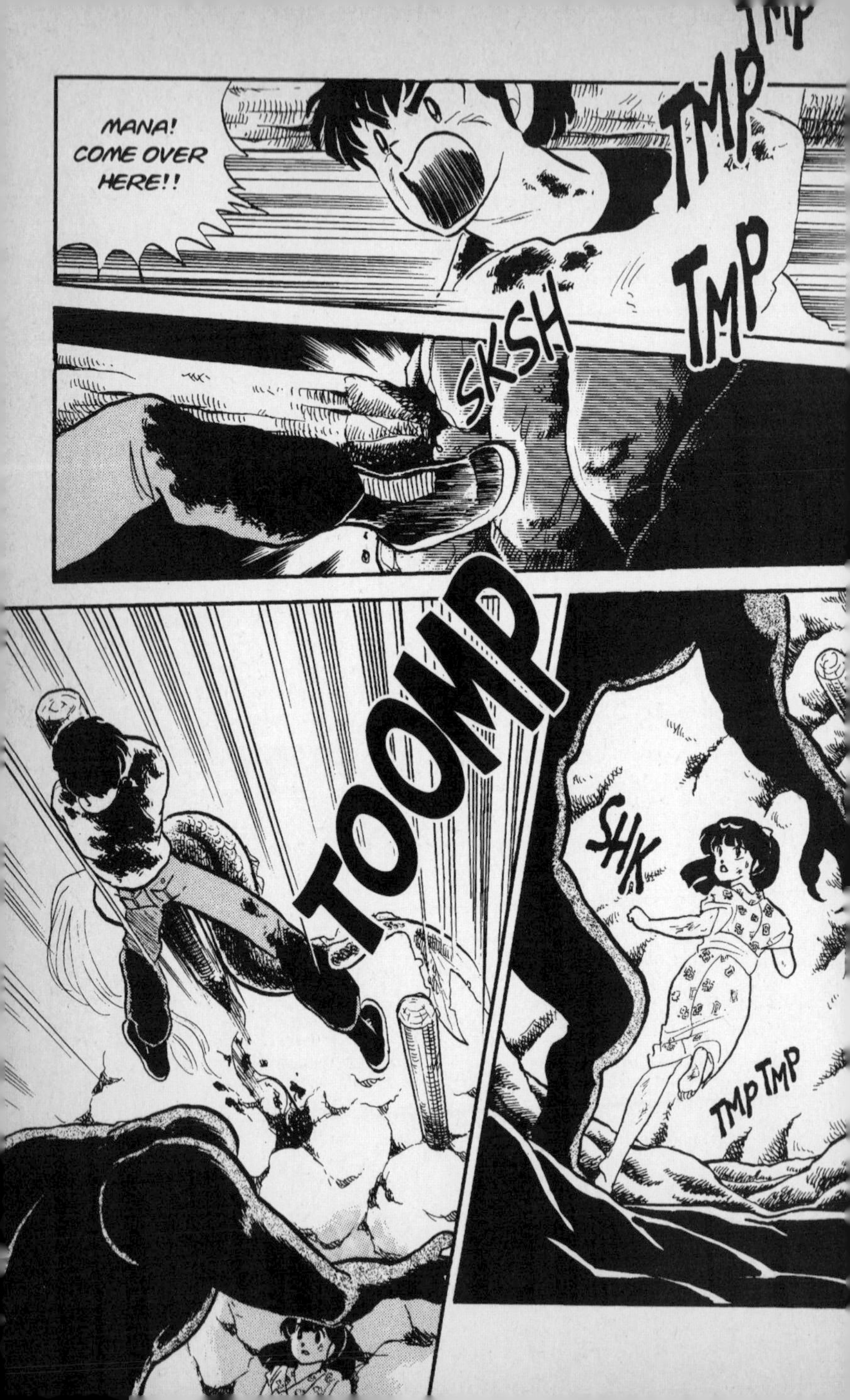
TMP TMP
TMP
MANA! COME OVER HERE!!
SKSH
SHK
TMP TMP
TOOMP

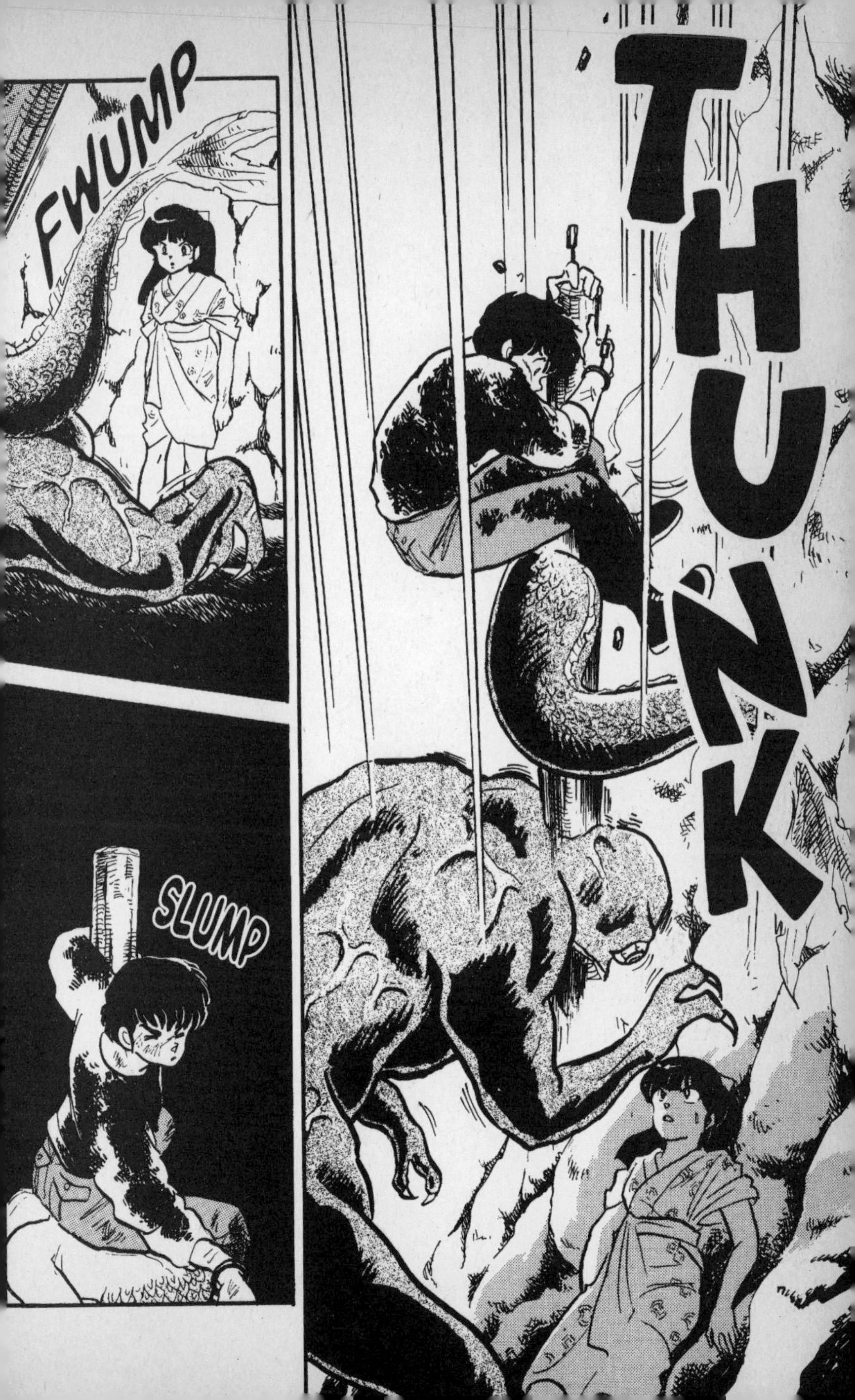
THUNK
FWUMP
SLUMP

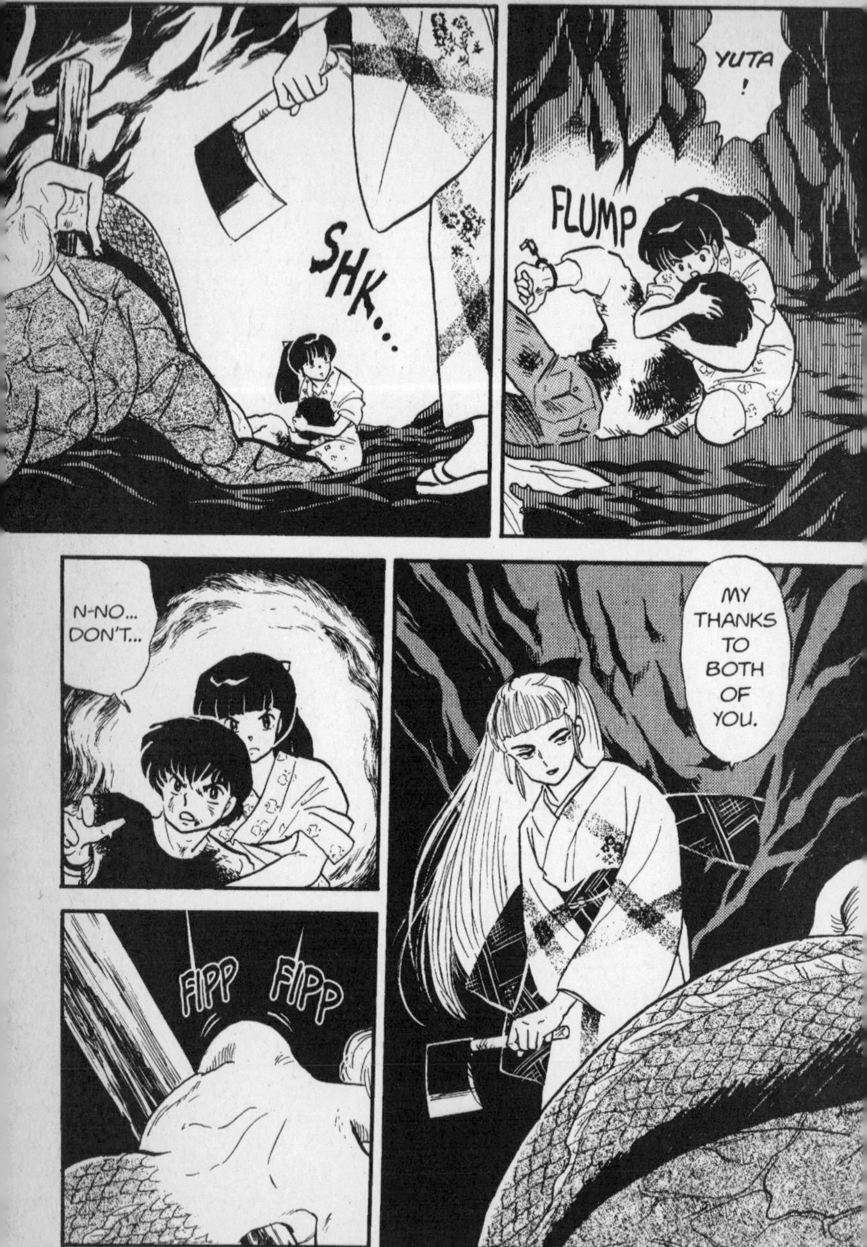
YUTA!
FLUMP
SHK...
MY THANKS TO BOTH OF YOU.
N-NO... DON'T...
FIPP FIPP

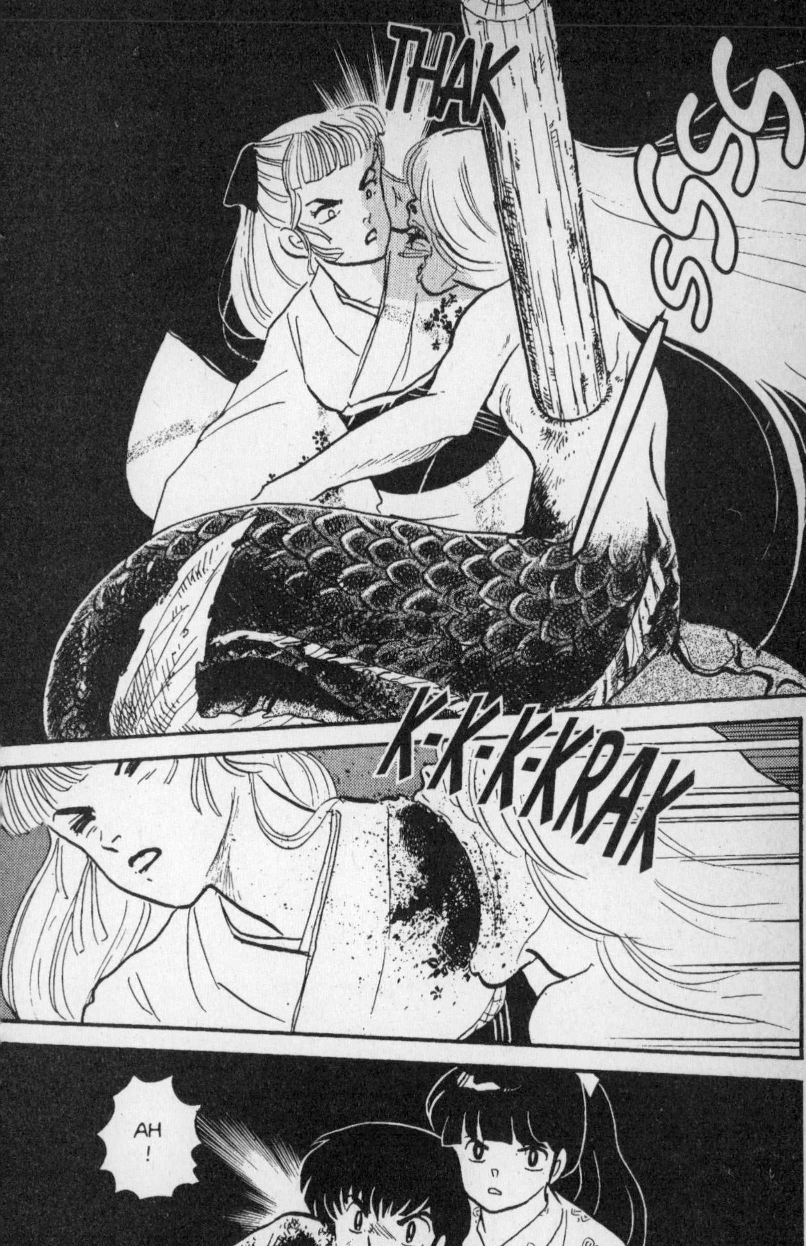
THAK
SSSS
K-K-K-KRAK
AH
!

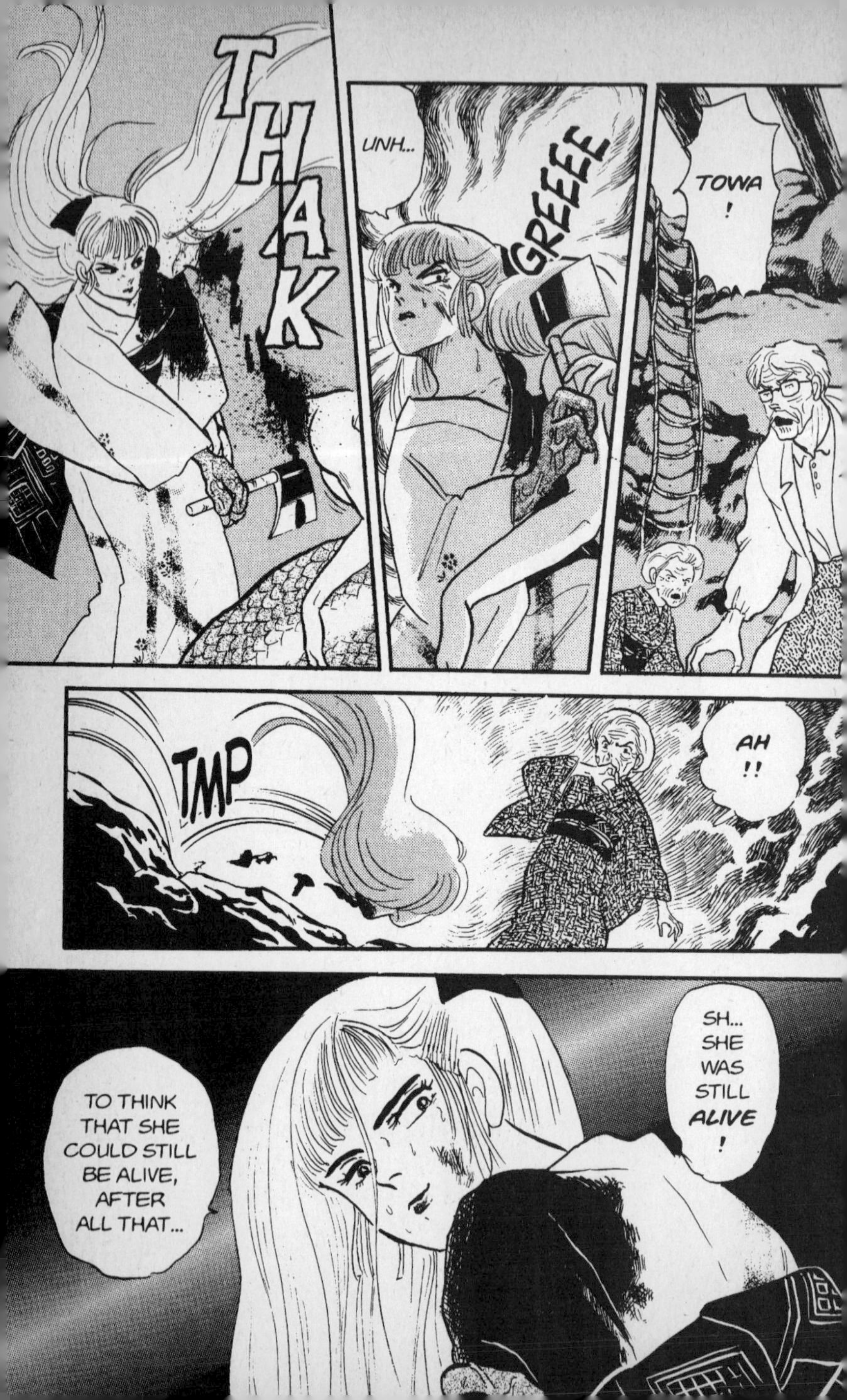
TOWA !
GREEEE
UNH...
THAK
AH !!
TMP
SH... SHE WAS STILL ALIVE !
TO THINK THAT SHE COULD STILL BE ALIVE, AFTER ALL THAT...

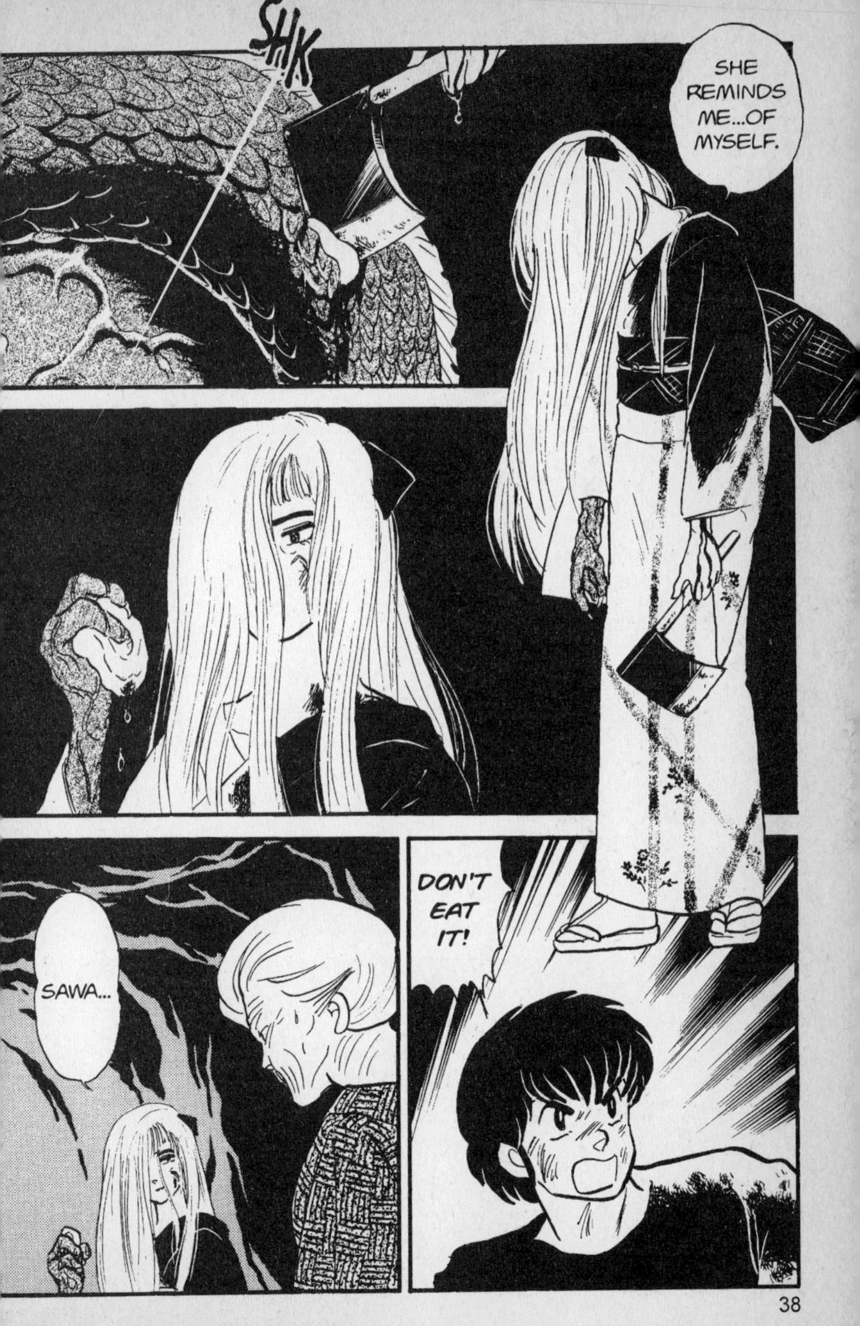
SHE REMINDS ME...OF MYSELF.
SHK
DON'T EAT IT!
SAWA...

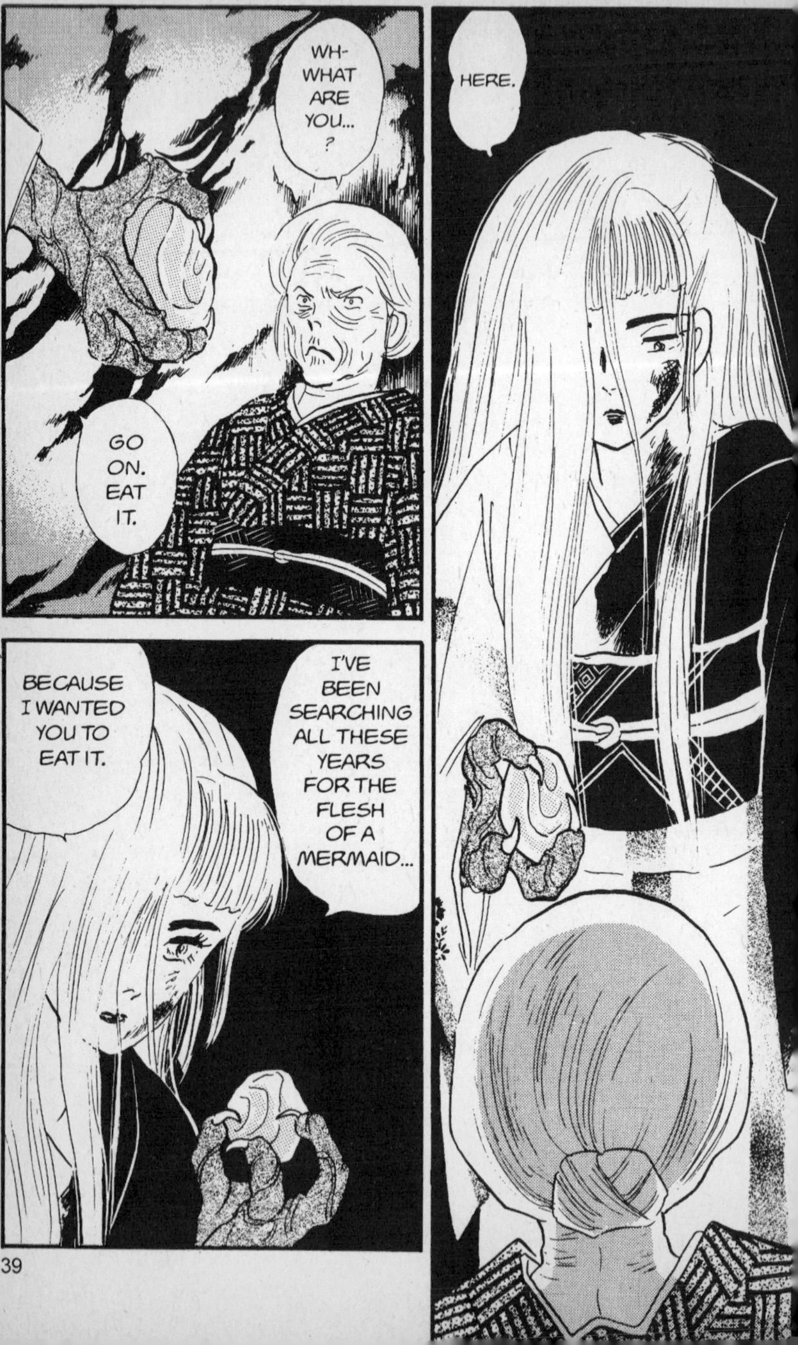
HERE.
WH- WHAT ARE YOU... ?
GO ON. EAT IT.
I'VE BEEN SEARCHING ALL THESE YEARS FOR THE FLESH OF A MERMAID...
BECAUSE I WANTED YOU TO EAT IT.

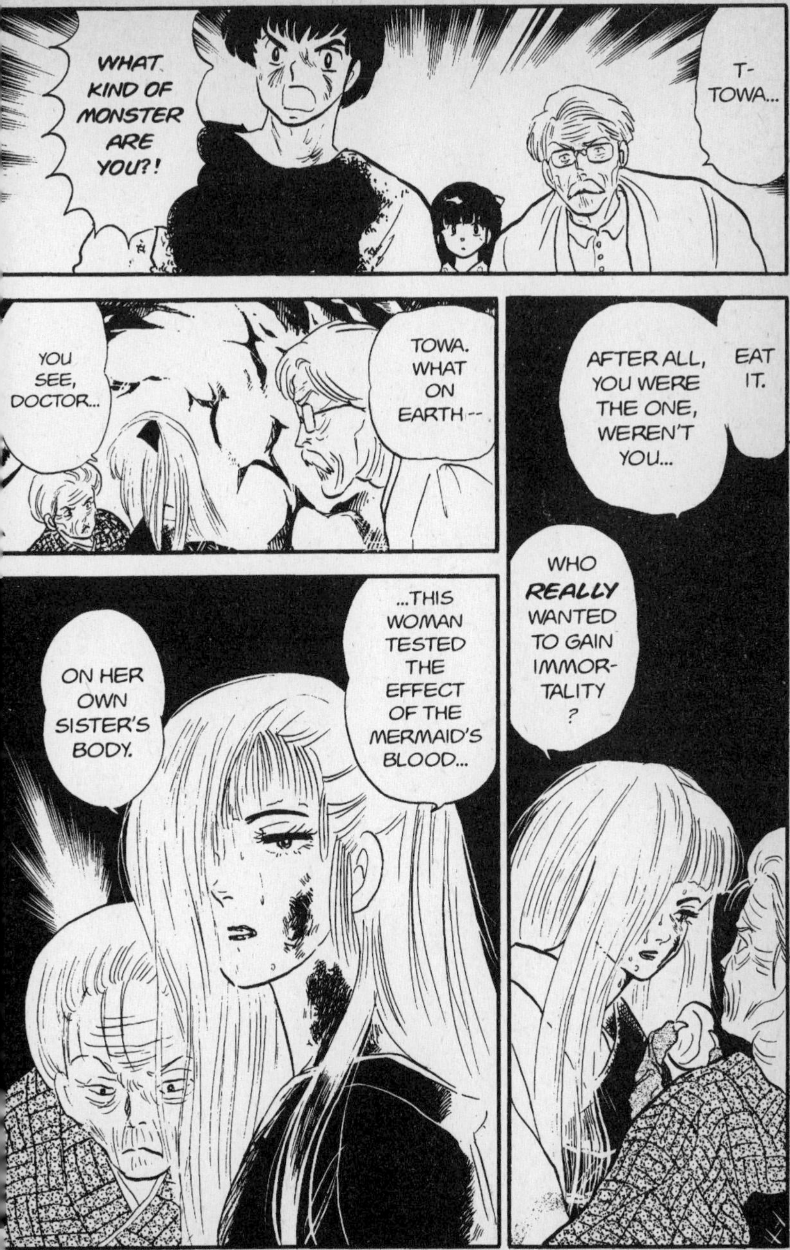
T- TOWA...
WHAT KIND OF MONSTER ARE YOU?!
EAT IT.
AFTER ALL, YOU WERE THE ONE, WEREN'T YOU...
WHO *REALLY* WANTED TO GAIN IMMORTALITY?
TOWA. WHAT ON EARTH--
YOU SEE, DOCTOR...
...THIS WOMAN TESTED THE EFFECT OF THE MERMAID'S BLOOD...
ON HER OWN SISTER'S BODY.

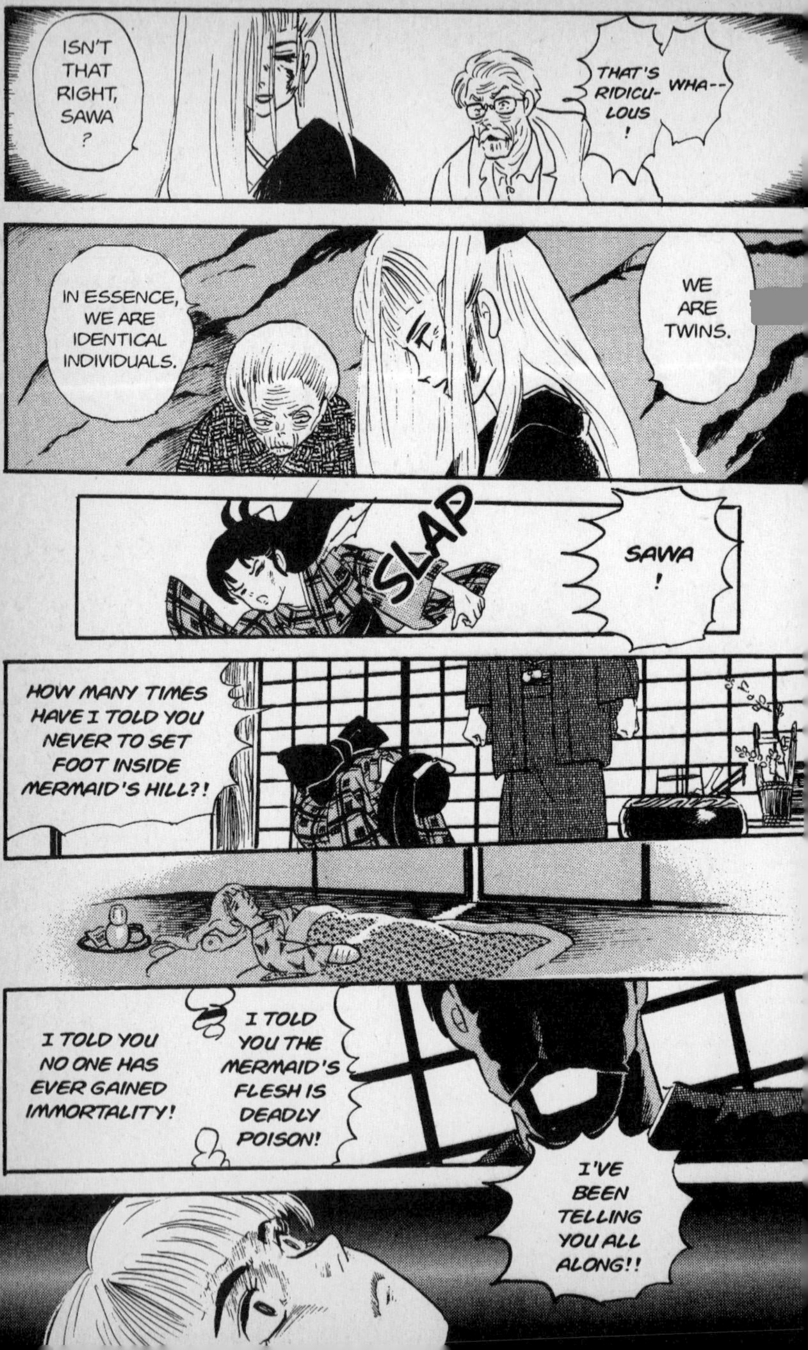
WHA--
THAT'S RIDICULOUS!
ISN'T THAT RIGHT, SAWA?
WE ARE TWINS.
IN ESSENCE, WE ARE IDENTICAL INDIVIDUALS.
SAWA!
SLAP
HOW MANY TIMES HAVE I TOLD YOU NEVER TO SET FOOT INSIDE MERMAID'S HILL?!
I TOLD YOU THE MERMAID'S FLESH IS DEADLY POISON!
I TOLD YOU NO ONE HAS EVER GAINED IMMORTALITY!
I'VE BEEN TELLING YOU ALL ALONG!!

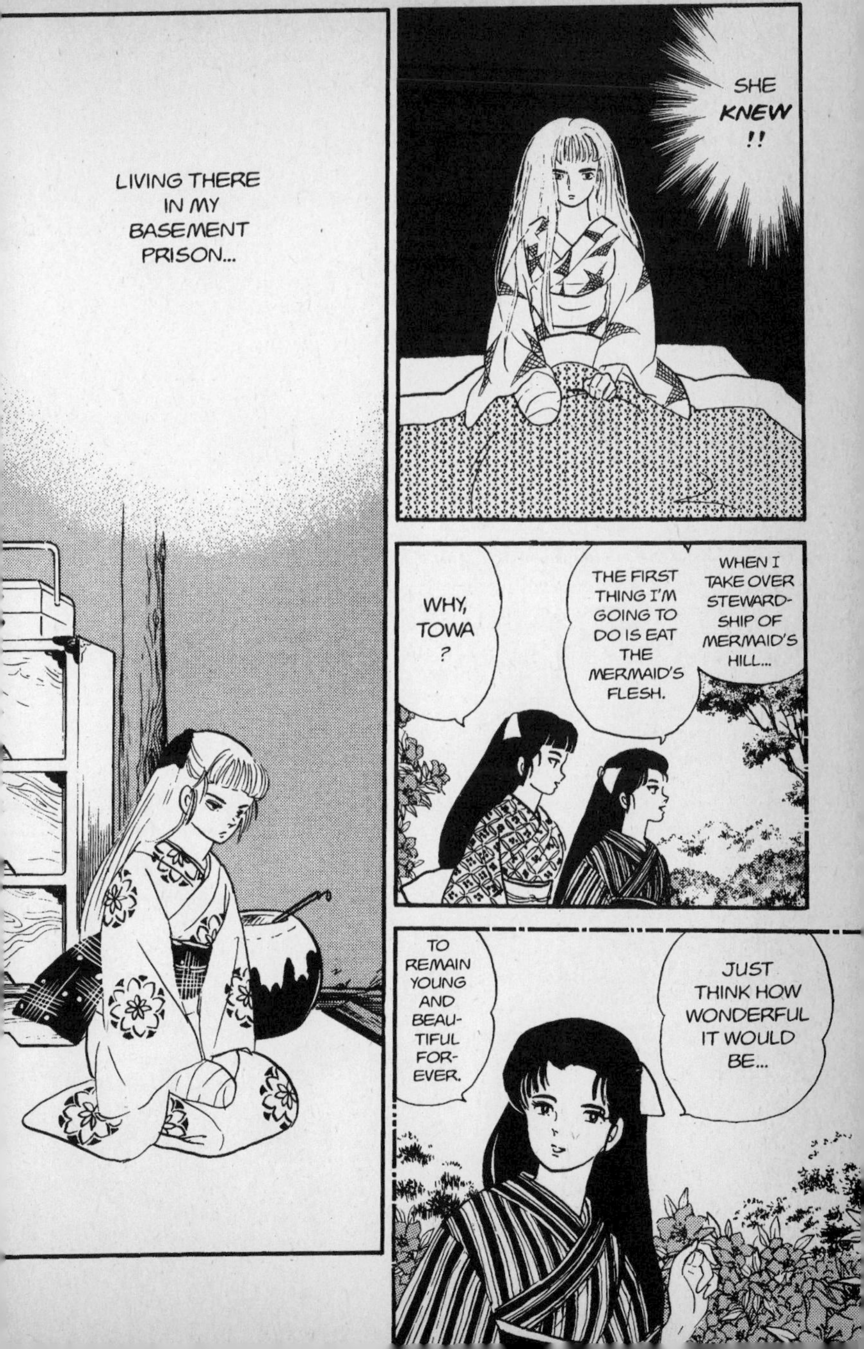
SHE KNEW !!
WHEN I TAKE OVER STEWARDSHIP OF MERMAID'S HILL...
THE FIRST THING I'M GOING TO DO IS EAT THE MERMAID'S FLESH.
WHY, TOWA?
JUST THINK HOW WONDERFUL IT WOULD BE...
TO REMAIN YOUNG AND BEAUTIFUL FOREVER.
LIVING THERE IN MY BASEMENT PRISON...

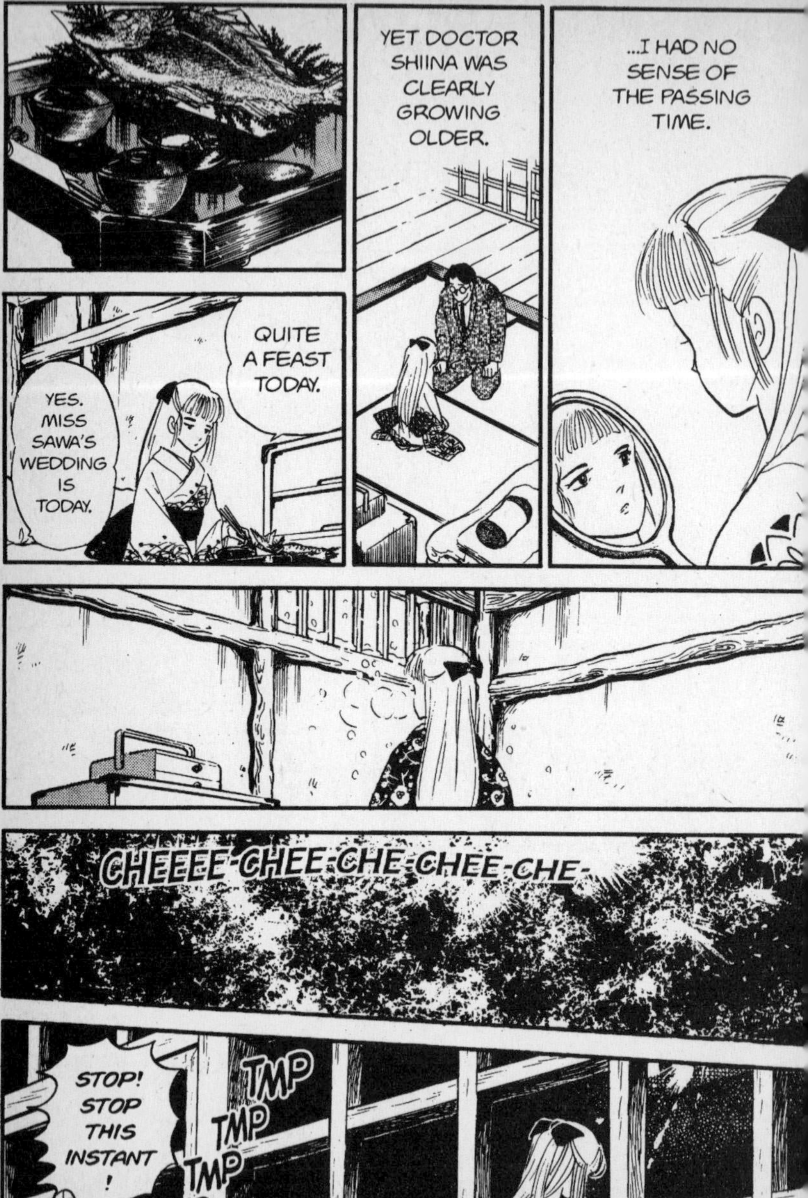
...I HAD NO SENSE OF THE PASSING TIME.
YET DOCTOR SHIINA WAS CLEARLY GROWING OLDER.
QUITE A FEAST TODAY.
YES. MISS SAWA'S WEDDING IS TODAY.
CHEEEE-CHEE-CHE-CHEE-CHE-
TMP TMP TMP TMP
STOP! STOP THIS INSTANT!

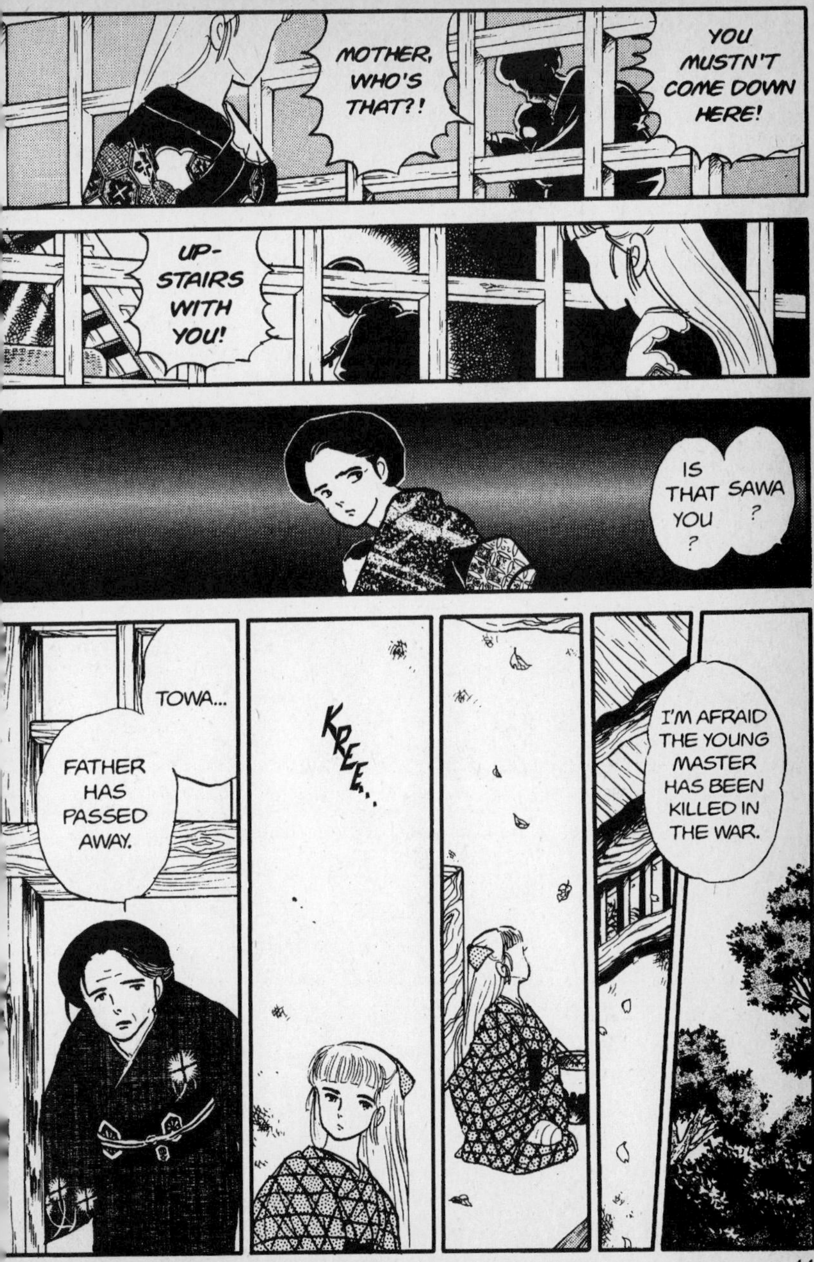
YOU MUSTN'T COME DOWN HERE!
MOTHER, WHO'S THAT?!
UP-STAIRS WITH YOU!
IS THAT YOU? SAWA?
I'M AFRAID THE YOUNG MASTER HAS BEEN KILLED IN THE WAR.
KREEE...
TOWA...
FATHER HAS PASSED AWAY.

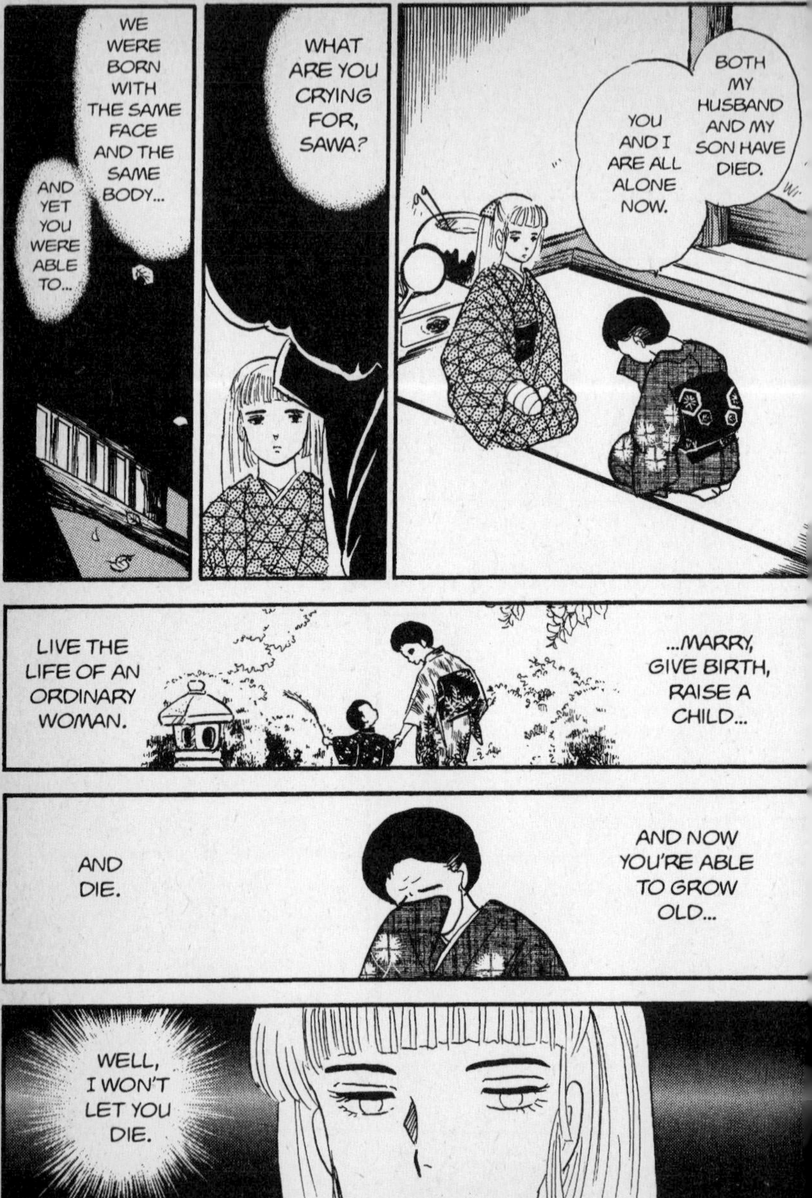
BOTH MY HUSBAND AND MY SON HAVE DIED.
YOU AND I ARE ALL ALONE NOW.
WHAT ARE YOU CRYING FOR, SAWA?
WE WERE BORN WITH THE SAME FACE AND THE SAME BODY...
AND YET YOU WERE ABLE TO...
...MARRY, GIVE BIRTH, RAISE A CHILD...
LIVE THE LIFE OF AN ORDINARY WOMAN.
AND NOW YOU'RE ABLE TO GROW OLD...
AND DIE.
WELL, I WON'T LET YOU DIE.

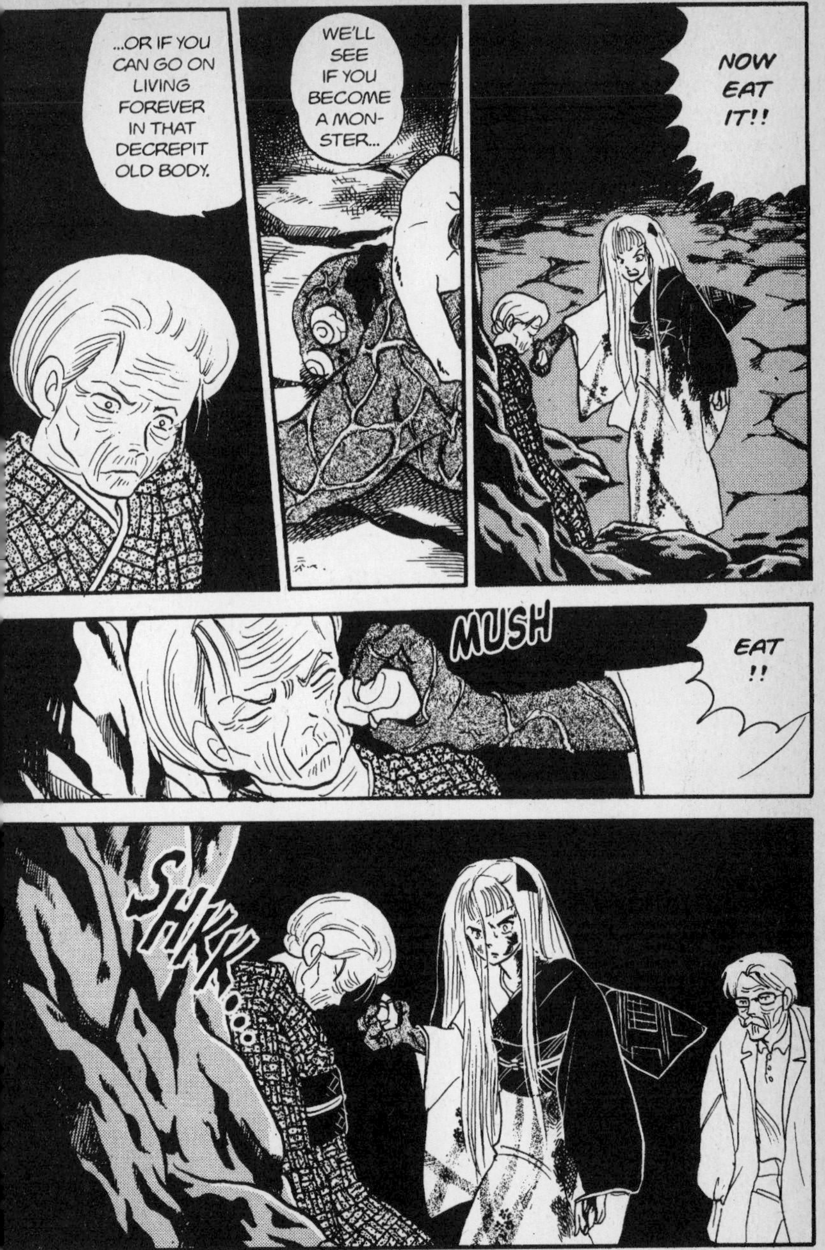
NOW EAT IT!!
WE'LL SEE IF YOU BECOME A MON-STER...
...OR IF YOU CAN GO ON LIVING FOREVER IN THAT DECREPIT OLD BODY.
EAT !!
MUSH
SHKKOOO

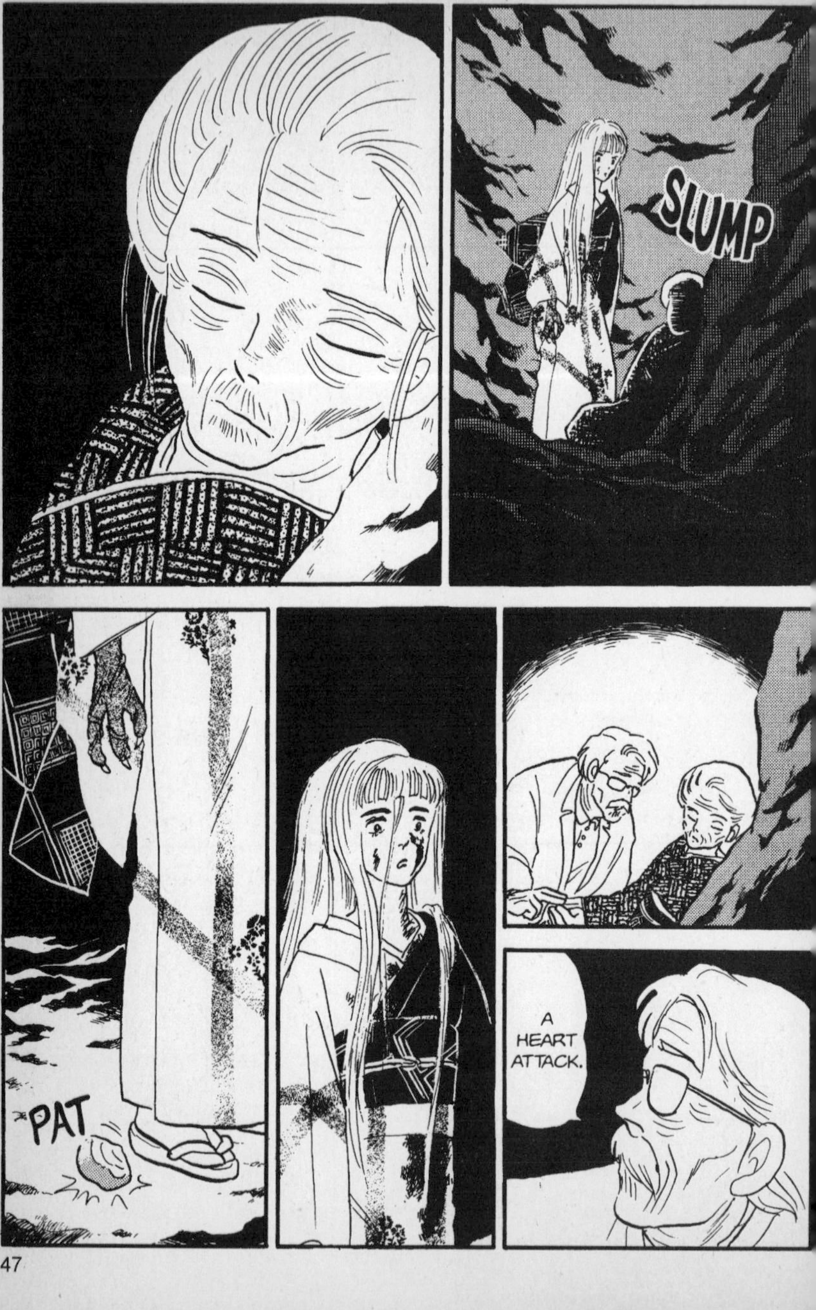
SLUMP
A HEART ATTACK.
PAT

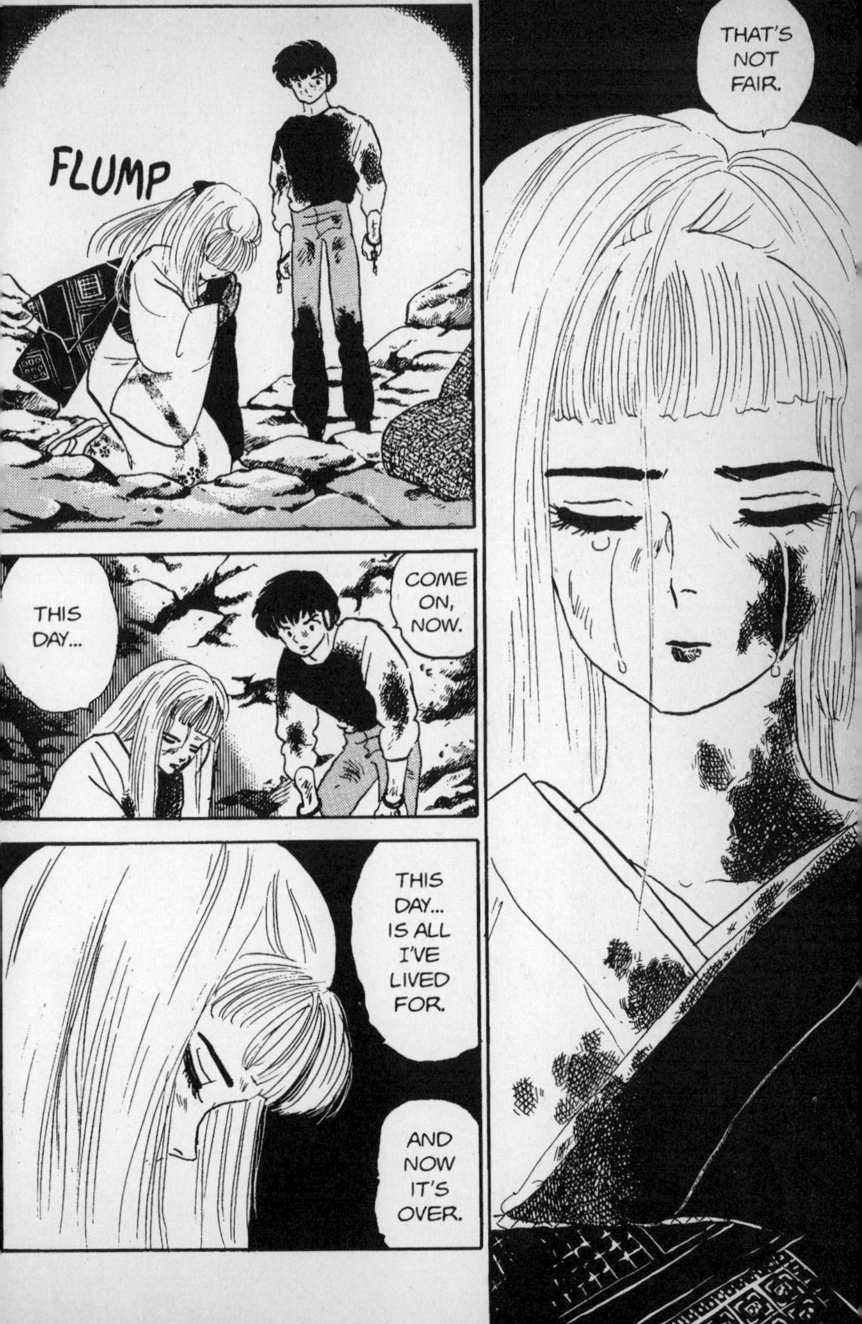
THAT'S NOT FAIR.
FLUMP
COME ON, NOW.
THIS DAY...
THIS DAY... IS ALL I'VE LIVED FOR.
AND NOW IT'S OVER.

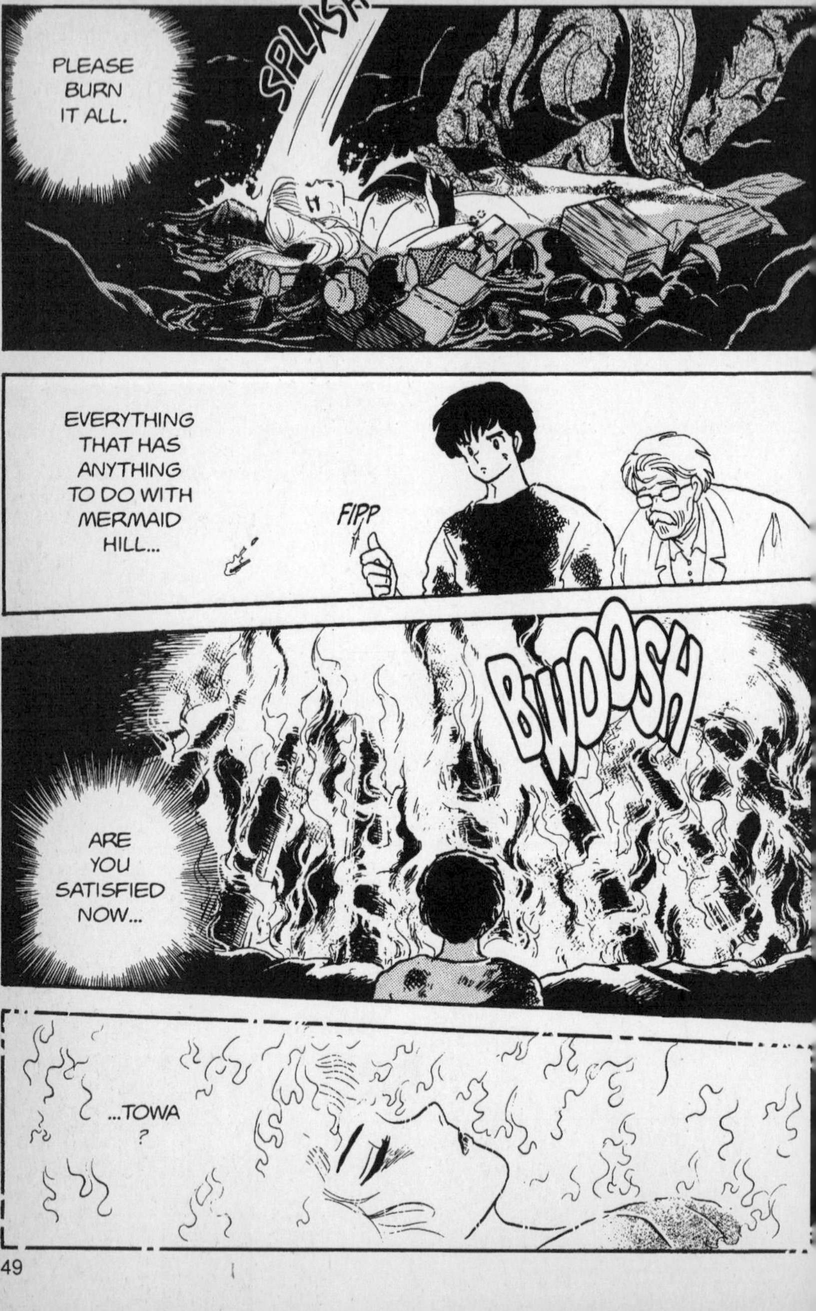
SPLASH
PLEASE BURN IT ALL.
EVERYTHING THAT HAS ANYTHING TO DO WITH MERMAID HILL...
FIPP
BWOOSH
ARE YOU SATISFIED NOW...
...TOWA ?

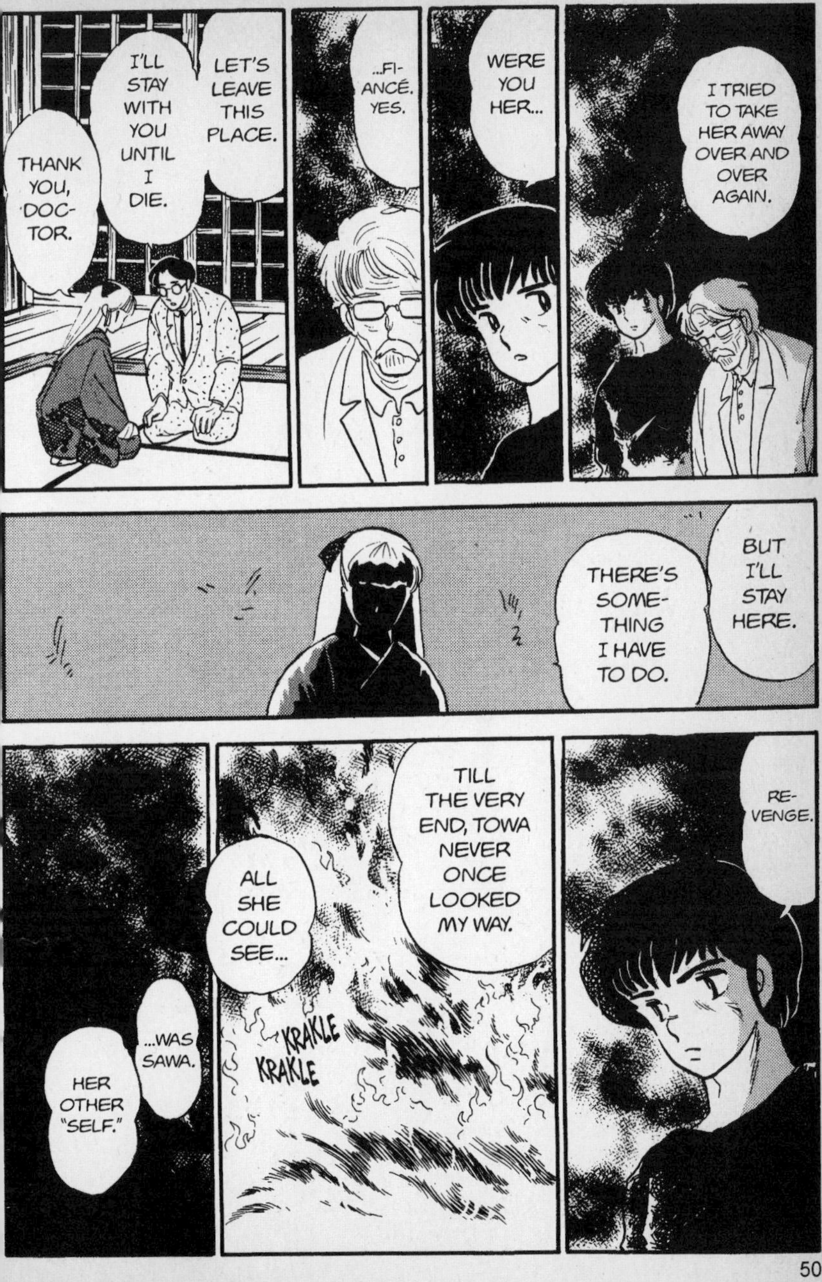
I TRIED TO TAKE HER AWAY OVER AND OVER AGAIN.
WERE YOU HER...
...FIANCÉ. YES.
LET'S LEAVE THIS PLACE.
I'LL STAY WITH YOU UNTIL I DIE.
THANK YOU, DOCTOR.
BUT I'LL STAY HERE.
THERE'S SOMETHING I HAVE TO DO.
REVENGE.
TILL THE VERY END, TOWA NEVER ONCE LOOKED MY WAY.
ALL SHE COULD SEE...
KRAKLE
KRAKLE
...WAS SAWA.
HER OTHER "SELF."

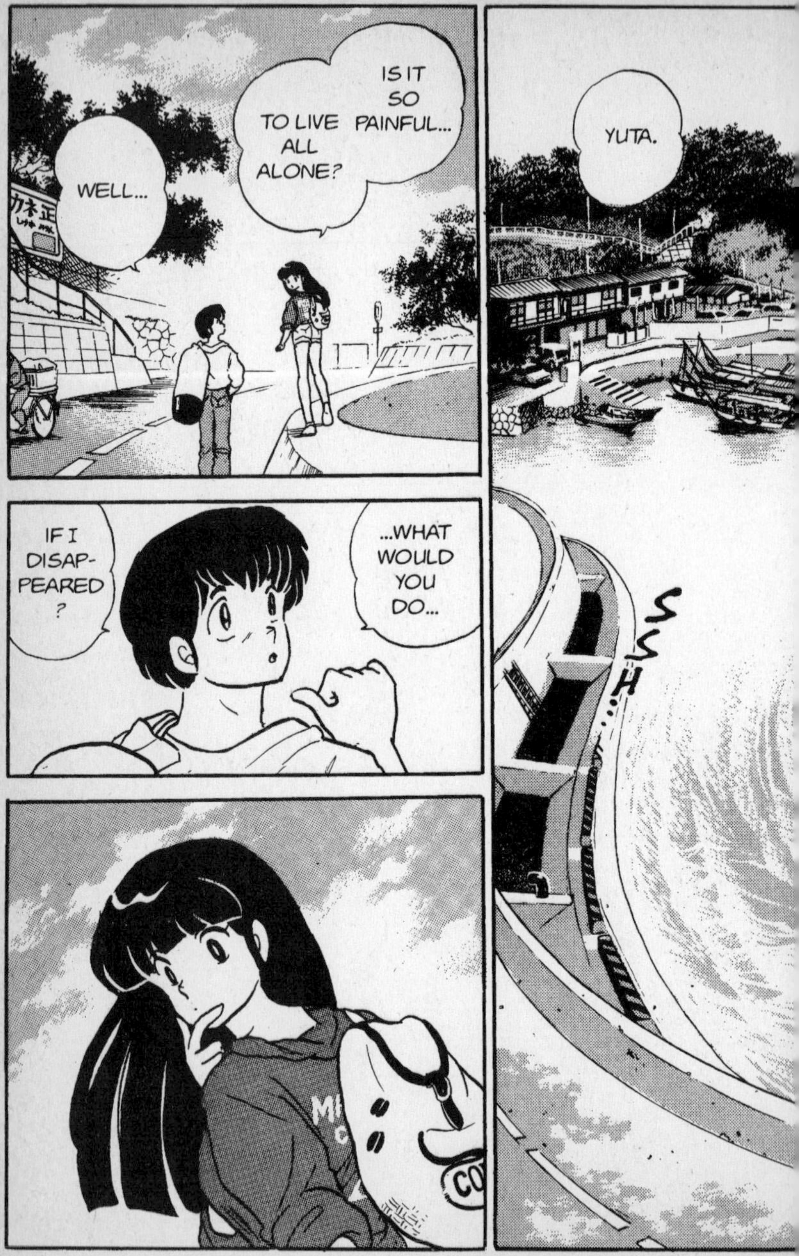
YUTA.
SSH...
IS IT SO PAINFUL... TO LIVE ALL ALONE?
WELL...
...WHAT WOULD YOU DO...
IF I DISAP-PEARED?

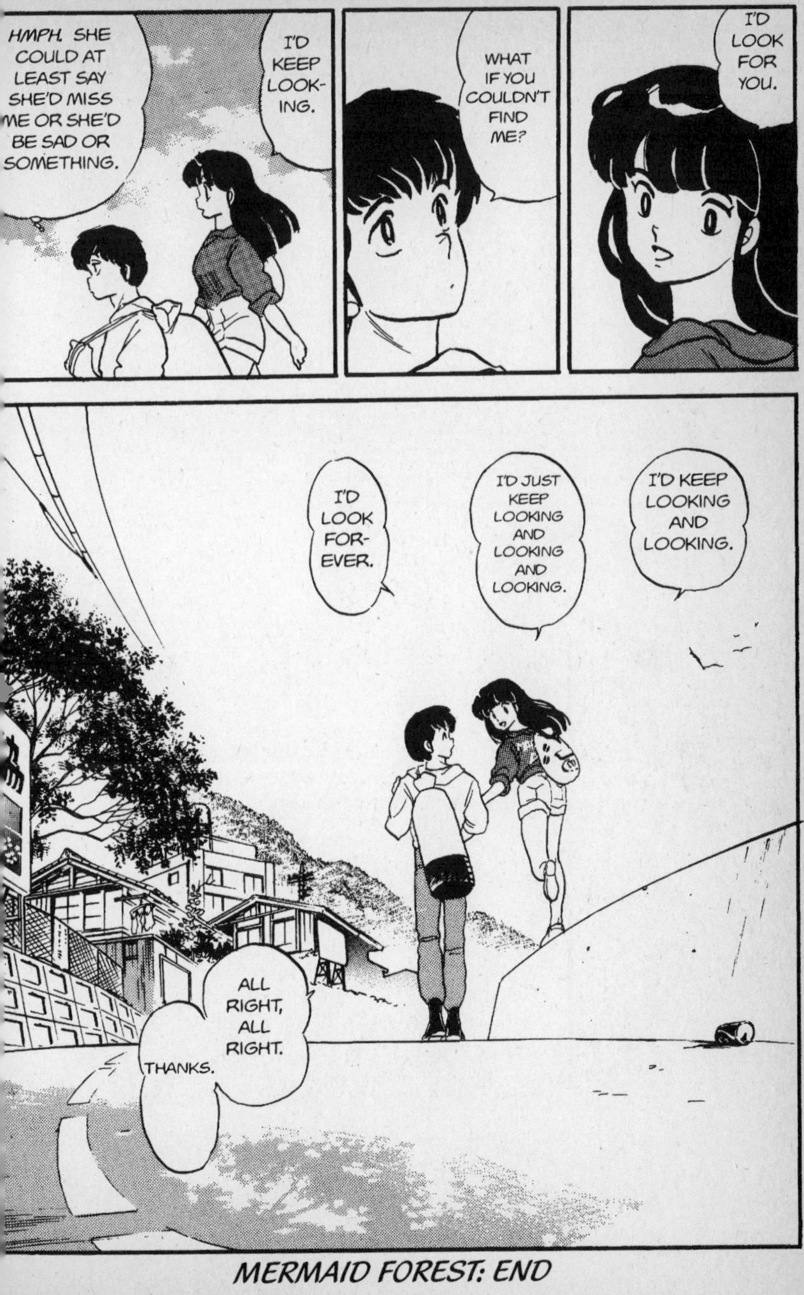
I'D LOOK FOR YOU.
WHAT IF YOU COULDN'T FIND ME?
I'D KEEP LOOKING.
HMPH. SHE COULD AT LEAST SAY SHE'D MISS ME OR SHE'D BE SAD OR SOMETHING.
I'D KEEP LOOKING AND LOOKING.
I'D JUST KEEP LOOKING AND LOOKING AND LOOKING.
I'D LOOK FOREVER.
ALL RIGHT, ALL RIGHT.
THANKS.

MERMAID FOREST: END

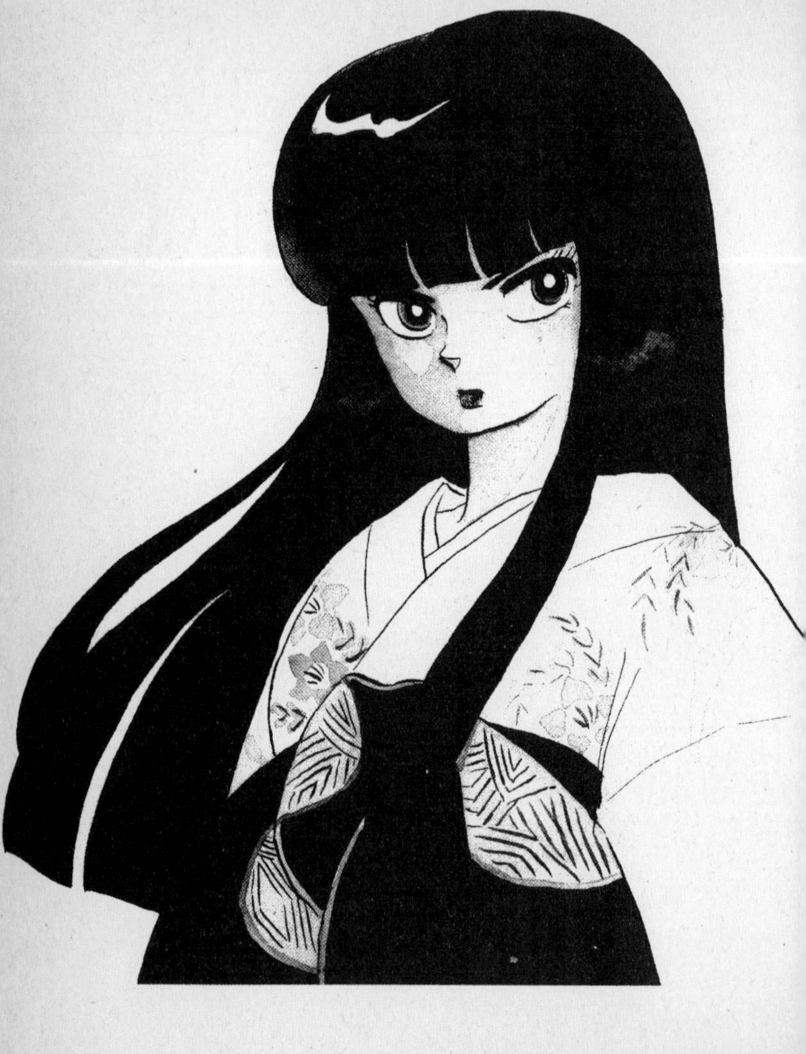

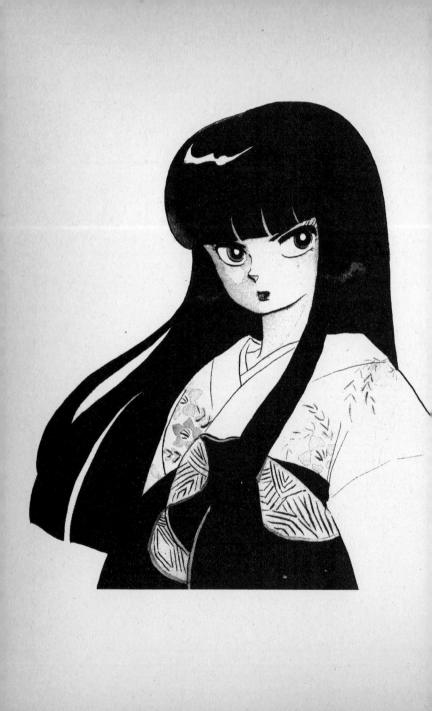

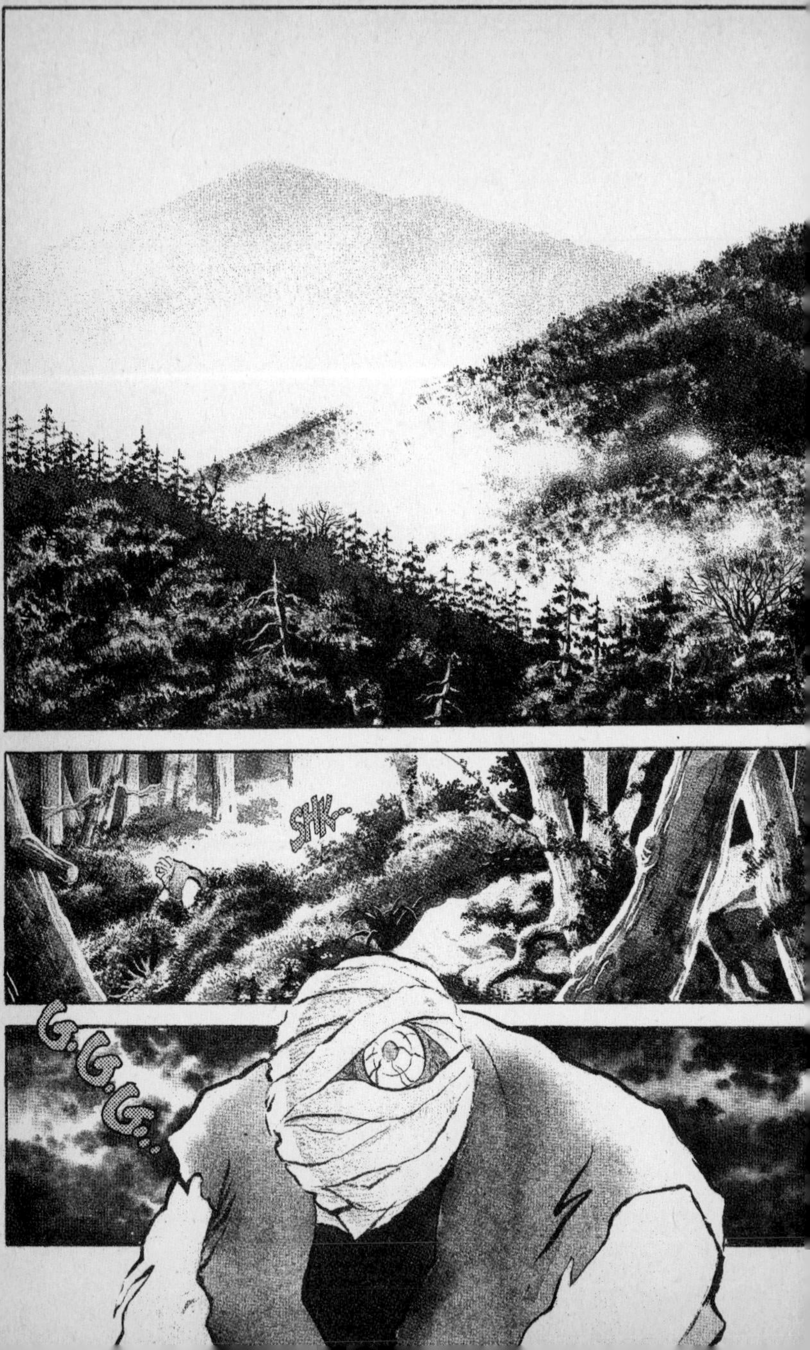
SHK...
G.G.G...

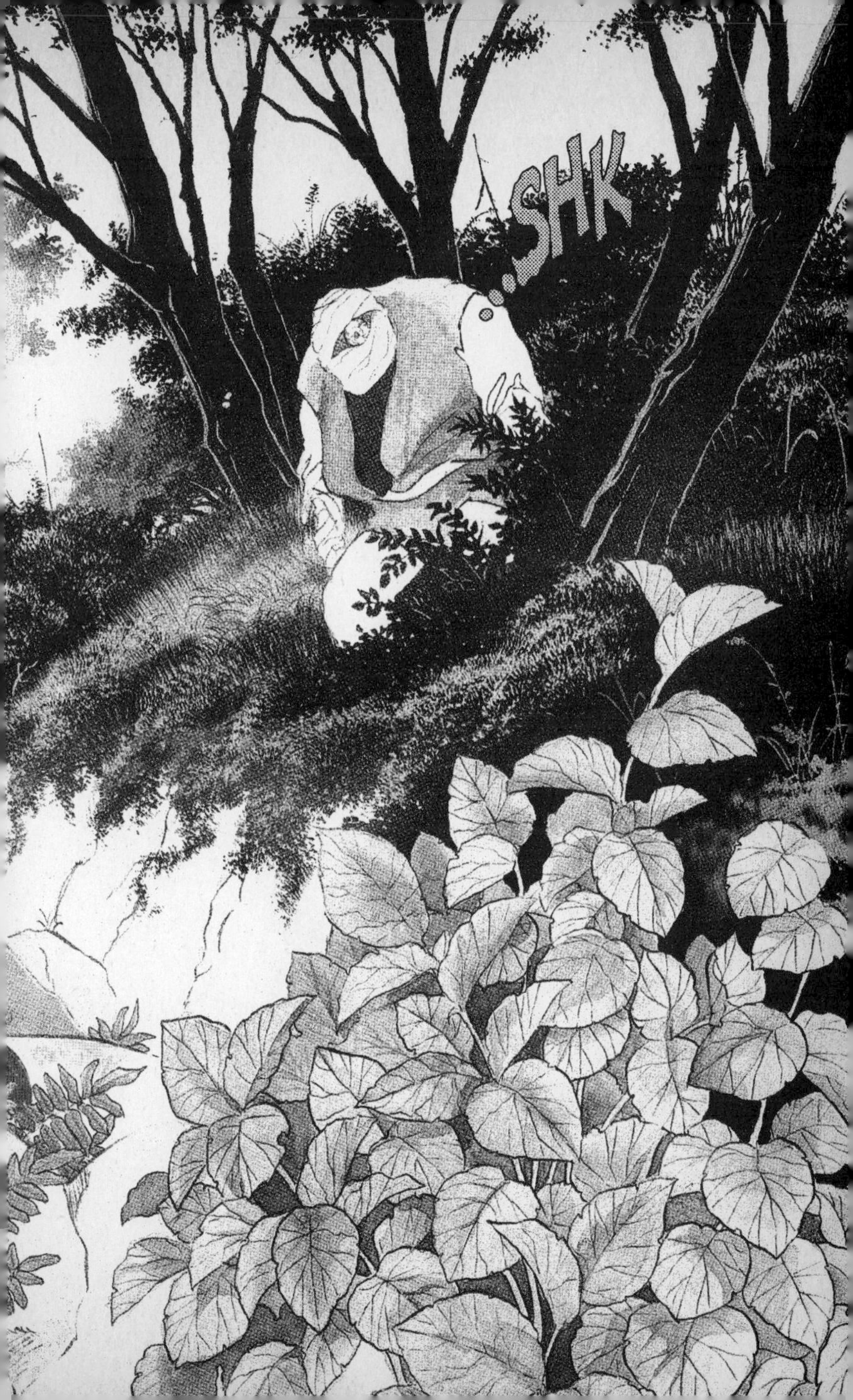
SHK

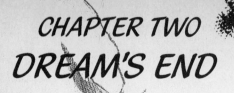

CHAPTER TWO
DREAM'S END

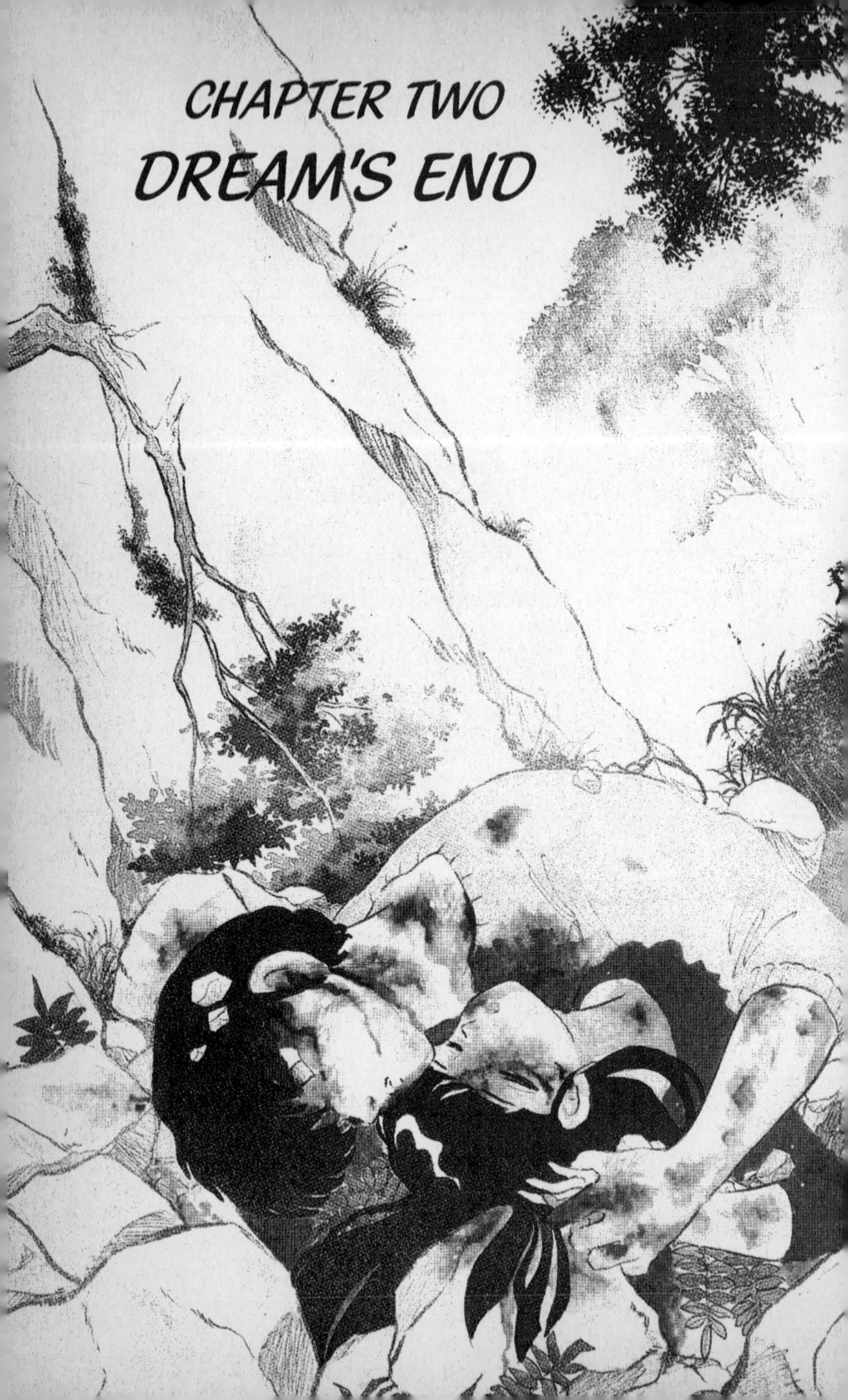

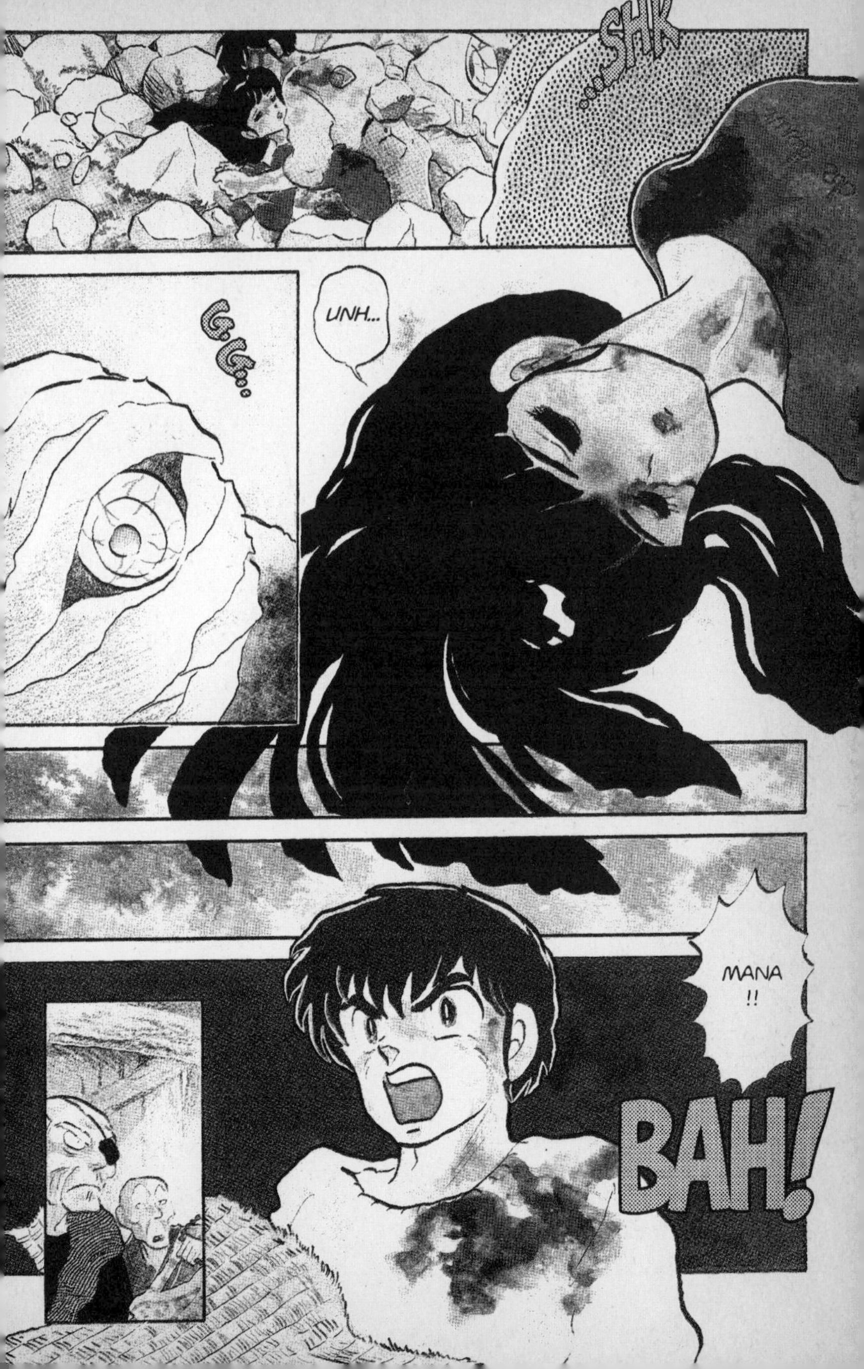
...SHK
UNH...
G.G...
MANA !!
BAH!

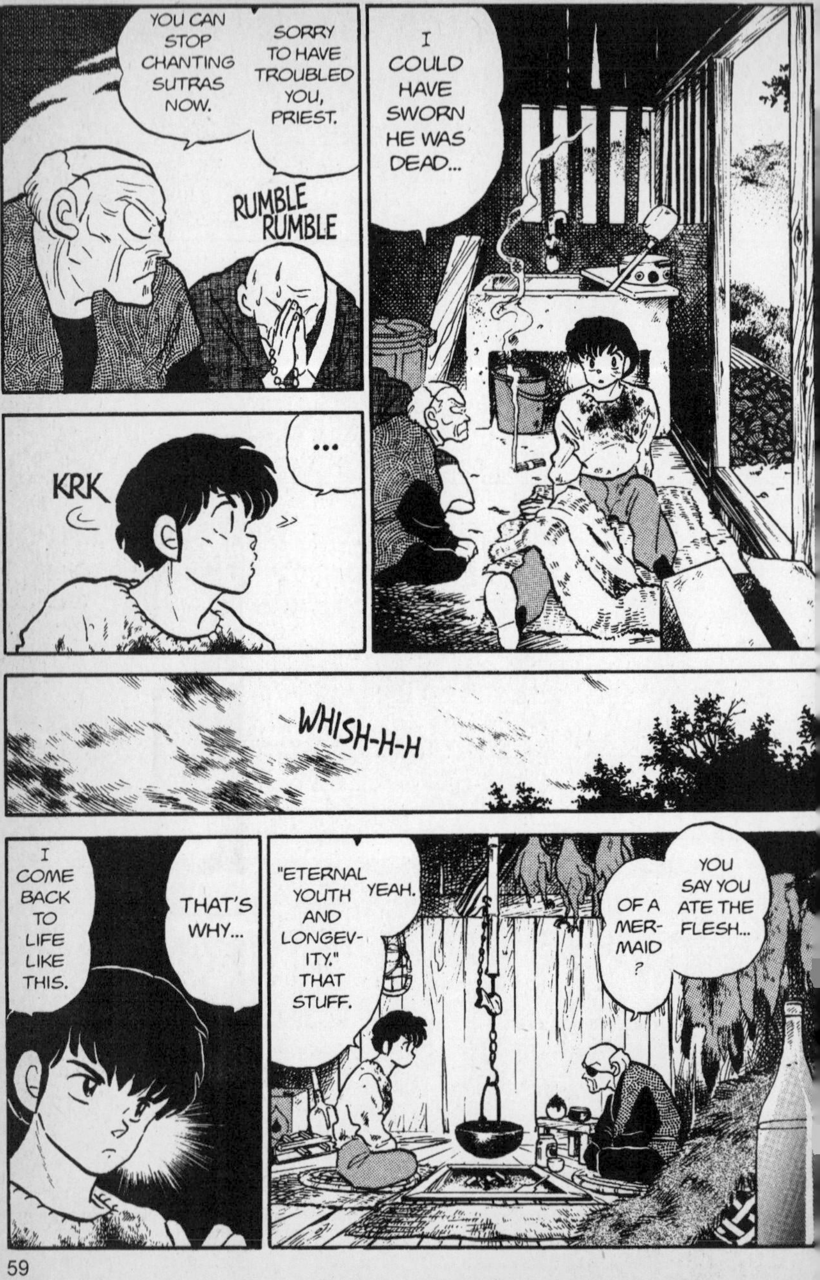
I COULD HAVE SWORN HE WAS DEAD...
SORRY TO HAVE TROUBLED YOU, PRIEST.
YOU CAN STOP CHANTING SUTRAS NOW.
RUMBLE RUMBLE
...
KRK
WHISH-H-H
YOU SAY YOU ATE THE FLESH...
OF A MERMAID?
YEAH.
"ETERNAL YOUTH AND LONGEVITY." THAT STUFF.
THAT'S WHY...
I COME BACK TO LIFE LIKE THIS.

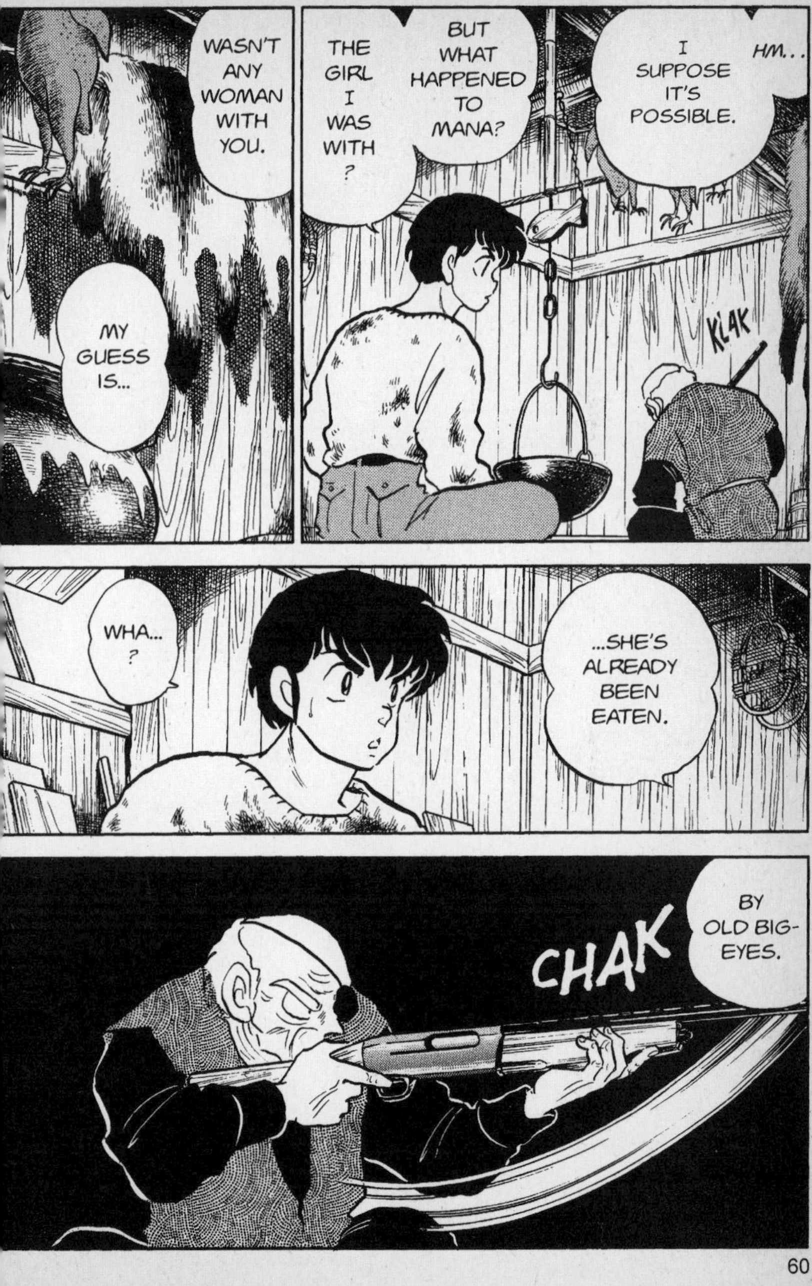
HM...
I SUPPOSE IT'S POSSIBLE.
BUT WHAT HAPPENED TO MANA?
THE GIRL I WAS WITH ?
KLAK
WASN'T ANY WOMAN WITH YOU.
MY GUESS IS...
...SHE'S ALREADY BEEN EATEN.
WHA... ?
BY OLD BIG-EYES.
CHAK

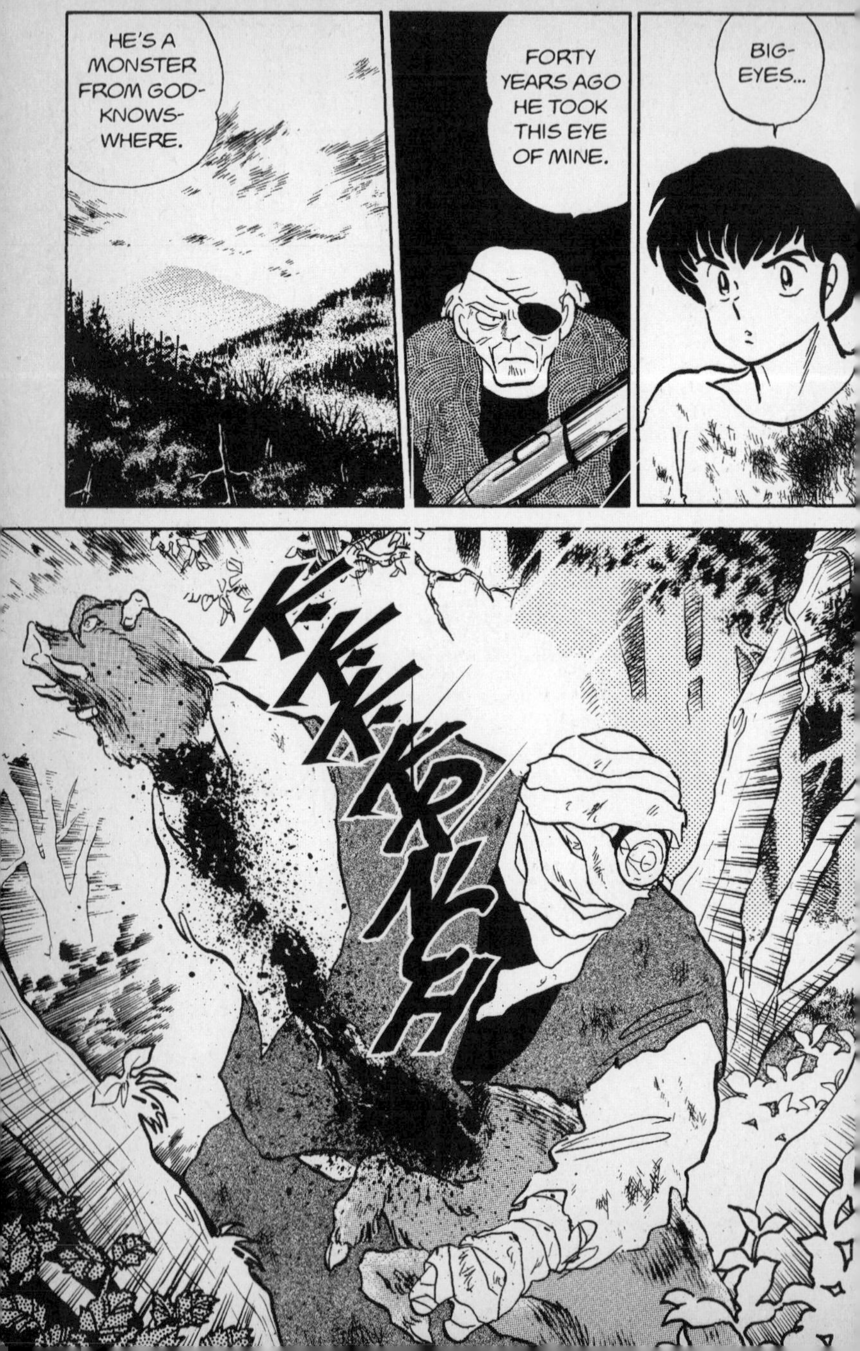
BIG-EYES...
FORTY YEARS AGO HE TOOK THIS EYE OF MINE.
HE'S A MONSTER FROM GOD-KNOWS-WHERE.
K-K-K-KRNCH

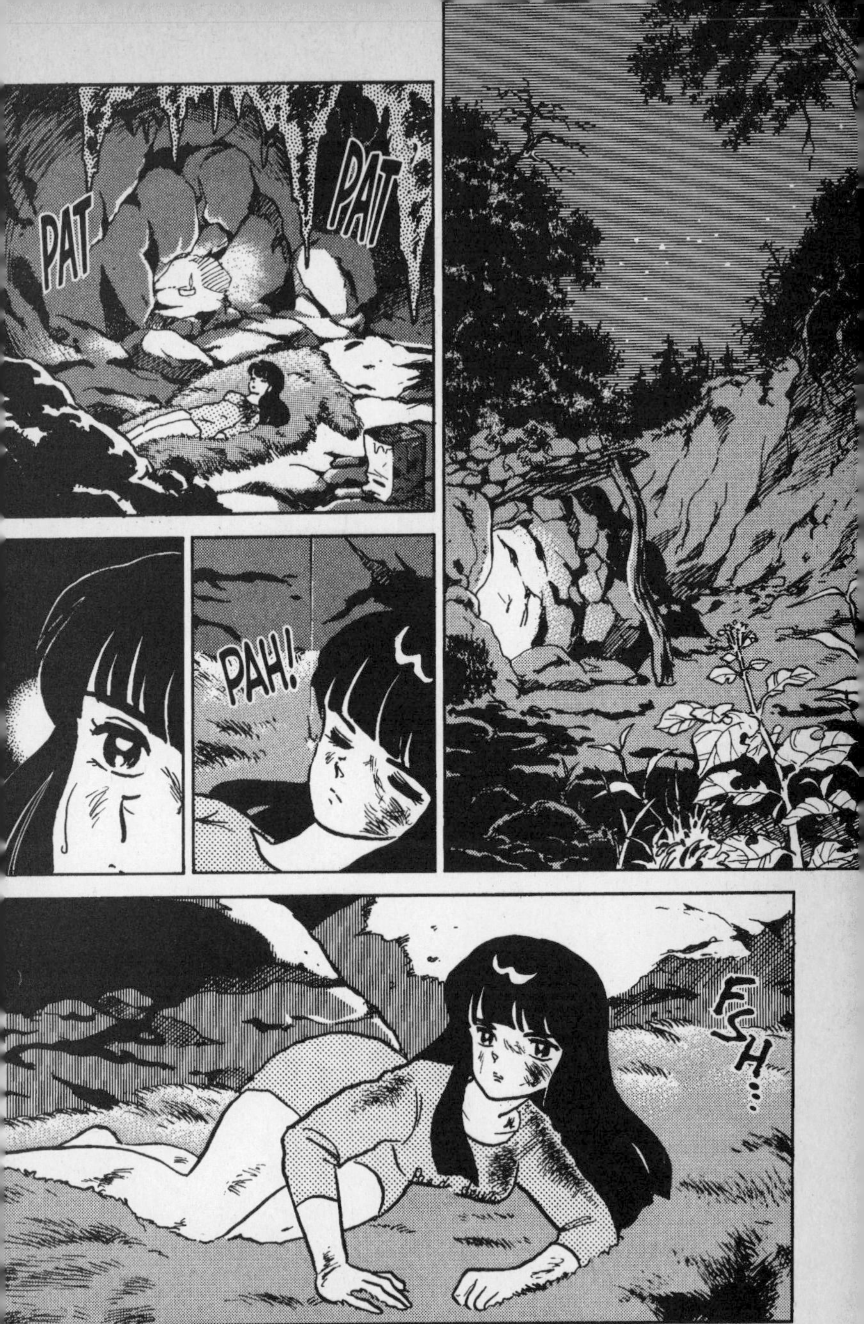
PAT
PAT
PAH!
FSH...

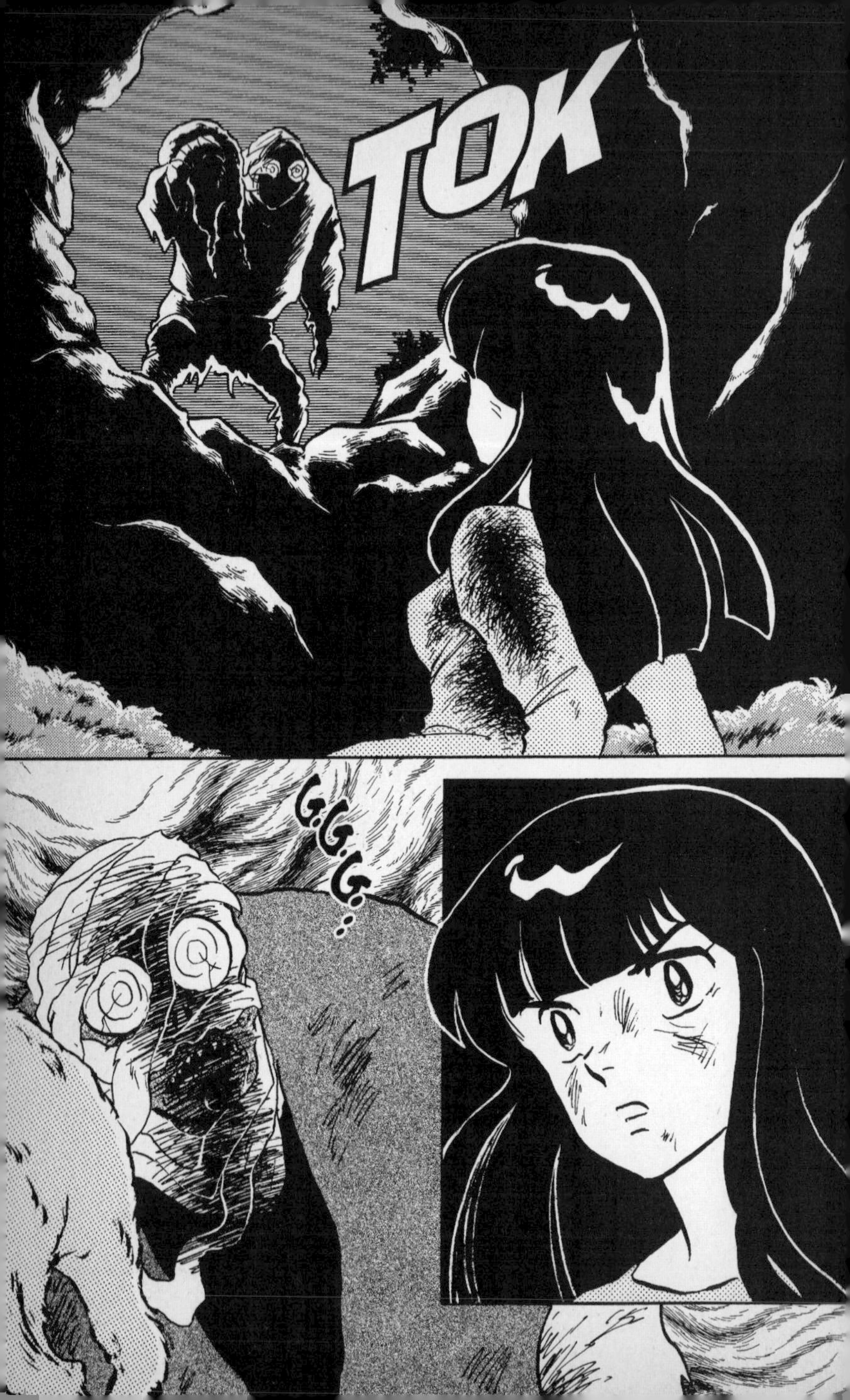
TOK
G.G.G..

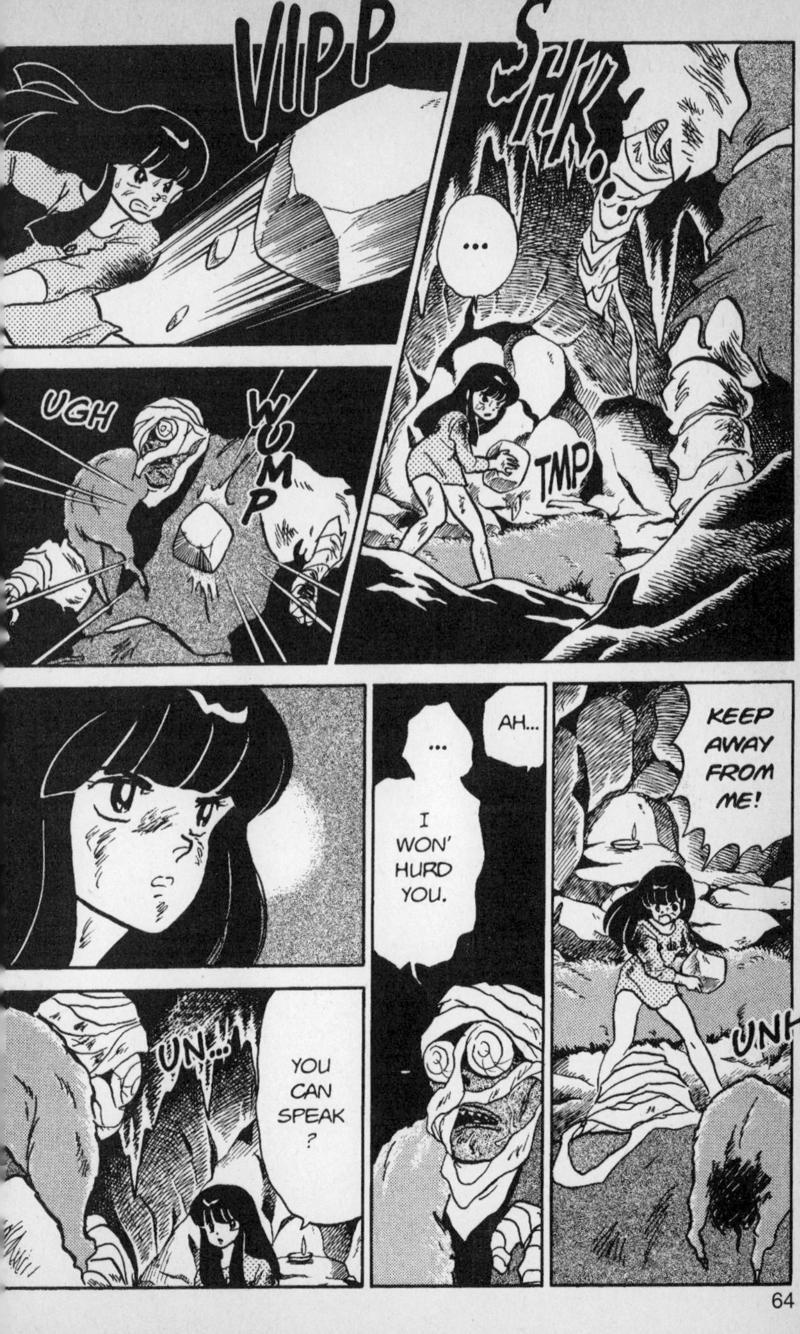
SHK
...
TMP
VIPP
UGH
WUMP
KEEP AWAY FROM ME!
UNH
AH...
...
I WON' HURD YOU.
UN...
YOU CAN SPEAK ?

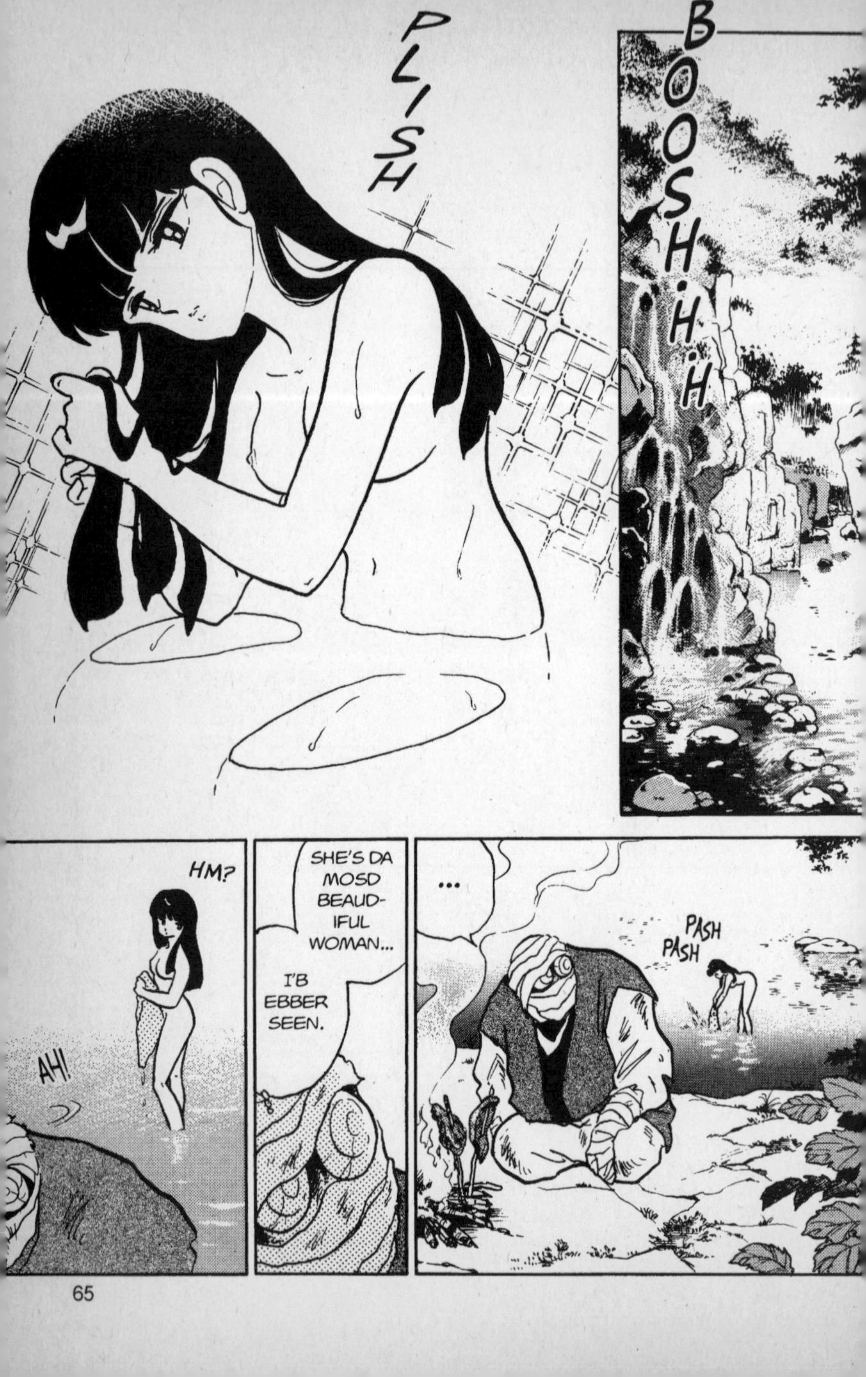
BOOSH.H.H.H
PLISH
...
PASH PASH
SHE'S DA MOSD BEAUD-IFUL WOMAN...
I'B EBBER SEEN.
HM?
AH!

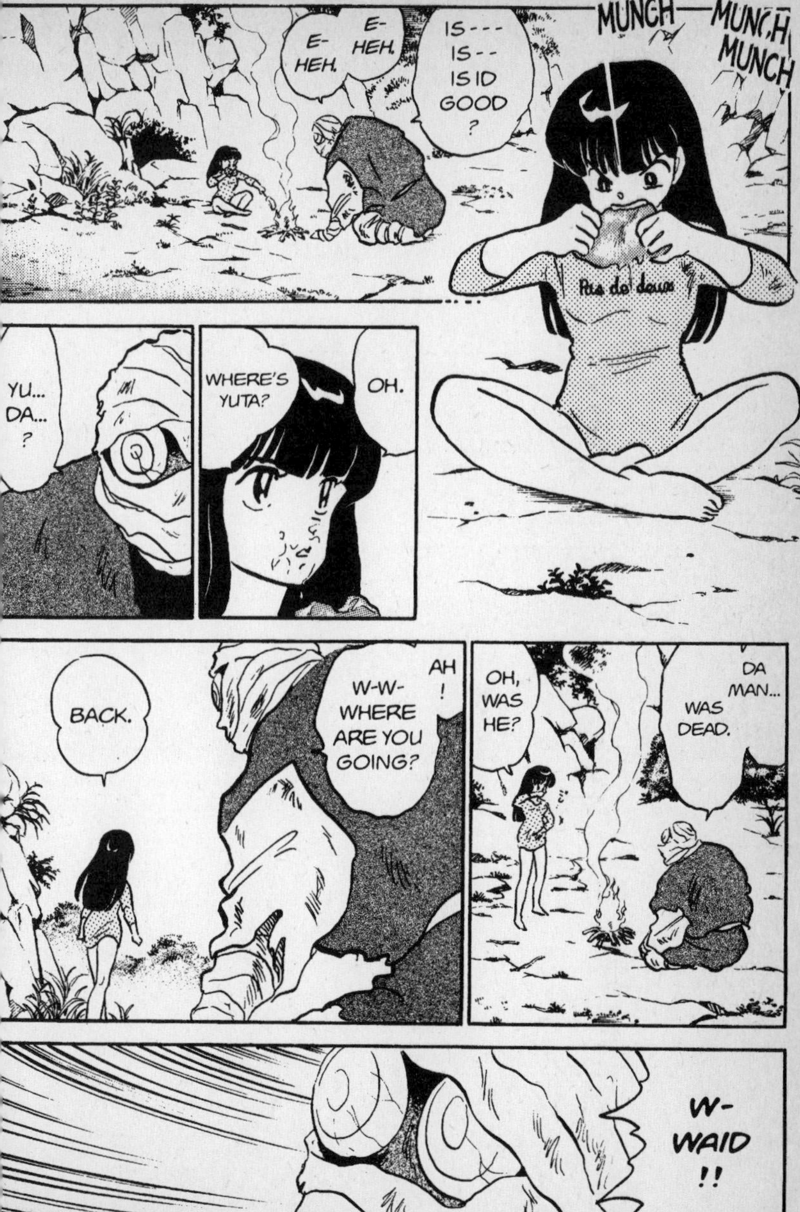
MUNCH MUNCH MUNCH
Pas de deux
IS--- IS-- IS ID GOOD?
E- HEH.
E- HEH.
OH.
WHERE'S YUTA?
YU... DA...?
DA MAN... WAS DEAD.
OH, WAS HE?
AH!
W-W-WHERE ARE YOU GOING?
BACK.
W-WAID!!

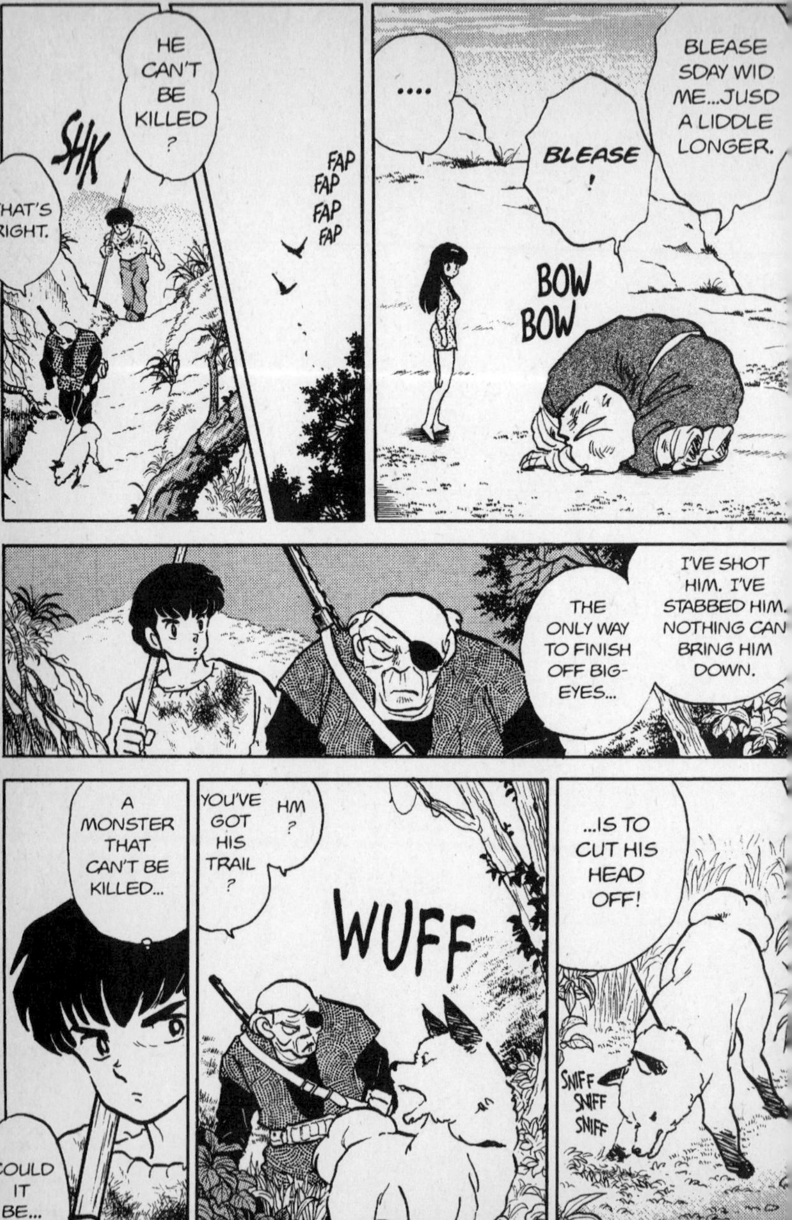
BLEASE SDAY WID ME...JUSD A LIDDLE LONGER.
BLEASE !
BOW BOW
....
FAP FAP FAP FAP
HE CAN'T BE KILLED ?
SHK
THAT'S RIGHT.
I'VE SHOT HIM. I'VE STABBED HIM. NOTHING CAN BRING HIM DOWN.
THE ONLY WAY TO FINISH OFF BIG-EYES...
...IS TO CUT HIS HEAD OFF!
SNIFF SNIFF SNIFF
HM ?
YOU'VE GOT HIS TRAIL ?
WUFF
A MONSTER THAT CAN'T BE KILLED...
COULD IT BE... ?

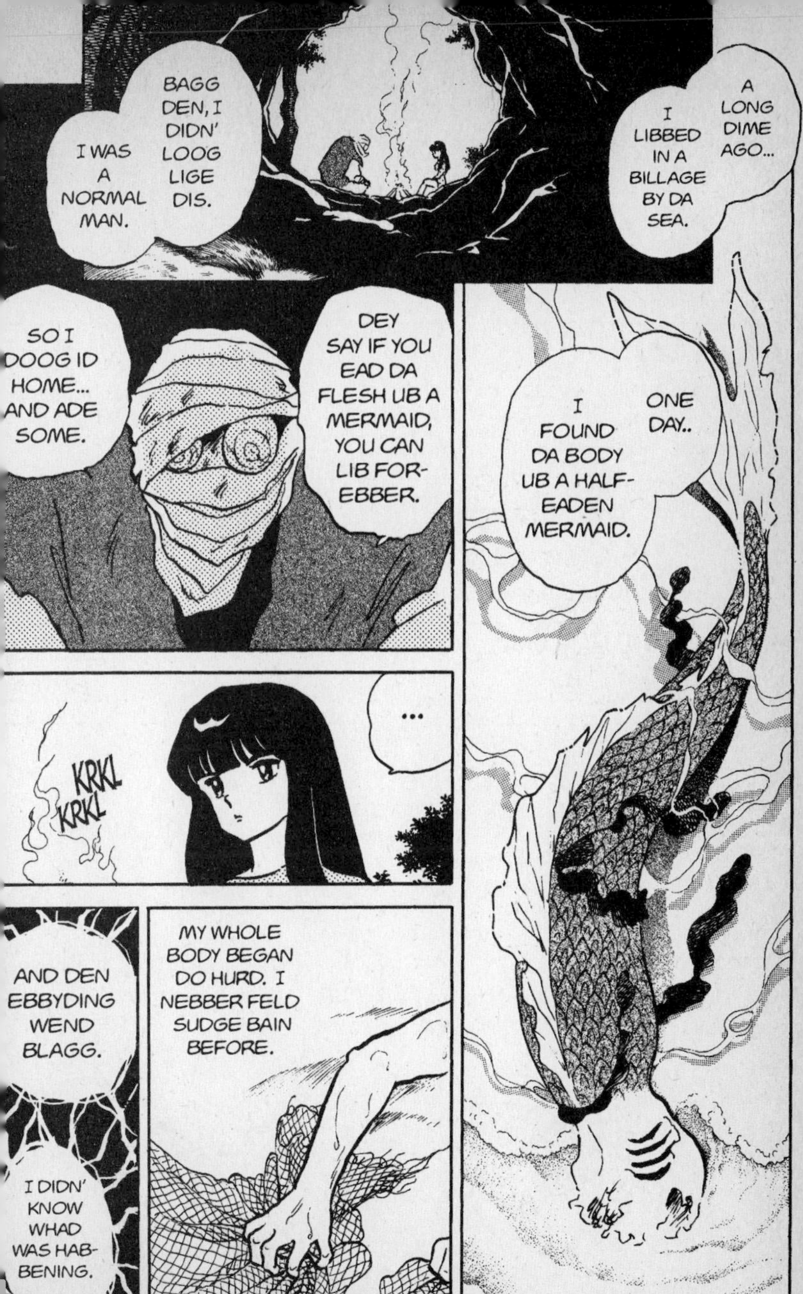
A LONG DIME AGO...
I LIBBED IN A BILLAGE BY DA SEA.
BAGG DEN, I DIDN' LOOG LIGE DIS.
I WAS A NORMAL MAN.
ONE DAY..
I FOUND DA BODY UB A HALF-EADEN MERMAID.
DEY SAY IF YOU EAD DA FLESH UB A MERMAID, YOU CAN LIB FOR-EBBER.
SO I DOOG ID HOME... AND ADE SOME.
...
KRKL
KRKL
MY WHOLE BODY BEGAN DO HURD. I NEBBER FELD SUDGE BAIN BEFORE.
AND DEN EBBYDING WEND BLAGG.
I DIDN' KNOW WHAD WAS HAB-BENING.

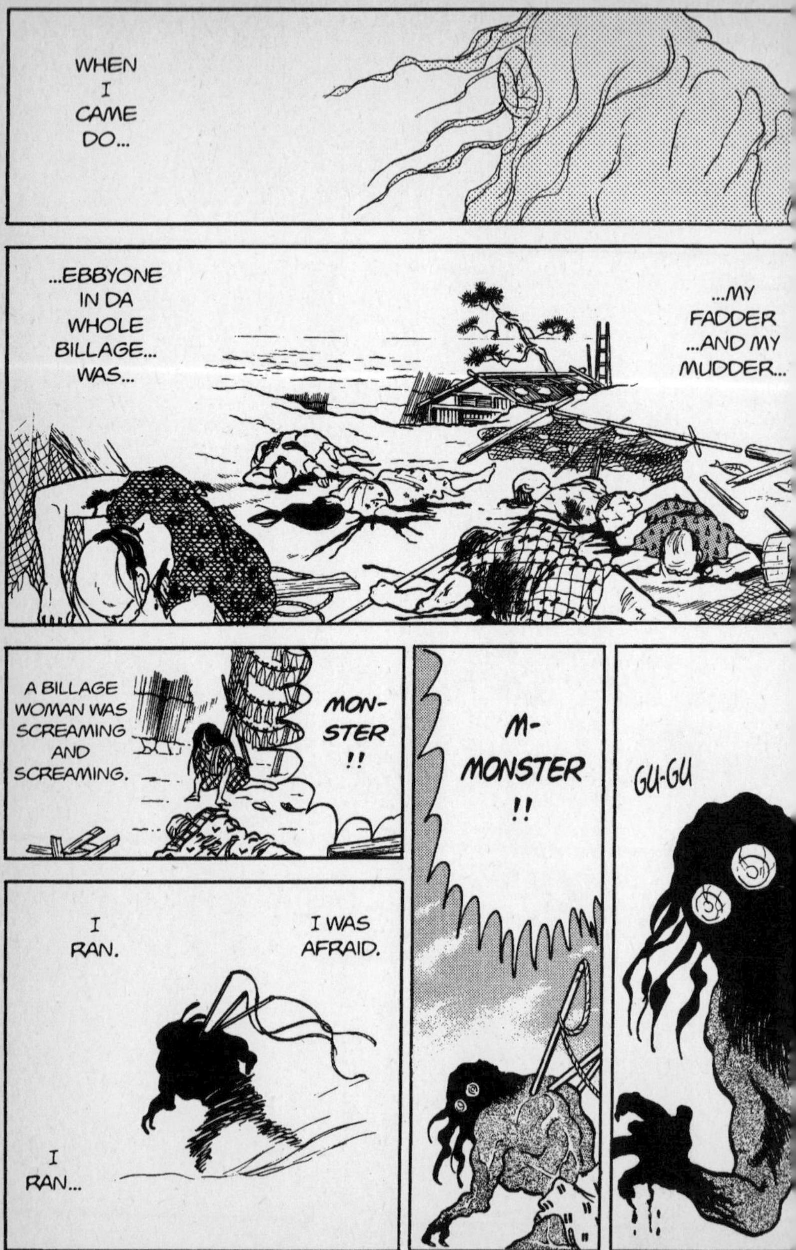
WHEN I CAME DO...
...EBBYONE IN DA WHOLE BILLAGE... WAS...
...MY FADDER ...AND MY MUDDER...
GU-GU
M- MONSTER !!
A BILLAGE WOMAN WAS SCREAMING AND SCREAMING.
MON-STER !!
I WAS AFRAID.
I RAN.
I RAN...

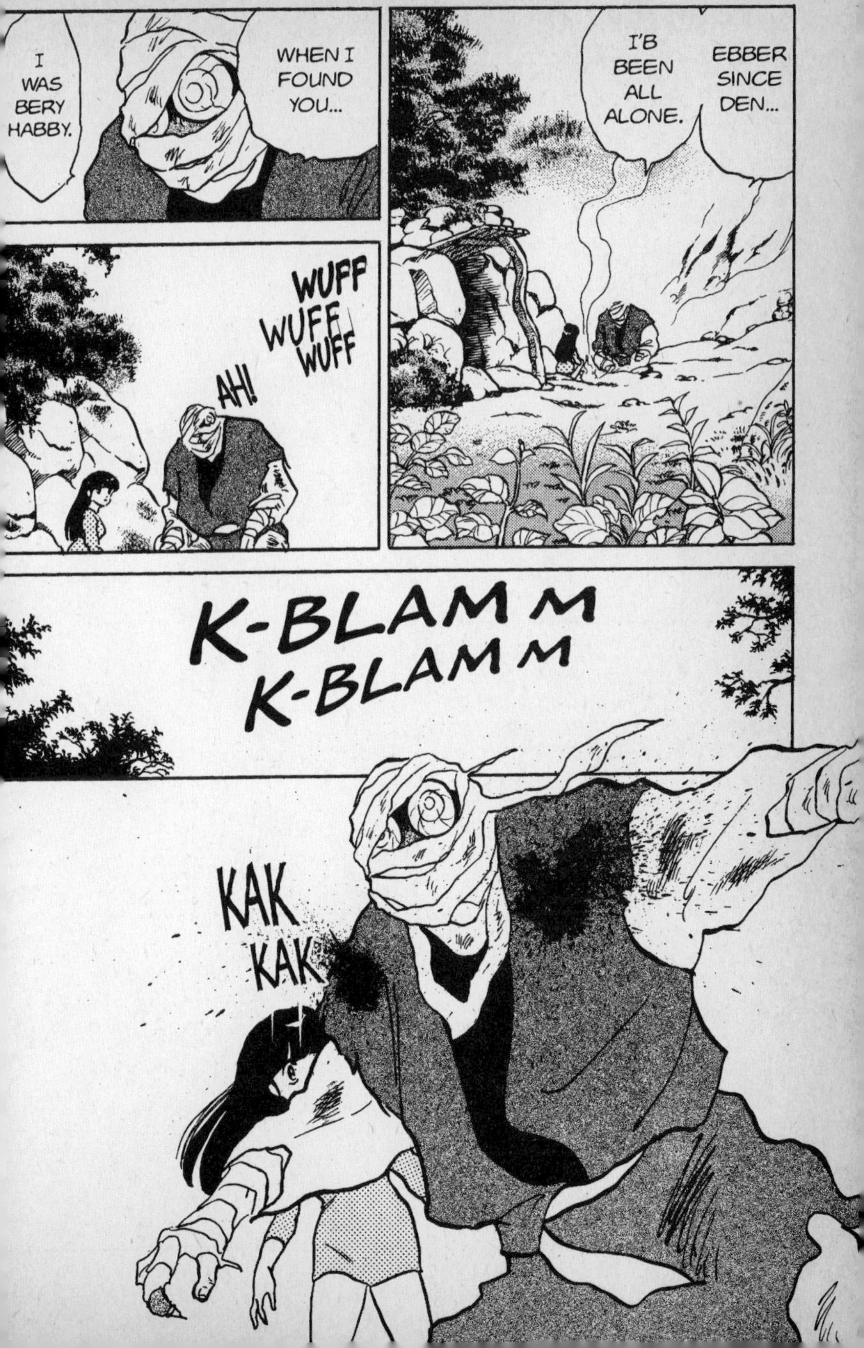
EBBER SINCE DEN...
I'B BEEN ALL ALONE.
WHEN I FOUND YOU...
I WAS BERY HABBY.
WUFF WUFF WUFF
AH!
K-BLAMM K-BLAMM
KAK KAK

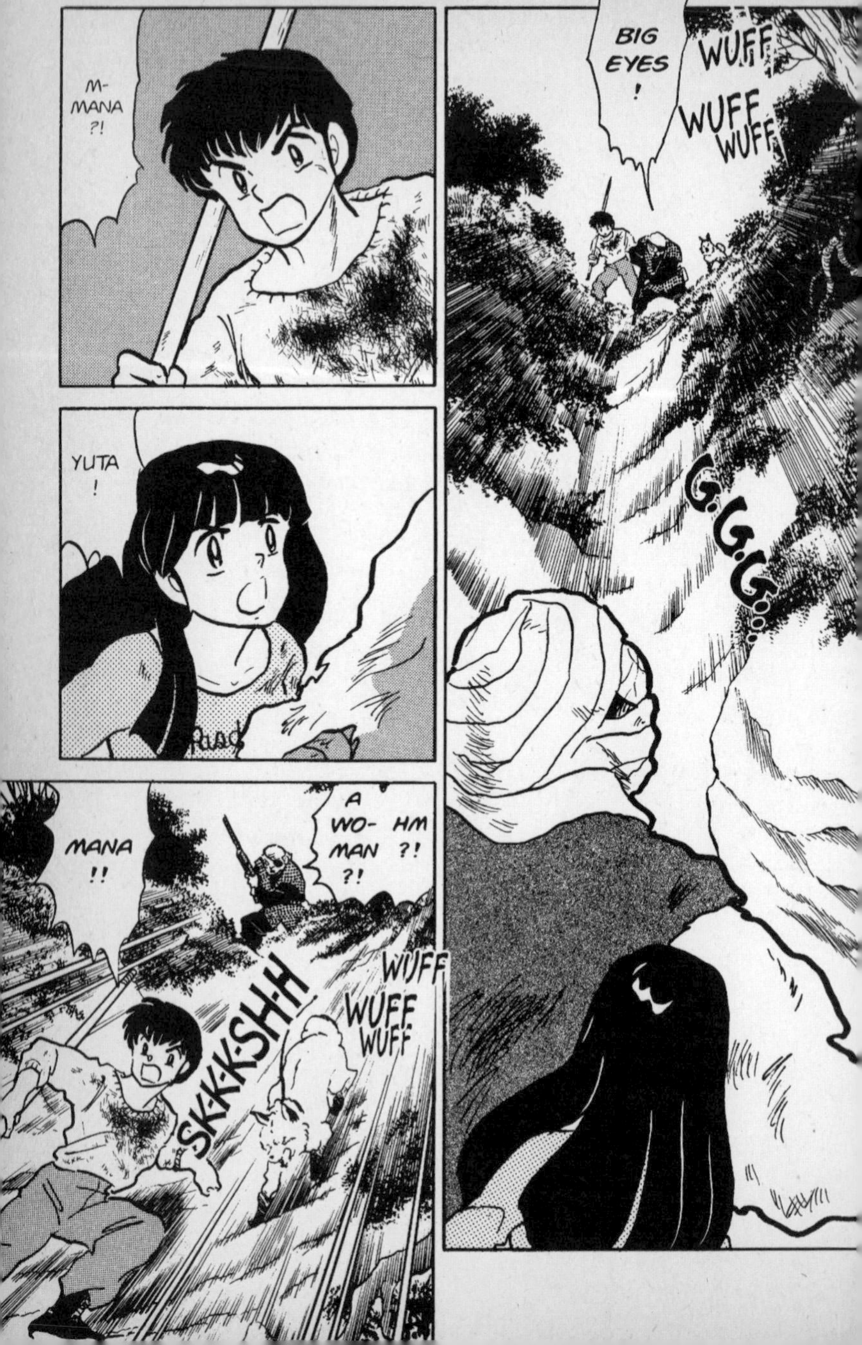
BIG EYES !
WUFF
WUFF WUFF
G.G.G...
M-MANA ?!
YUTA !
HM ?!
A WO-MAN ?!
MANA !!
WUFF
WUFF WUFF
SK-K-KSH-H

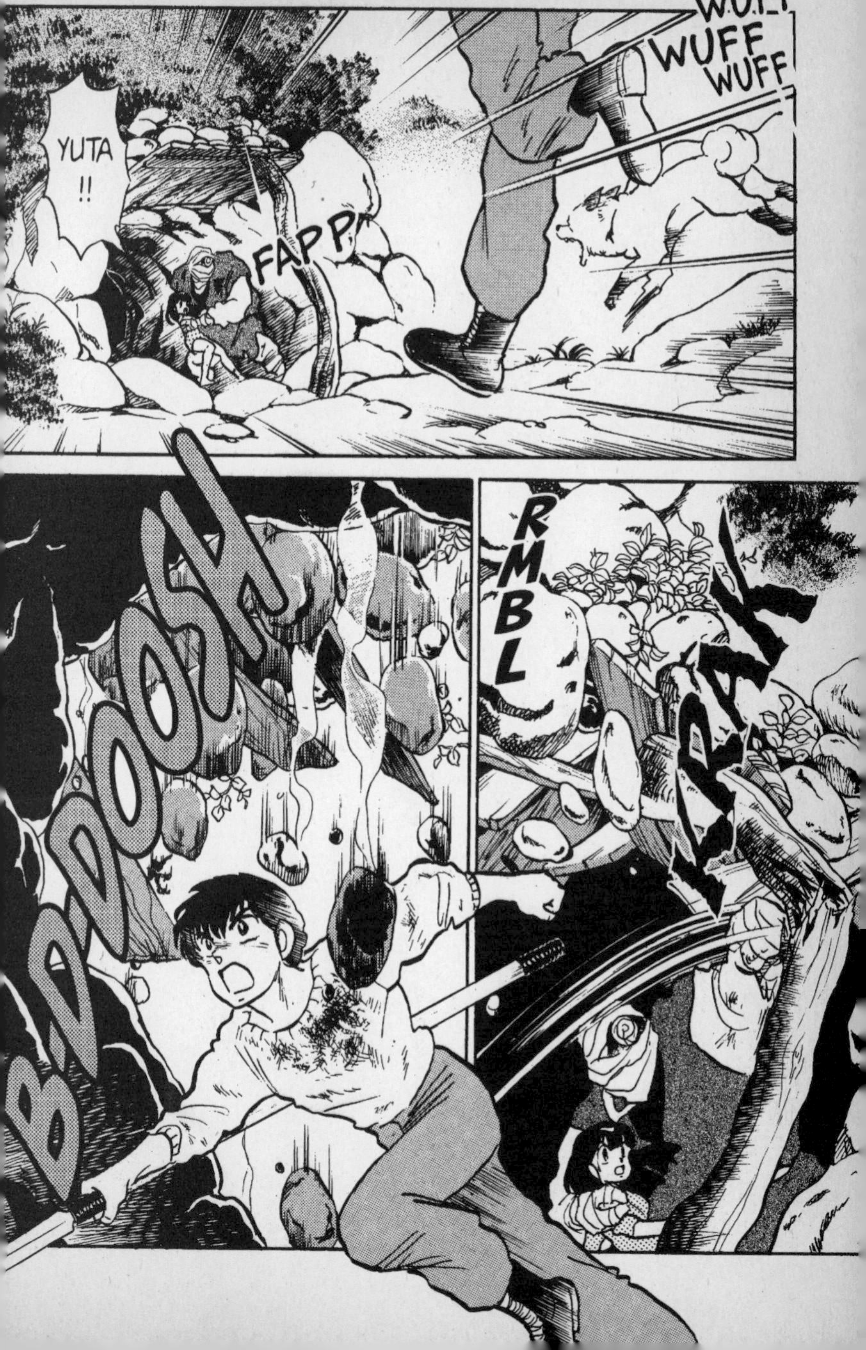
WUFF
WUFF
WUFF
FAPP
YUTA !!
RMBL
KRAK
BDOOSH

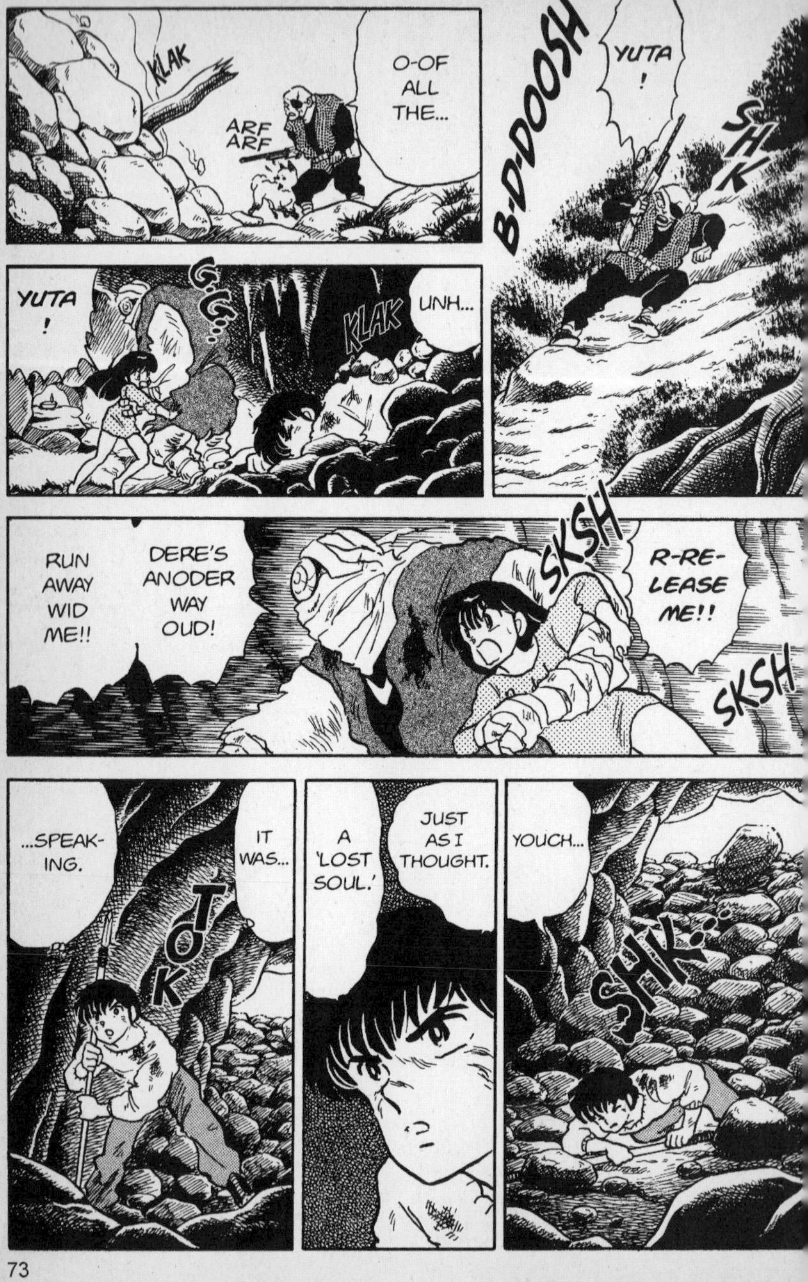
B-D-DOOSH
YUTA!
SHK
O-OF ALL THE...
KLAK
ARF ARF
UNH...
KLAK
G G..
YUTA!
R-RE-LEASE ME!!
SKSH
SKSH
DERE'S ANODER WAY OUD!
RUN AWAY WID ME!!
YOUCH...
SHK..
JUST AS I THOUGHT.
A 'LOST SOUL.'
IT WAS...
...SPEAK-ING.
TOK

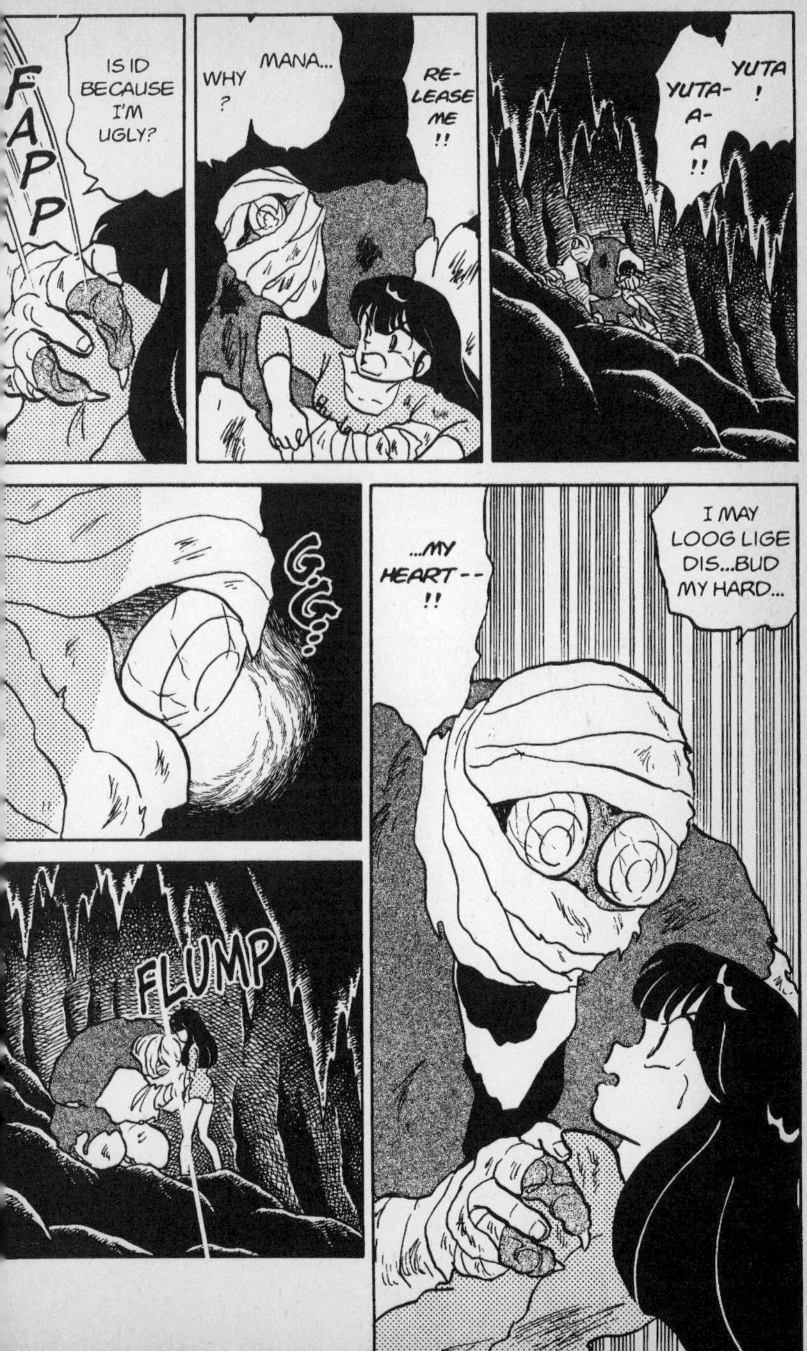

YUTA!
YUTA-A-A!!
RE-LEASE ME!!
MANA... WHY?
IS ID BECAUSE I'M UGLY?
FAPP
I MAY LOOG LIGE DIS...BUD MY HARD...
...MY HEART--!!
G.G.G...
FLUMP

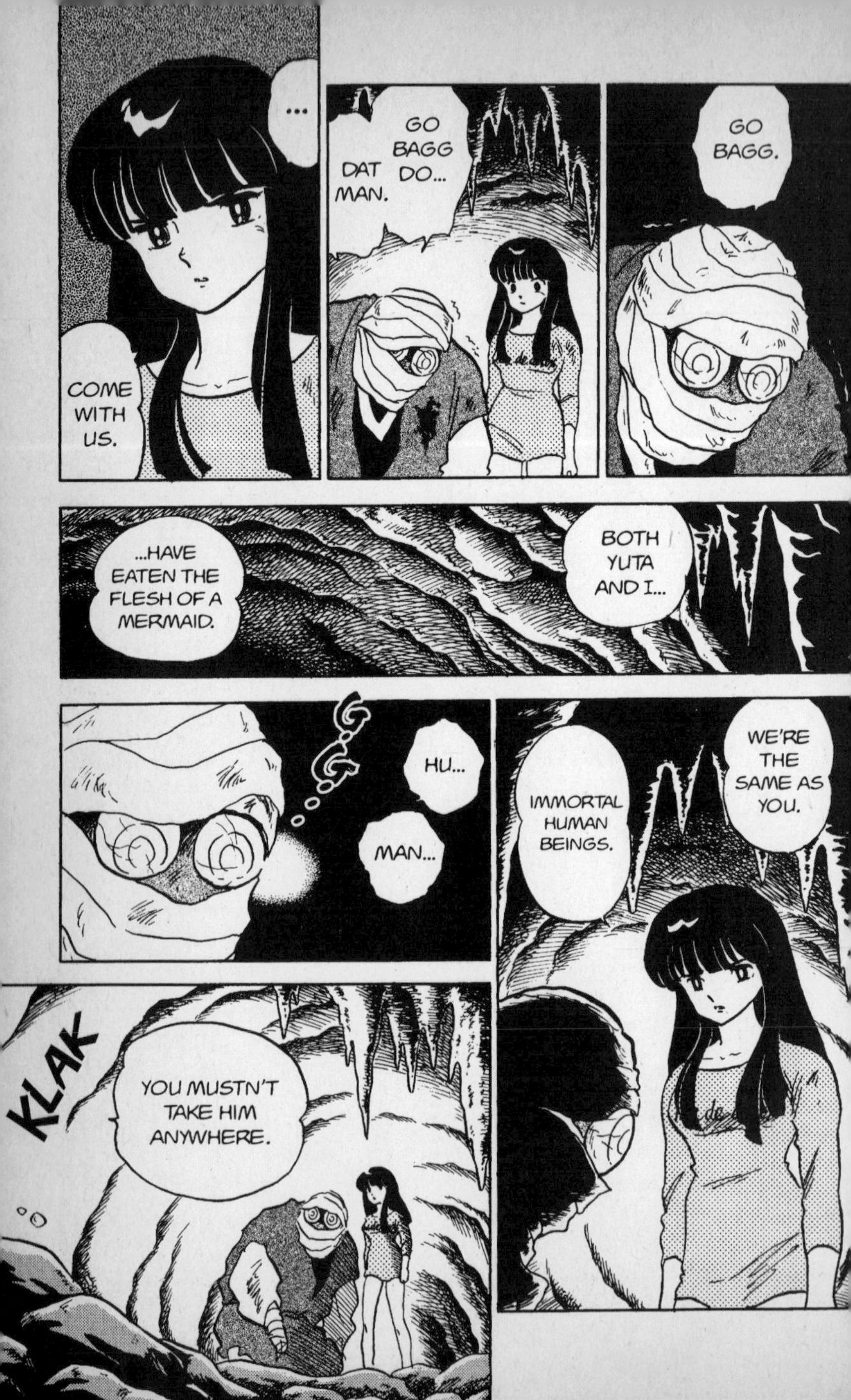
GO BAGG.
GO BAGG DO... DAT MAN.
...
COME WITH US.
BOTH YUTA AND I...
...HAVE EATEN THE FLESH OF A MERMAID.
WE'RE THE SAME AS YOU.
IMMORTAL HUMAN BEINGS.
HU...
MAN...
KLAK
YOU MUSTN'T TAKE HIM ANYWHERE.

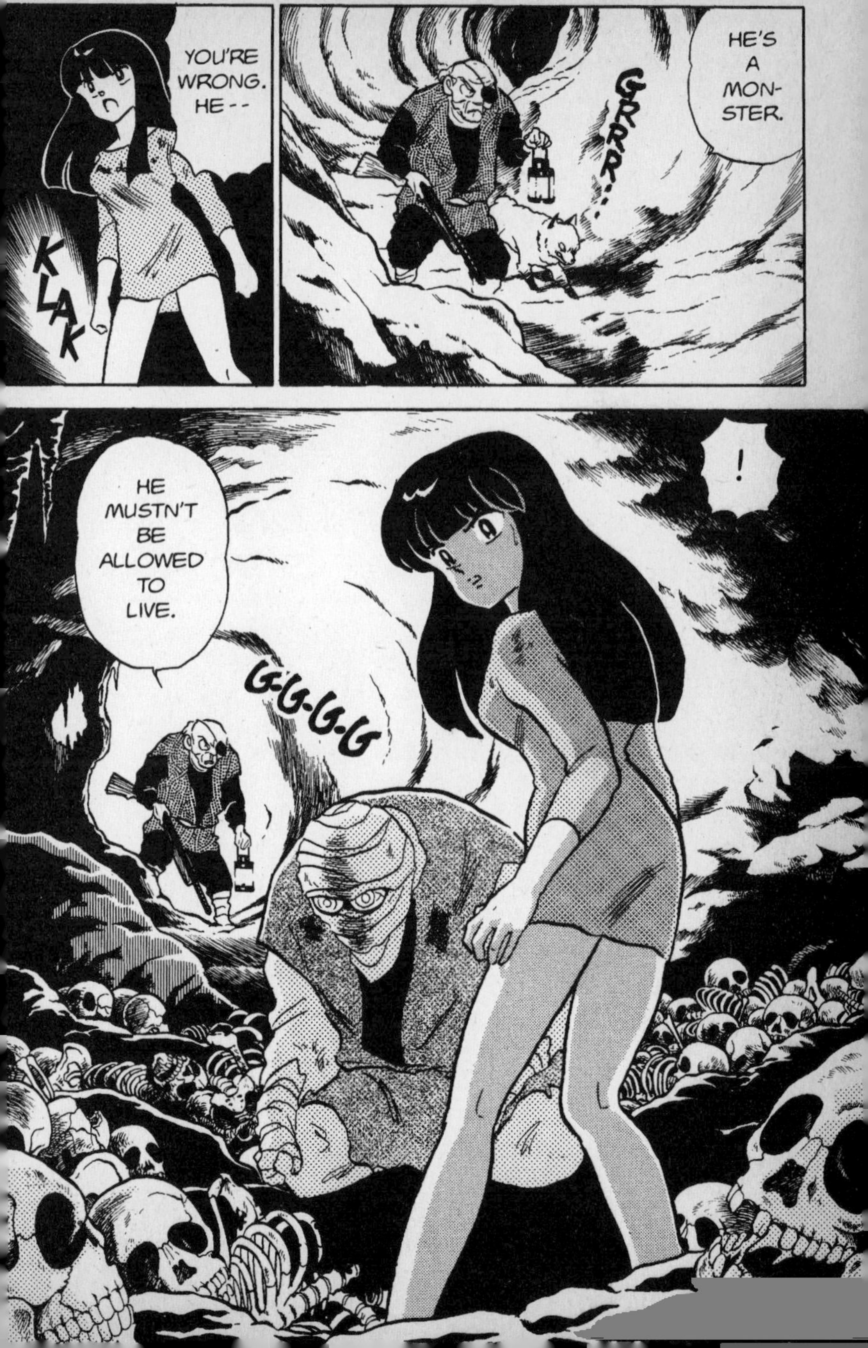
HE'S A MONSTER.
GRRR..
YOU'RE WRONG. HE--
KLAK
!
HE MUSTN'T BE ALLOWED TO LIVE.
G-G-G-G

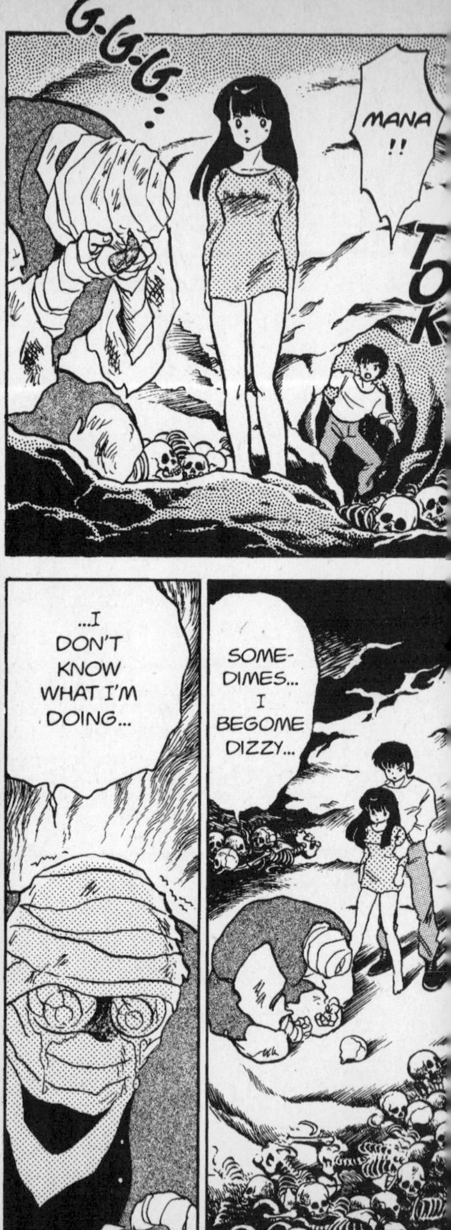
G-G-G...
MANA !!
TOK
SOME-DIMES... I BEGOME DIZZY...
...I DON'T KNOW WHAT I'M DOING...
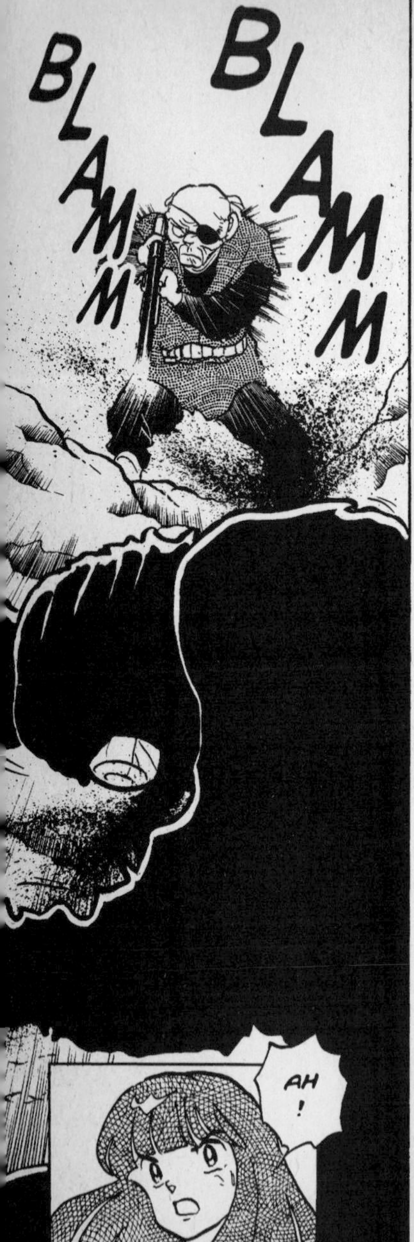
BLAMM
BLAMM
AH !

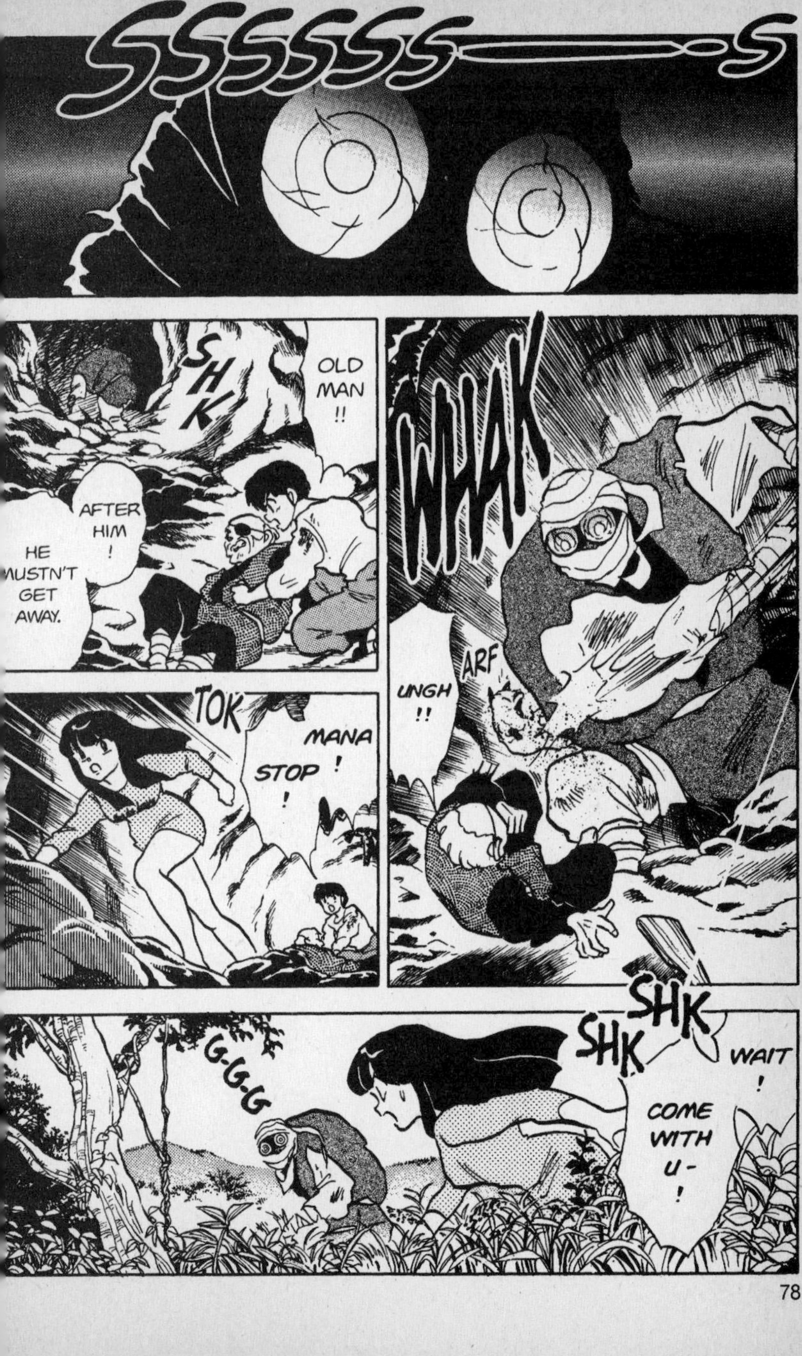

SSSSSSS—S
WHAK
ARF
UNGH !!
SHK
OLD MAN !!
AFTER HIM !
HE MUSTN'T GET AWAY.
TOK
MANA !
STOP !
SHK
SHK
WAIT !
COME WITH U- !
G-G-G

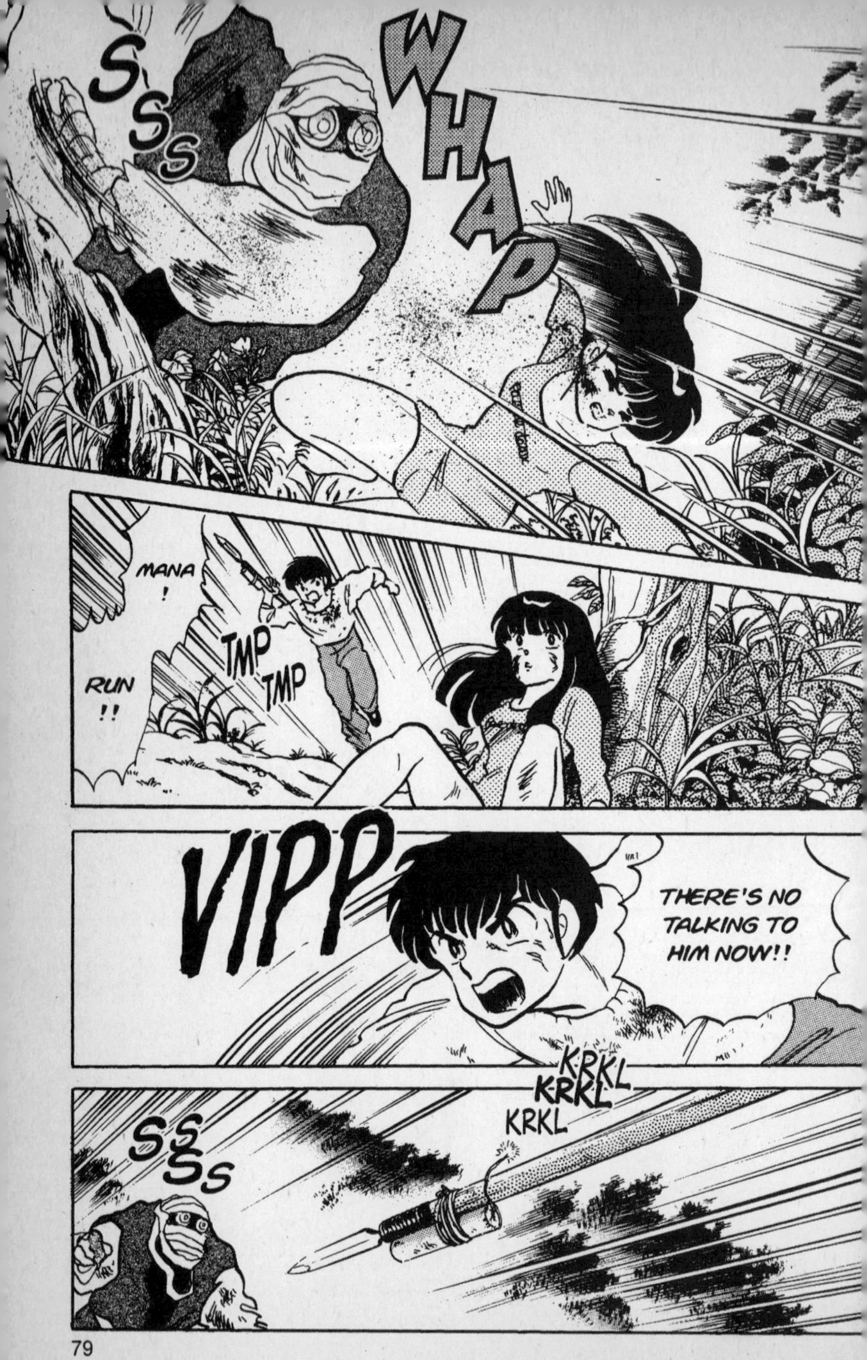
WHAP
SSS
MANA !
TMP TMP
RUN !!
THERE'S NO TALKING TO HIM NOW!!
VIPP
K-RKL K-RKL KRKL
SSSS

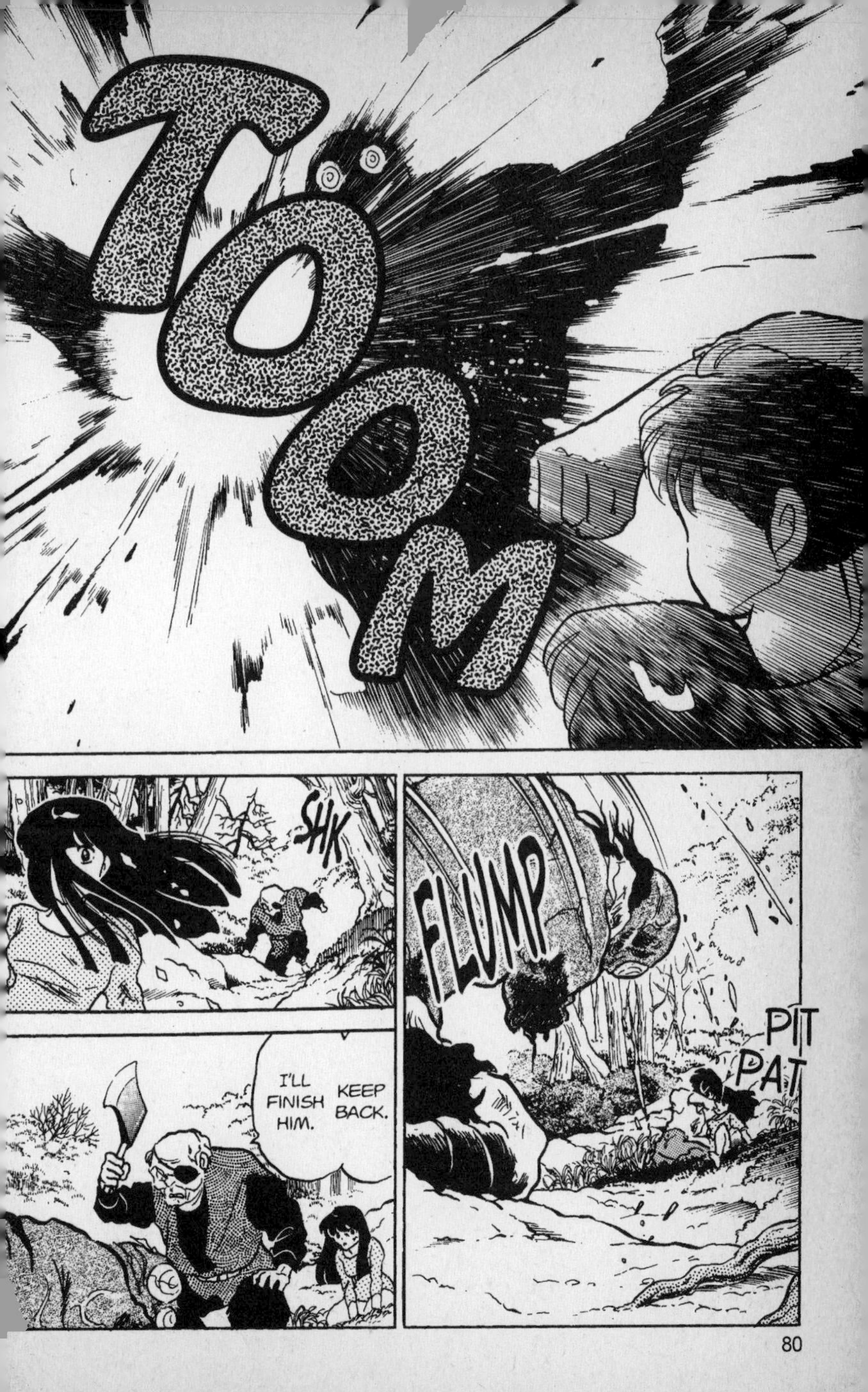
TOOM
FLUMP
PIT PAT
SHK
I'LL FINISH HIM. KEEP BACK.

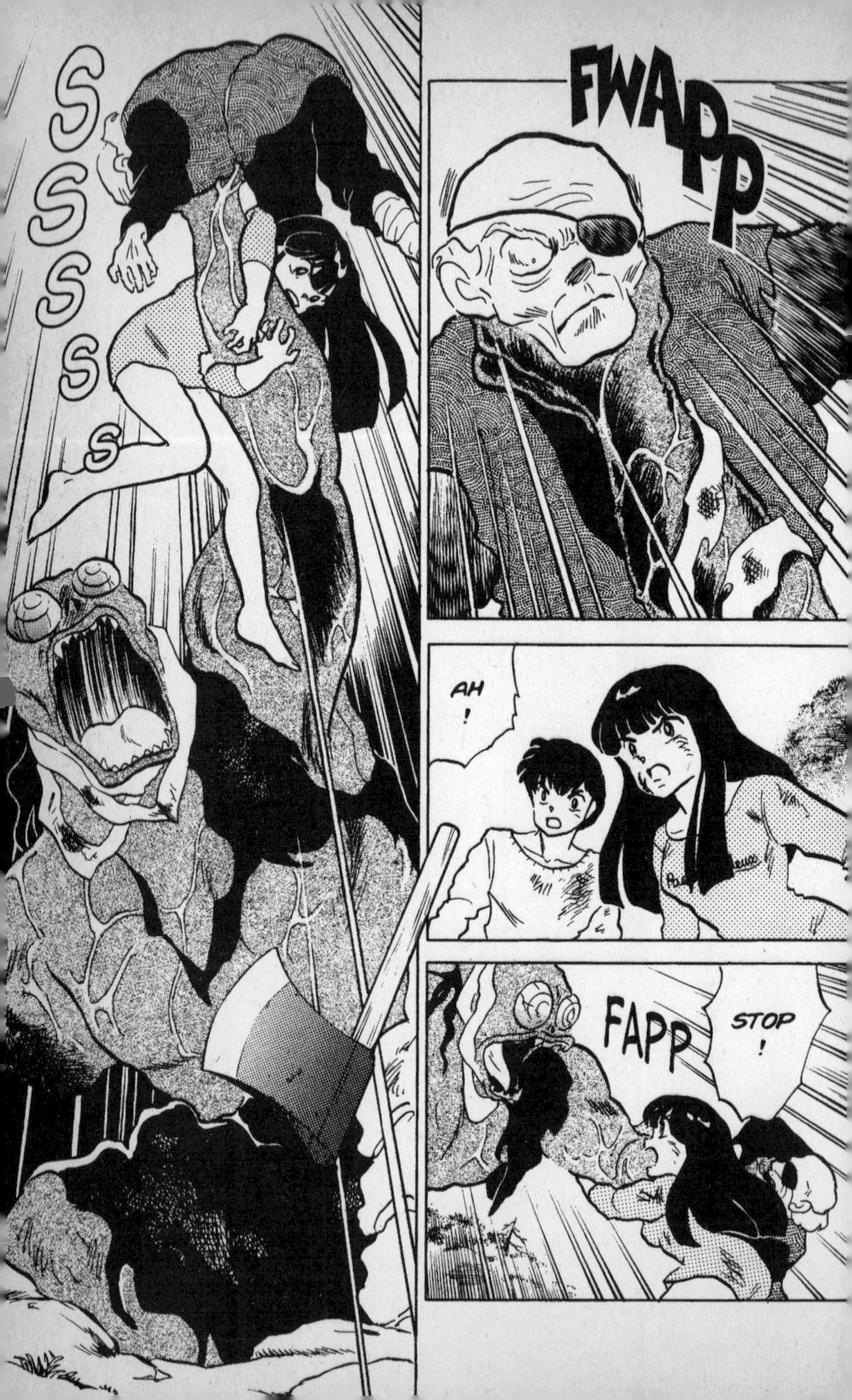
FWAPP
AH!
FAPP
STOP!
SSSSSs

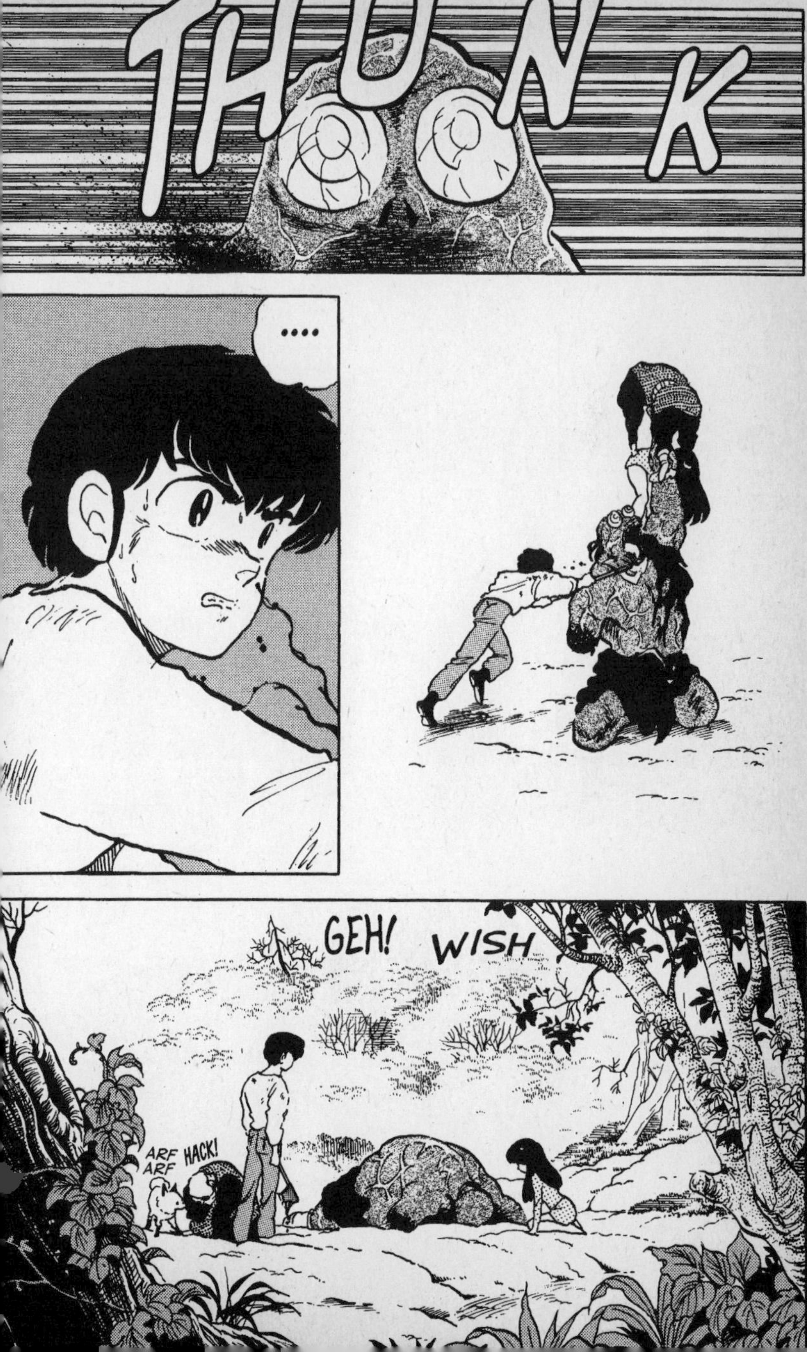
THUNK
....
GEH!
WISH
HACK!
ARF ARF

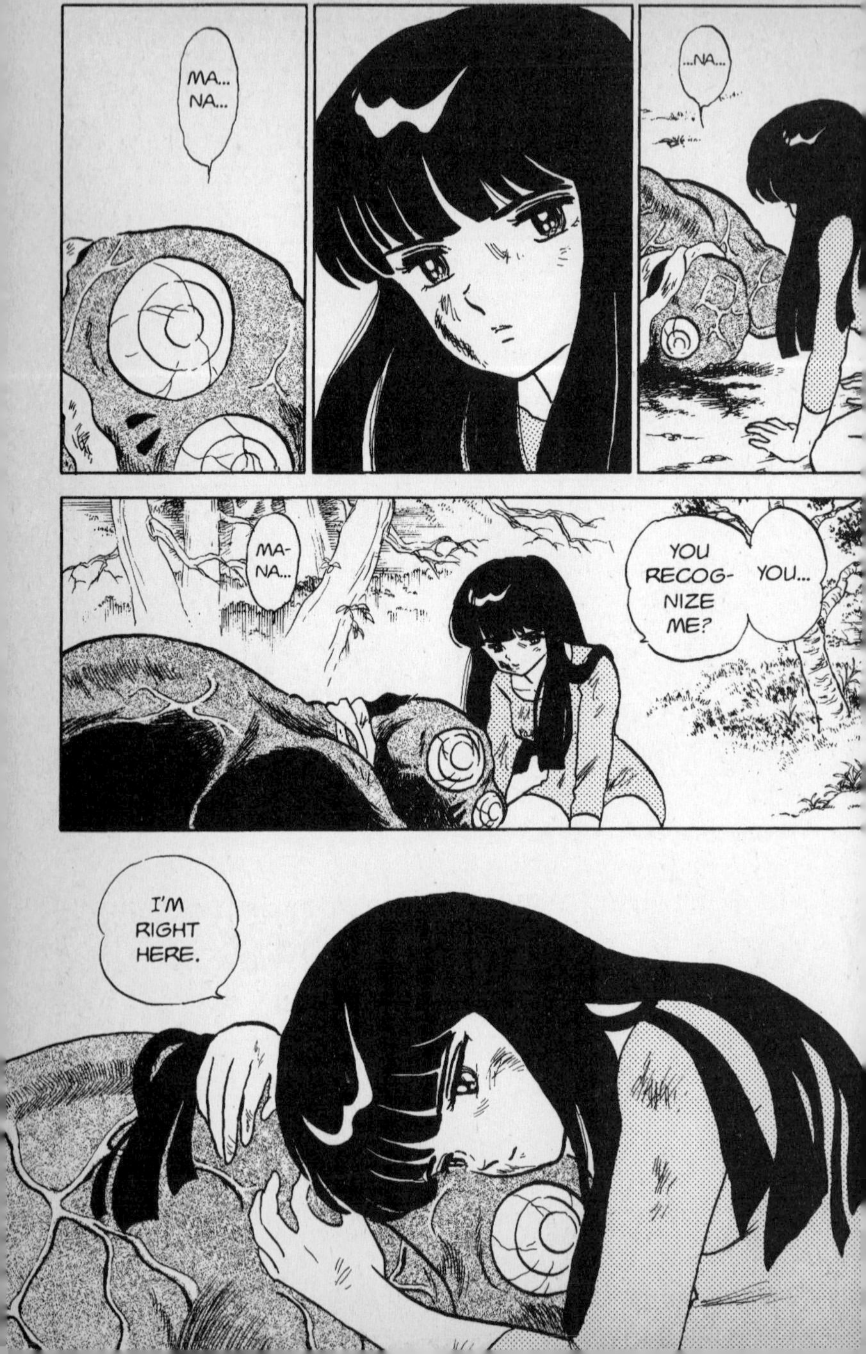
...NA...
MA... NA...
YOU...
YOU RECOG-NIZE ME?
MA-NA...
I'M RIGHT HERE.

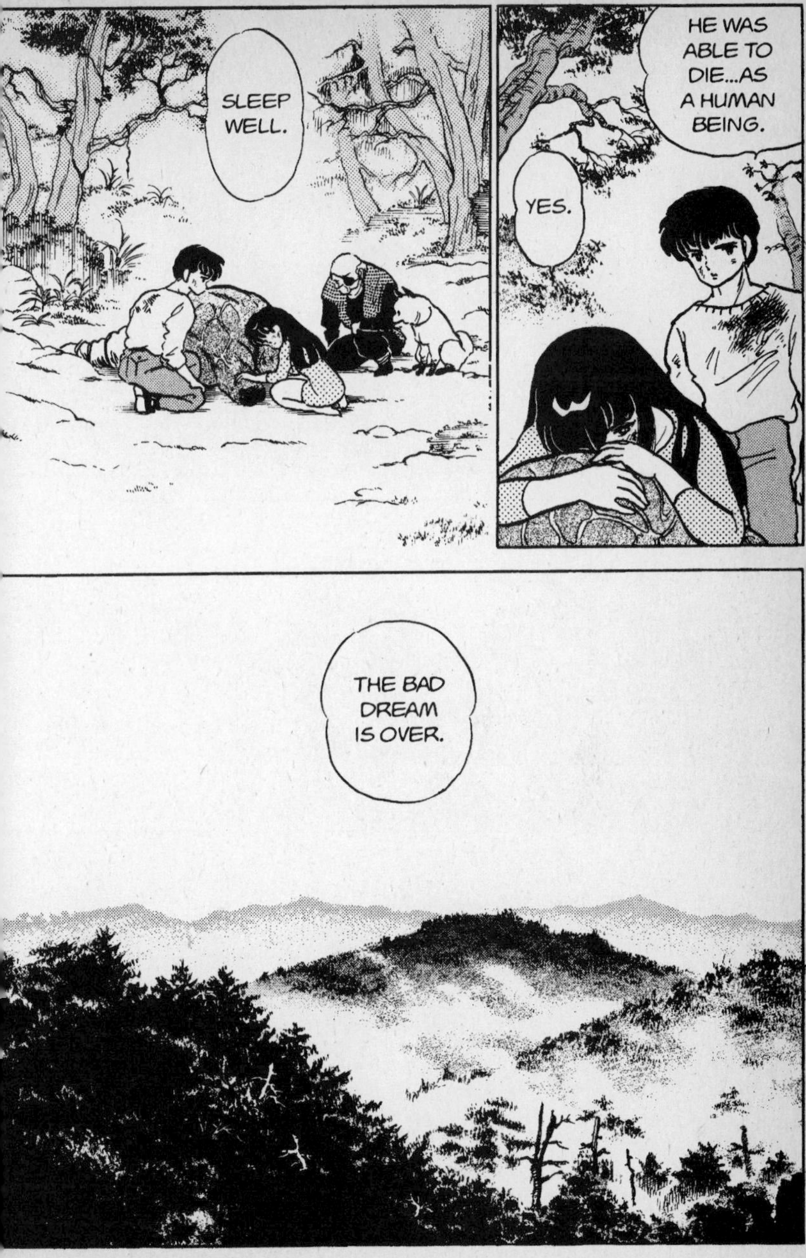
HE WAS ABLE TO DIE...AS A HUMAN BEING.
YES.
SLEEP WELL.
THE BAD DREAM IS OVER.

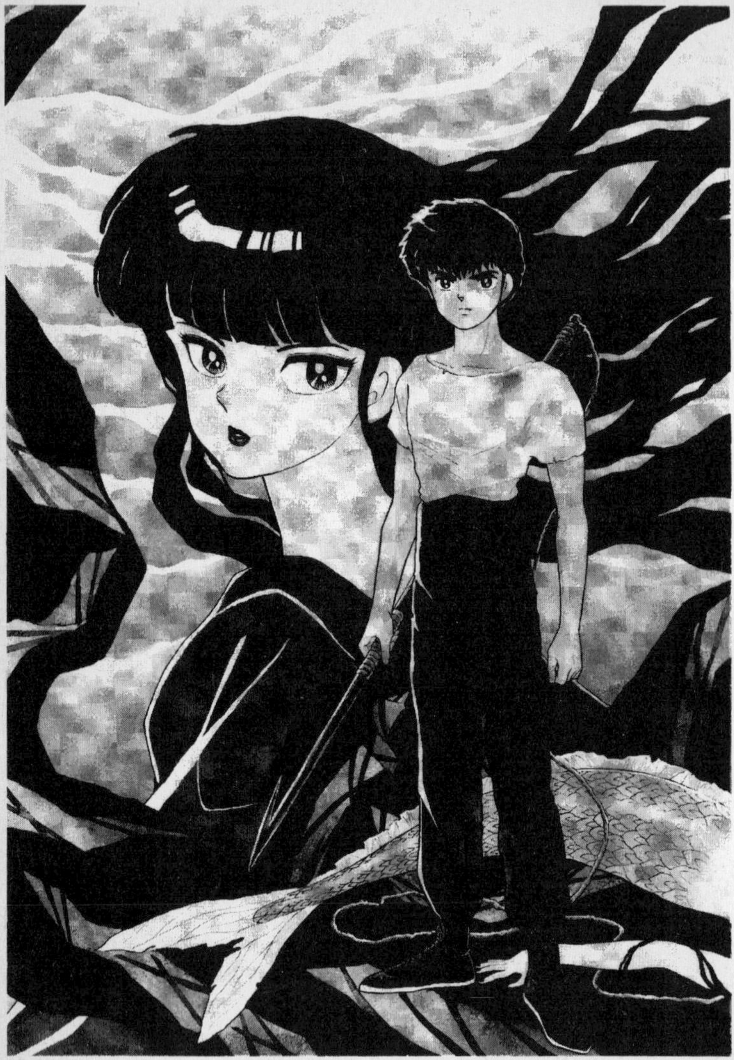

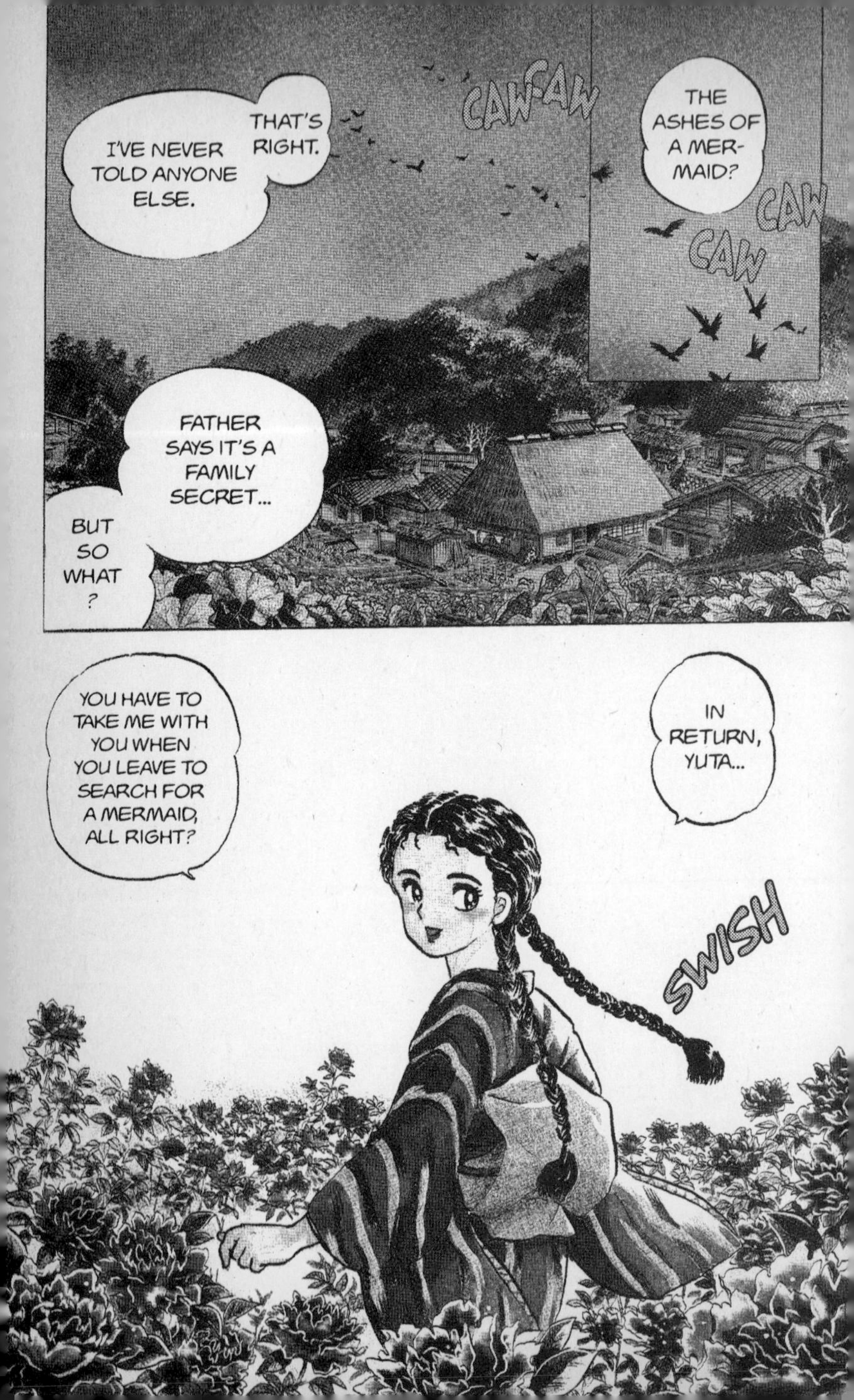
THE ASHES OF A MERMAID?
CAWCAW
CAW
CAW
THAT'S RIGHT.
I'VE NEVER TOLD ANYONE ELSE.
FATHER SAYS IT'S A FAMILY SECRET...
BUT SO WHAT?
IN RETURN, YUTA...
YOU HAVE TO TAKE ME WITH YOU WHEN YOU LEAVE TO SEARCH FOR A MERMAID, ALL RIGHT?
SWISH

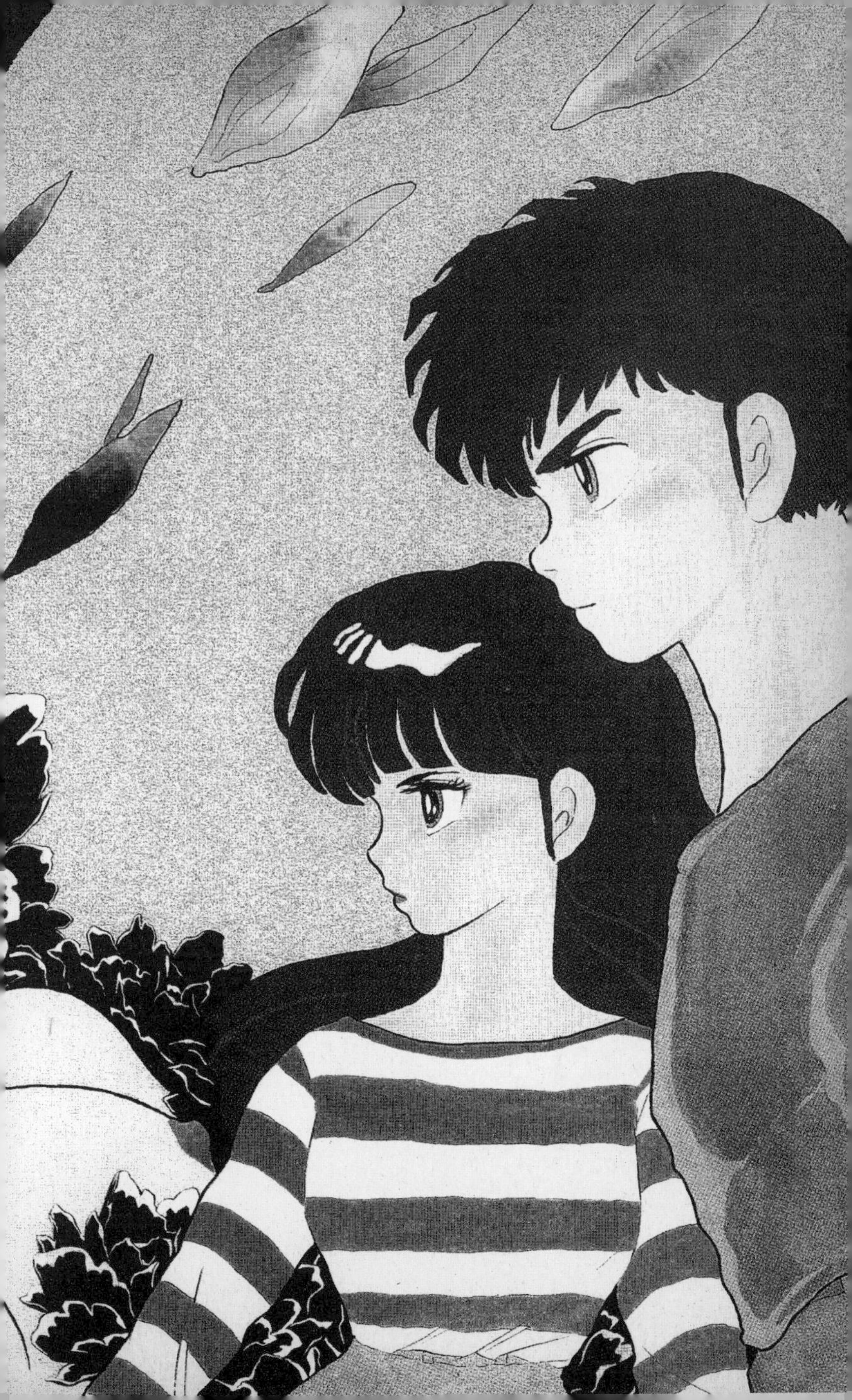

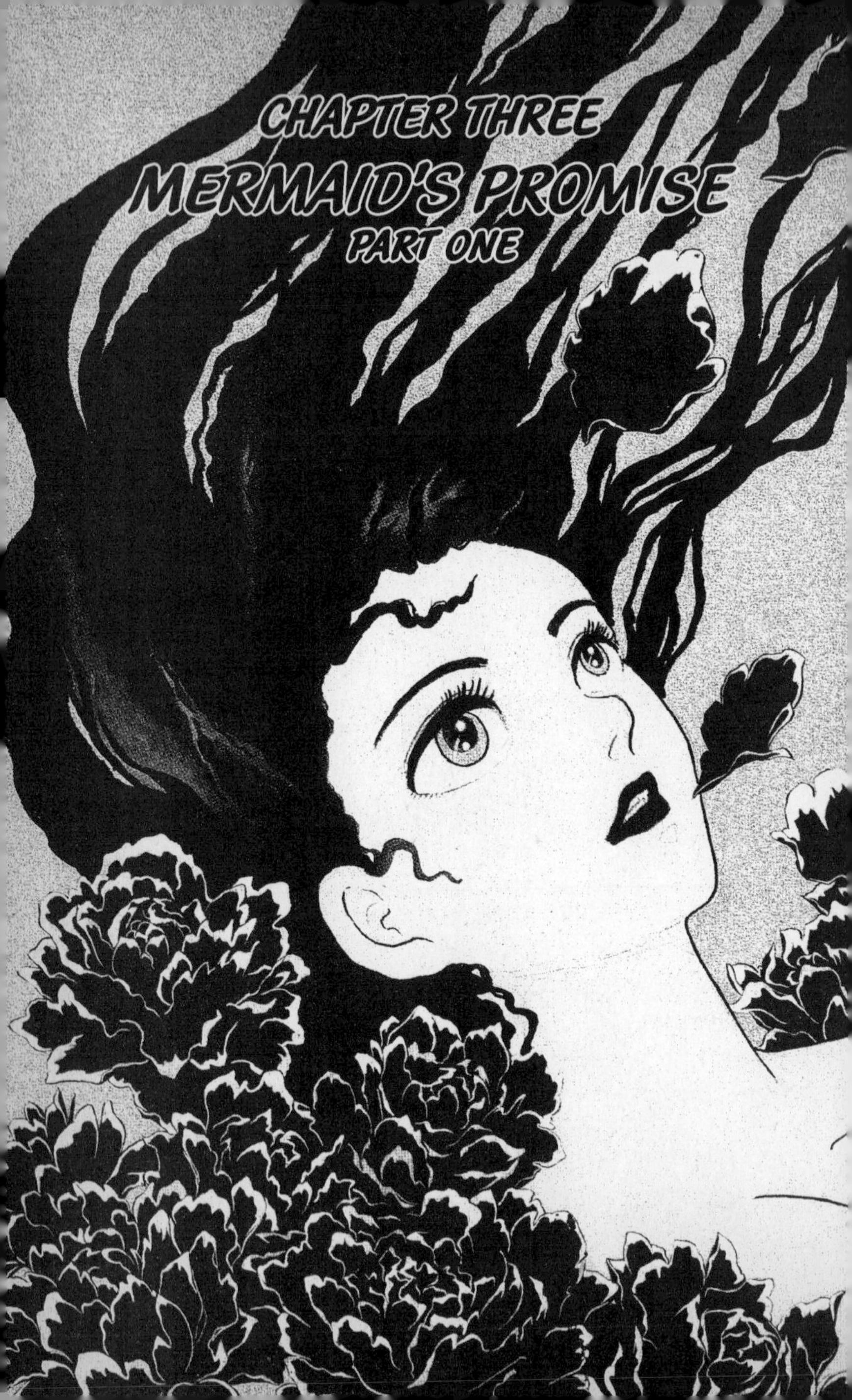
CHAPTER THREE
MERMAID'S PROMISE
PART ONE

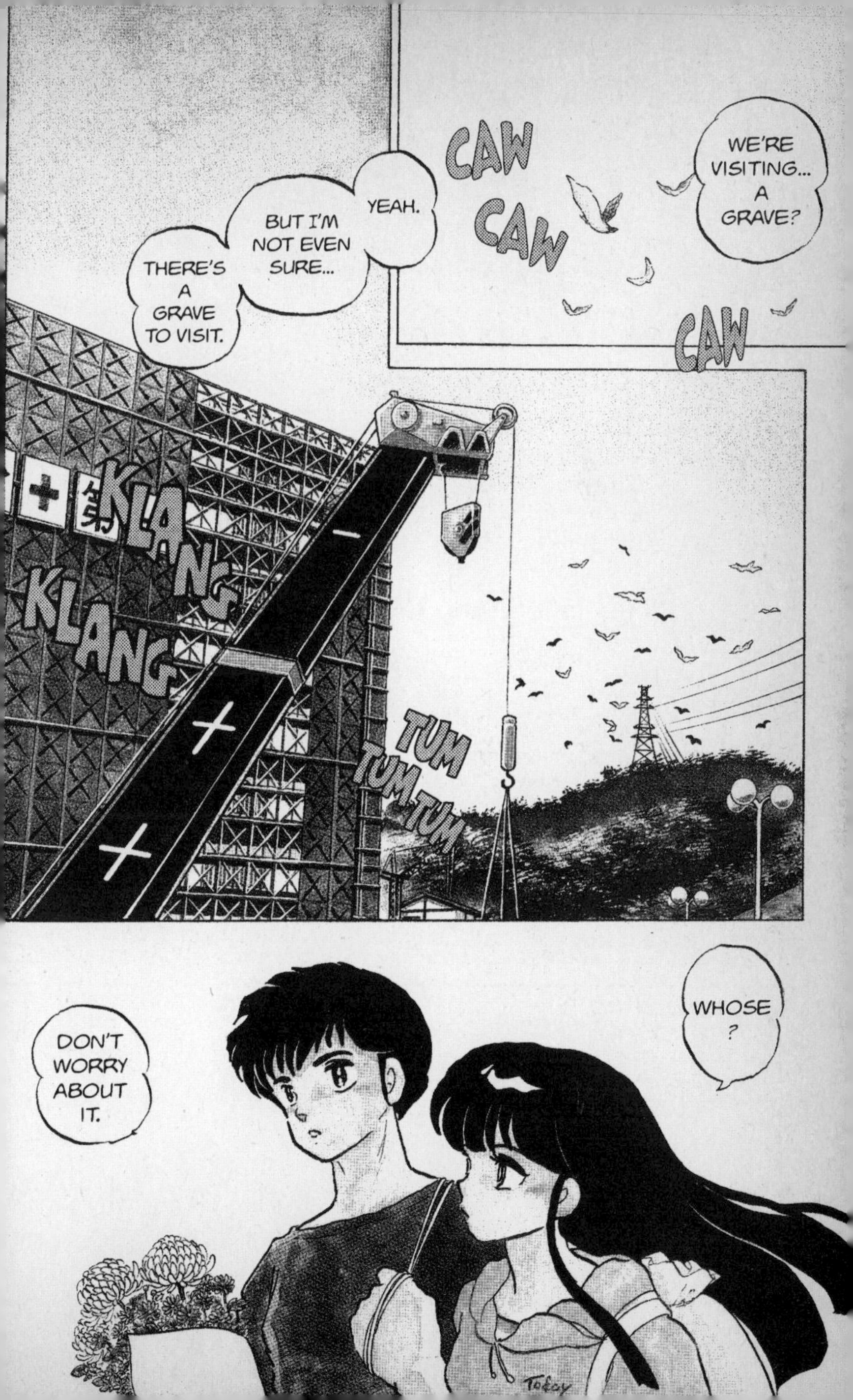
WE'RE VISITING... A GRAVE?
CAW
CAW
CAW
TUM TUM TUM
YEAH.
BUT I'M NOT EVEN SURE...
THERE'S A GRAVE TO VISIT.
KLANG
KLANG
WHOSE?
DON'T WORRY ABOUT IT.

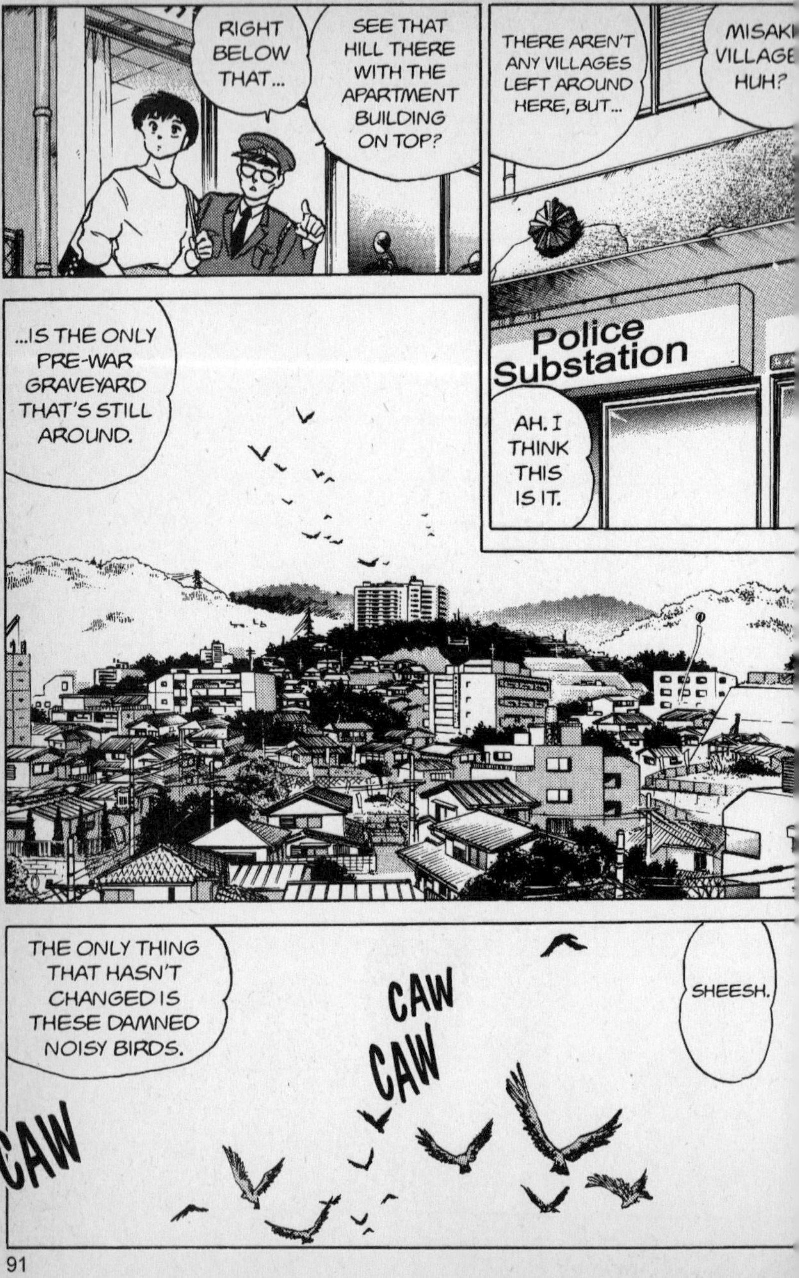
MISAK VILLAG HUH?
THERE AREN'T ANY VILLAGES LEFT AROUND HERE, BUT...
Police Substation
AH. I THINK THIS IS IT.
SEE THAT HILL THERE WITH THE APARTMENT BUILDING ON TOP?
RIGHT BELOW THAT...
...IS THE ONLY PRE-WAR GRAVEYARD THAT'S STILL AROUND.
SHEESH.
CAW
CAW
THE ONLY THING THAT HASN'T CHANGED IS THESE DAMNED NOISY BIRDS.
CAW

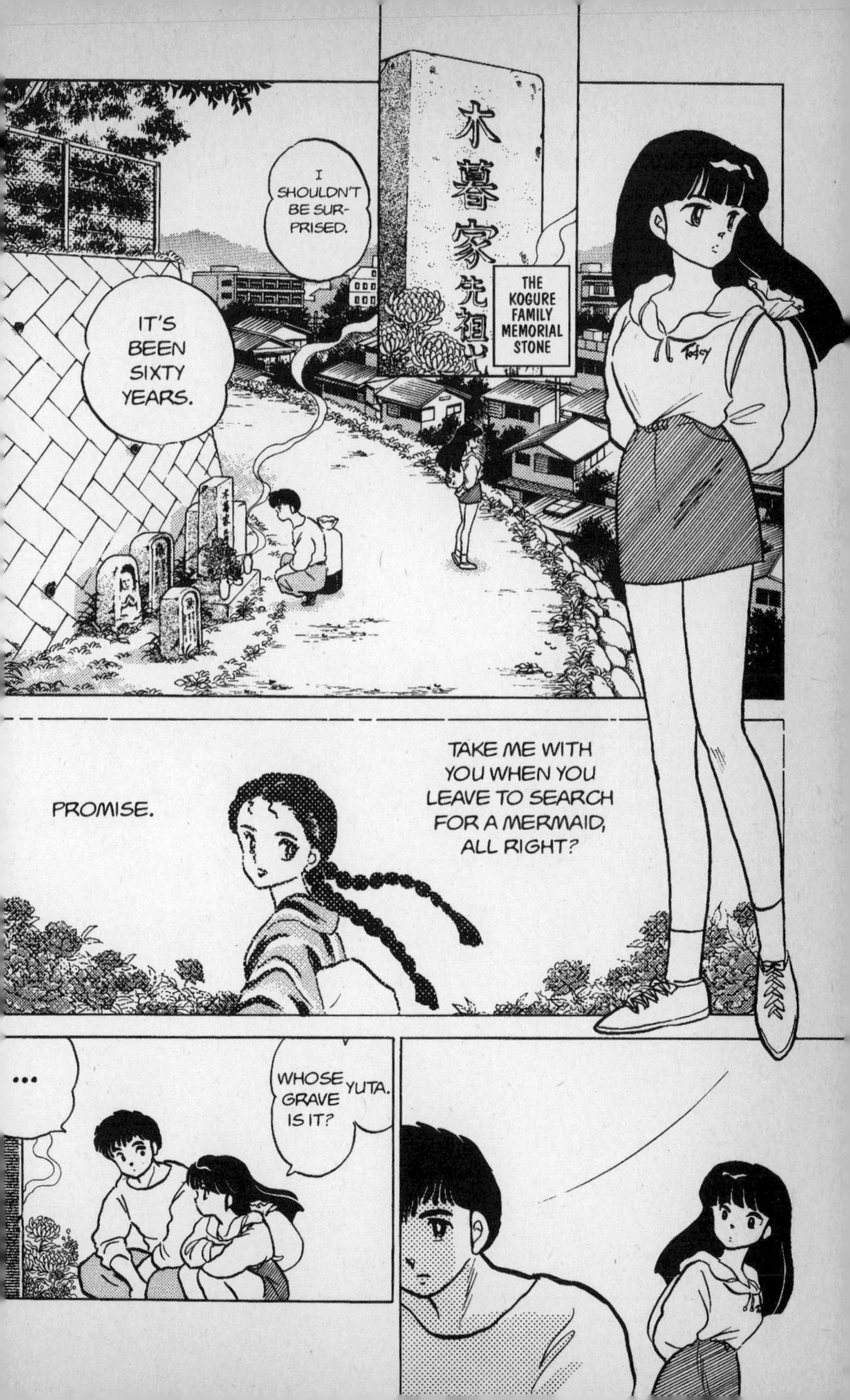
木暮家先祖
THE KOGURE FAMILY MEMORIAL STONE
I SHOULDN'T BE SUR- PRISED.
IT'S BEEN SIXTY YEARS.
TAKE ME WITH YOU WHEN YOU LEAVE TO SEARCH FOR A MERMAID, ALL RIGHT?
PROMISE.
YUTA.
WHOSE GRAVE IS IT?
...

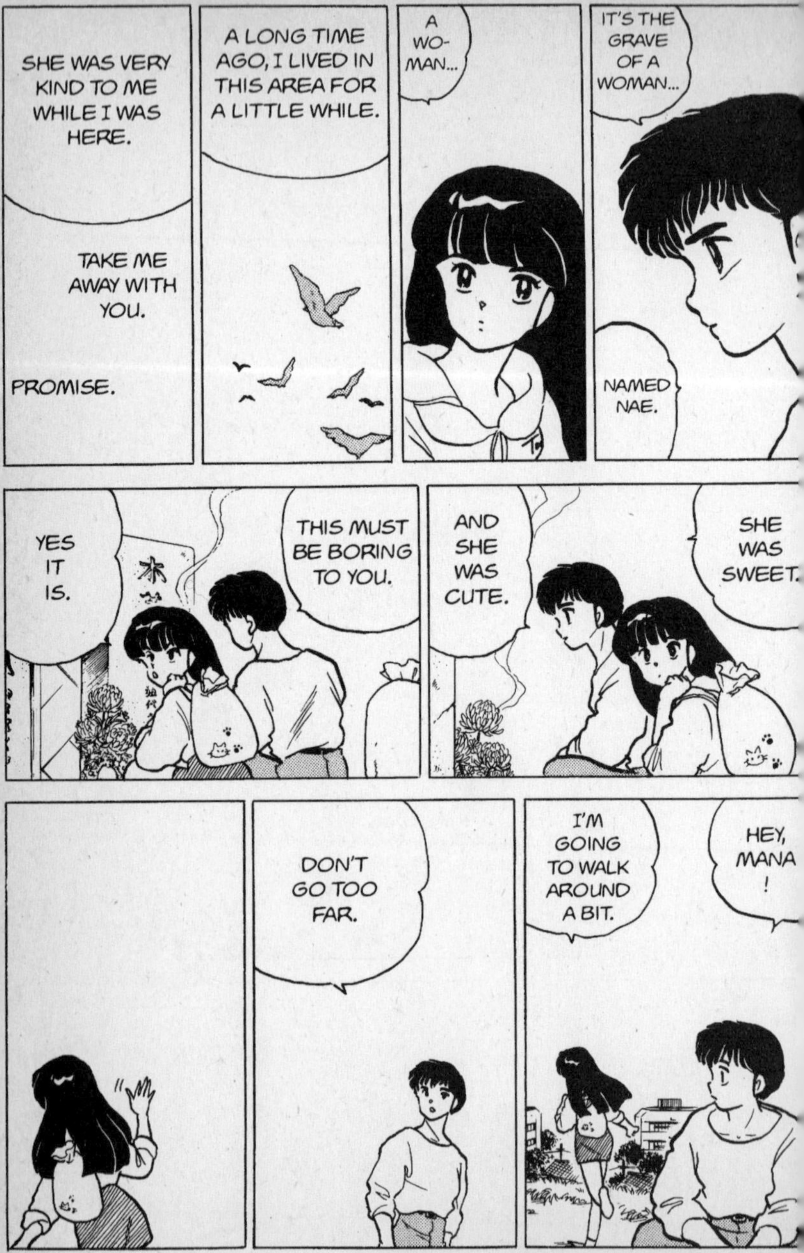
IT'S THE GRAVE OF A WOMAN...
NAMED NAE.
A WO-MAN...
A LONG TIME AGO, I LIVED IN THIS AREA FOR A LITTLE WHILE.
SHE WAS VERY KIND TO ME WHILE I WAS HERE.
TAKE ME AWAY WITH YOU.
PROMISE.
SHE WAS SWEET.
AND SHE WAS CUTE.
THIS MUST BE BORING TO YOU.
YES IT IS.
HEY, MANA!
I'M GOING TO WALK AROUND A BIT.
DON'T GO TOO FAR.

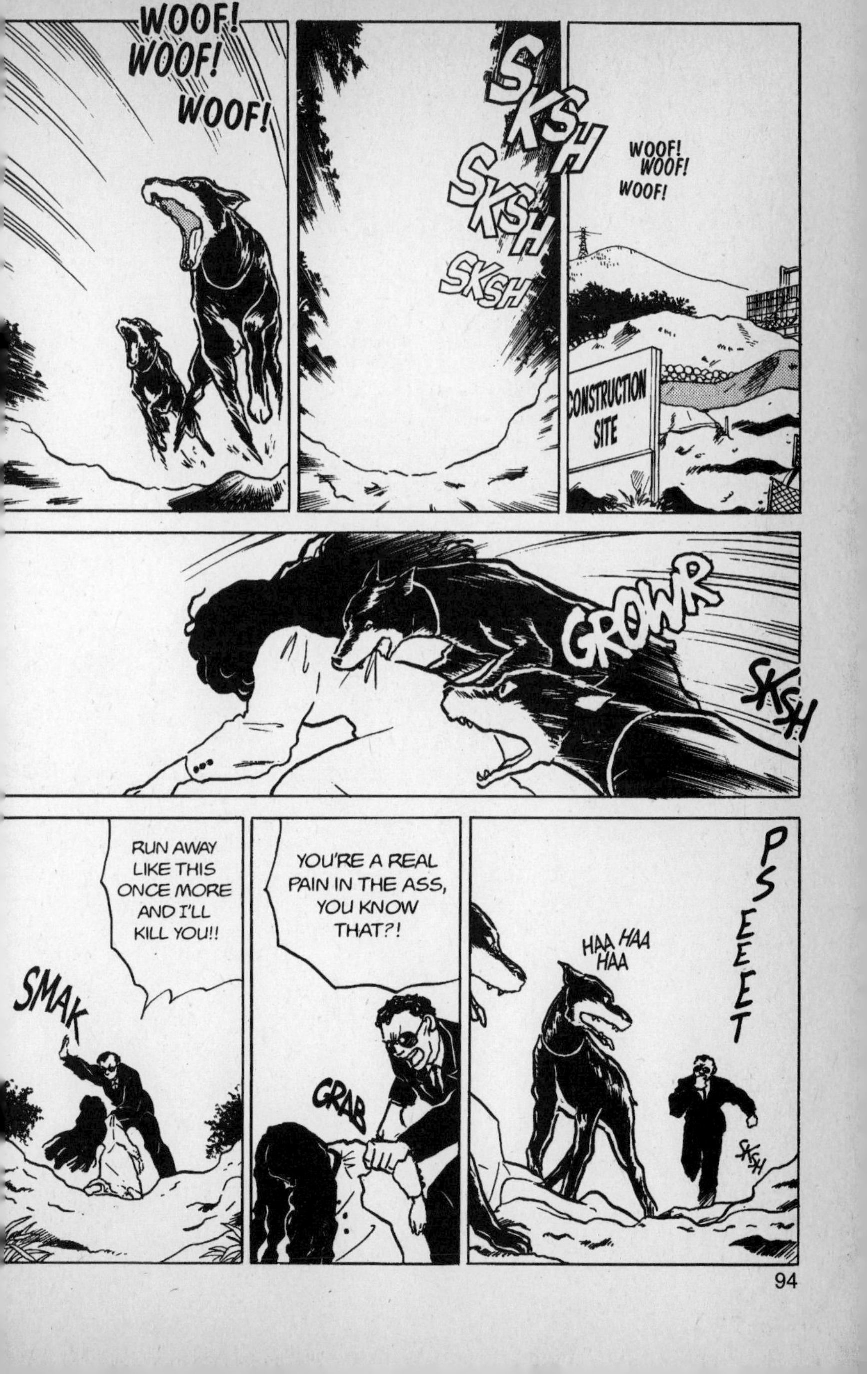
WOOF!
WOOF!
WOOF!
CONSTRUCTION SITE
SKSH
SKSH
SKSH
WOOF!
WOOF!
WOOF!
GROWR
SKSH
PSEEEET
HAA HAA HAA
SKSH
YOU'RE A REAL PAIN IN THE ASS, YOU KNOW THAT?!
GRAB
RUN AWAY LIKE THIS ONCE MORE AND I'LL KILL YOU!!
SMAK

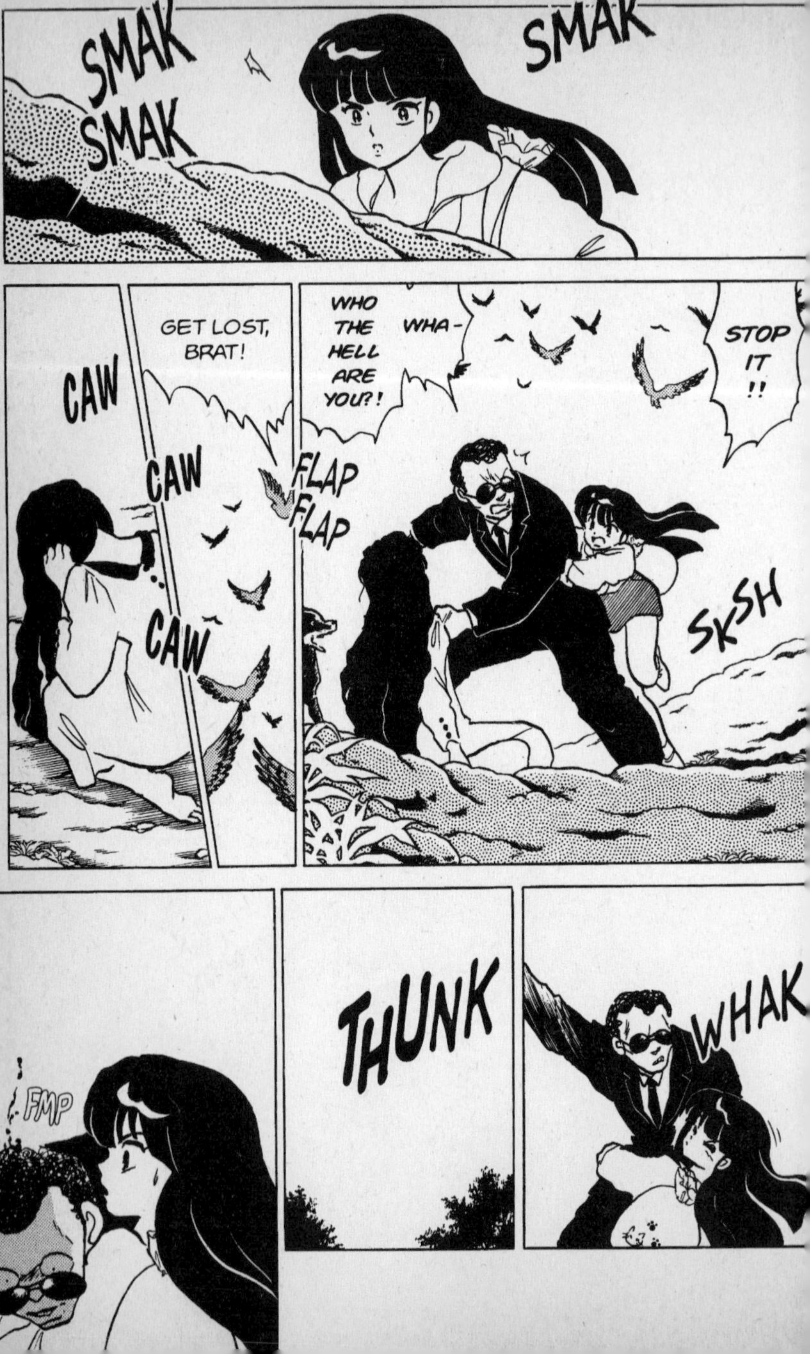
SMAK
SMAK
SMAK
STOP IT!!
WHA-
WHO THE HELL ARE YOU?!
FLAP FLAP
SKSH
GET LOST, BRAT!
CAW
CAW
CAW
WHAK
THUNK
FMP

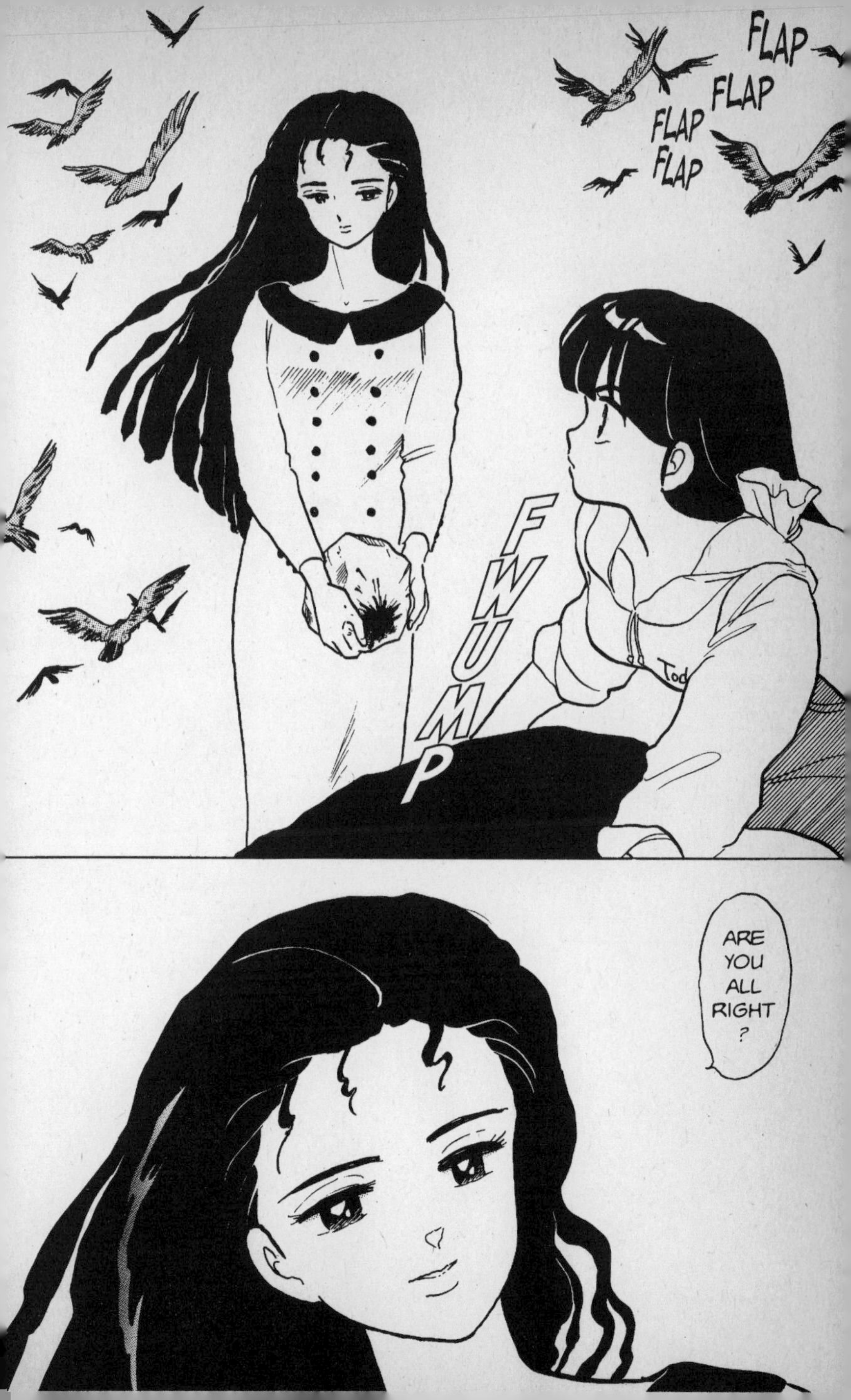
FLAP
FLAP
FLAP
FLAP
FWUMP
ARE YOU ALL RIGHT?

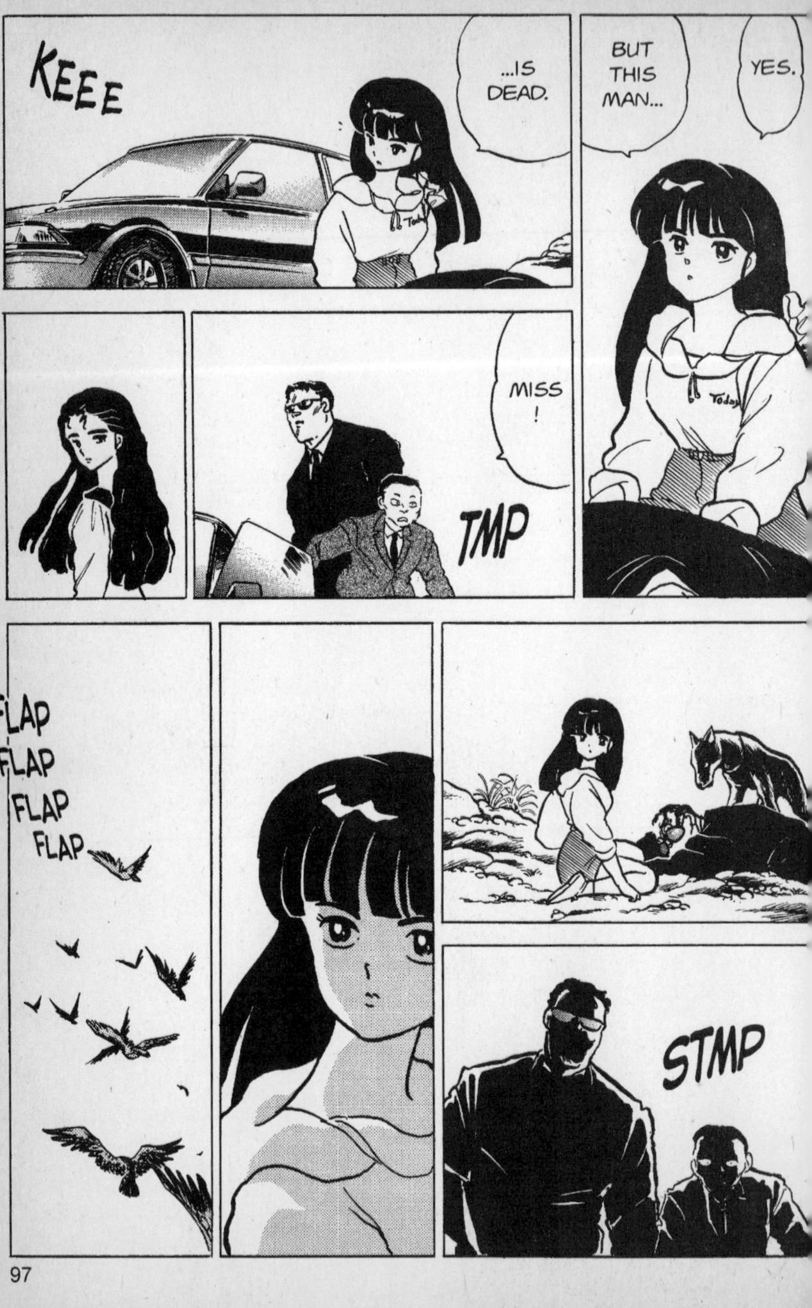
YES.
BUT THIS MAN...
...IS DEAD.
KEEE
MISS!
TMP
STMP
FLAP
FLAP
FLAP
FLAP

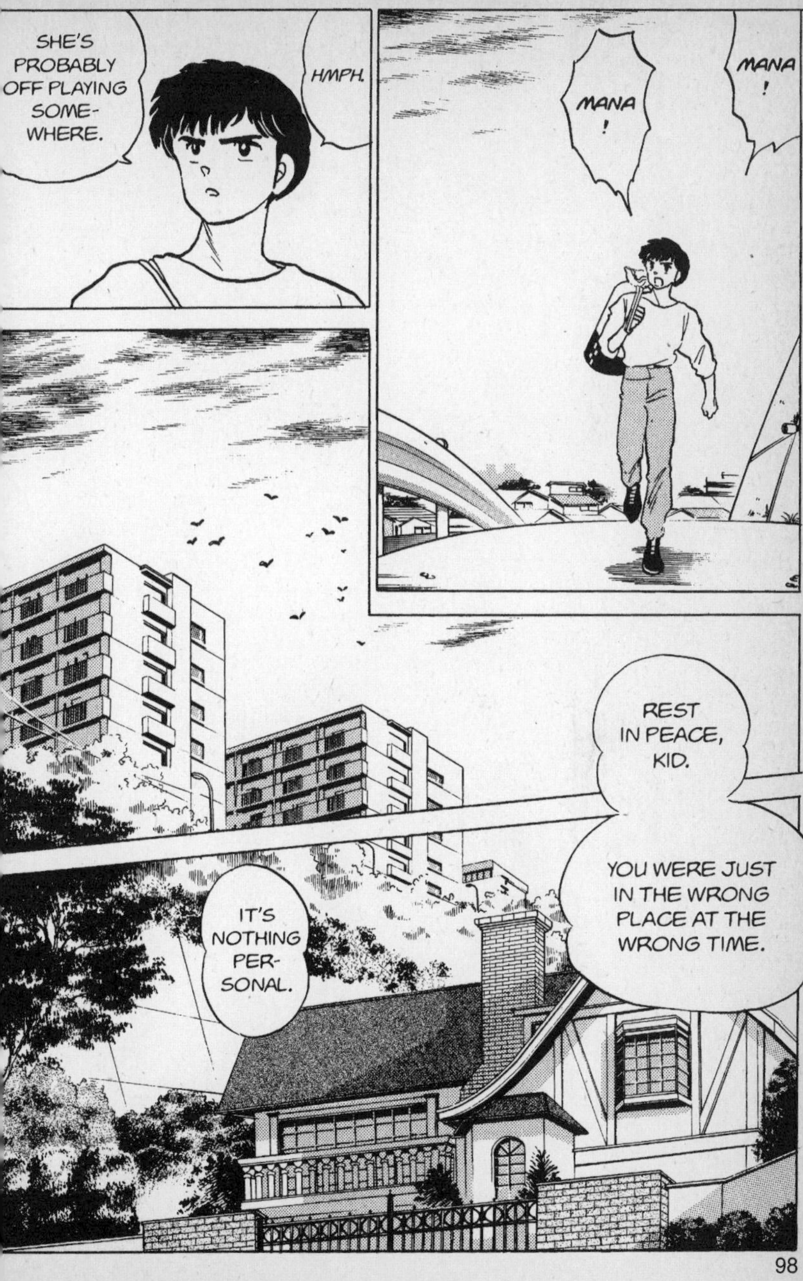
MANA!
MANA!
HMPH.
SHE'S PROBABLY OFF PLAYING SOME-WHERE.
REST IN PEACE, KID.
YOU WERE JUST IN THE WRONG PLACE AT THE WRONG TIME.
IT'S NOTHING PER-SONAL.

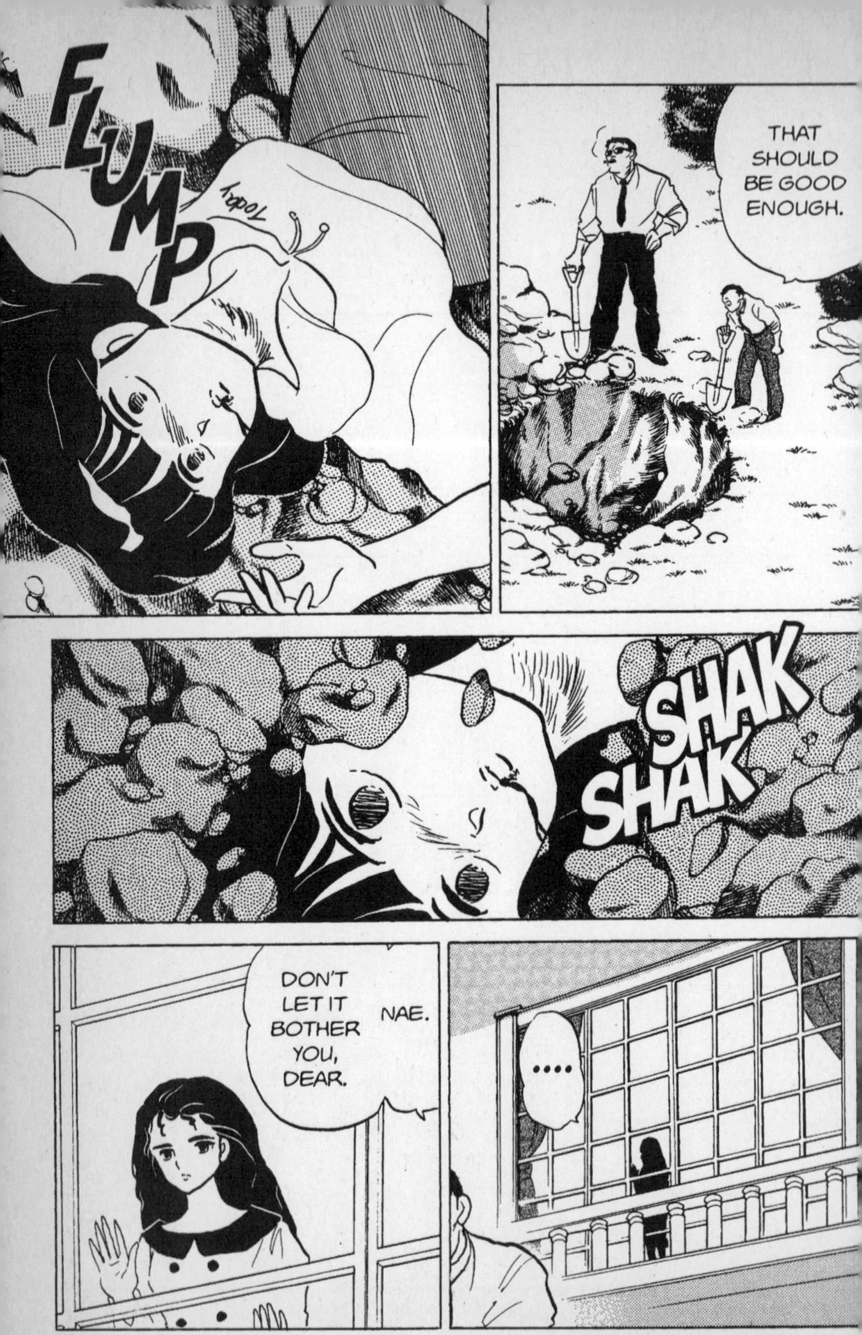
THAT SHOULD BE GOOD ENOUGH.
FLUMP
SHAK SHAK
....
NAE.
DON'T LET IT BOTHER YOU, DEAR.

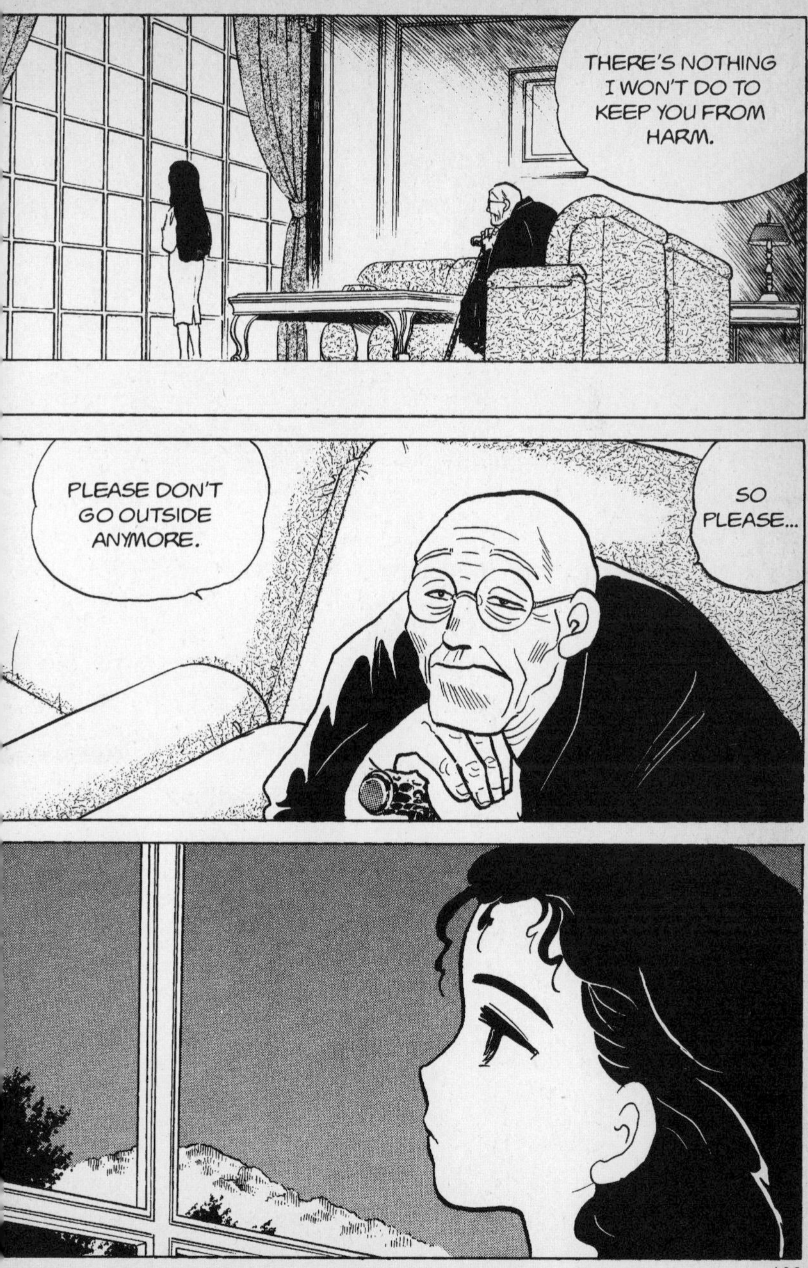
THERE'S NOTHING I WON'T DO TO KEEP YOU FROM HARM.
SO PLEASE...
PLEASE DON'T GO OUTSIDE ANYMORE.

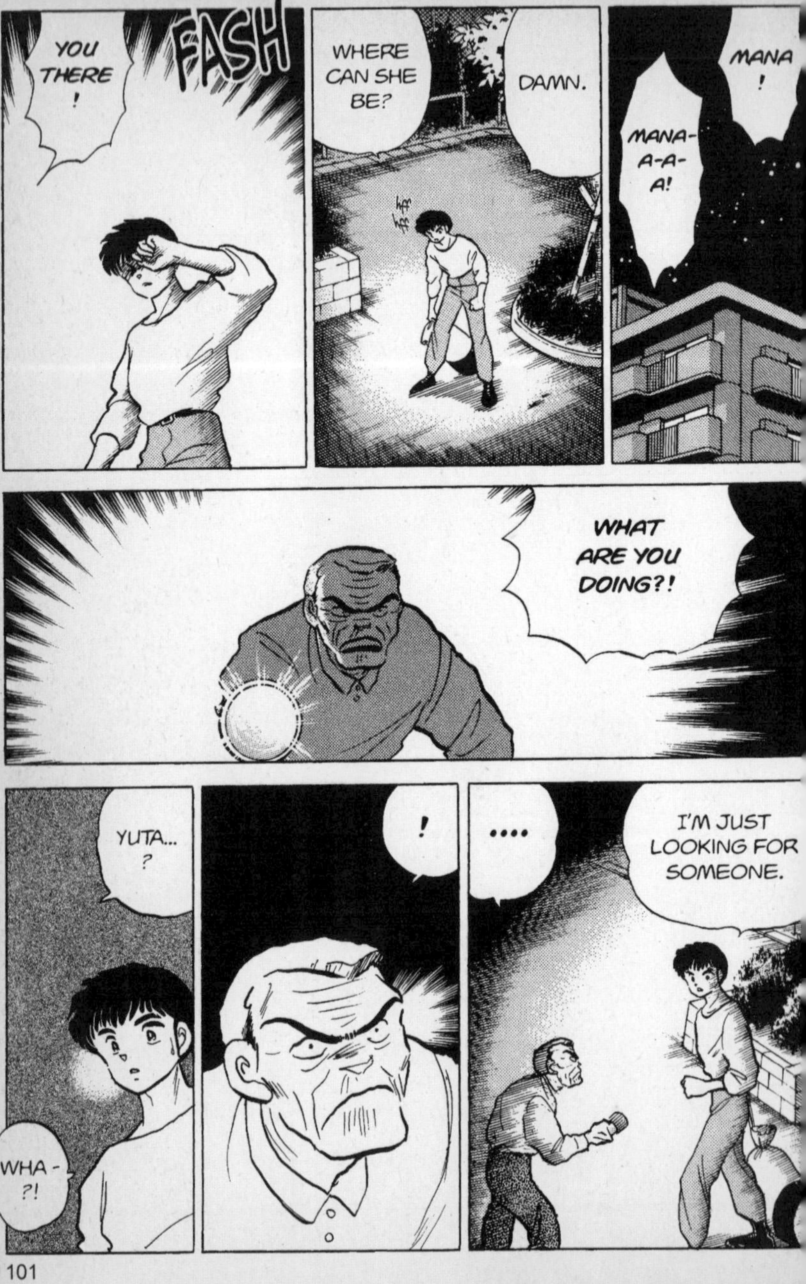
MANA!
MANA-A-A-A!
DAMN.
WHERE CAN SHE BE?
hff hff
FASH
YOU THERE!
WHAT ARE YOU DOING?!
I'M JUST LOOKING FOR SOMEONE.
....
!
YUTA...?
WHA-?!

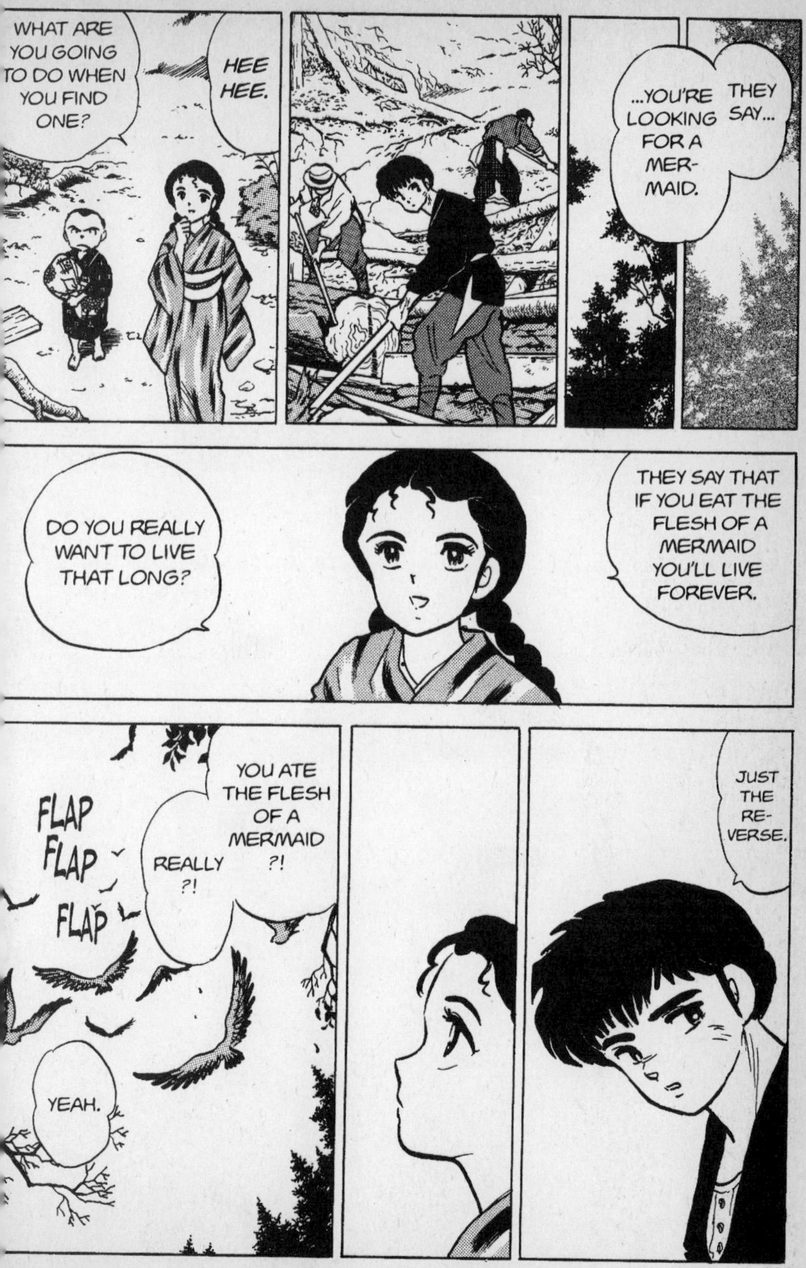
THEY SAY...
...YOU'RE LOOKING FOR A MERMAID.
HEE HEE.
WHAT ARE YOU GOING TO DO WHEN YOU FIND ONE?
THEY SAY THAT IF YOU EAT THE FLESH OF A MERMAID YOU'LL LIVE FOREVER.
DO YOU REALLY WANT TO LIVE THAT LONG?
JUST THE REVERSE.
YOU ATE THE FLESH OF A MERMAID ?!
REALLY ?!
FLAP FLAP FLAP
YEAH.

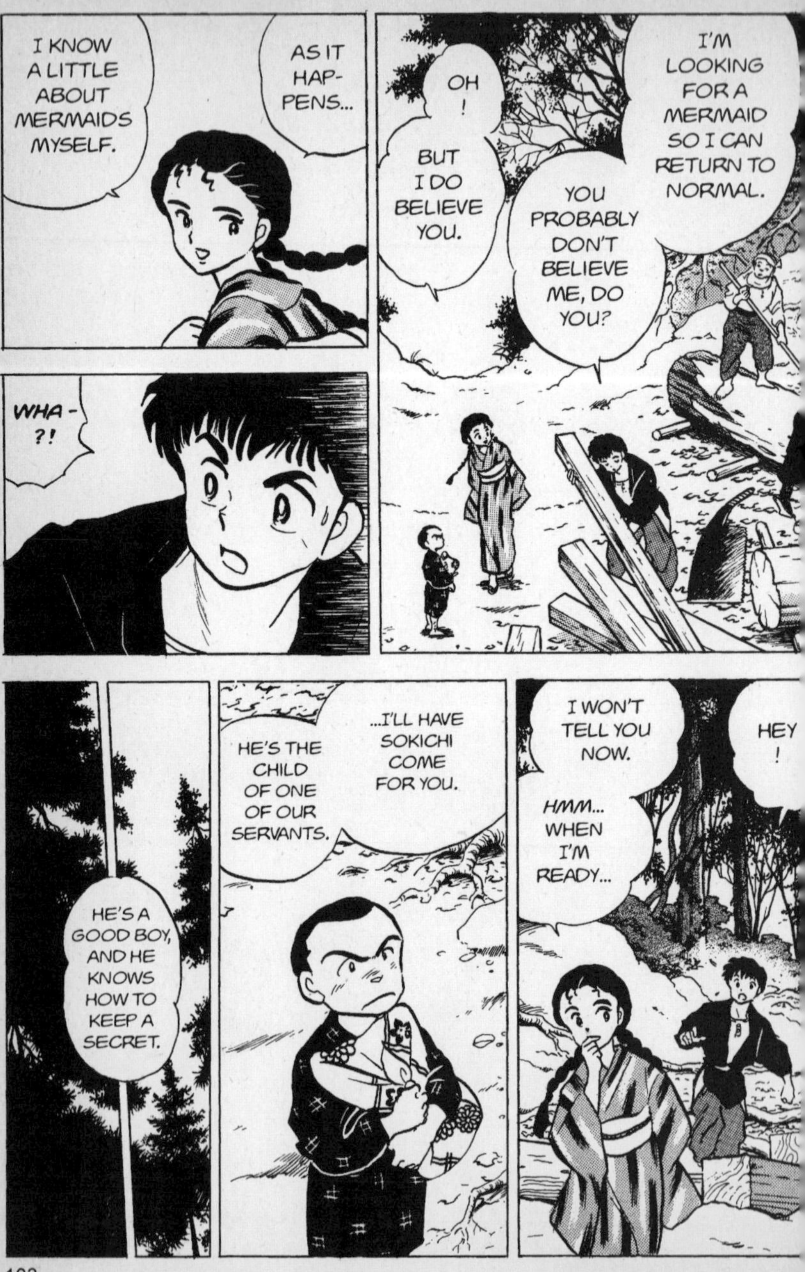
I'M LOOKING FOR A MERMAID SO I CAN RETURN TO NORMAL.
YOU PROBABLY DON'T BELIEVE ME, DO YOU?
OH! BUT I DO BELIEVE YOU.
AS IT HAP-PENS...
I KNOW A LITTLE ABOUT MERMAIDS MYSELF.
WHA-?!
HEY!
I WON'T TELL YOU NOW.
HMM... WHEN I'M READY...
...I'LL HAVE SOKICHI COME FOR YOU.
HE'S THE CHILD OF ONE OF OUR SERVANTS.
HE'S A GOOD BOY, AND HE KNOWS HOW TO KEEP A SECRET.

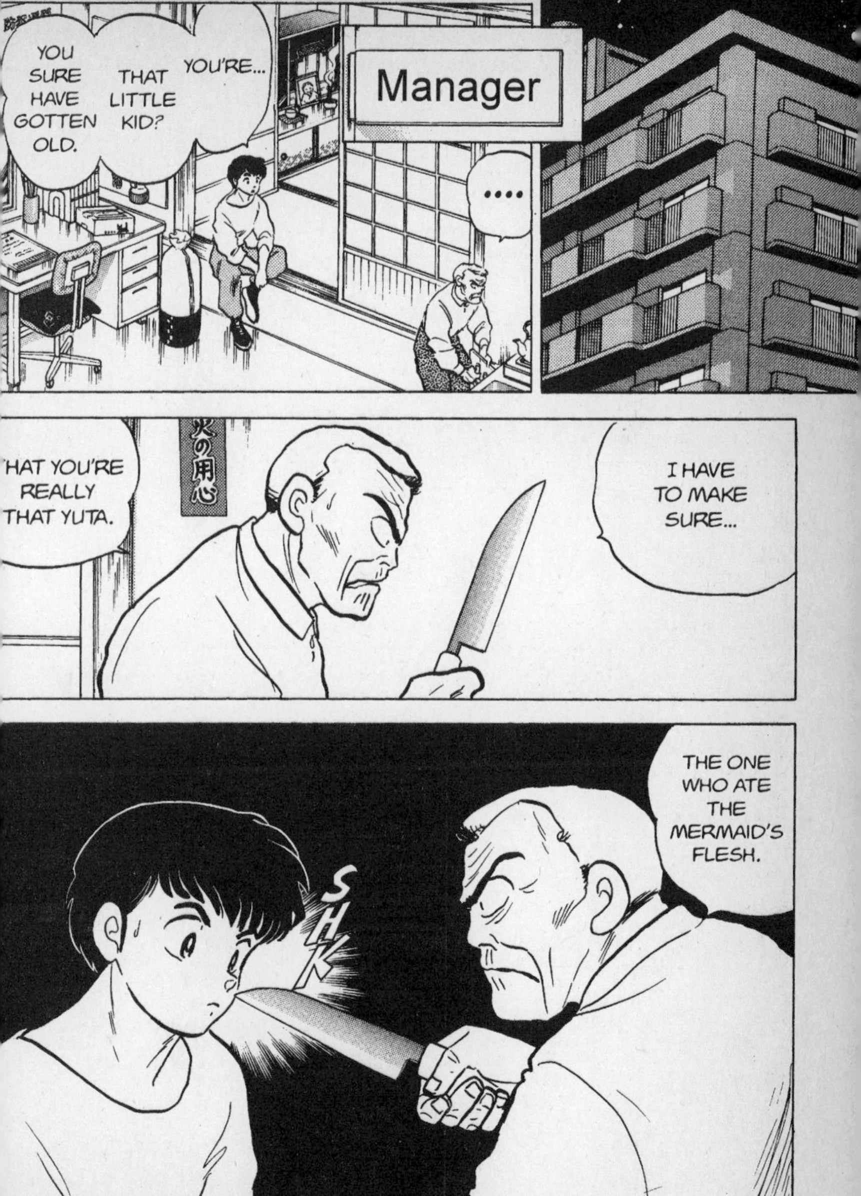
Manager
YOU'RE... THAT LITTLE KID?
YOU SURE HAVE GOTTEN OLD.
....
I HAVE TO MAKE SURE...
HAT YOU'RE REALLY THAT YUTA.
火の用心
THE ONE WHO ATE THE MERMAID'S FLESH.
SHK

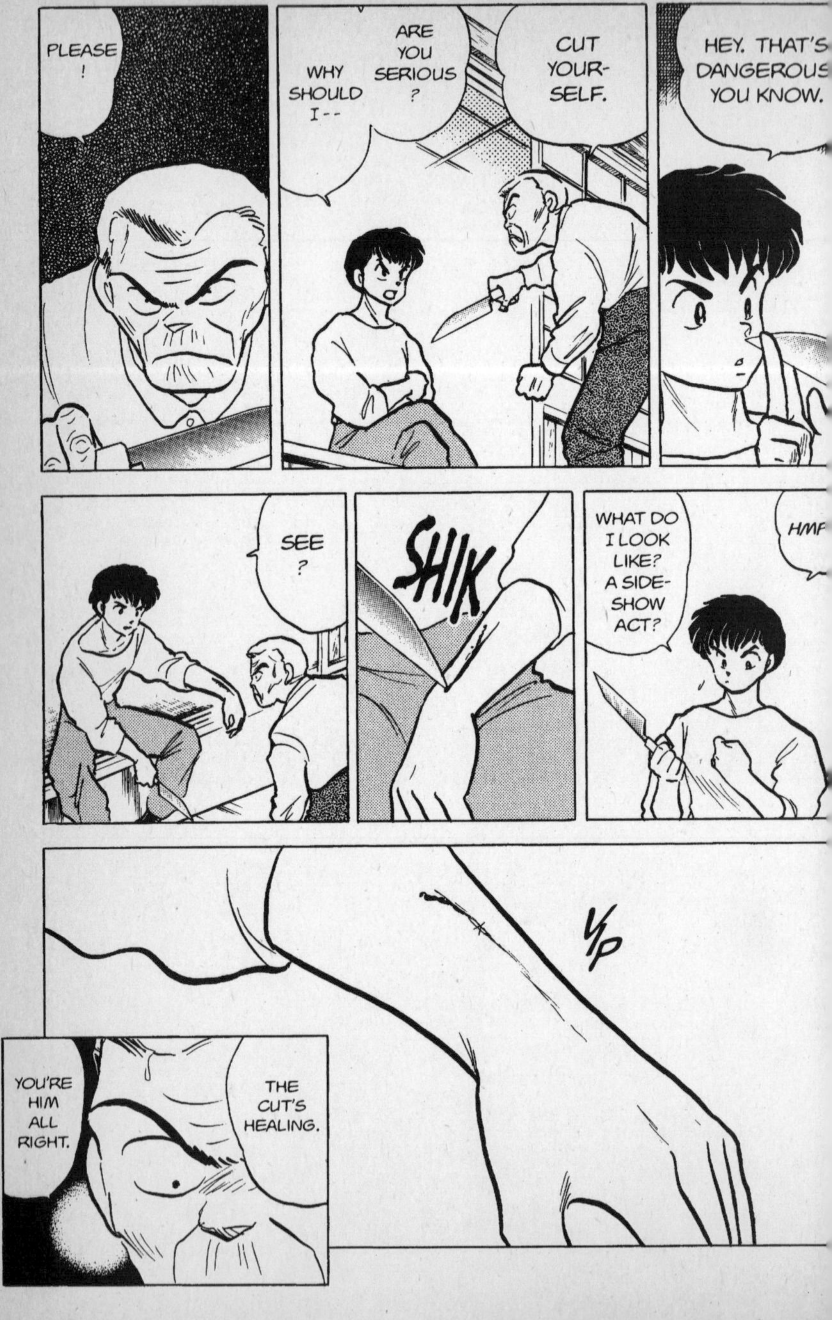
HEY. THAT'S DANGEROUS YOU KNOW.
CUT YOUR-SELF.
ARE YOU SERIOUS?
WHY SHOULD I--
PLEASE!
HMF
WHAT DO I LOOK LIKE? A SIDE-SHOW ACT?
SHIK
SEE?
VIP
THE CUT'S HEALING.
YOU'RE HIM ALL RIGHT.

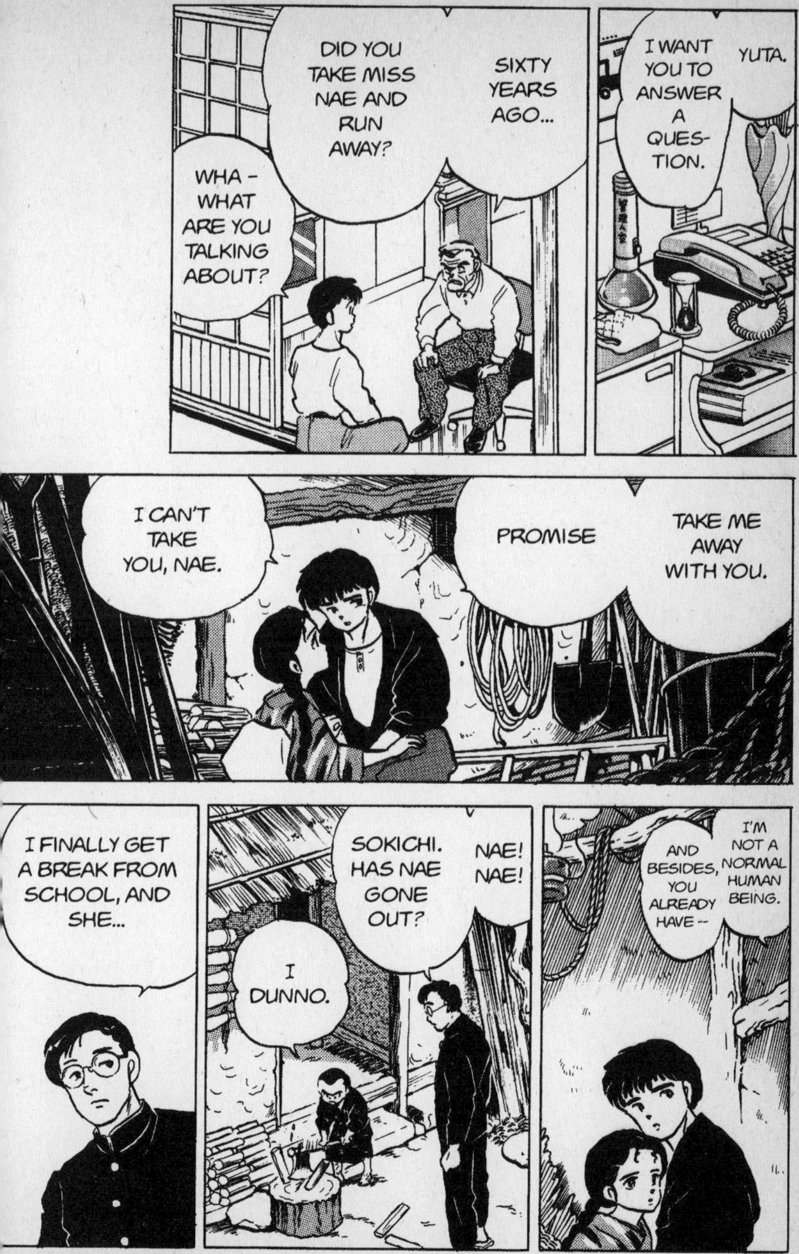
YUTA.
I WANT YOU TO ANSWER A QUESTION.
SIXTY YEARS AGO...
DID YOU TAKE MISS NAE AND RUN AWAY?
WHA-WHAT ARE YOU TALKING ABOUT?
TAKE ME AWAY WITH YOU.
PROMISE
I CAN'T TAKE YOU, NAE.
I'M NOT A NORMAL HUMAN BEING.
AND BESIDES, YOU ALREADY HAVE --
NAE! NAE!
SOKICHI. HAS NAE GONE OUT?
I DUNNO.
I FINALLY GET A BREAK FROM SCHOOL, AND SHE...

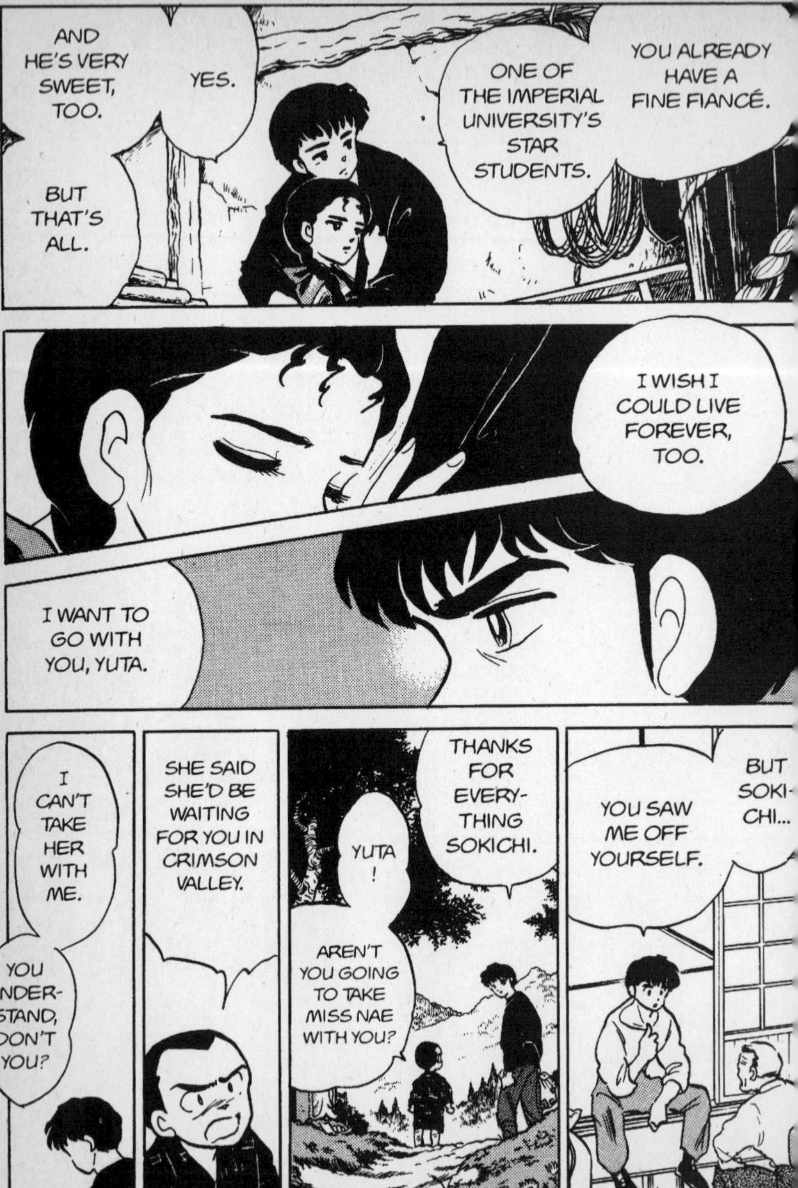
YOU ALREADY HAVE A FINE FIANCÉ.
ONE OF THE IMPERIAL UNIVERSITY'S STAR STUDENTS.
YES.
AND HE'S VERY SWEET, TOO.
BUT THAT'S ALL.
I WISH I COULD LIVE FOREVER, TOO.
I WANT TO GO WITH YOU, YUTA.
BUT SOKI-CHI...
YOU SAW ME OFF YOURSELF.
THANKS FOR EVERY-THING SOKICHI.
YUTA!
AREN'T YOU GOING TO TAKE MISS NAE WITH YOU?
SHE SAID SHE'D BE WAITING FOR YOU IN CRIMSON VALLEY.
I CAN'T TAKE HER WITH ME.
YOU UNDER-STAND, DON'T YOU?

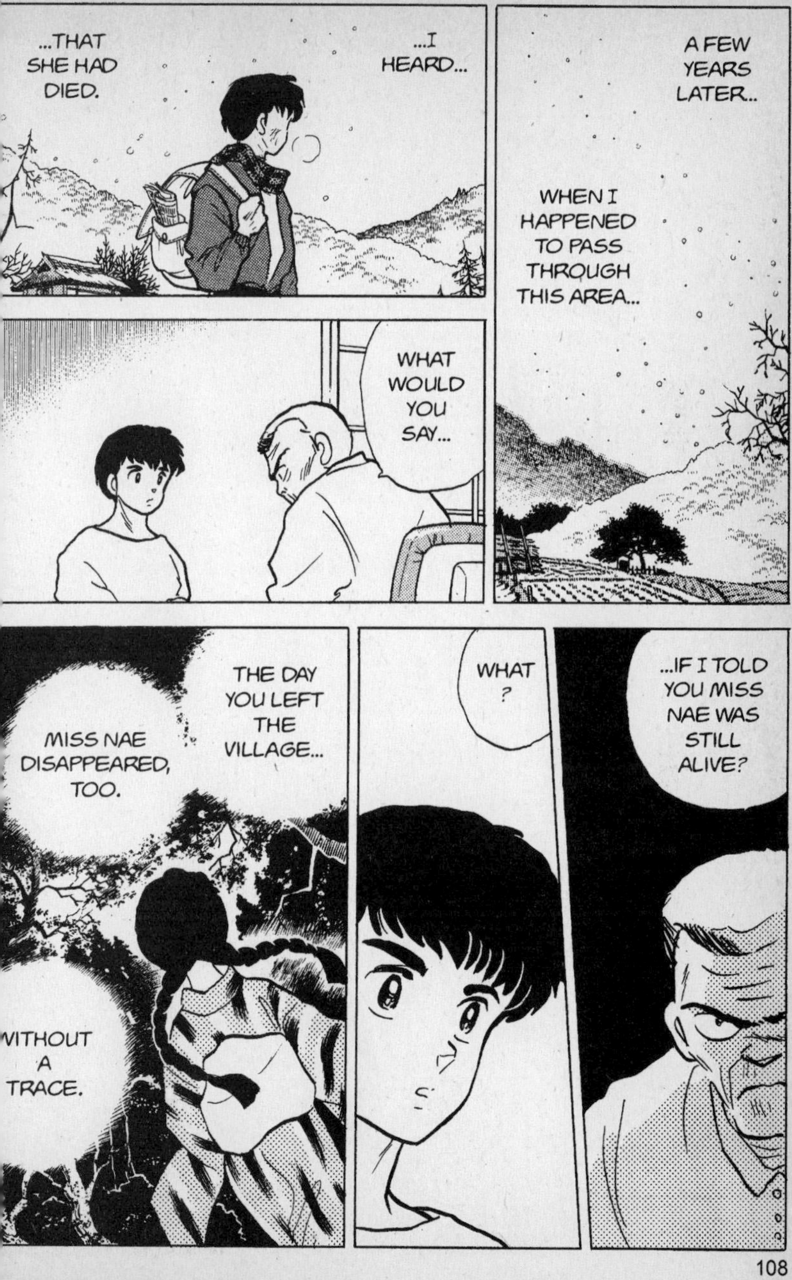
A FEW YEARS LATER..
WHEN I HAPPENED TO PASS THROUGH THIS AREA...
...I HEARD...
...THAT SHE HAD DIED.
WHAT WOULD YOU SAY...
...IF I TOLD YOU MISS NAE WAS STILL ALIVE?
WHAT ?
THE DAY YOU LEFT THE VILLAGE...
MISS NAE DISAPPEARED, TOO.
WITHOUT A TRACE.

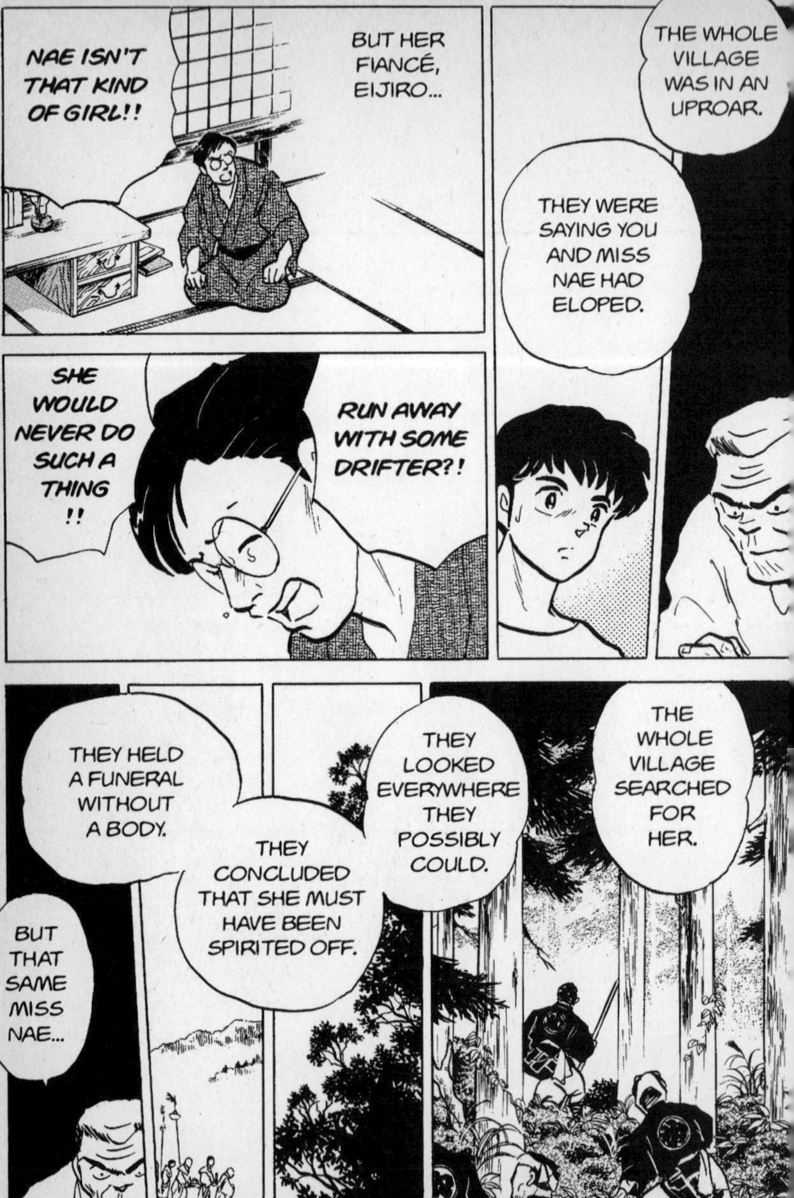
THE WHOLE VILLAGE WAS IN AN UPROAR.
THEY WERE SAYING YOU AND MISS NAE HAD ELOPED.
BUT HER FIANCÉ, EIJIRO...
NAE ISN'T THAT KIND OF GIRL!!
RUN AWAY WITH SOME DRIFTER?!
SHE WOULD NEVER DO SUCH A THING!!
THE WHOLE VILLAGE SEARCHED FOR HER.
THEY LOOKED EVERYWHERE THEY POSSIBLY COULD.
THEY CONCLUDED THAT SHE MUST HAVE BEEN SPIRITED OFF.
THEY HELD A FUNERAL WITHOUT A BODY.
BUT THAT SAME MISS NAE...

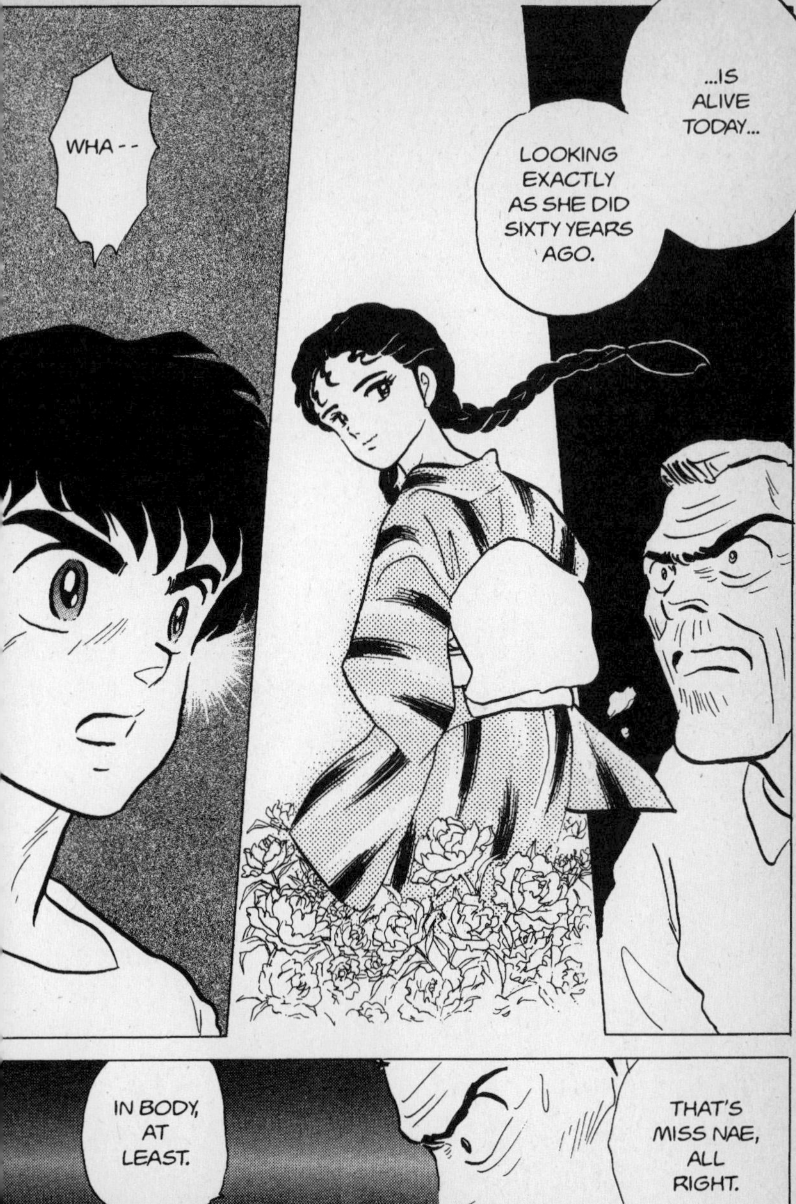
...IS ALIVE TODAY...
LOOKING EXACTLY AS SHE DID SIXTY YEARS AGO.
WHA - -
THAT'S MISS NAE, ALL RIGHT.
IN BODY, AT LEAST.

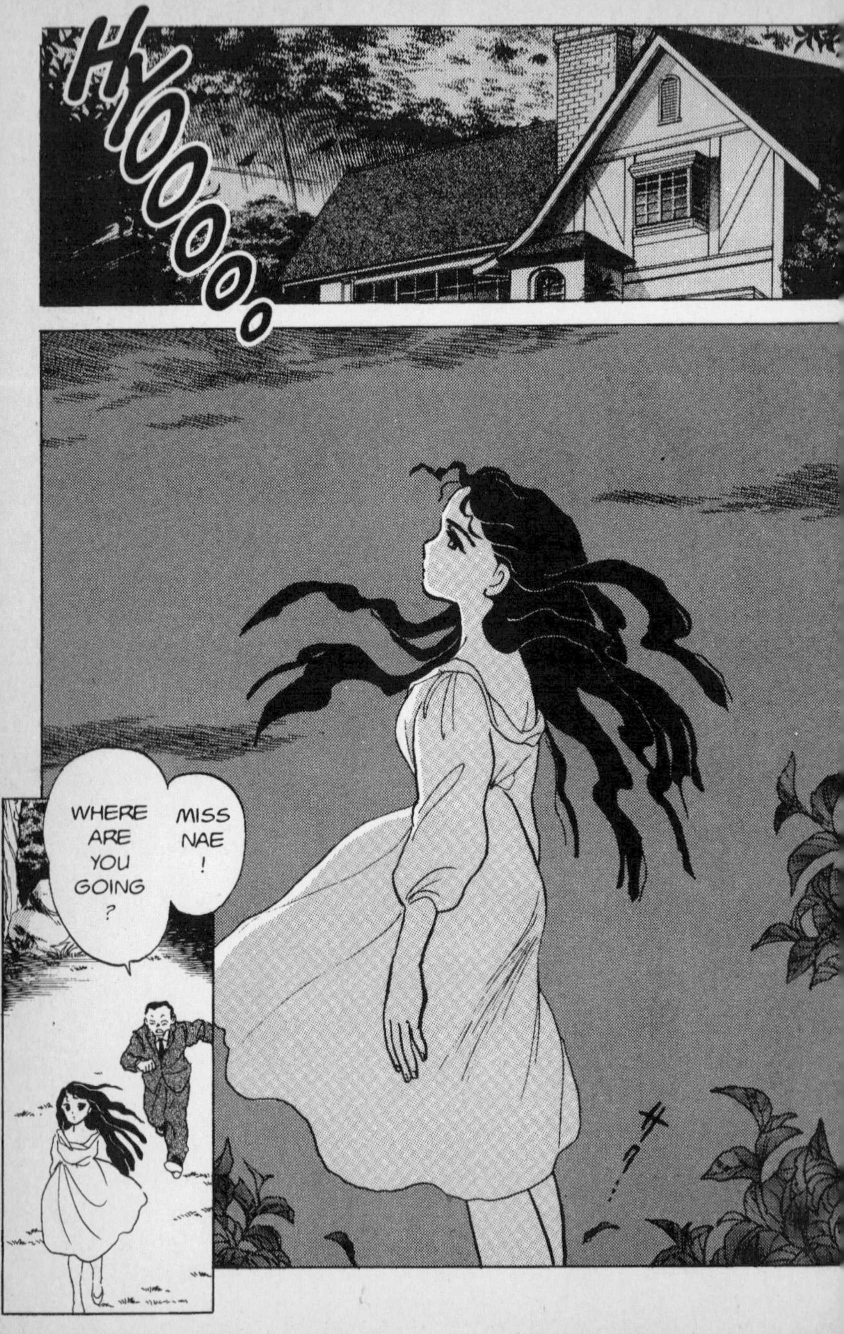
HYOOOOOO
MISS NAE!
WHERE ARE YOU GOING?

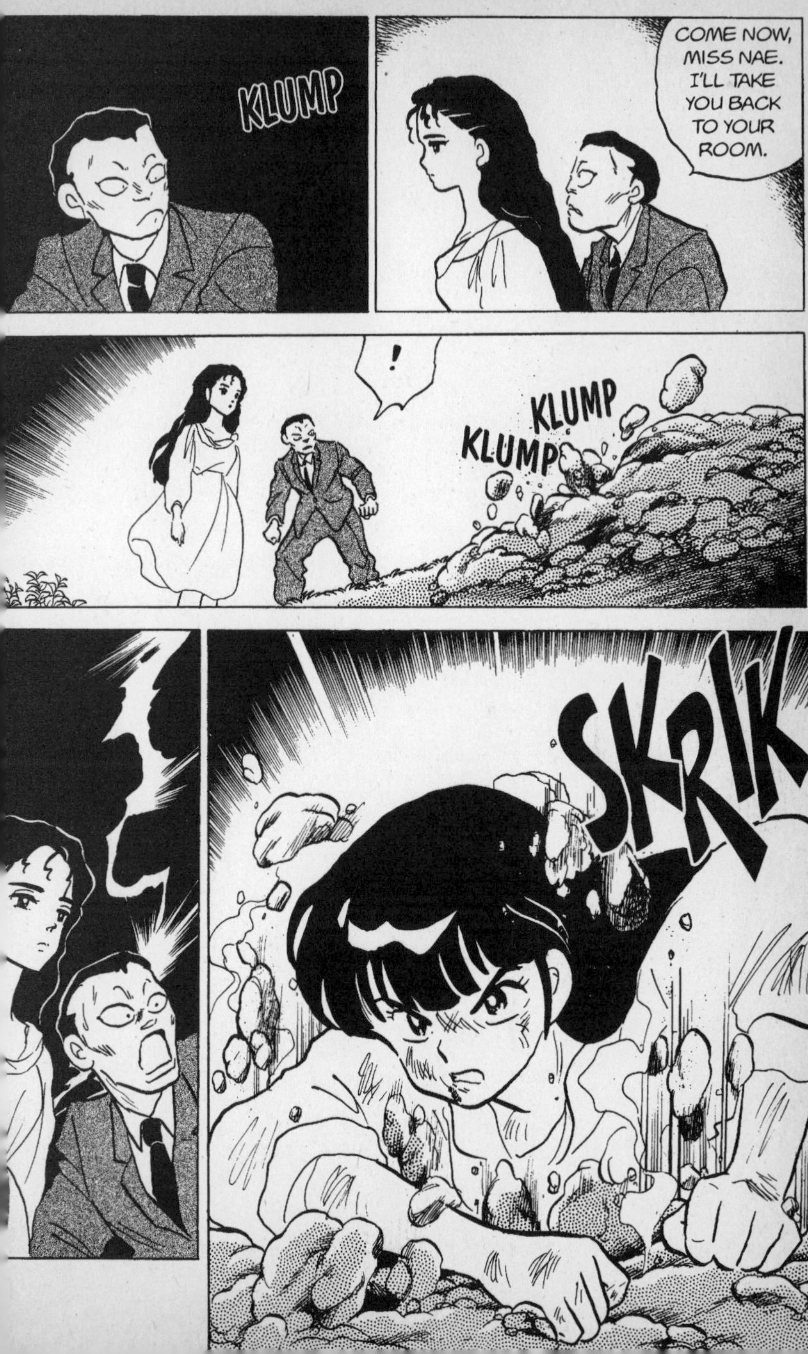
COME NOW, MISS NAE. I'LL TAKE YOU BACK TO YOUR ROOM.
KLUMP
!
KLUMP
KLUMP
SKRIK

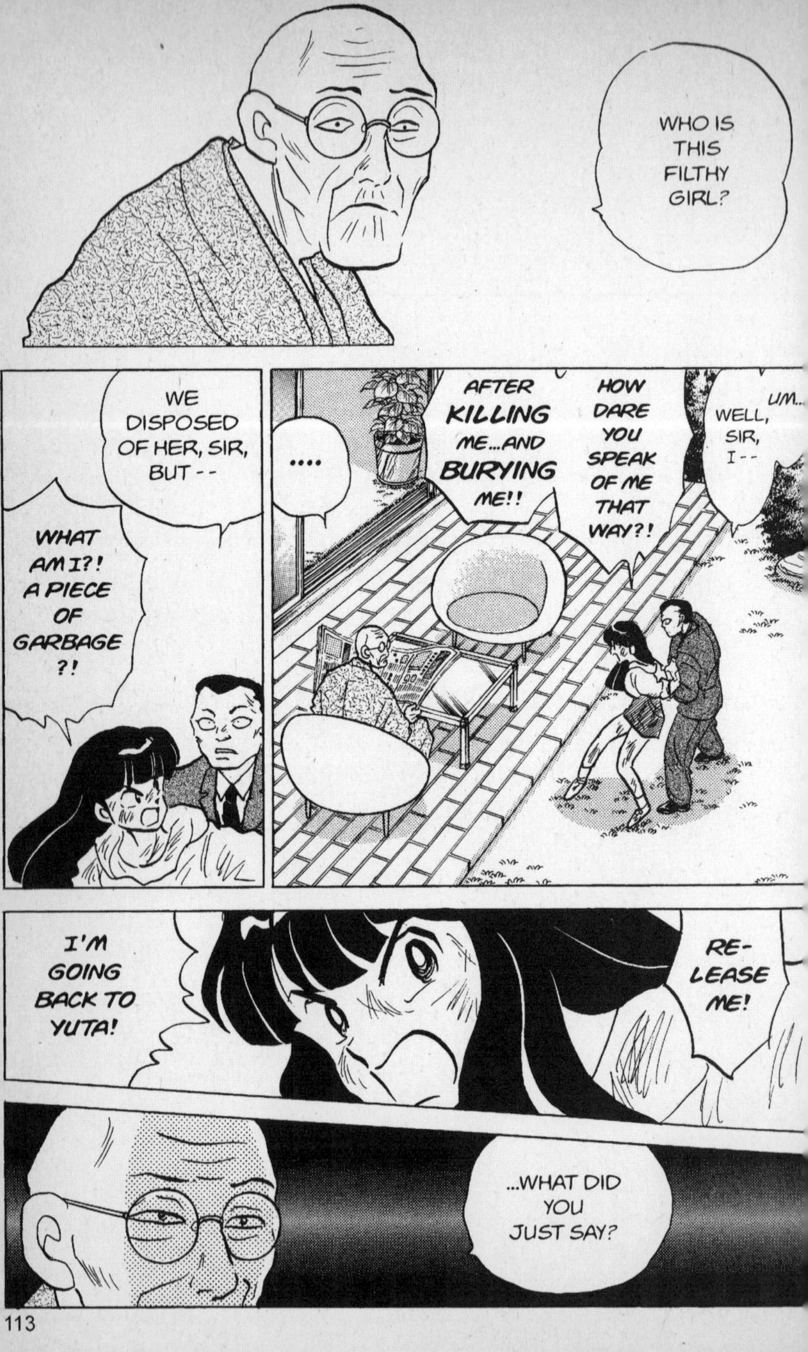
WHO IS THIS FILTHY GIRL?
WE DISPOSED OF HER, SIR, BUT --
WHAT AM I?! A PIECE OF GARBAGE?!
....
AFTER KILLING ME...AND BURYING ME!!
HOW DARE YOU SPEAK OF ME THAT WAY?!
UM... WELL, SIR, I --
I'M GOING BACK TO YUTA!
RE-LEASE ME!
...WHAT DID YOU JUST SAY?

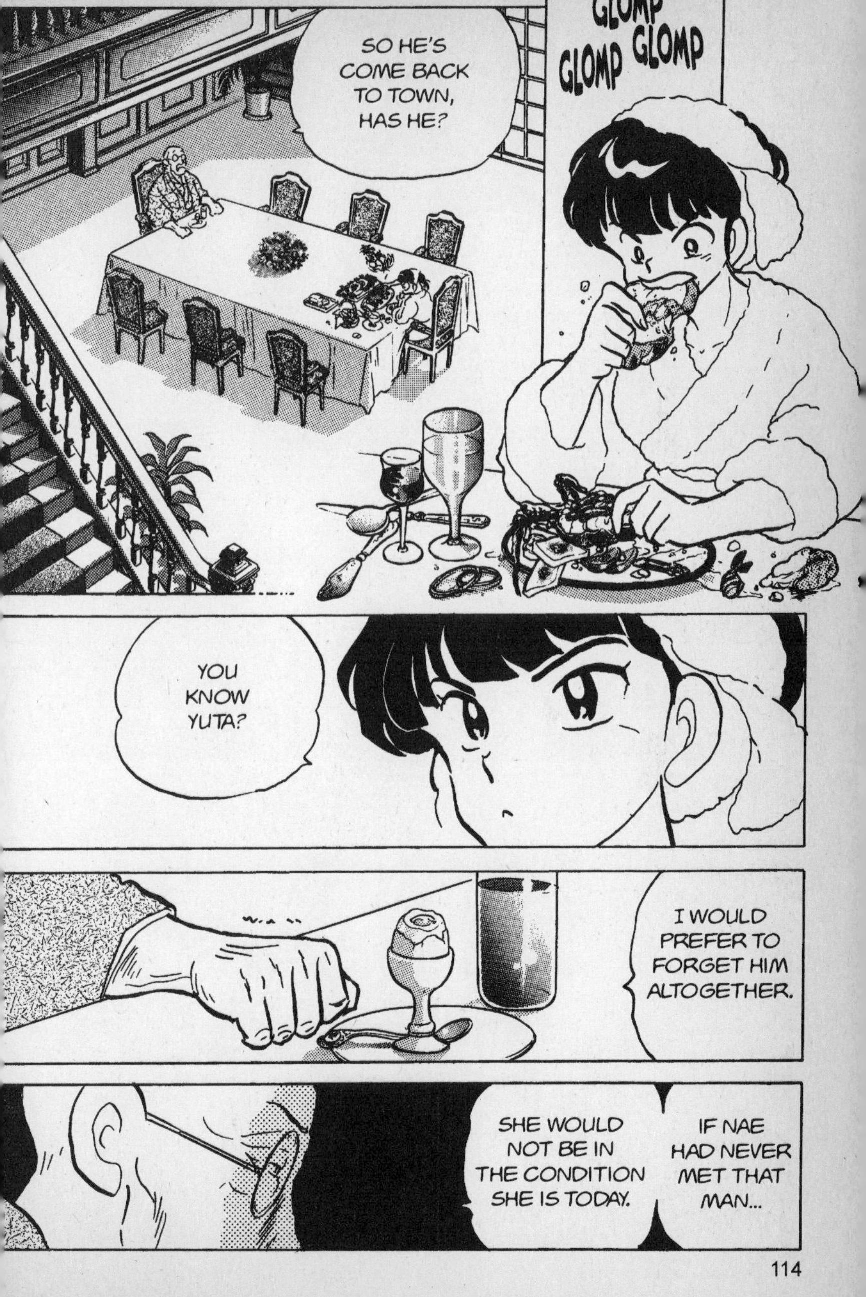
GLOMP GLOMP GLOMP
SO HE'S COME BACK TO TOWN, HAS HE?
YOU KNOW YUTA?
I WOULD PREFER TO FORGET HIM ALTOGETHER.
IF NAE HAD NEVER MET THAT MAN...
SHE WOULD NOT BE IN THE CONDITION SHE IS TODAY.

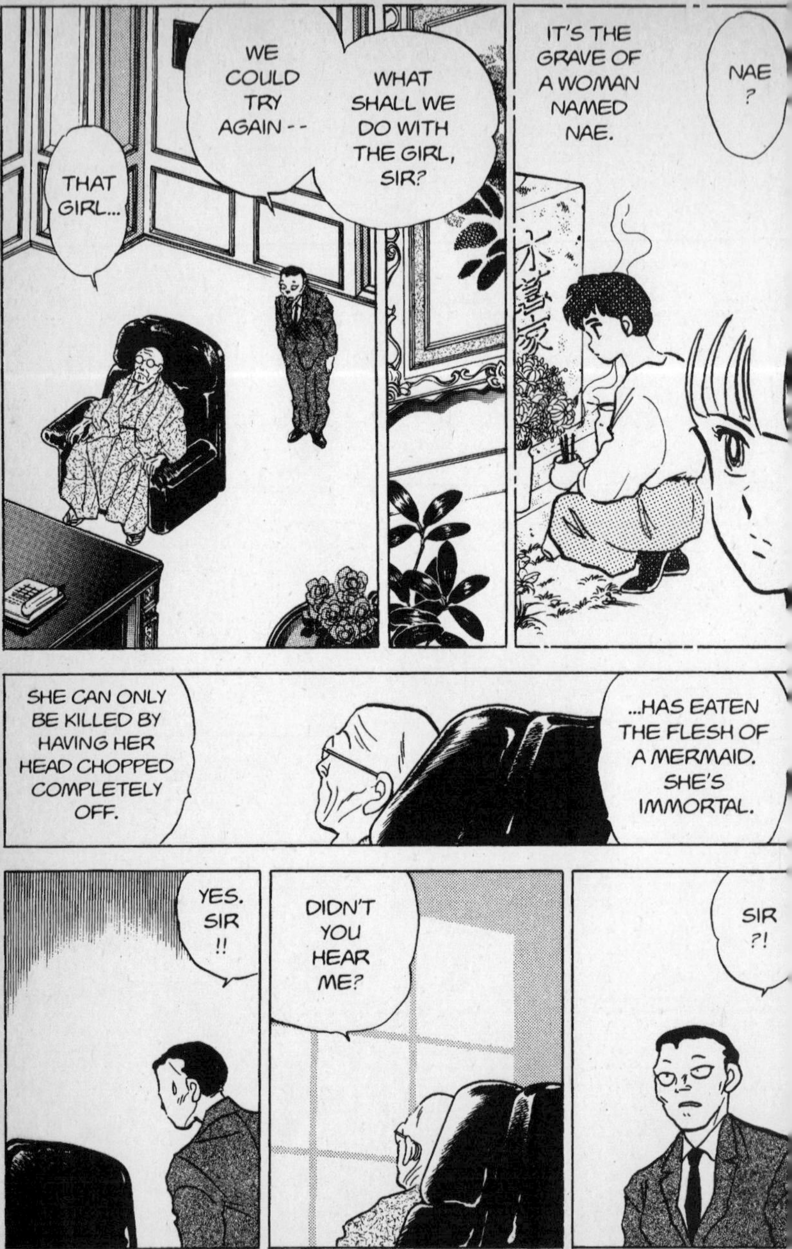
NAE ?
IT'S THE GRAVE OF A WOMAN NAMED NAE.
WE COULD TRY AGAIN --
WHAT SHALL WE DO WITH THE GIRL, SIR?
THAT GIRL...
...HAS EATEN THE FLESH OF A MERMAID. SHE'S IMMORTAL.
SHE CAN ONLY BE KILLED BY HAVING HER HEAD CHOPPED COMPLETELY OFF.
SIR ?!
DIDN'T YOU HEAR ME?
YES. SIR !!

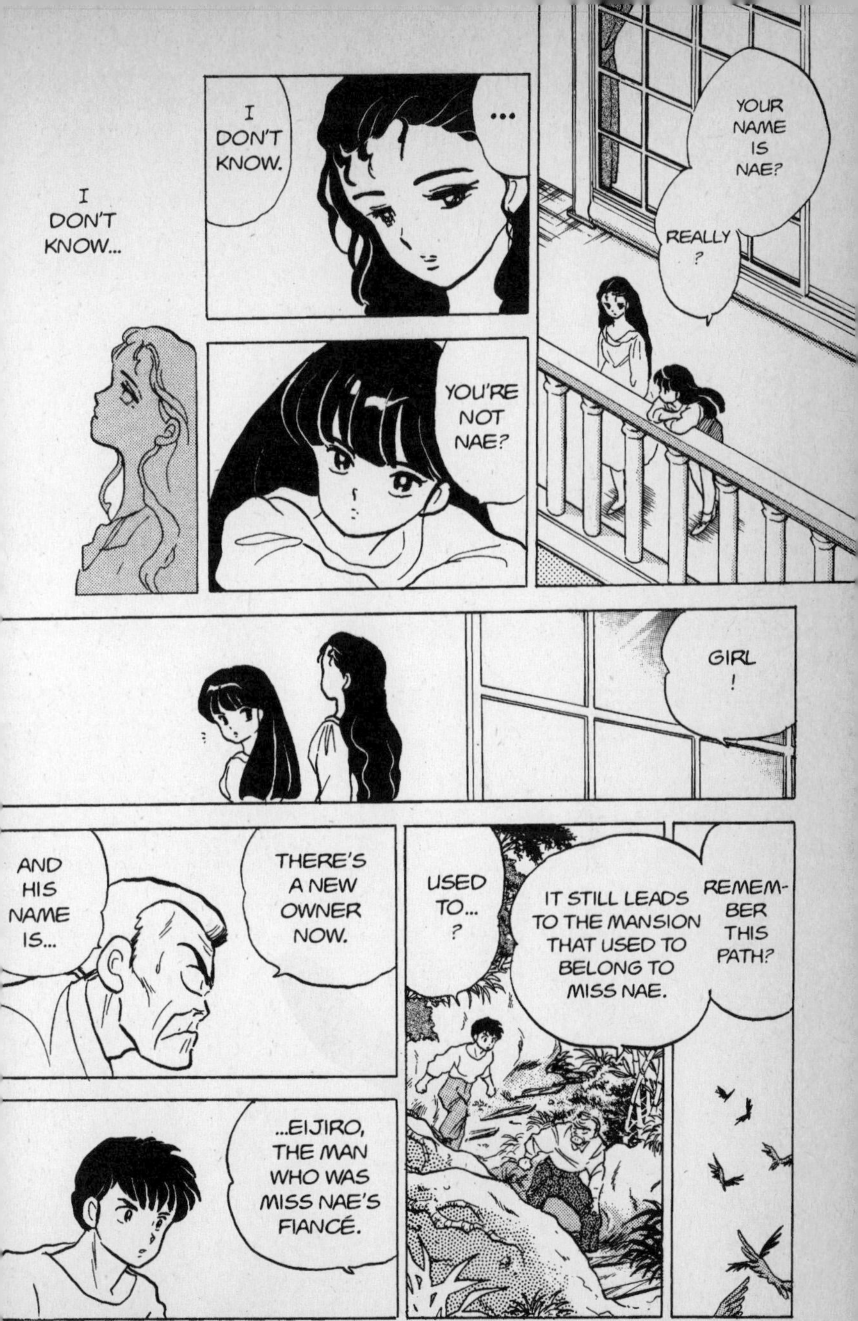
YOUR NAME IS NAE?
REALLY?
...
I DON'T KNOW.
I DON'T KNOW...
YOU'RE NOT NAE?
GIRL!
REMEM-BER THIS PATH?
IT STILL LEADS TO THE MANSION THAT USED TO BELONG TO MISS NAE.
USED TO...?
THERE'S A NEW OWNER NOW.
AND HIS NAME IS...
...EIJIRO, THE MAN WHO WAS MISS NAE'S FIANCÉ.

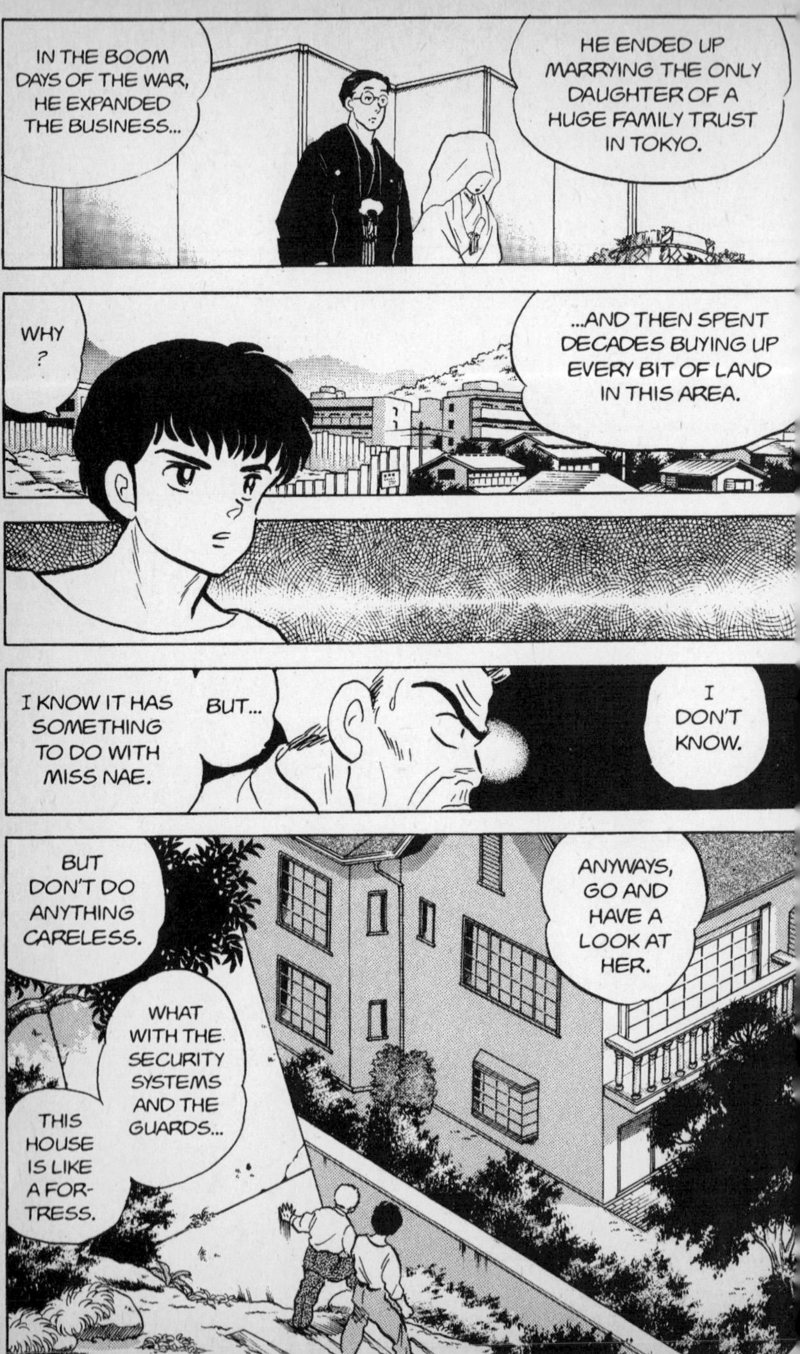
HE ENDED UP MARRYING THE ONLY DAUGHTER OF A HUGE FAMILY TRUST IN TOKYO.
IN THE BOOM DAYS OF THE WAR, HE EXPANDED THE BUSINESS...
...AND THEN SPENT DECADES BUYING UP EVERY BIT OF LAND IN THIS AREA.
WHY ?
I DON'T KNOW.
BUT...
I KNOW IT HAS SOMETHING TO DO WITH MISS NAE.
ANYWAYS, GO AND HAVE A LOOK AT HER.
BUT DON'T DO ANYTHING CARELESS.
WHAT WITH THE SECURITY SYSTEMS AND THE GUARDS...
THIS HOUSE IS LIKE A FOR-TRESS.

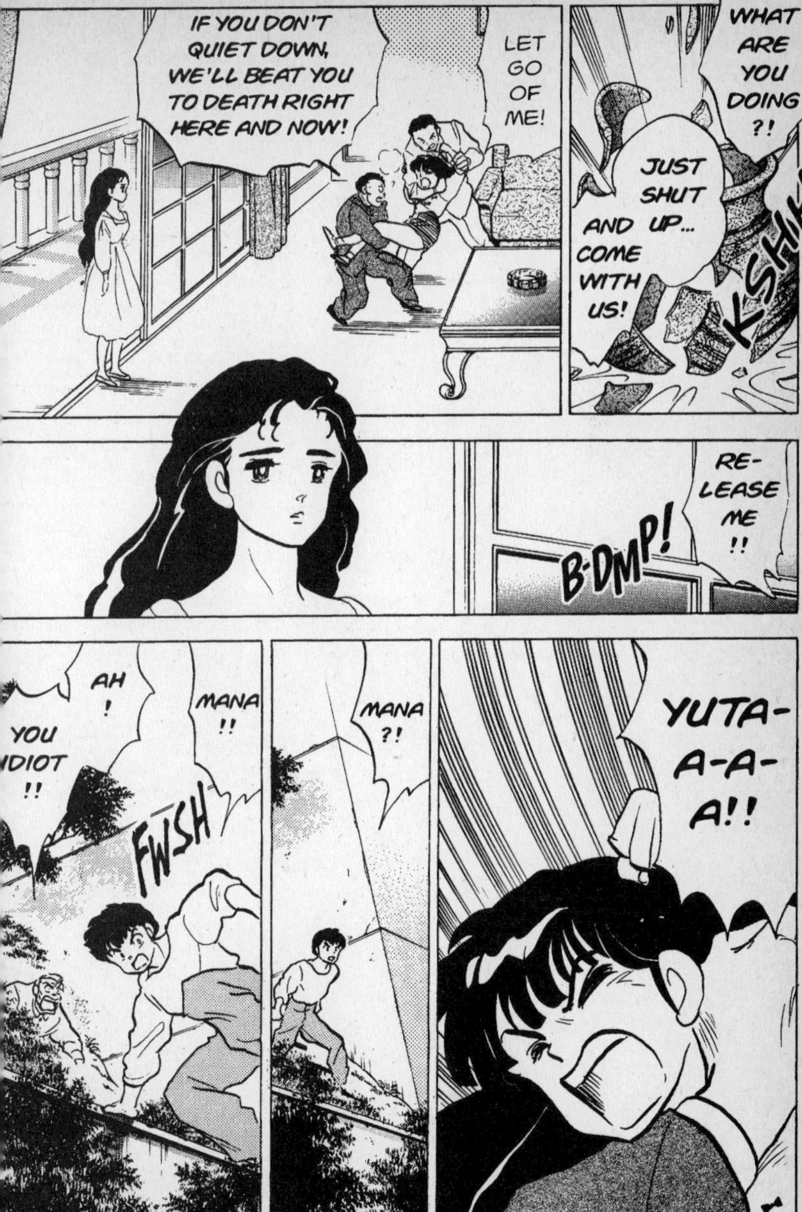
WHAT ARE YOU DOING?!
JUST SHUT UP... AND COME WITH US!
KSHHHH
LET GO OF ME!
IF YOU DON'T QUIET DOWN, WE'LL BEAT YOU TO DEATH RIGHT HERE AND NOW!
RE-LEASE ME!!
B-DMP!
YUTA-A-A-A!!
MANA?!
MANA!!
AH!
YOU IDIOT!!
FWSH

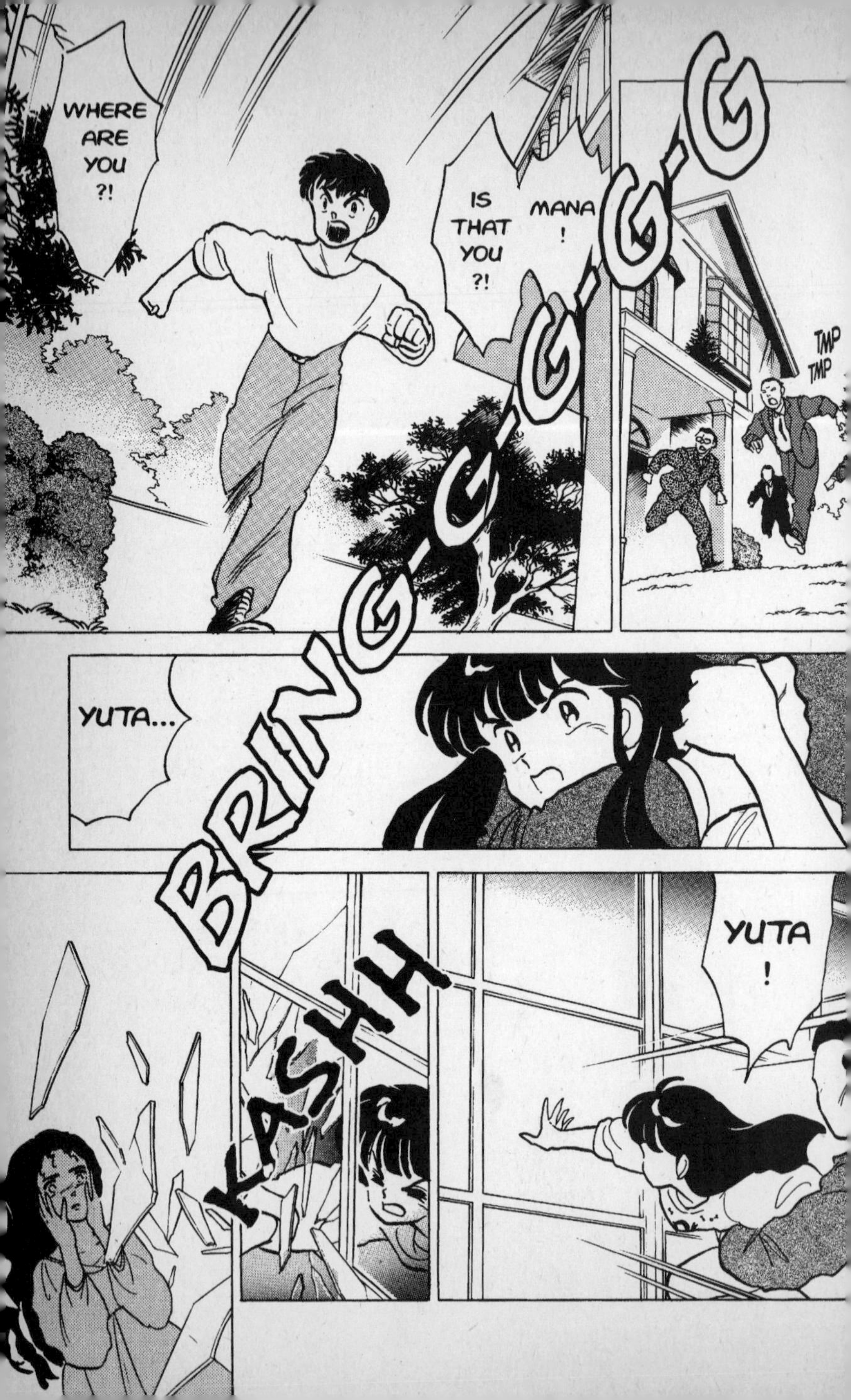
TMP TMP
MANA !
IS THAT YOU ?!
WHERE ARE YOU ?!
BRING-G-G-G
YUTA...
YUTA !
KASHH

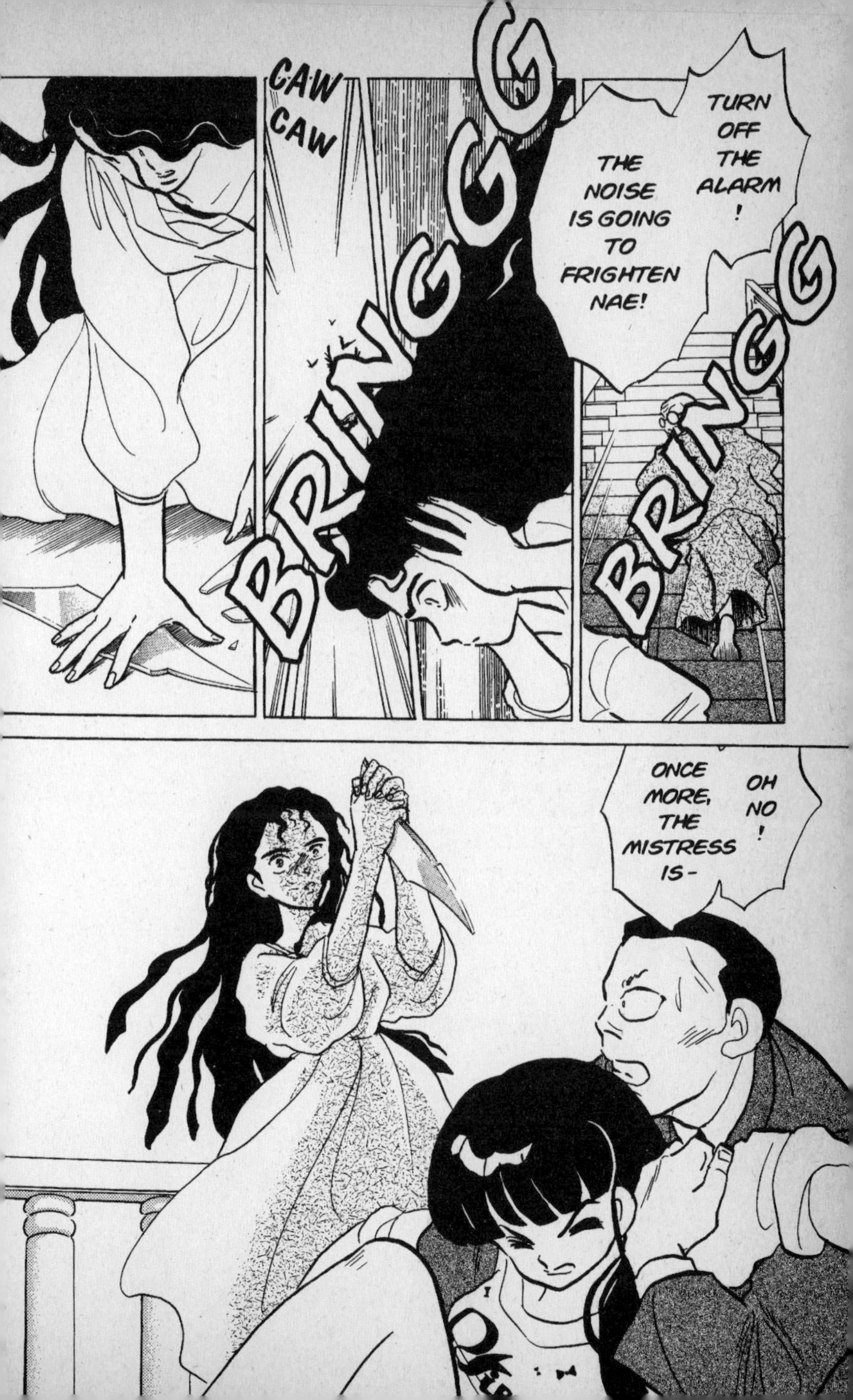
TURN OFF THE ALARM!
THE NOISE IS GOING TO FRIGHTEN NAE!
BRINGG
BRINGGG
CAW CAW
OH NO!
ONCE MORE, THE MISTRESS IS-

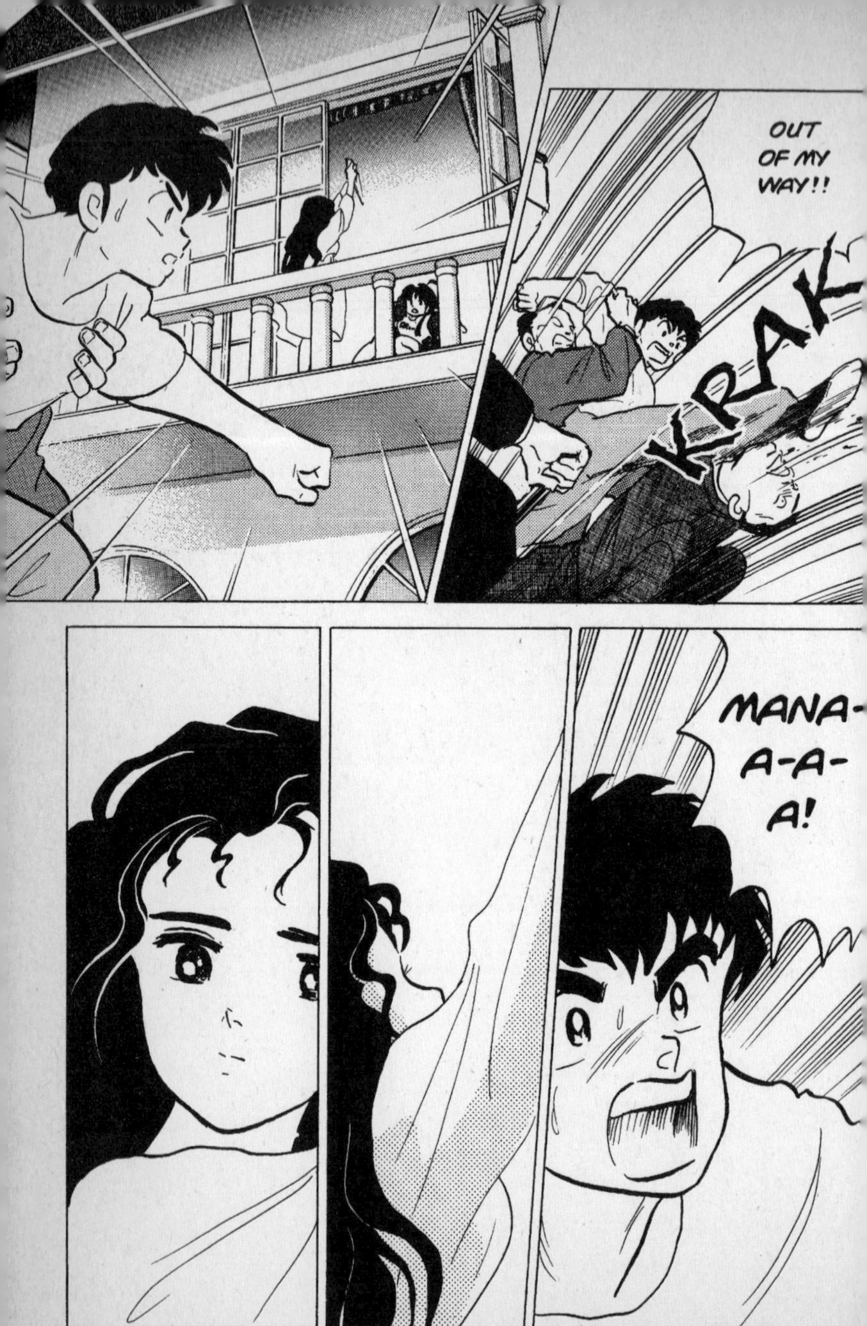
OUT OF MY WAY!!
KRAK
MANA-A-A-A!

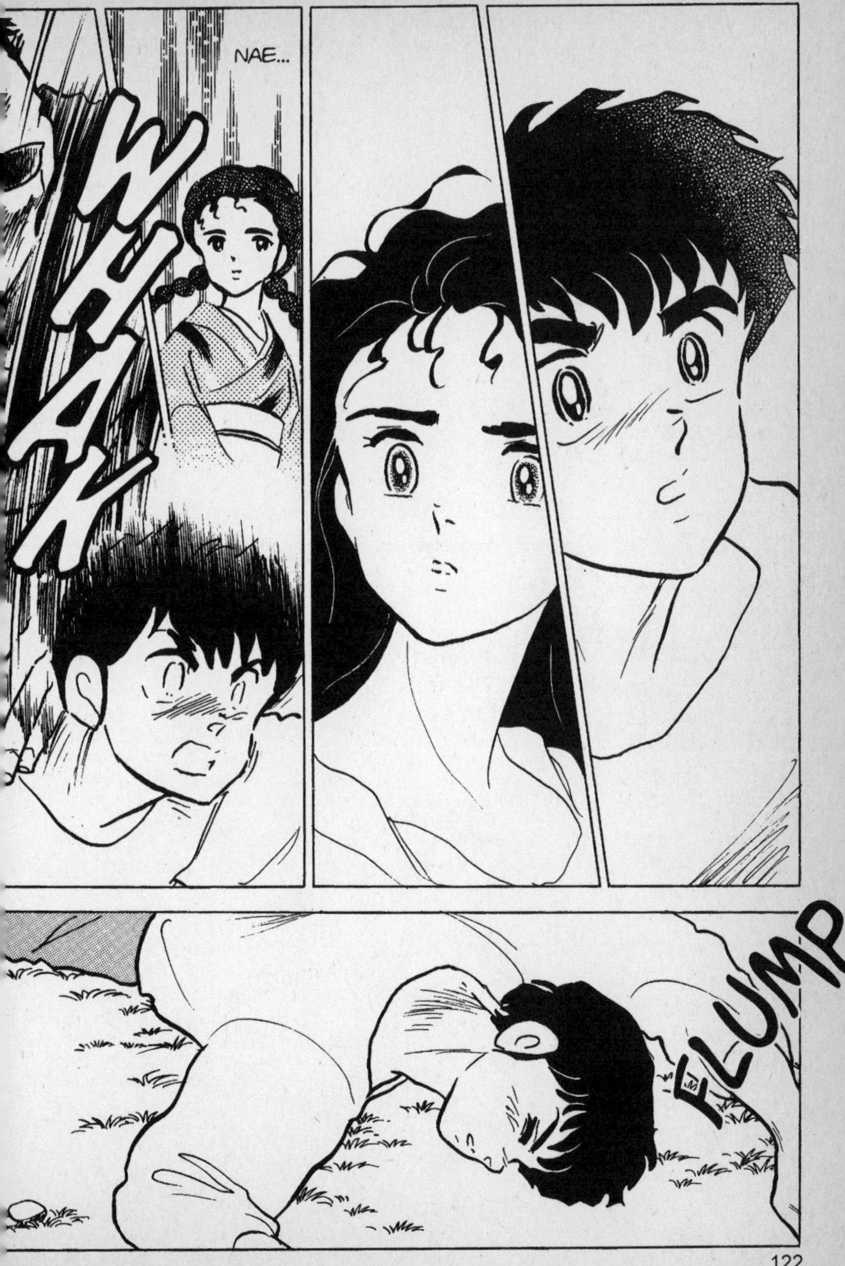
NAE...
WHAK
FLUMP

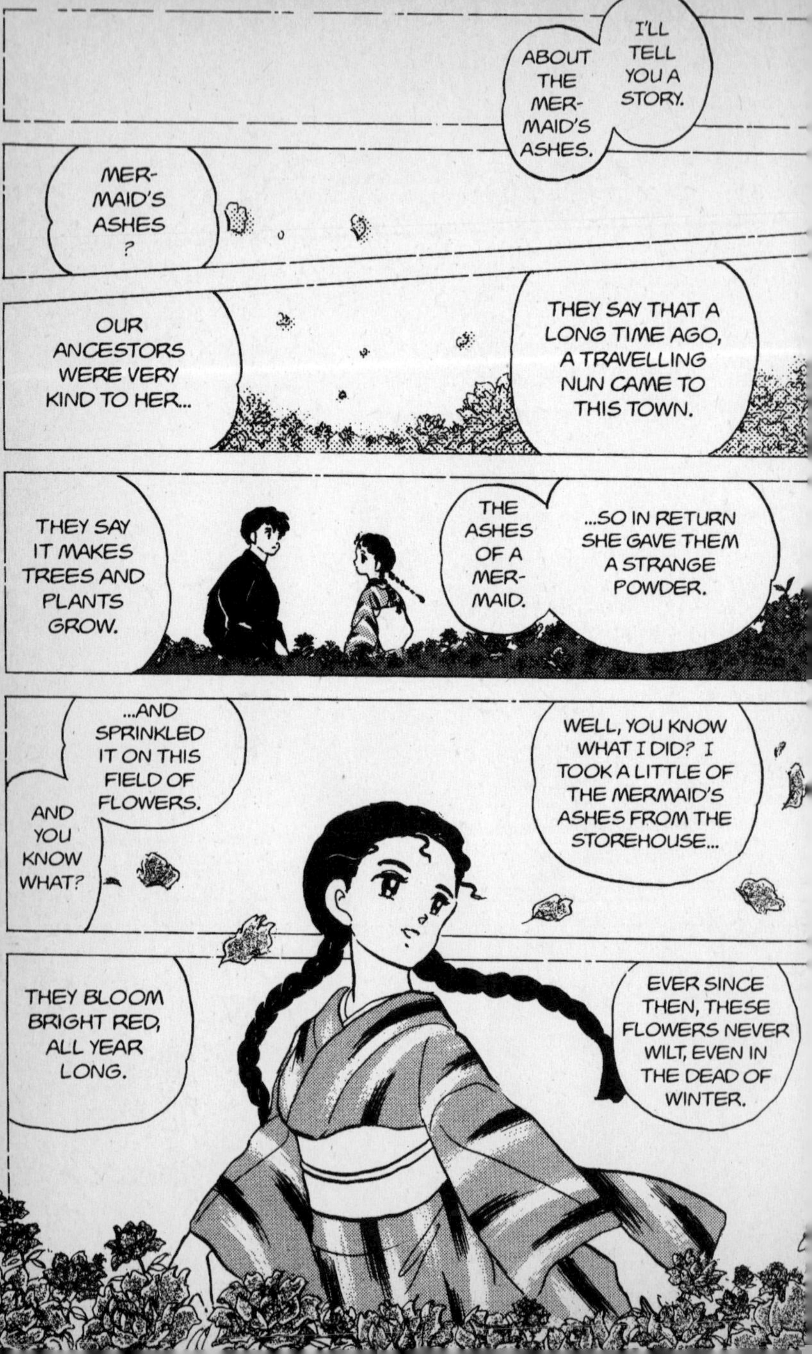
I'LL TELL YOU A STORY.
ABOUT THE MER-MAID'S ASHES.
MER-MAID'S ASHES?
THEY SAY THAT A LONG TIME AGO, A TRAVELLING NUN CAME TO THIS TOWN.
OUR ANCESTORS WERE VERY KIND TO HER...
...SO IN RETURN SHE GAVE THEM A STRANGE POWDER.
THE ASHES OF A MER-MAID.
THEY SAY IT MAKES TREES AND PLANTS GROW.
WELL, YOU KNOW WHAT I DID? I TOOK A LITTLE OF THE MERMAID'S ASHES FROM THE STOREHOUSE...
...AND SPRINKLED IT ON THIS FIELD OF FLOWERS.
AND YOU KNOW WHAT?
EVER SINCE THEN, THESE FLOWERS NEVER WILT, EVEN IN THE DEAD OF WINTER.
THEY BLOOM BRIGHT RED, ALL YEAR LONG.

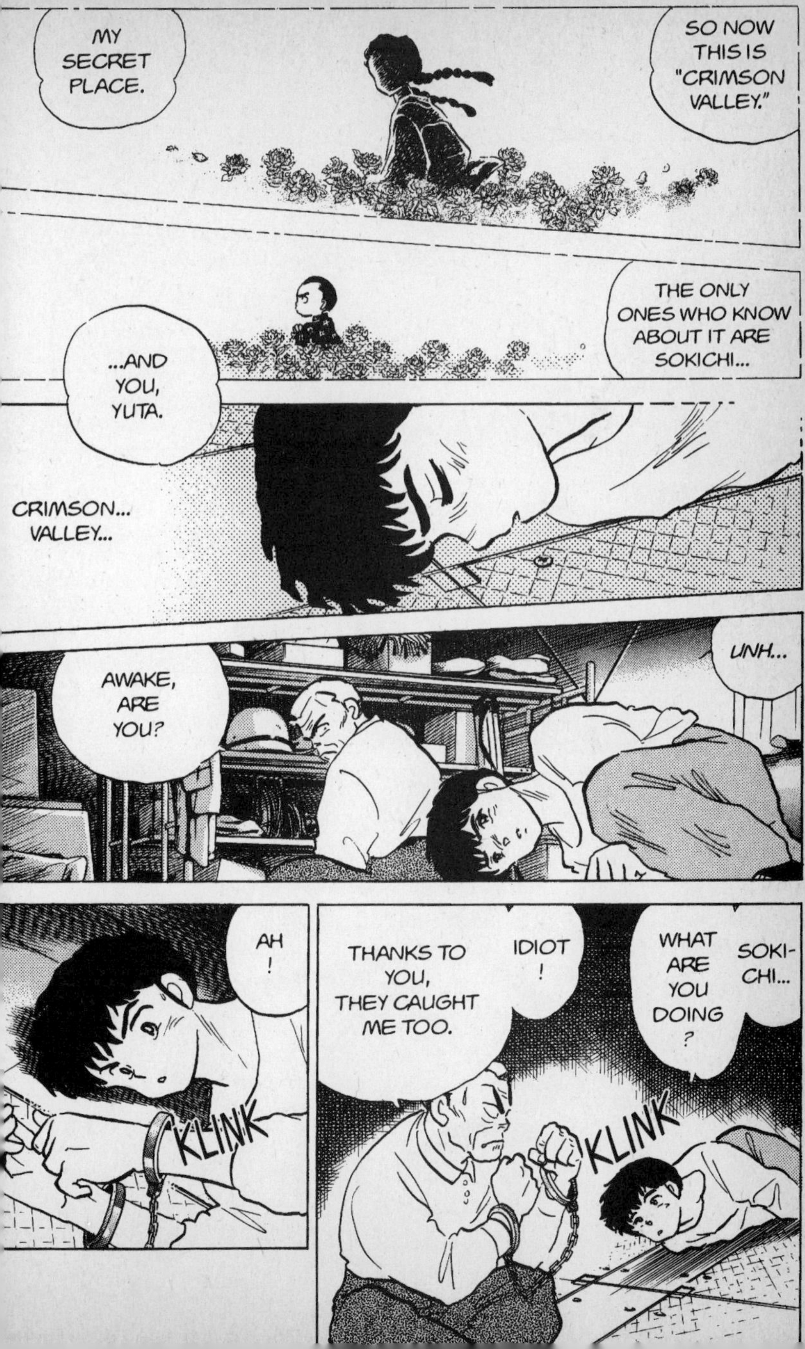
SO NOW THIS IS "CRIMSON VALLEY."
MY SECRET PLACE.
THE ONLY ONES WHO KNOW ABOUT IT ARE SOKICHI...
...AND YOU, YUTA.
CRIMSON... VALLEY...
UNH...
AWAKE, ARE YOU?
SOKI-CHI...
WHAT ARE YOU DOING?
IDIOT!
THANKS TO YOU, THEY CAUGHT ME TOO.
KLINK
AH!
KLINK

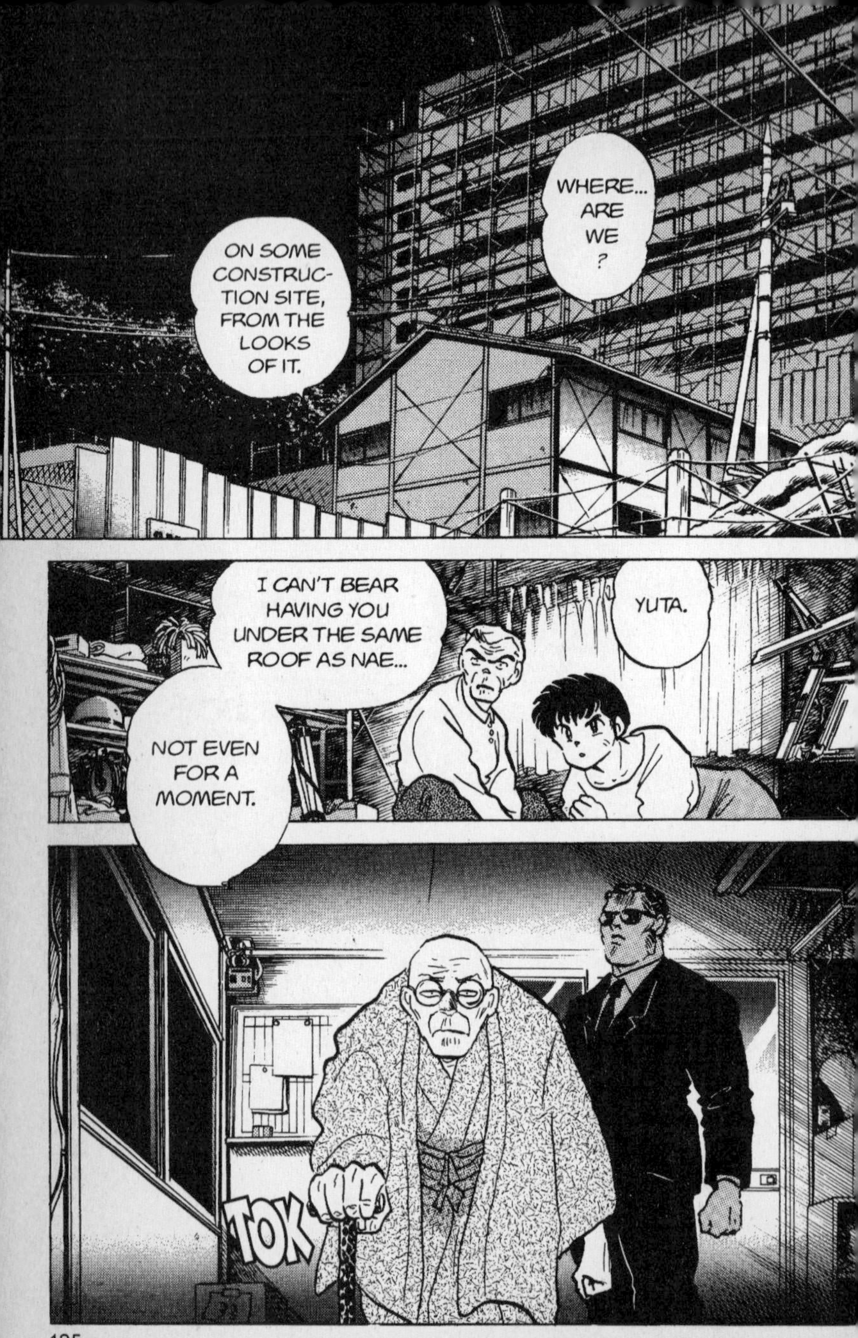
WHERE... ARE WE ?
ON SOME CONSTRUCTION SITE, FROM THE LOOKS OF IT.
YUTA.
I CAN'T BEAR HAVING YOU UNDER THE SAME ROOF AS NAE...
NOT EVEN FOR A MOMENT.
TOK

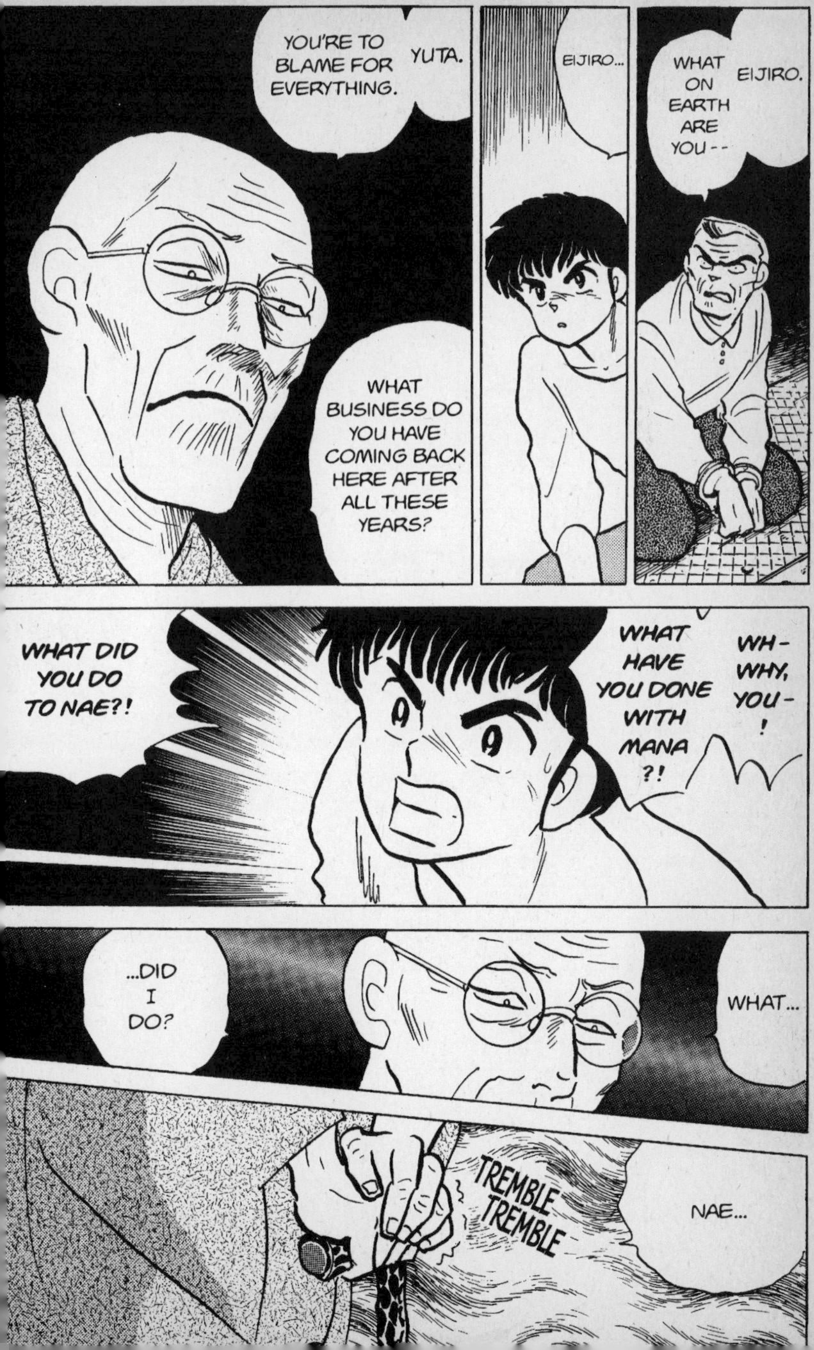
EIJIRO.
WHAT ON EARTH ARE YOU --
EIJIRO...
YUTA.
YOU'RE TO BLAME FOR EVERYTHING.
WHAT BUSINESS DO YOU HAVE COMING BACK HERE AFTER ALL THESE YEARS?
WH-WHY, YOU-!
WHAT HAVE YOU DONE WITH MANA?!
WHAT DID YOU DO TO NAE?!
WHAT...
...DID I DO?
NAE...
TREMBLE TREMBLE

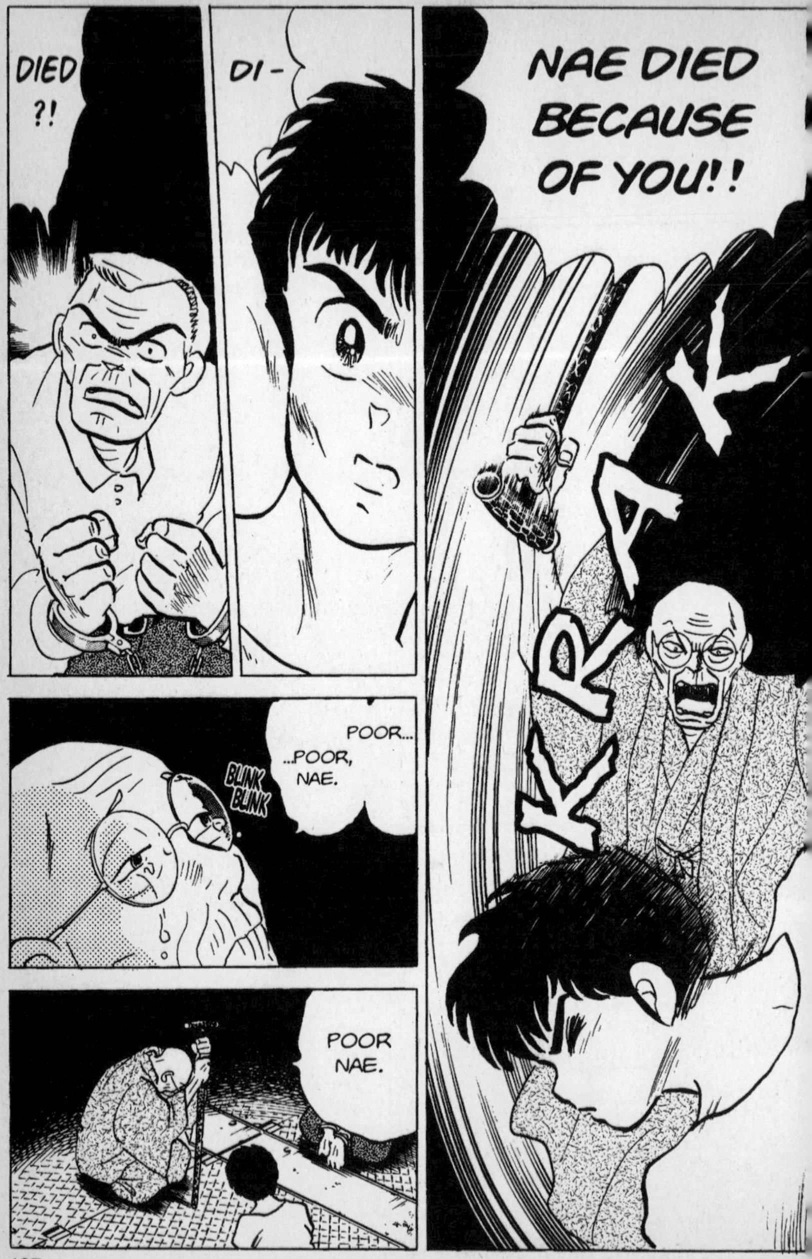
NAE DIED BECAUSE OF YOU!!
KRAK
DI-
DIED ?!
POOR...
...POOR, NAE.
BLINK BLINK
POOR NAE.

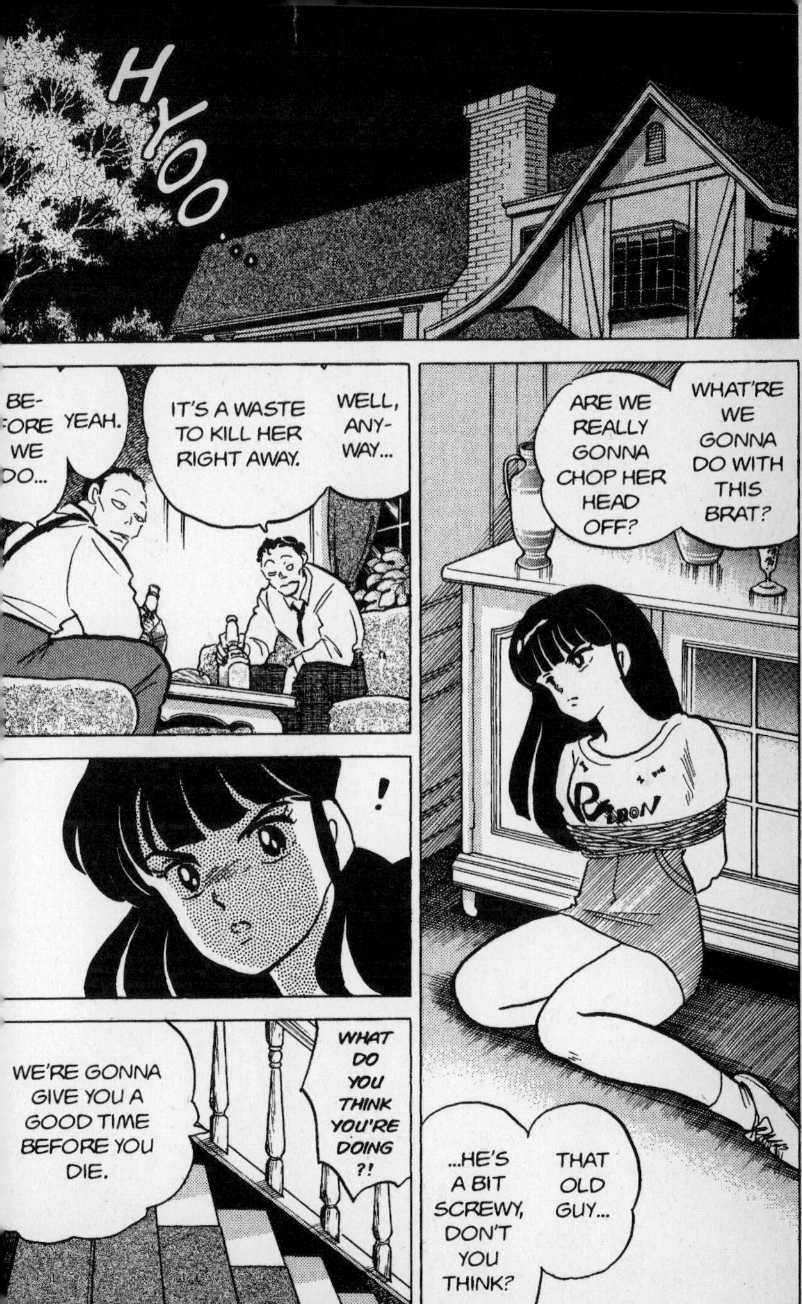
HYOO...
WHAT'RE WE GONNA DO WITH THIS BRAT?
ARE WE REALLY GONNA CHOP HER HEAD OFF?
THAT OLD GUY...
...HE'S A BIT SCREWY, DON'T YOU THINK?
WELL, ANYWAY...
IT'S A WASTE TO KILL HER RIGHT AWAY.
YEAH.
BEFORE WE DO...
!
WHAT DO YOU THINK YOU'RE DOING?!
WE'RE GONNA GIVE YOU A GOOD TIME BEFORE YOU DIE.

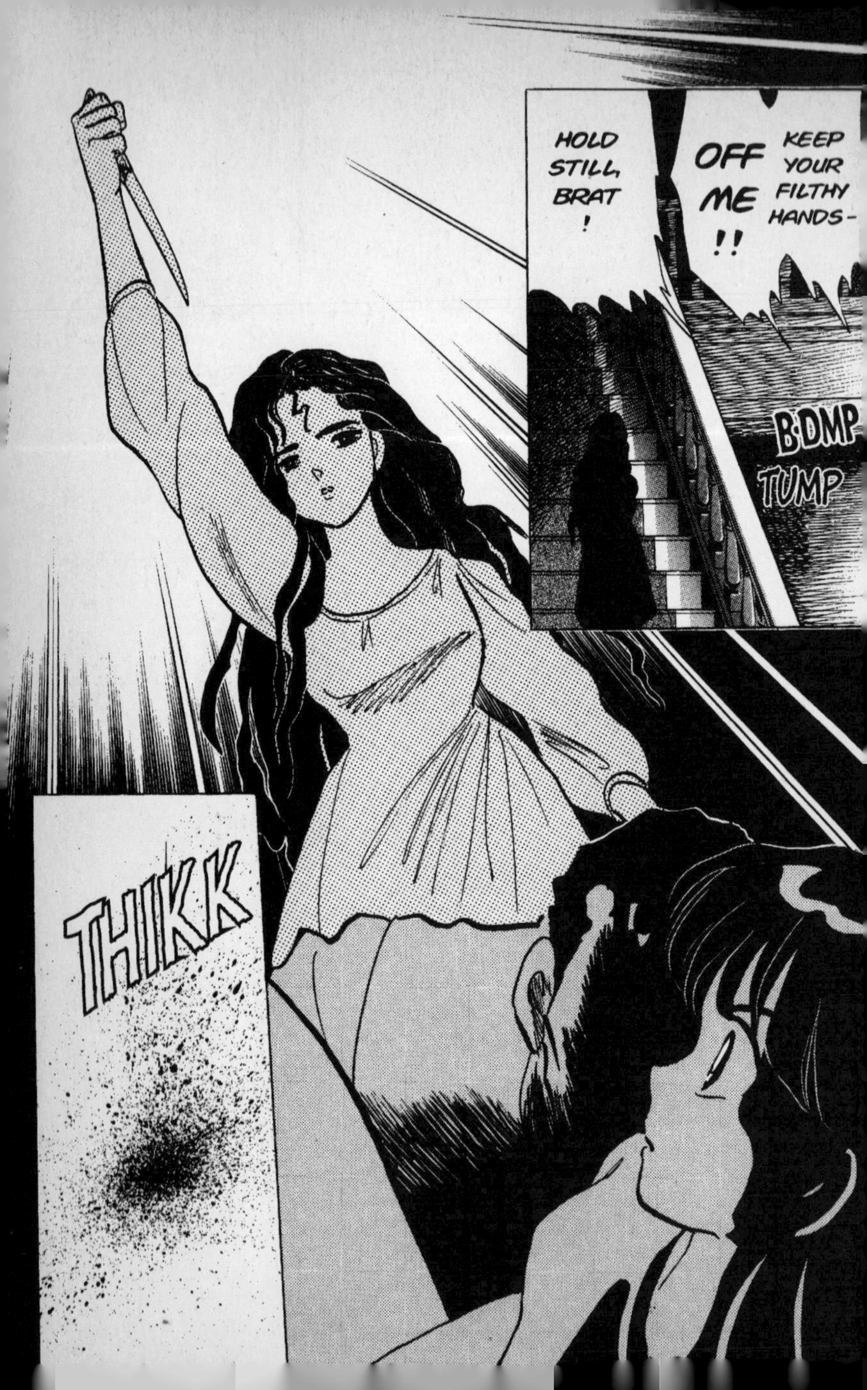
KEEP YOUR FILTHY HANDS-
OFF ME !!
HOLD STILL, BRAT !
B-DMP
TUMP
THIKK

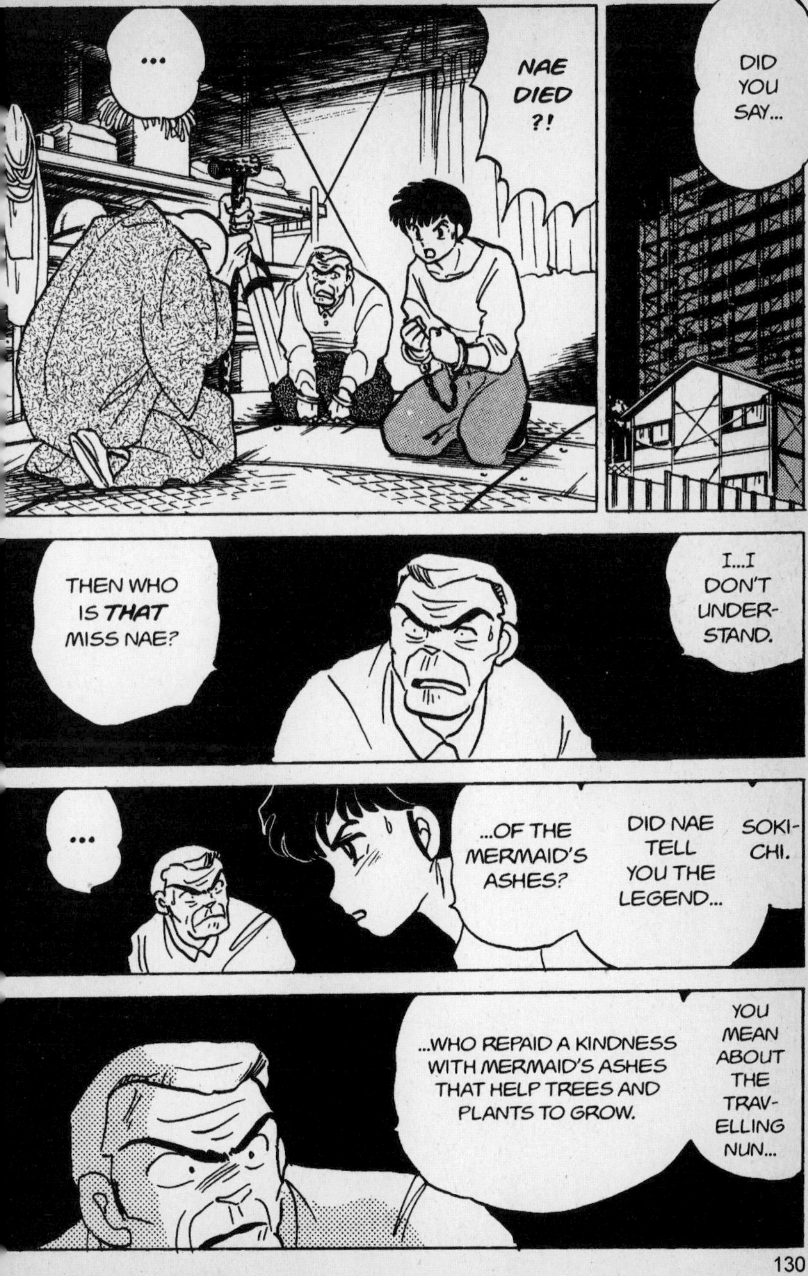

DID YOU SAY...
NAE DIED ?!
...
I...I DON'T UNDER-STAND.
THEN WHO IS *THAT* MISS NAE?
SOKI-CHI.
DID NAE TELL YOU THE LEGEND...
...OF THE MERMAID'S ASHES?
...
YOU MEAN ABOUT THE TRAV-ELLING NUN...
...WHO REPAID A KINDNESS WITH MERMAID'S ASHES THAT HELP TREES AND PLANTS TO GROW.

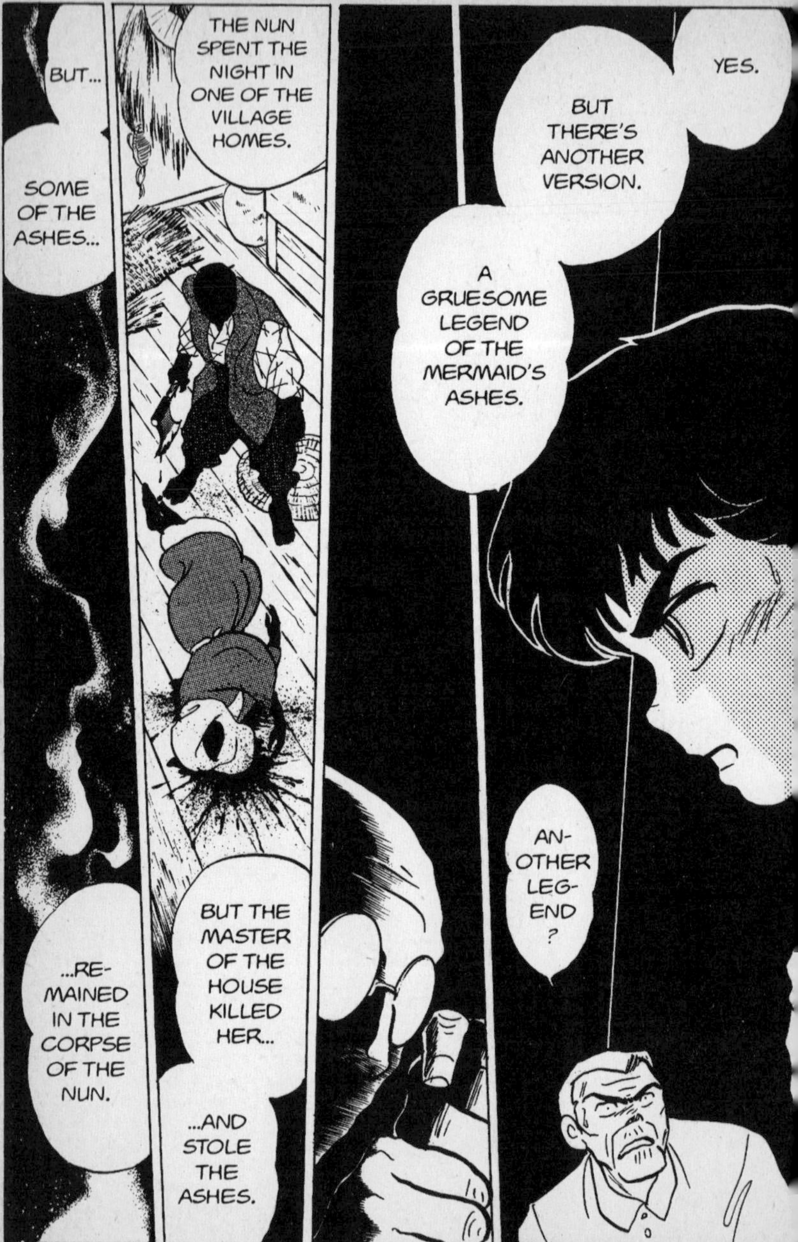
YES.
BUT THERE'S ANOTHER VERSION.
A GRUESOME LEGEND OF THE MERMAID'S ASHES.
AN-OTHER LEG-END?
THE NUN SPENT THE NIGHT IN ONE OF THE VILLAGE HOMES.
BUT THE MASTER OF THE HOUSE KILLED HER...
...AND STOLE THE ASHES.
BUT...
SOME OF THE ASHES...
...RE-MAINED IN THE CORPSE OF THE NUN.

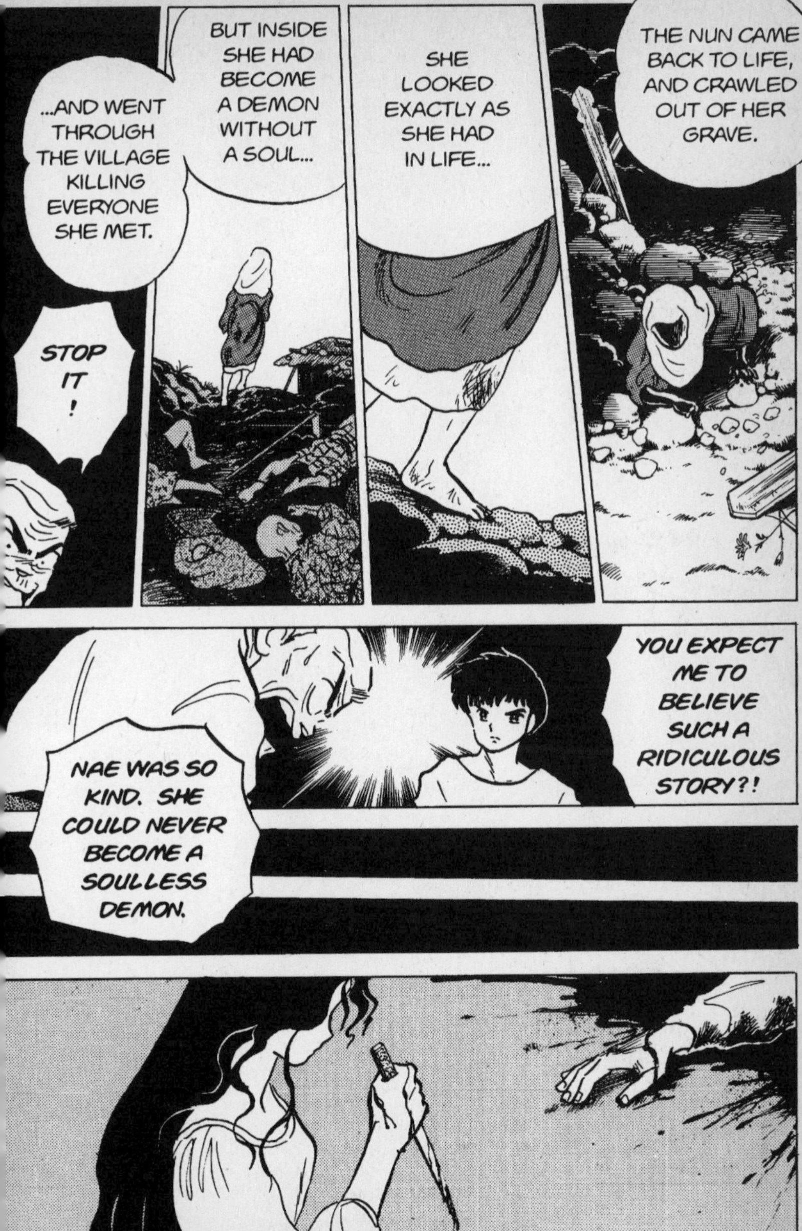
THE NUN CAME BACK TO LIFE, AND CRAWLED OUT OF HER GRAVE.
SHE LOOKED EXACTLY AS SHE HAD IN LIFE...
BUT INSIDE SHE HAD BECOME A DEMON WITHOUT A SOUL...
...AND WENT THROUGH THE VILLAGE KILLING EVERYONE SHE MET.
STOP IT!
YOU EXPECT ME TO BELIEVE SUCH A RIDICULOUS STORY?!
NAE WAS SO KIND. SHE COULD NEVER BECOME A SOULLESS DEMON.

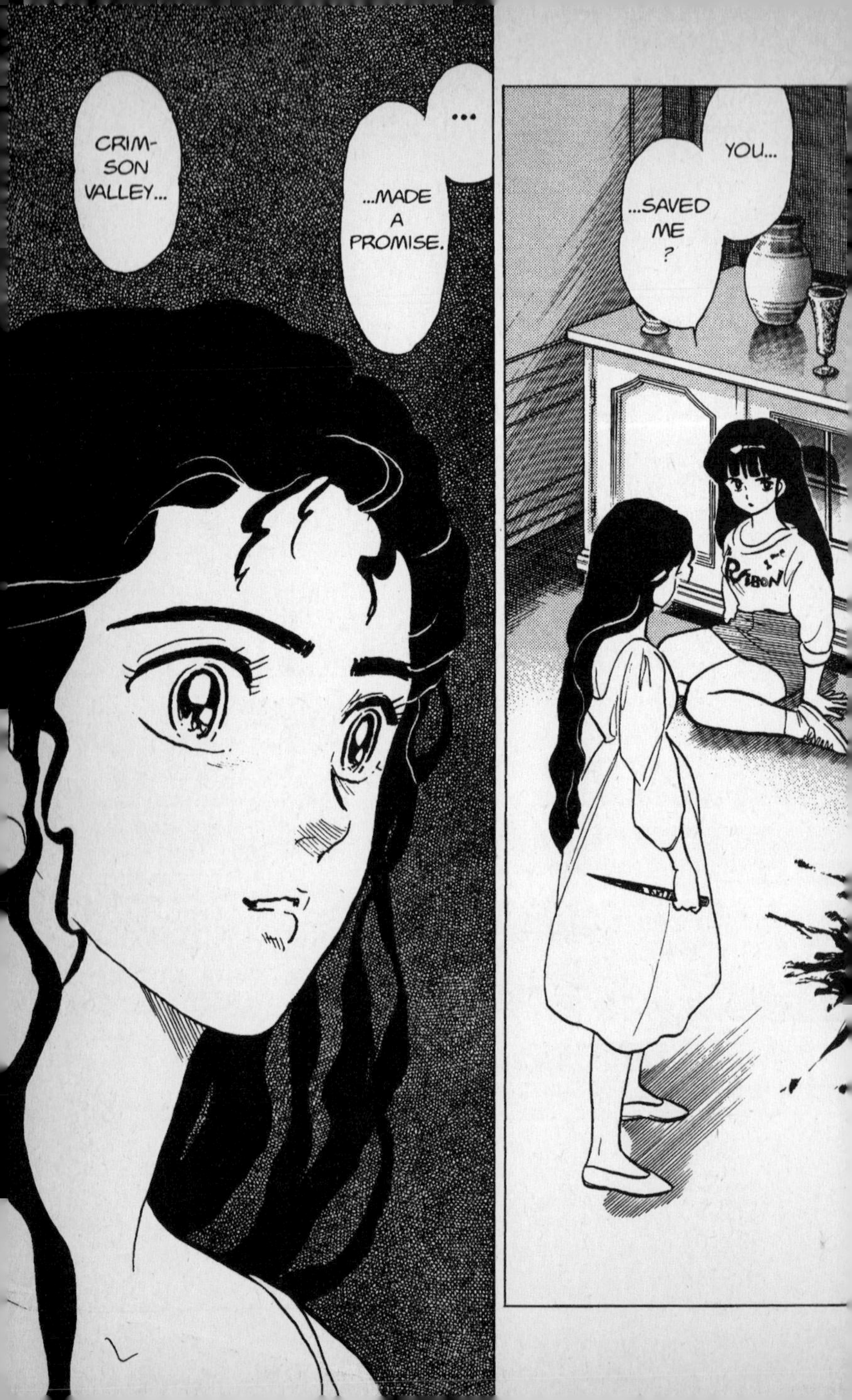
YOU...
...SAVED ME ?
...
...MADE A PROMISE.
CRIM-SON VALLEY...

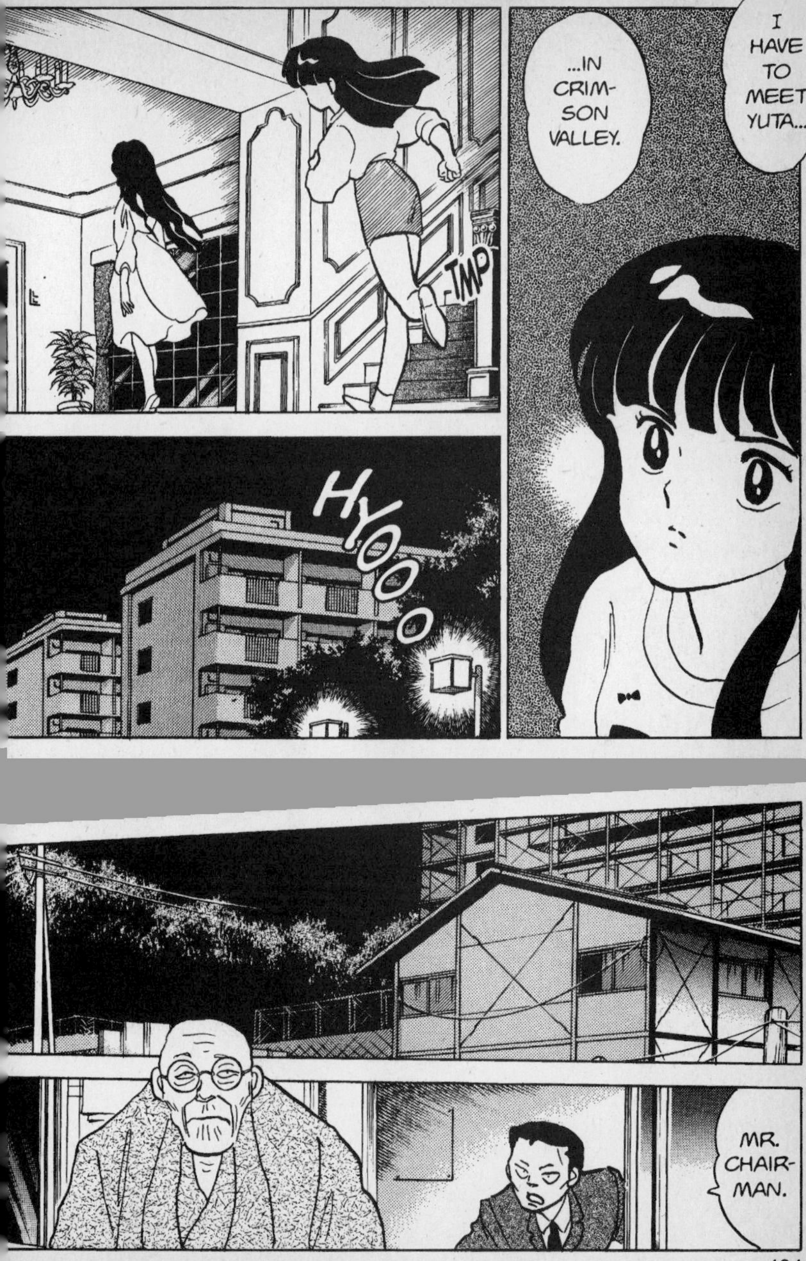
I HAVE TO MEET YUTA...
...IN CRIM-SON VALLEY.
TMP
HYOOOO
MR. CHAIR-MAN.

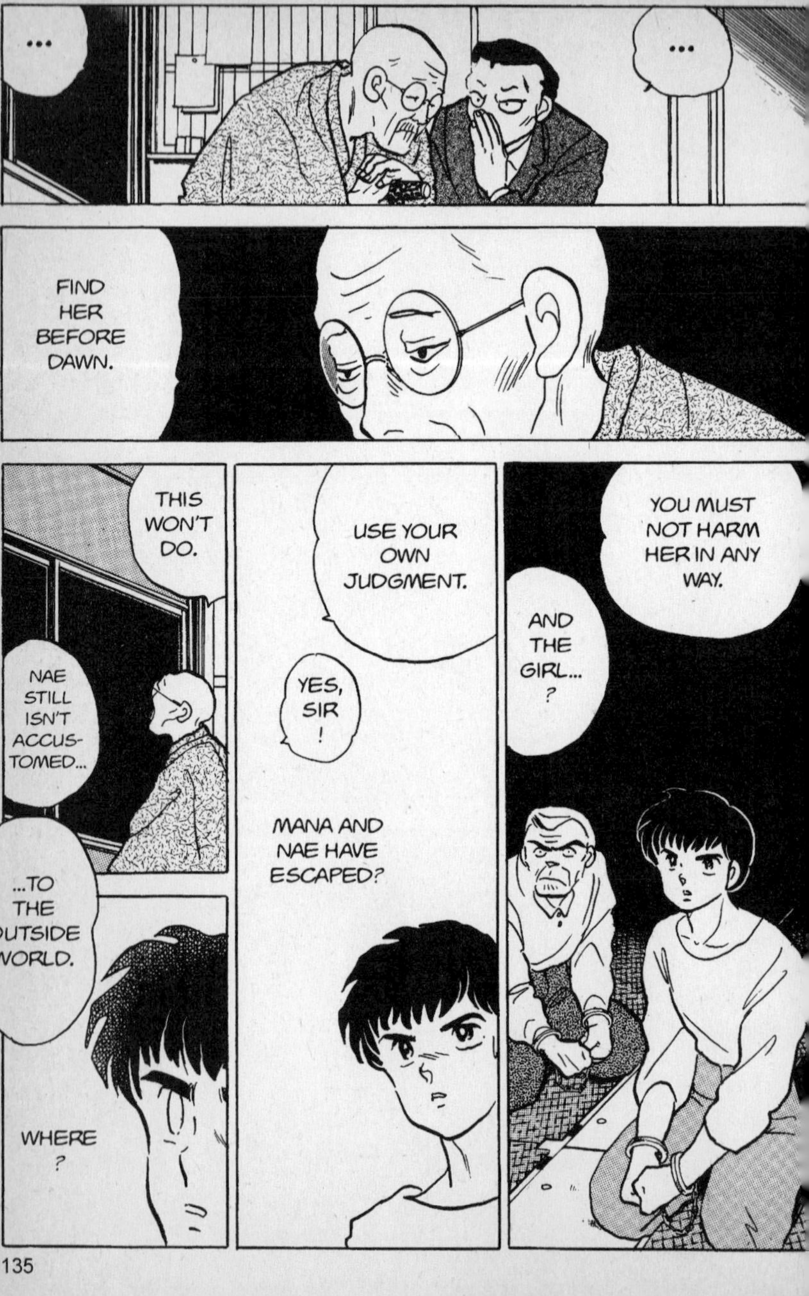
...
...
FIND HER BEFORE DAWN.
YOU MUST NOT HARM HER IN ANY WAY.
AND THE GIRL...?
USE YOUR OWN JUDGMENT.
YES, SIR!
MANA AND NAE HAVE ESCAPED?
THIS WON'T DO.
NAE STILL ISN'T ACCUS-TOMED...
...TO THE OUTSIDE WORLD.
WHERE?

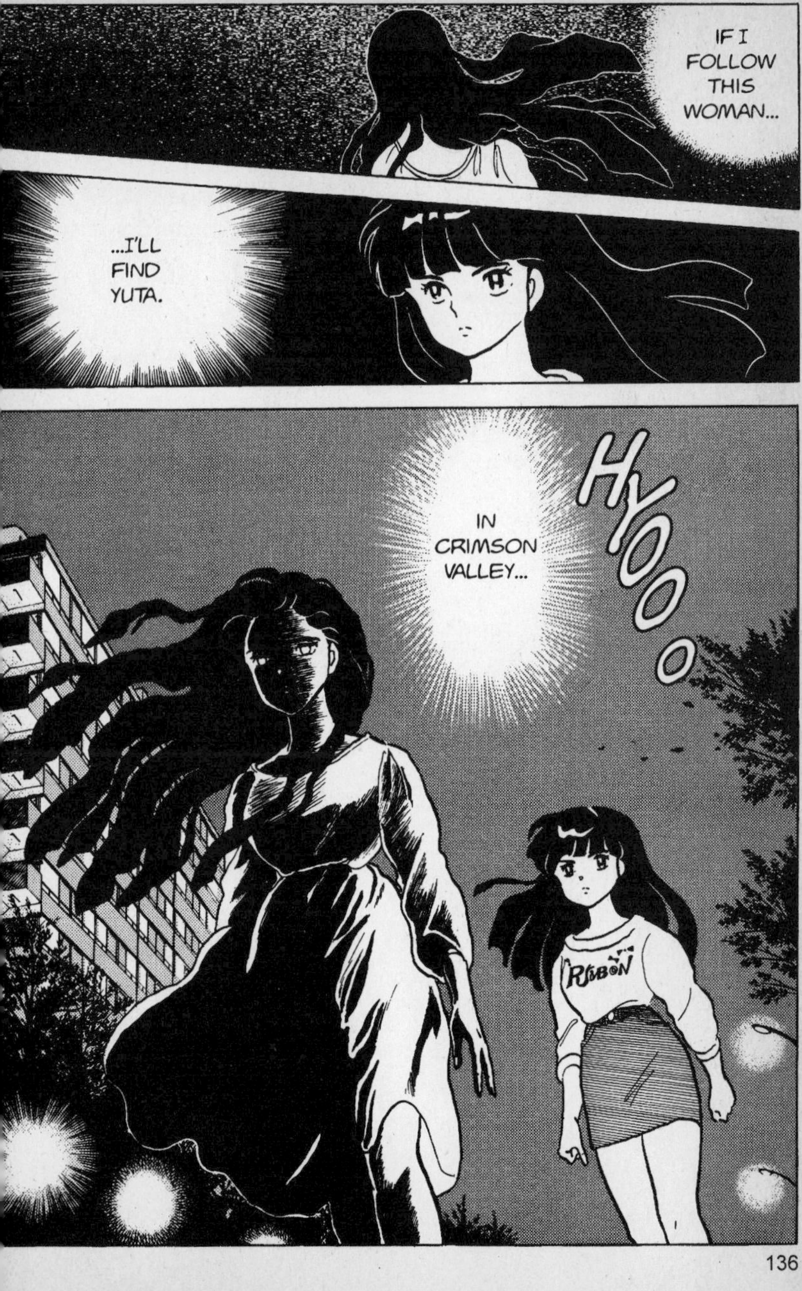
IF I FOLLOW THIS WOMAN...
...I'LL FIND YUTA.
HYOOOO
IN CRIMSON VALLEY...

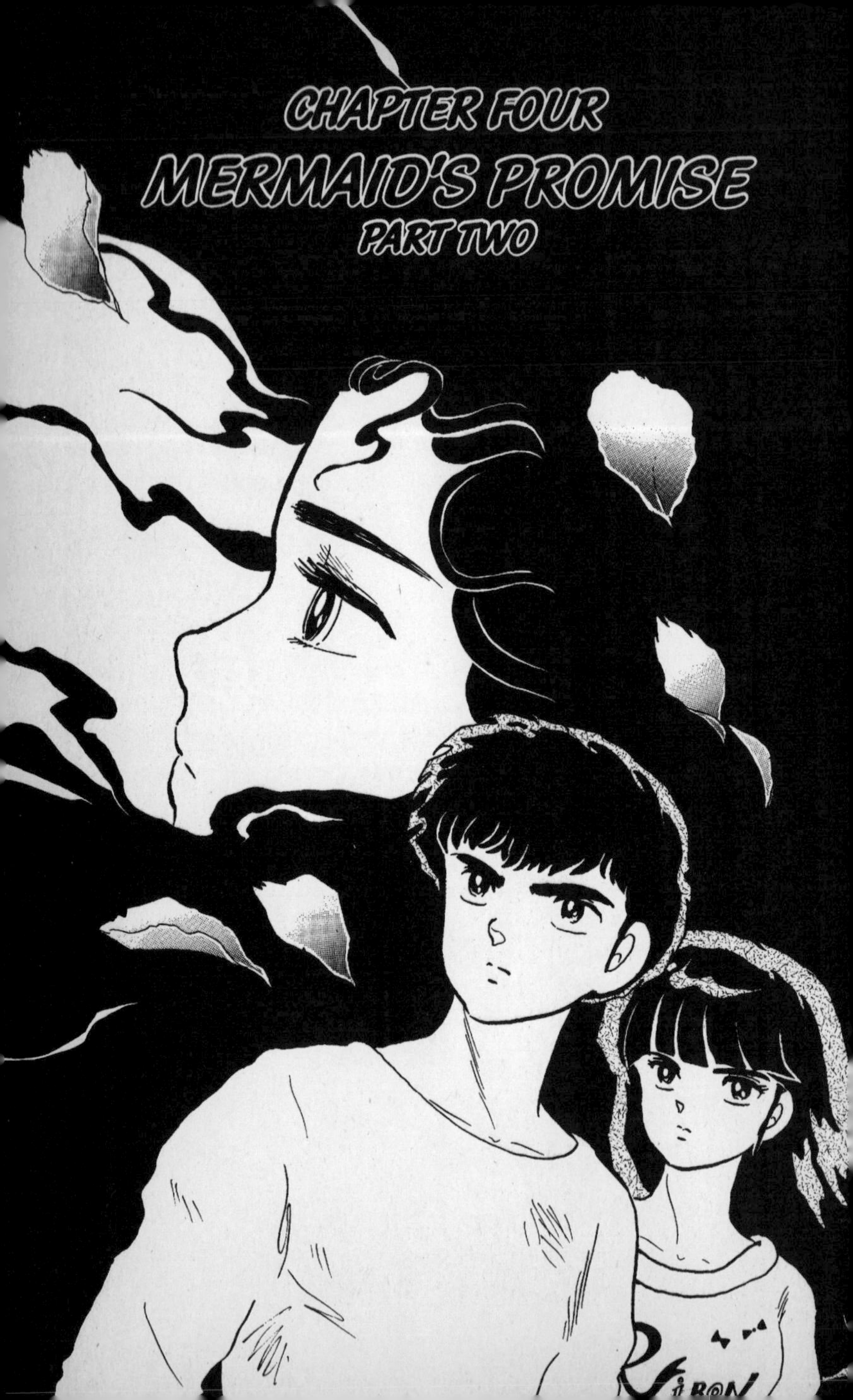
CHAPTER FOUR
MERMAID'S PROMISE
PART TWO

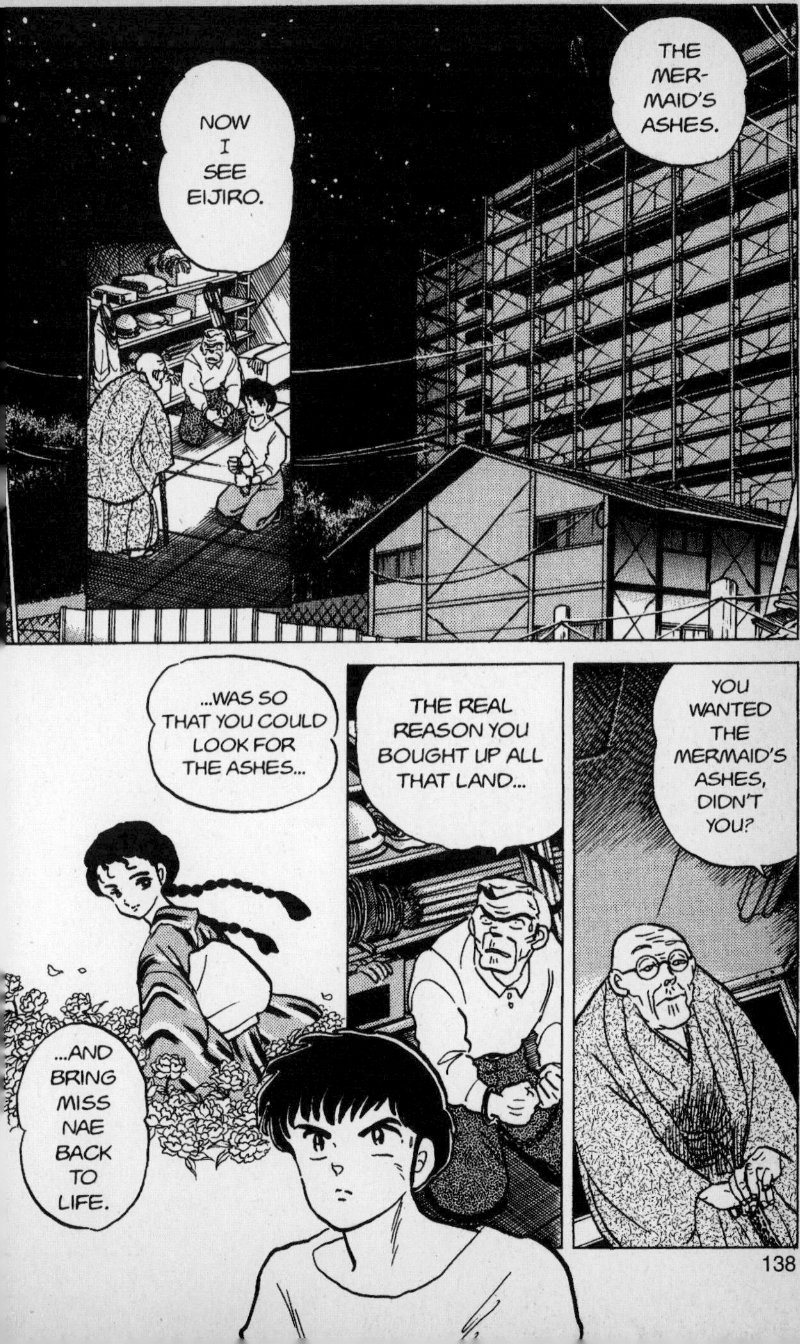
THE MER-MAID'S ASHES.
NOW I SEE EIJIRO.
YOU WANTED THE MERMAID'S ASHES, DIDN'T YOU?
THE REAL REASON YOU BOUGHT UP ALL THAT LAND...
...WAS SO THAT YOU COULD LOOK FOR THE ASHES...
...AND BRING MISS NAE BACK TO LIFE.

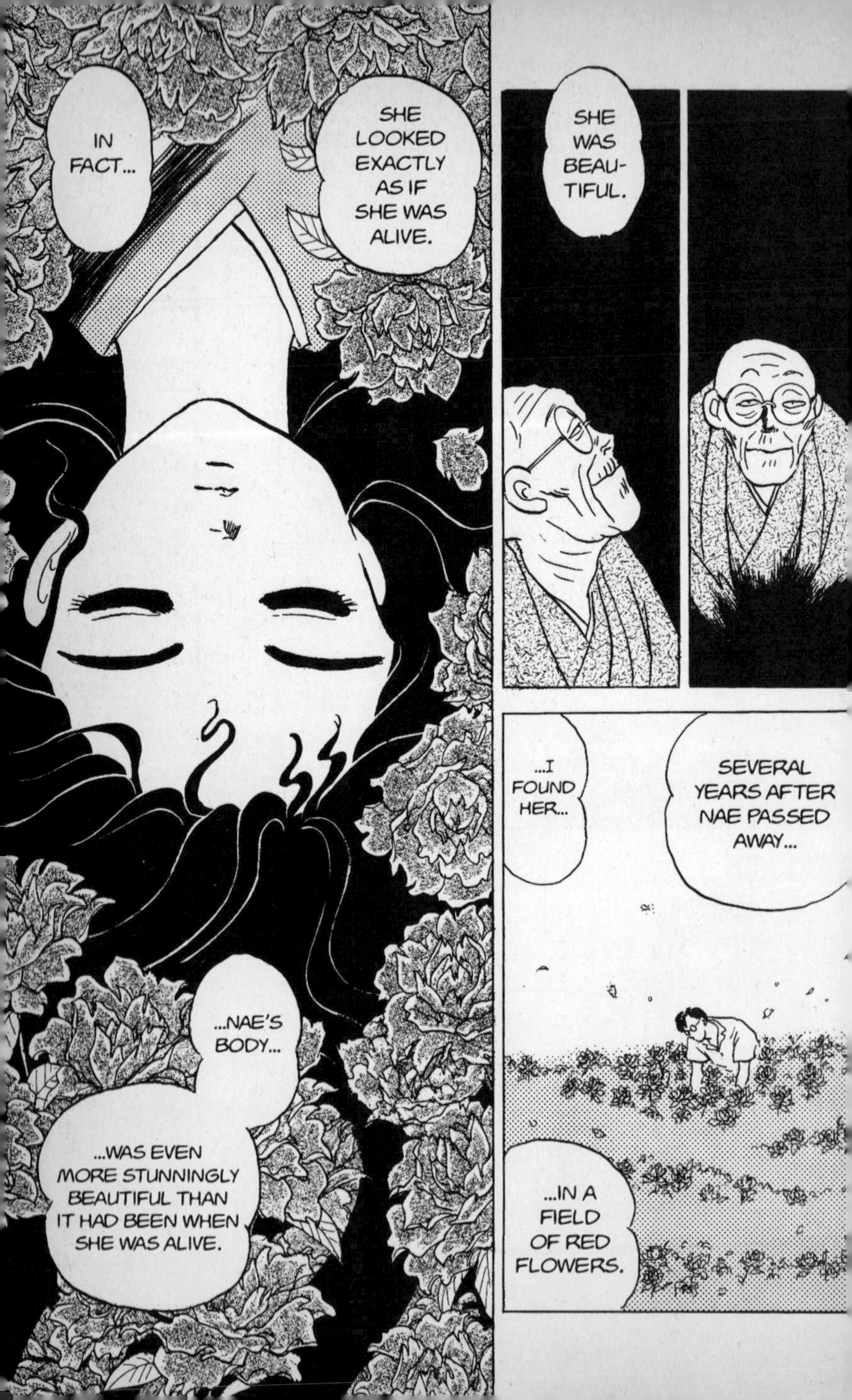
SHE WAS BEAU-TIFUL.
SEVERAL YEARS AFTER NAE PASSED AWAY...
...I FOUND HER...
...IN A FIELD OF RED FLOWERS.
SHE LOOKED EXACTLY AS IF SHE WAS ALIVE.
IN FACT...
...NAE'S BODY...
...WAS EVEN MORE STUNNINGLY BEAUTIFUL THAN IT HAD BEEN WHEN SHE WAS ALIVE.

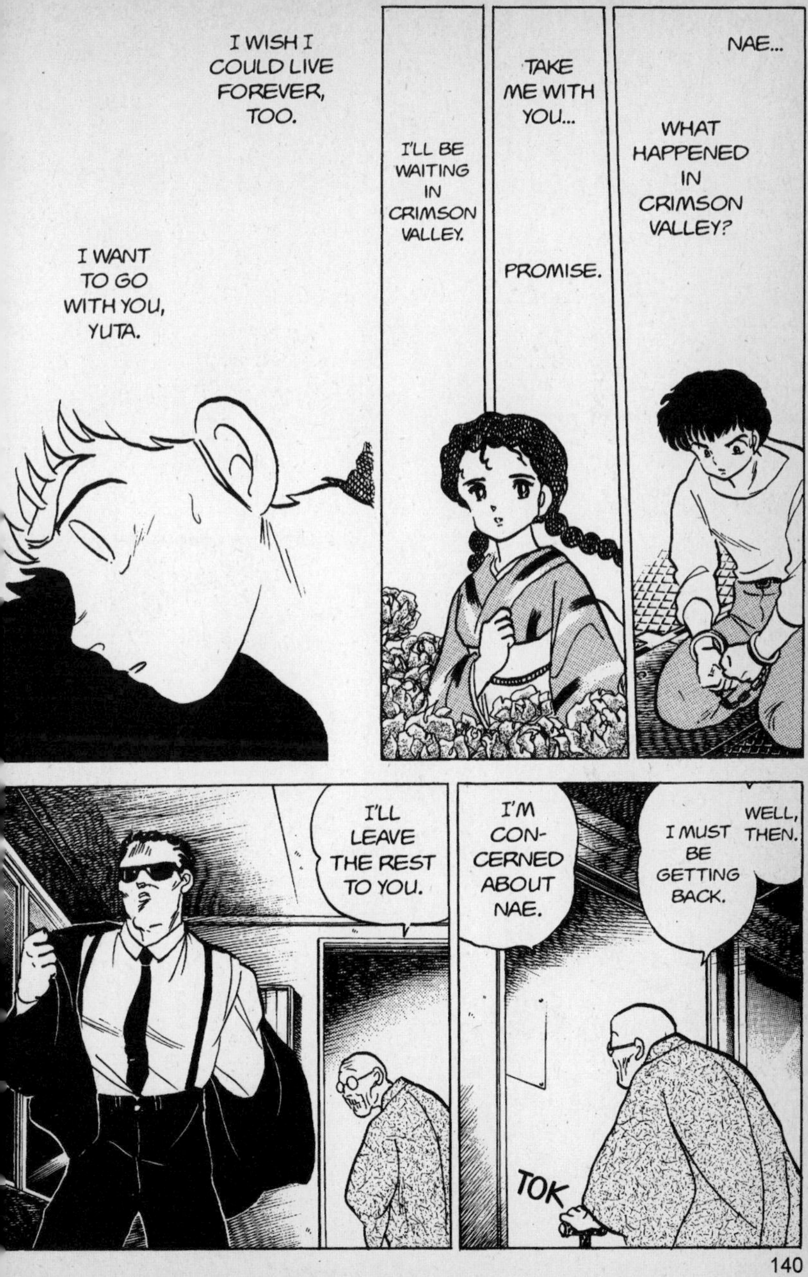
NAE...
WHAT HAPPENED IN CRIMSON VALLEY?
TAKE ME WITH YOU...
PROMISE.
I'LL BE WAITING IN CRIMSON VALLEY.
I WISH I COULD LIVE FOREVER, TOO.
I WANT TO GO WITH YOU, YUTA.
WELL, THEN.
I MUST BE GETTING BACK.
I'M CON-CERNED ABOUT NAE.
TOK
I'LL LEAVE THE REST TO YOU.

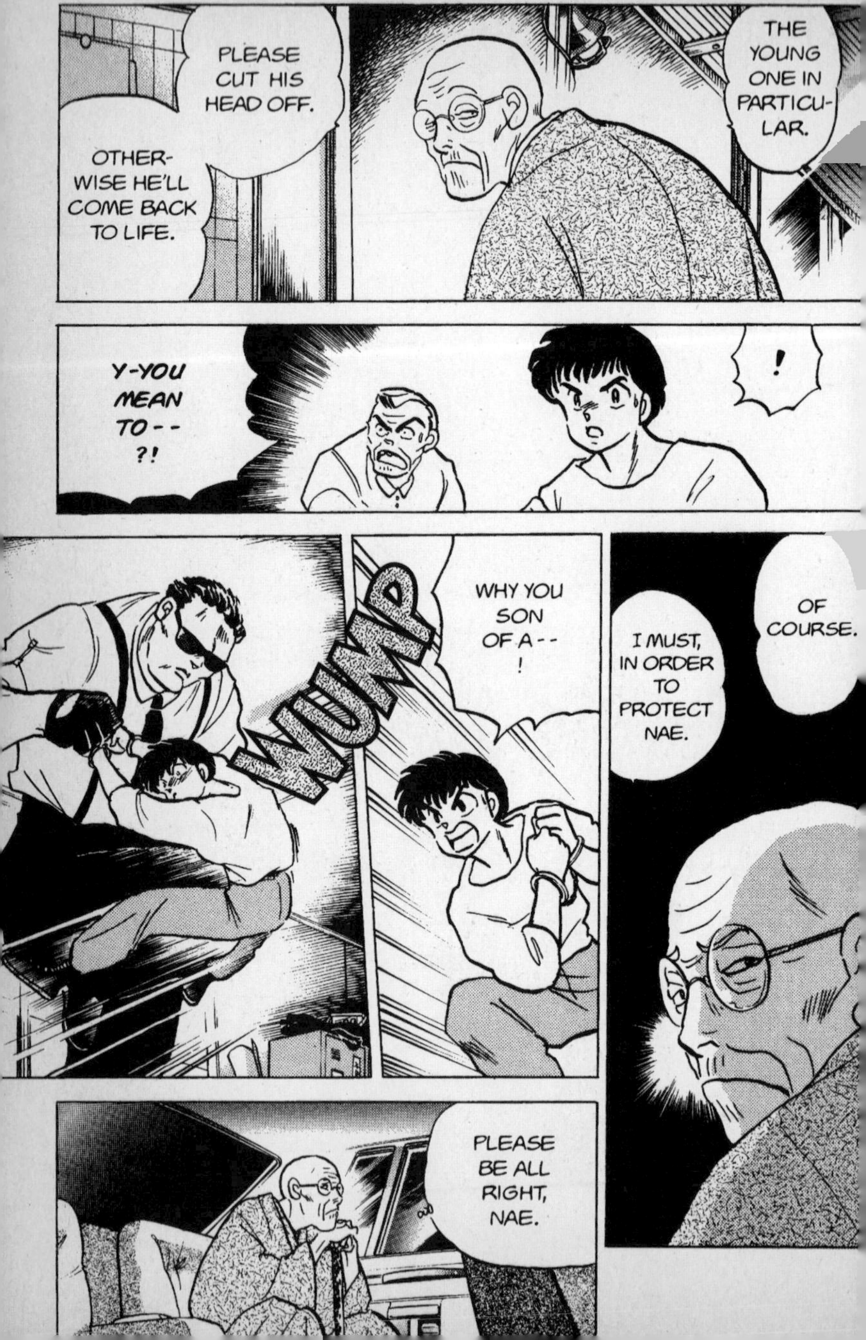
THE YOUNG ONE IN PARTICULAR.
PLEASE CUT HIS HEAD OFF.
OTHERWISE HE'LL COME BACK TO LIFE.
!
Y-YOU MEAN TO--?!
OF COURSE.
I MUST, IN ORDER TO PROTECT NAE.
WHY YOU SON OF A--!
WUMP
PLEASE BE ALL RIGHT, NAE.

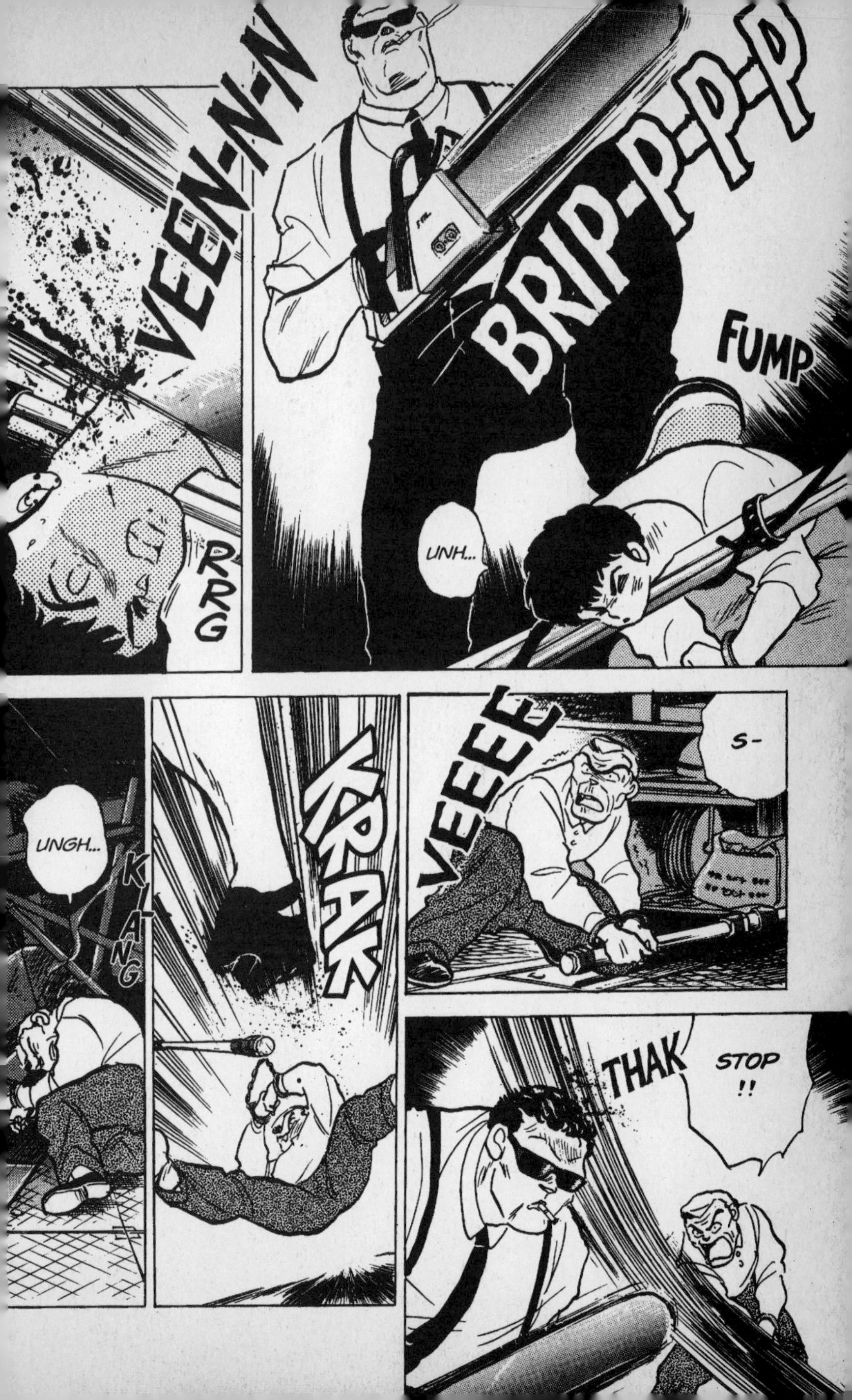
BRIP-P-P-P-P
FUMP
UNH...
VEEN-N-N
RRG
S-
VEEEE
THAK
STOP !!
KRAK
UNGH...
KLANG

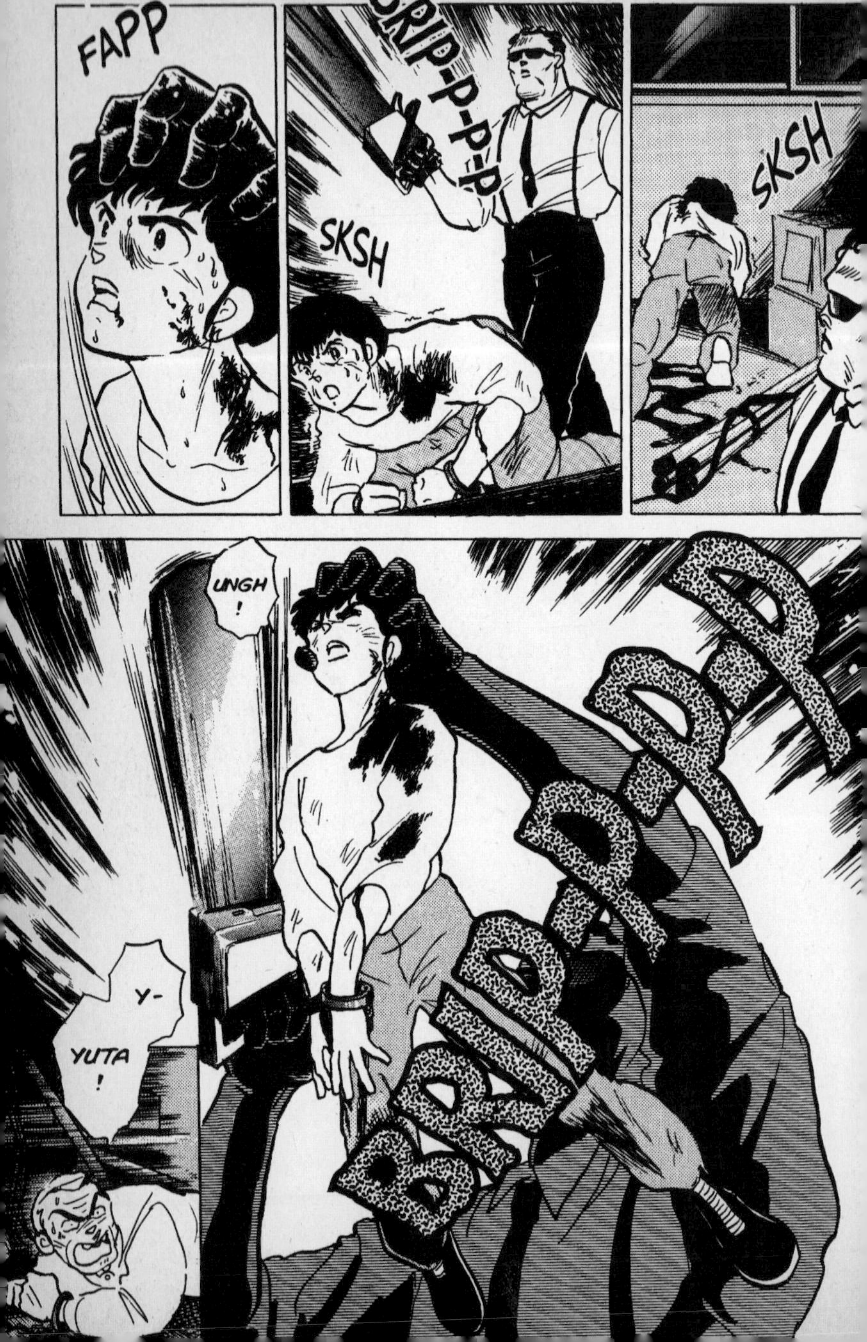
SKSH
BRIP-P-P-P
SKSH
FAPP
UNGH!
BRIP-P-P-P
Y- YUTA!

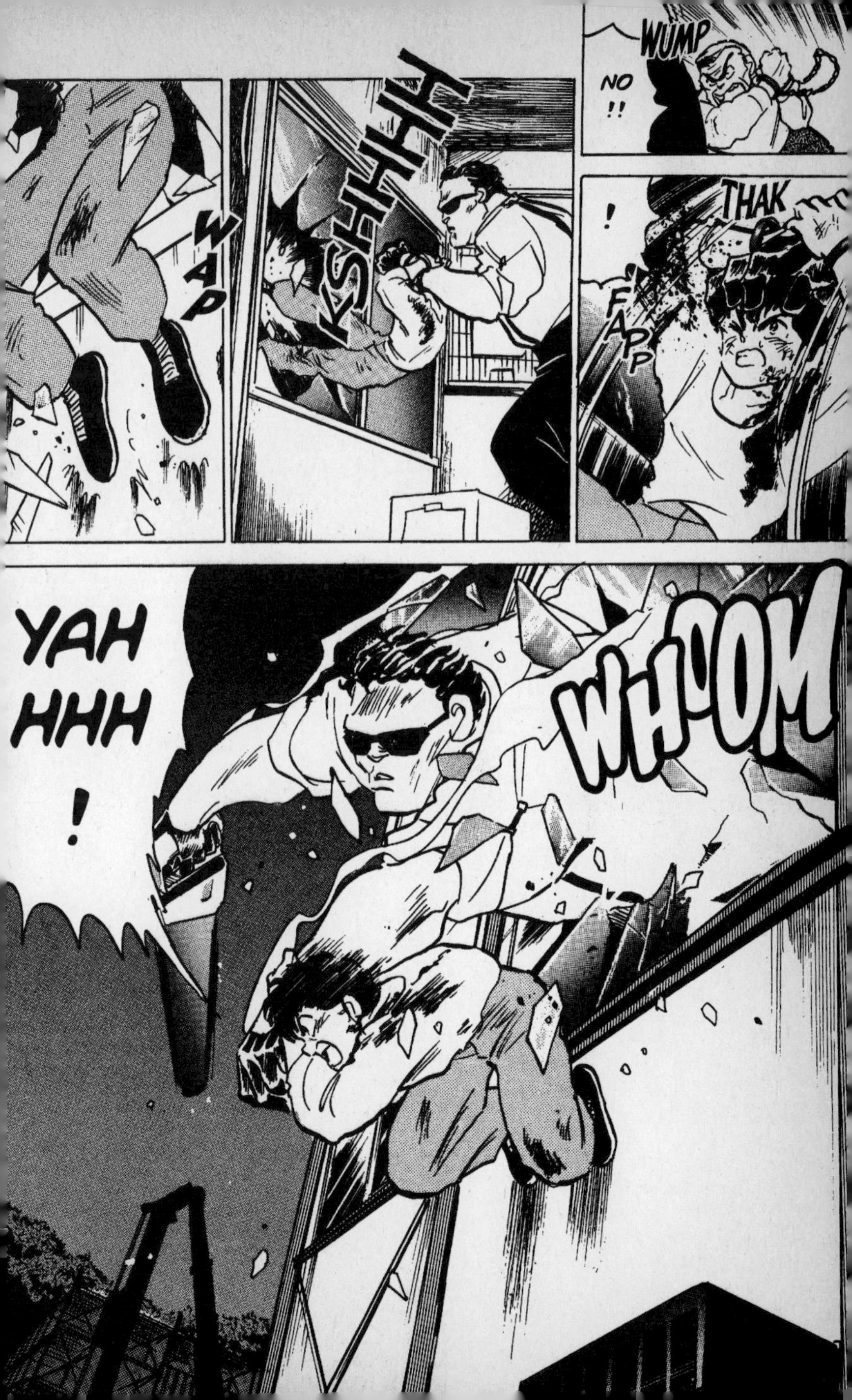
NO !!
WUMP
!
THAK
FAPP
KSHHHHH
WAP
YAH HHH !
WHOOM

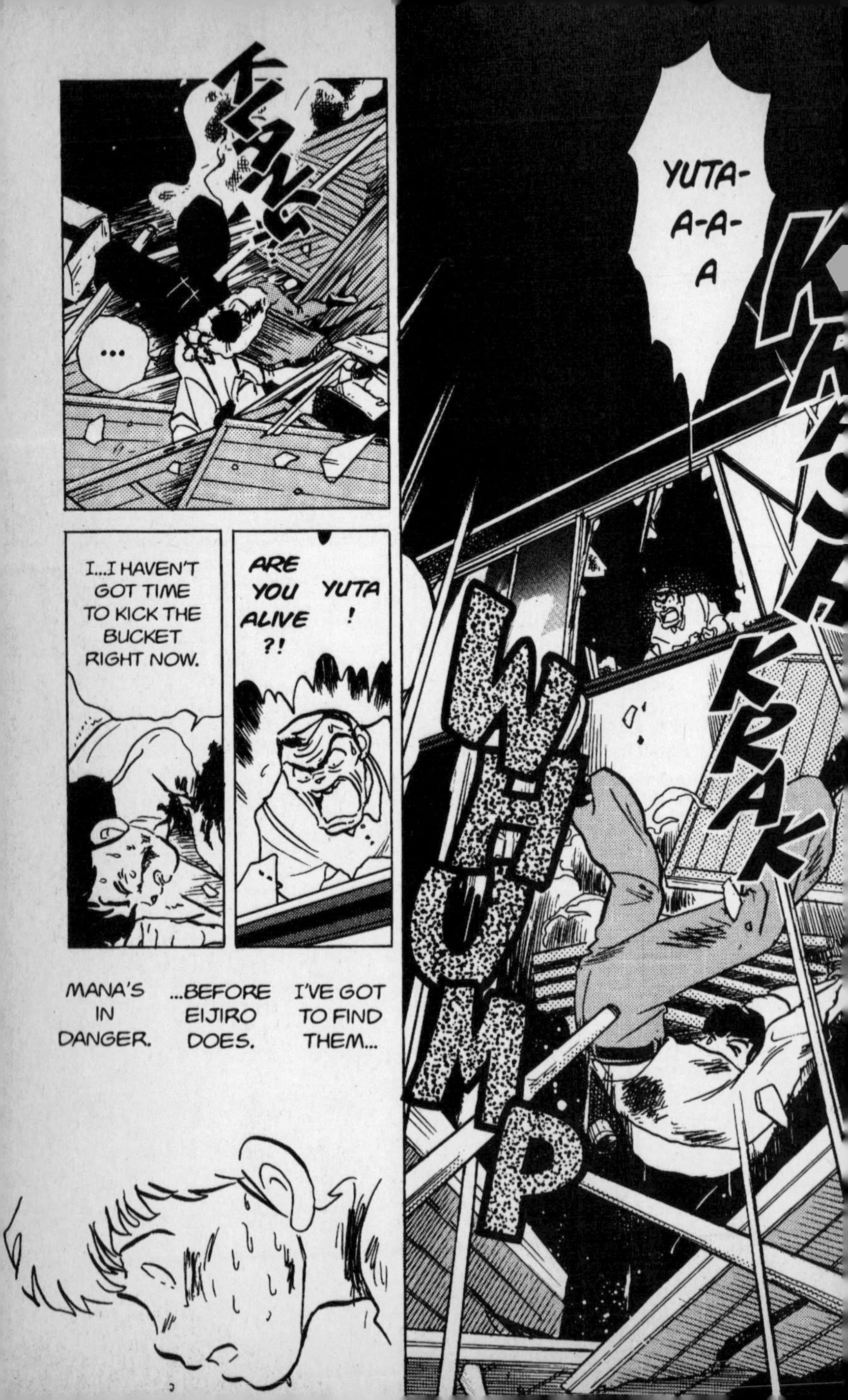
YUTA-A-A-A
KRAK
WHUMP
KLANG
...
YUTA!
ARE YOU ALIVE?!
I...I HAVEN'T GOT TIME TO KICK THE BUCKET RIGHT NOW.
I'VE GOT TO FIND THEM...
...BEFORE EIJIRO DOES.
MANA'S IN DANGER.

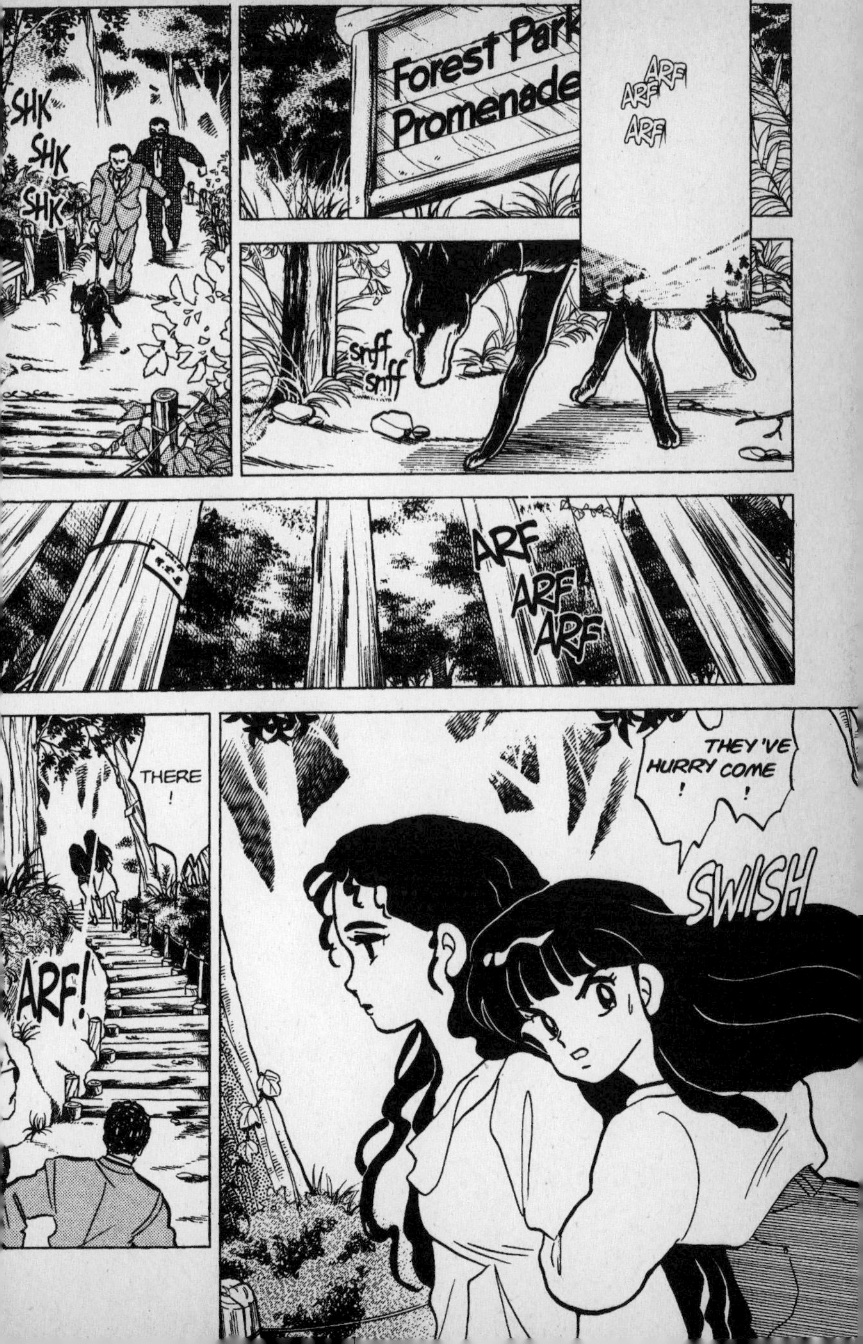
ARF ARF ARF
Forest Park Promenade
snff snff
SHK SHK SHK
ARF ARF ARF
THEY'VE COME!
HURRY!
SWISH
THERE!
ARF!

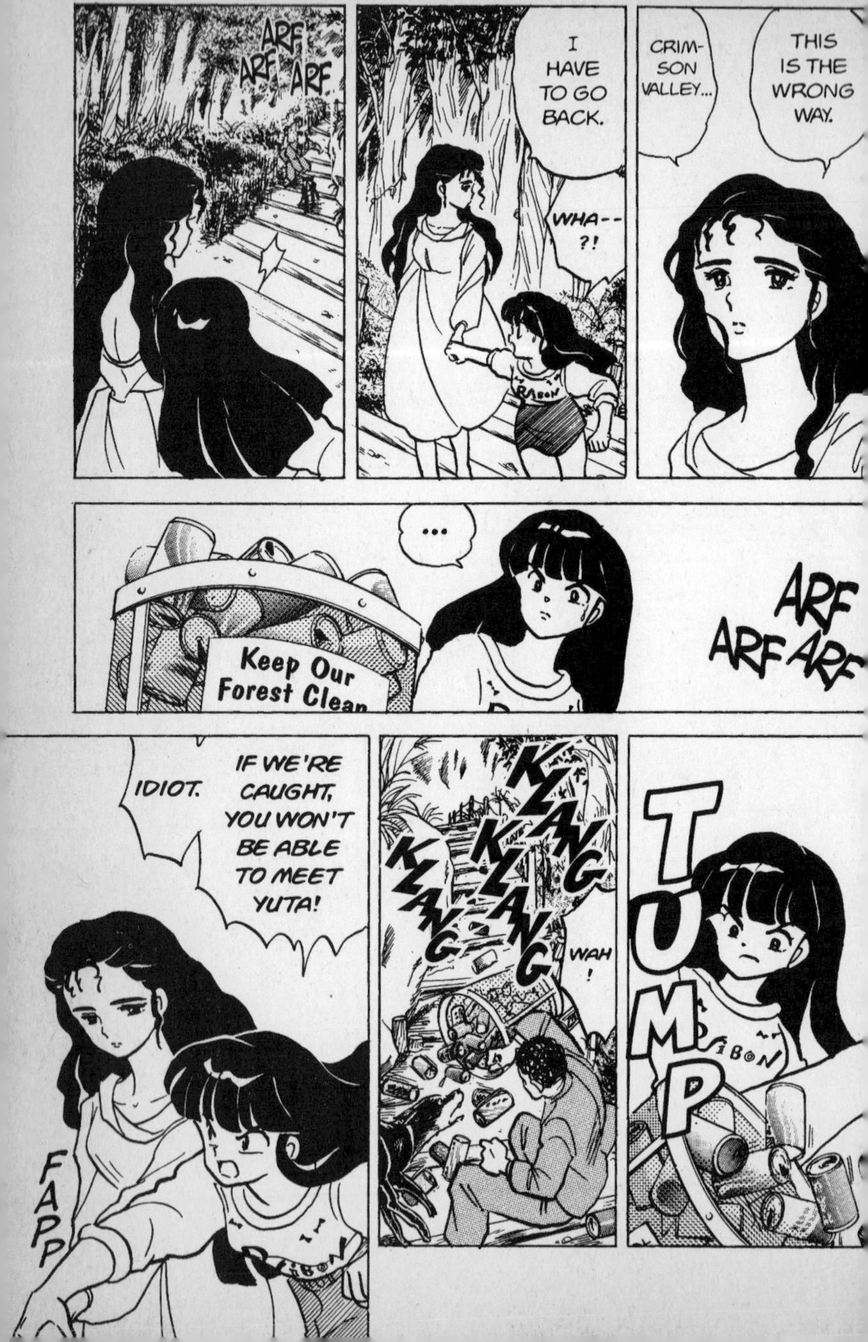
THIS IS THE WRONG WAY.
CRIM-SON VALLEY...
I HAVE TO GO BACK.
WHA--?!
ARF ARF ARF
ARF ARF ARF
...
Keep Our Forest Clea
TUMP
KLANG KLANG KLANG
WAH!
IF WE'RE CAUGHT, YOU WON'T BE ABLE TO MEET YUTA!
IDIOT.
FAPP

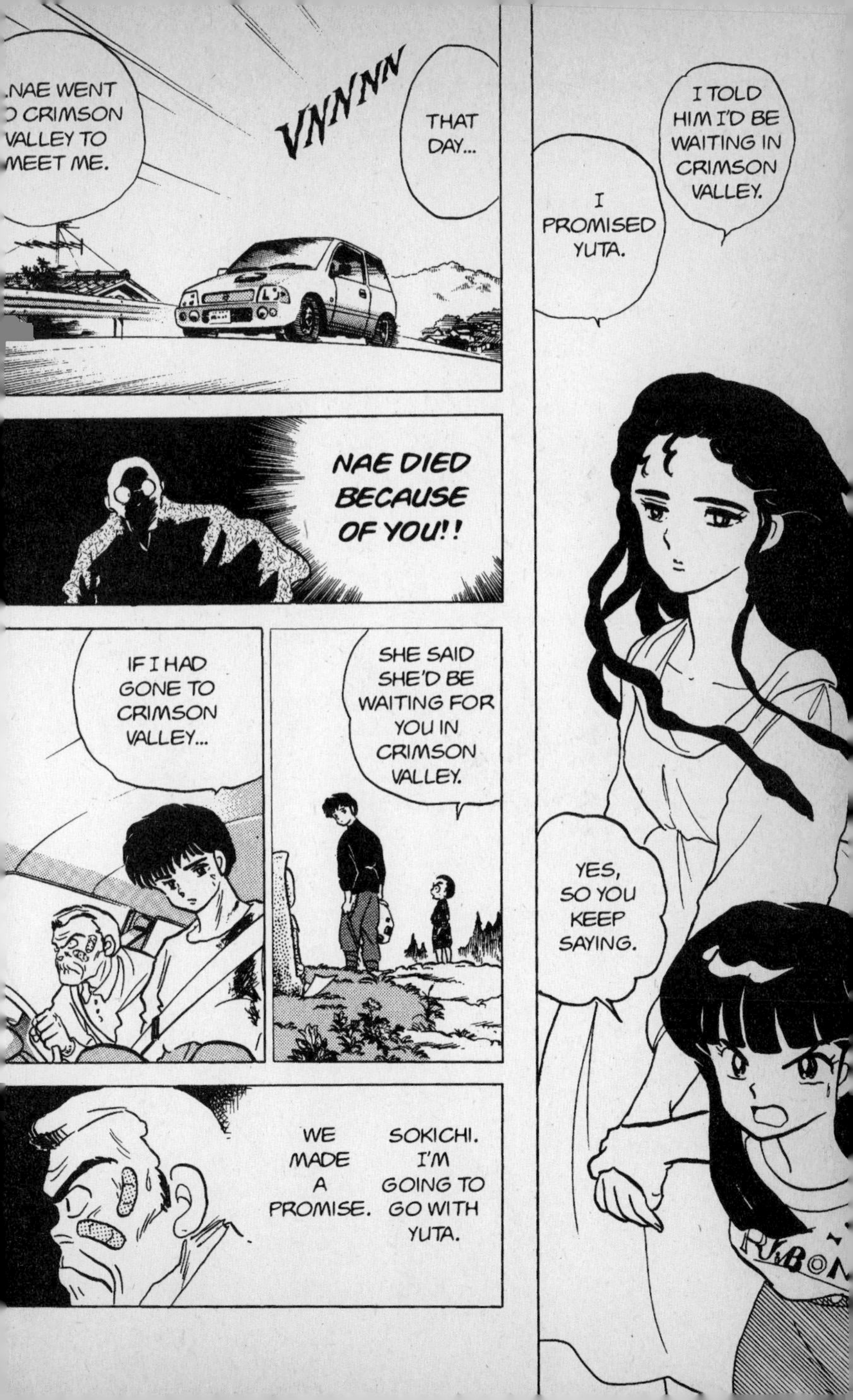
I TOLD HIM I'D BE WAITING IN CRIMSON VALLEY.
I PROMISED YUTA.
YES, SO YOU KEEP SAYING.
VNNNN
THAT DAY...
NAE WENT CRIMSON VALLEY TO MEET ME.
NAE DIED BECAUSE OF YOU!!
SHE SAID SHE'D BE WAITING FOR YOU IN CRIMSON VALLEY.
IF I HAD GONE TO CRIMSON VALLEY...
SOKICHI. I'M GOING TO GO WITH YUTA.
WE MADE A PROMISE.

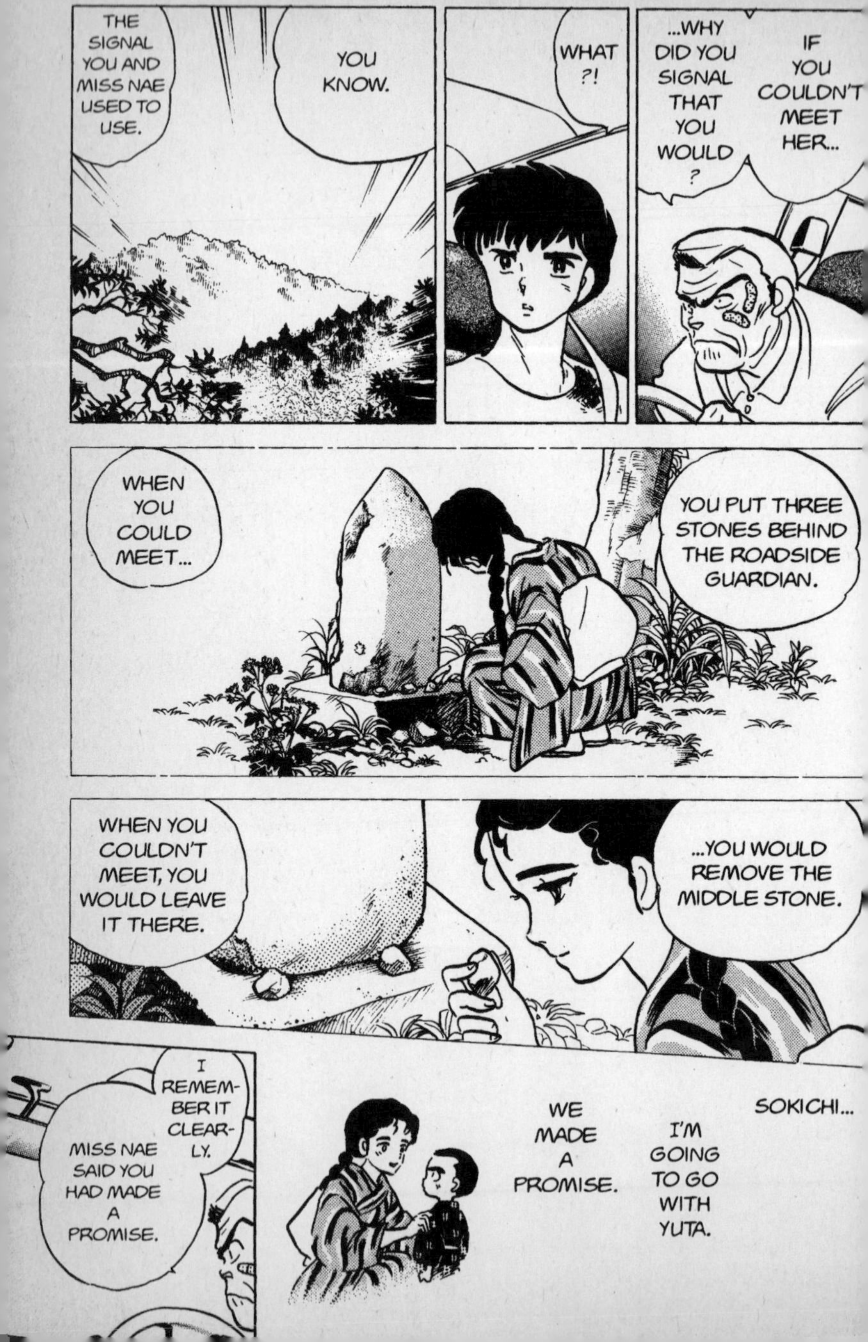

IF YOU COULDN'T MEET HER...
...WHY DID YOU SIGNAL THAT YOU WOULD?
WHAT?!
YOU KNOW.
THE SIGNAL YOU AND MISS NAE USED TO USE.
YOU PUT THREE STONES BEHIND THE ROADSIDE GUARDIAN.
WHEN YOU COULD MEET...
...YOU WOULD REMOVE THE MIDDLE STONE.
WHEN YOU COULDN'T MEET, YOU WOULD LEAVE IT THERE.
SOKICHI...
I'M GOING TO GO WITH YUTA.
WE MADE A PROMISE.
I REMEMBER IT CLEARLY.
MISS NAE SAID YOU HAD MADE A PROMISE.

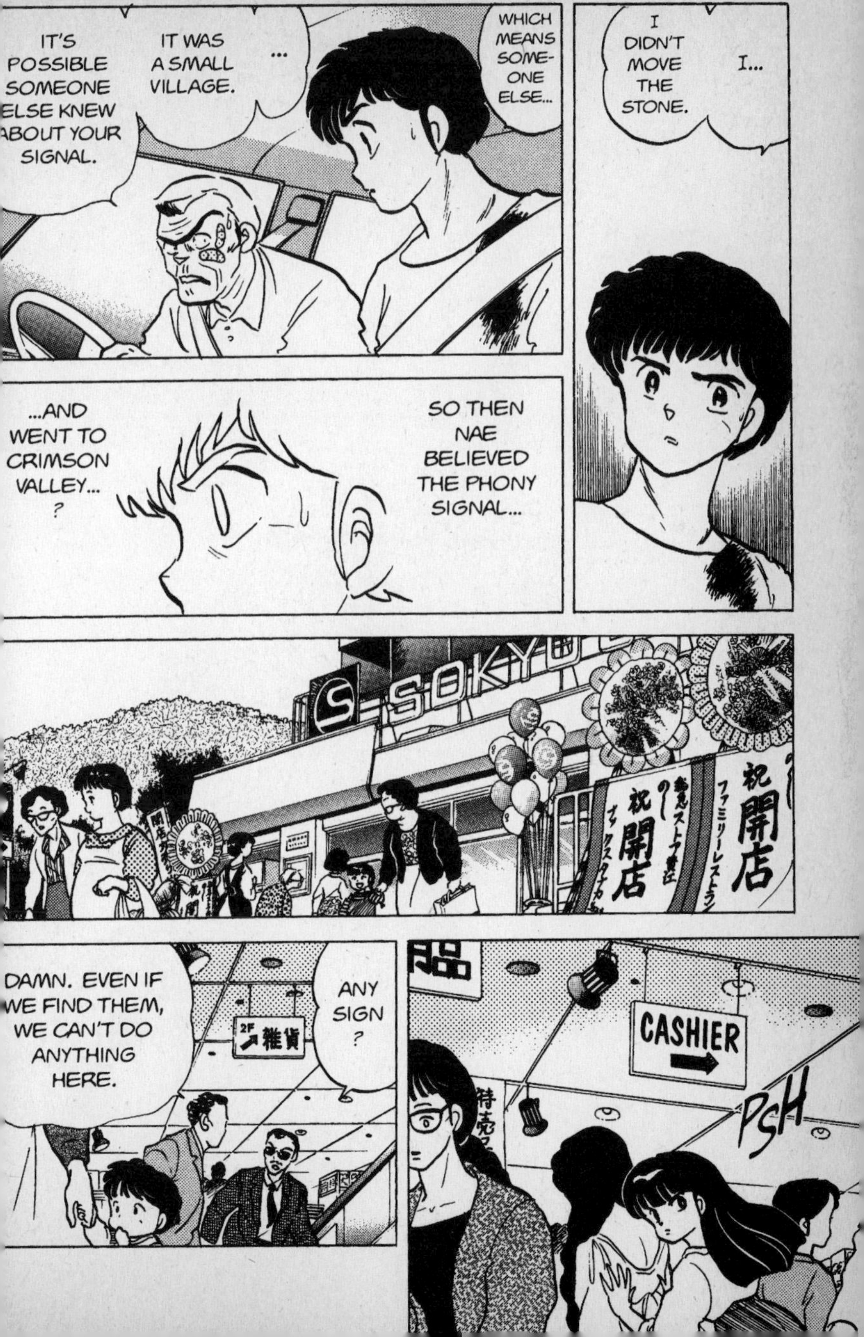
I...
I DIDN'T MOVE THE STONE.
WHICH MEANS SOME-ONE ELSE...
...
IT WAS A SMALL VILLAGE.
IT'S POSSIBLE SOMEONE ELSE KNEW ABOUT YOUR SIGNAL.
SO THEN NAE BELIEVED THE PHONY SIGNAL...
...AND WENT TO CRIMSON VALLEY... ?
SOKYU
祝開店
祝開店
CASHIER
PSH
ANY SIGN ?
DAMN. EVEN IF WE FIND THEM, WE CAN'T DO ANYTHING HERE.
2F 雑貨

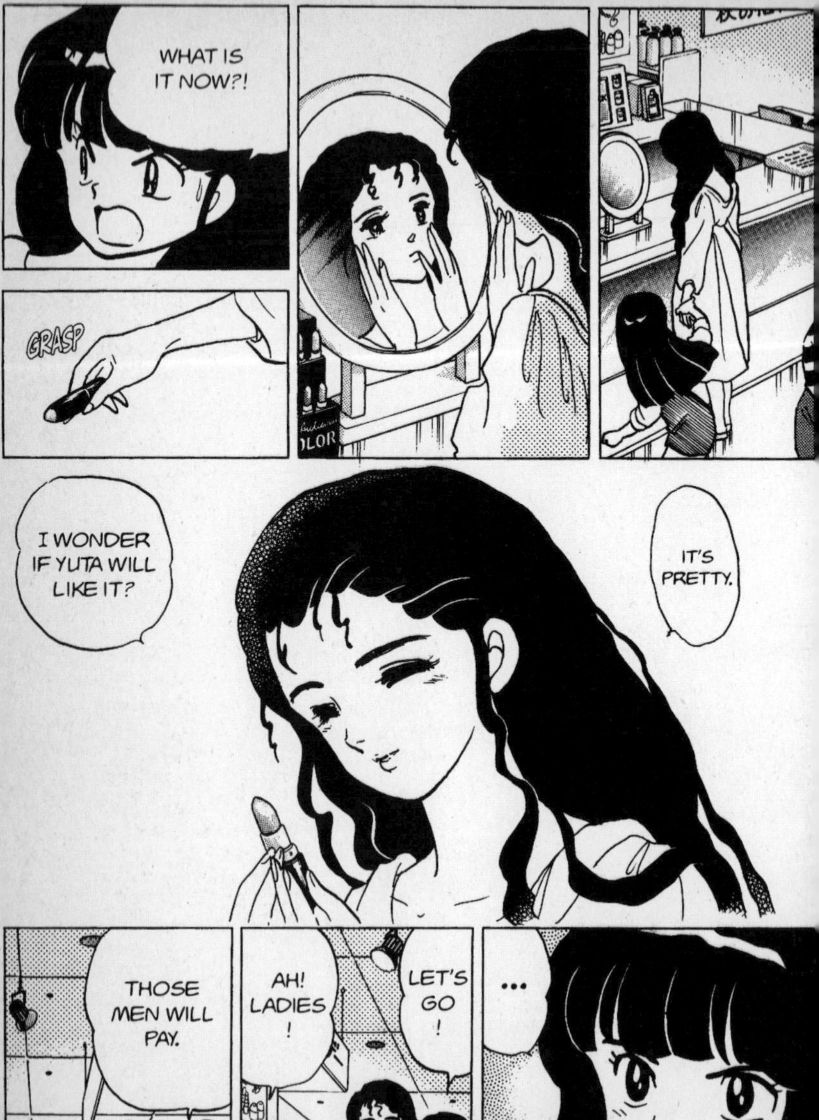
WHAT IS IT NOW?!
GRASP
IT'S PRETTY.
I WONDER IF YUTA WILL LIKE IT?
...
LET'S GO!
AH! LADIES!
THOSE MEN WILL PAY.

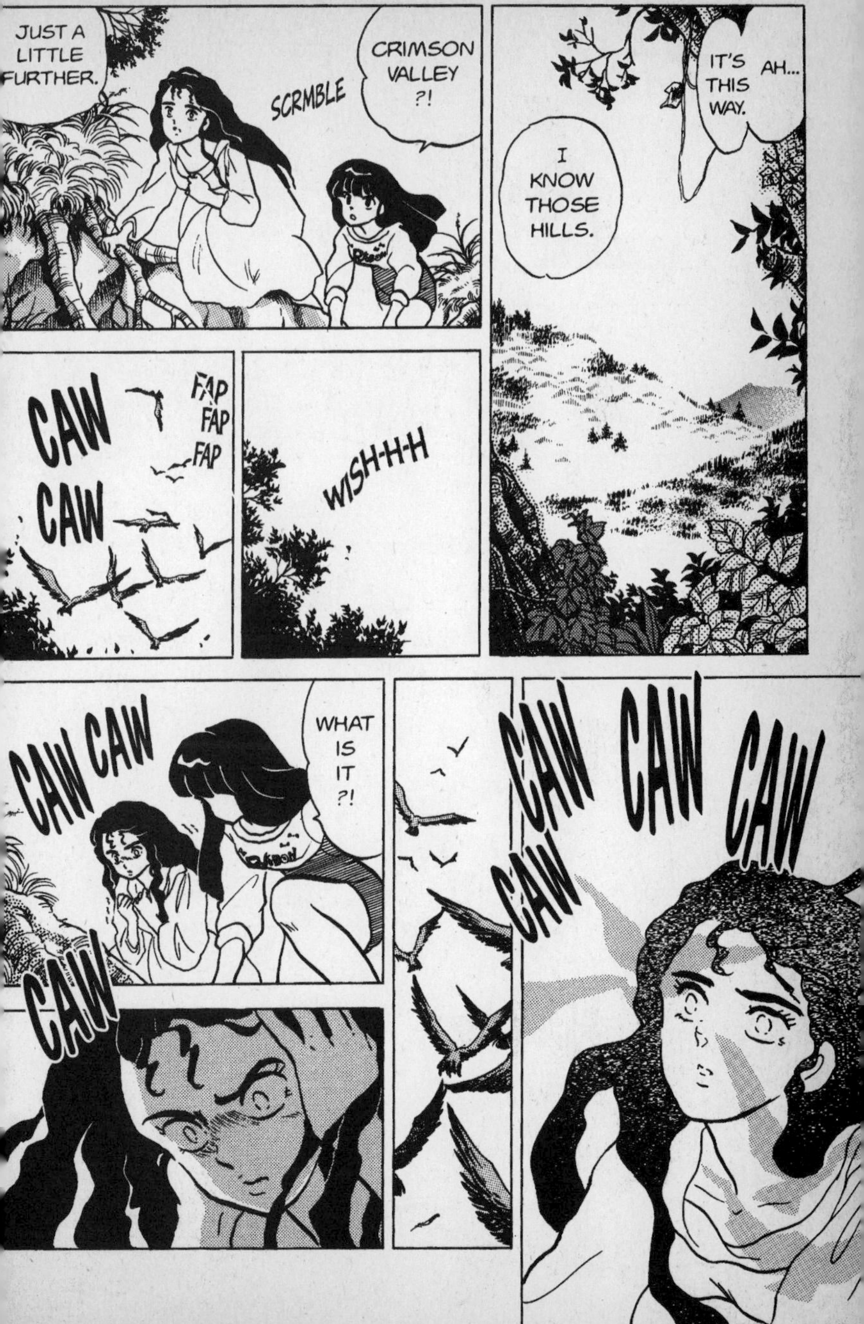
AH...
IT'S THIS WAY.
I KNOW THOSE HILLS.
CRIMSON VALLEY ?!
SCRMBLE
JUST A LITTLE FURTHER.
WISH-H-H
FAP FAP FAP
CAW CAW
CAW CAW CAW CAW CAW
WHAT IS IT ?!
CAW CAW
CAW

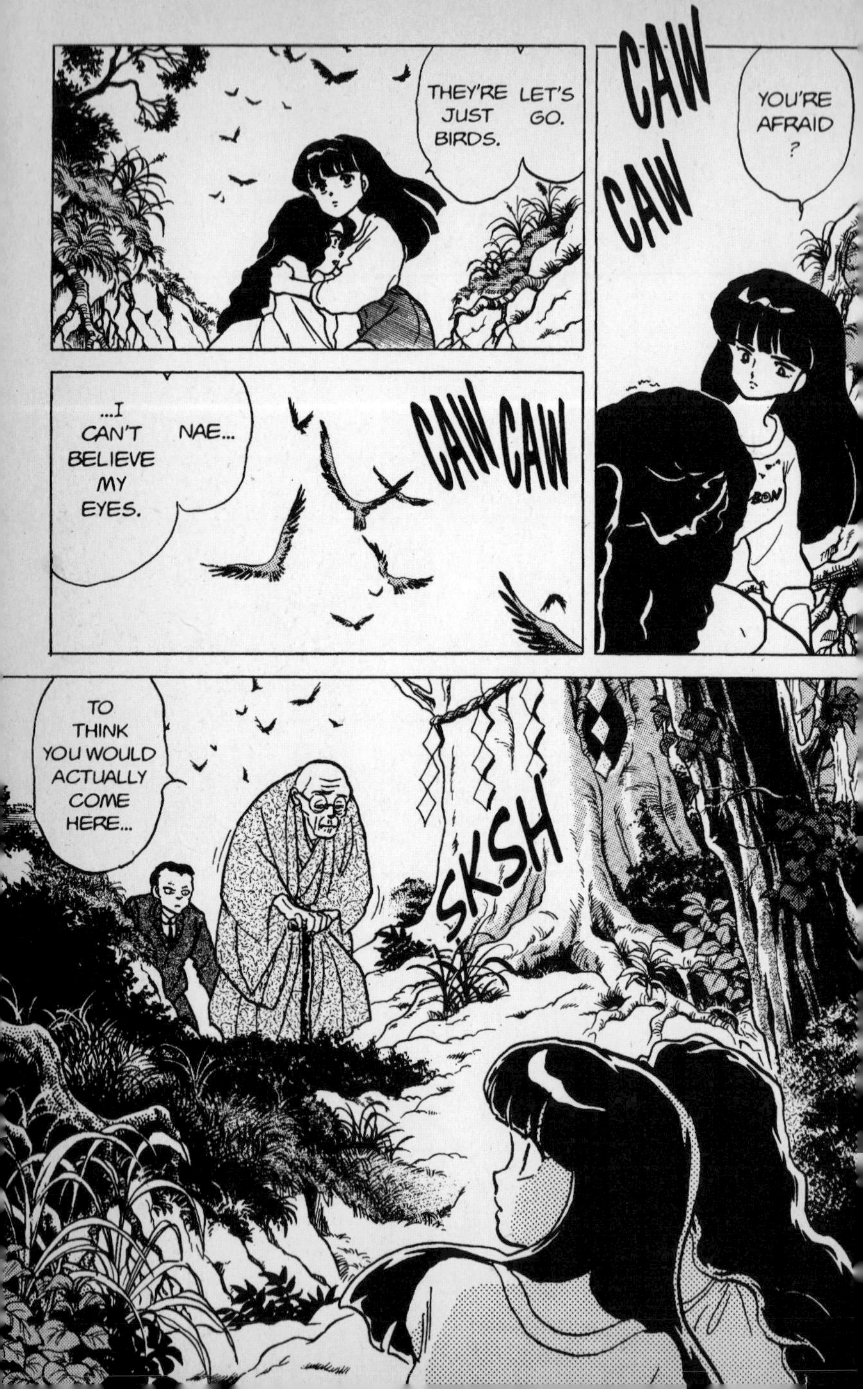
CAW
CAW
YOU'RE AFRAID?
LET'S GO.
THEY'RE JUST BIRDS.
CAW
CAW
NAE...
...I CAN'T BELIEVE MY EYES.
SKSH
TO THINK YOU WOULD ACTUALLY COME HERE...

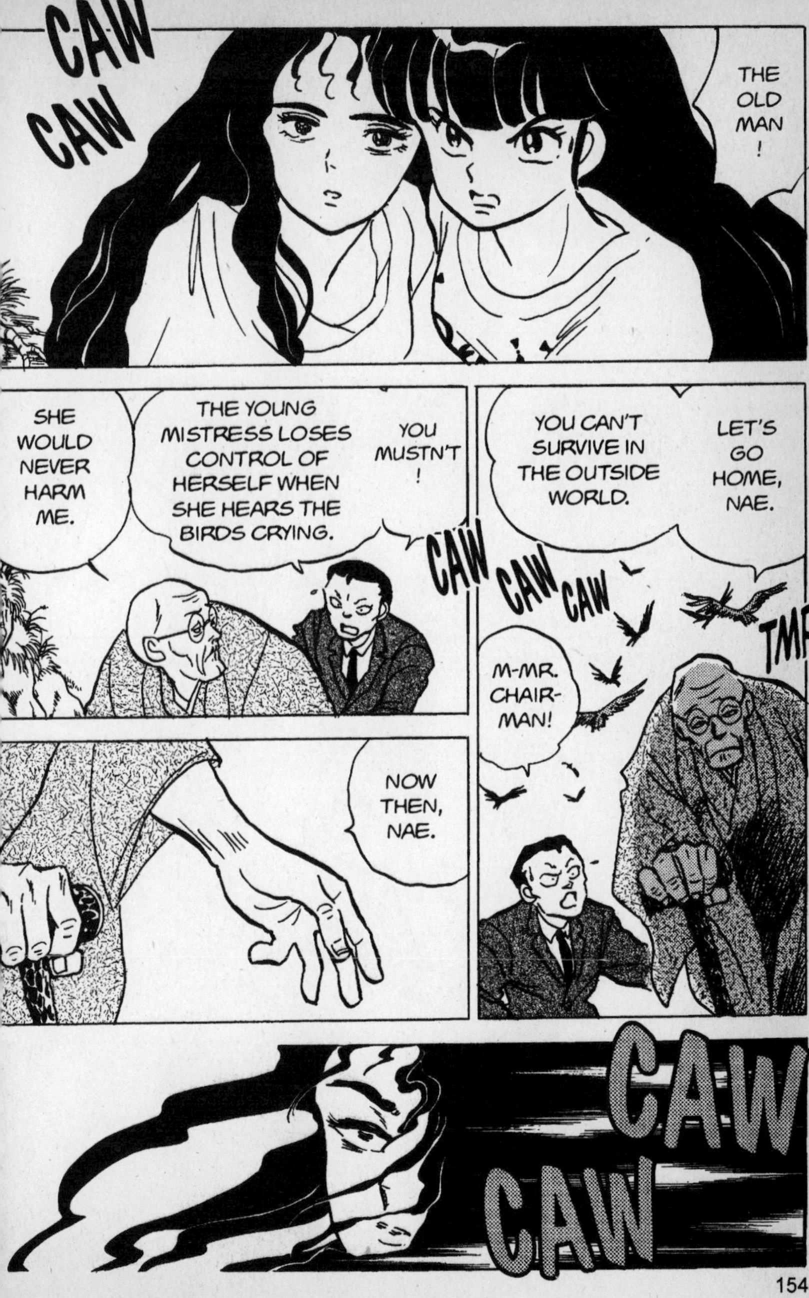
THE OLD MAN !
CAW CAW
LET'S GO HOME, NAE.
YOU CAN'T SURVIVE IN THE OUTSIDE WORLD.
CAW CAW CAW
TMP
M-MR. CHAIRMAN!
YOU MUSTN'T !
THE YOUNG MISTRESS LOSES CONTROL OF HERSELF WHEN SHE HEARS THE BIRDS CRYING.
SHE WOULD NEVER HARM ME.
NOW THEN, NAE.
CAW CAW

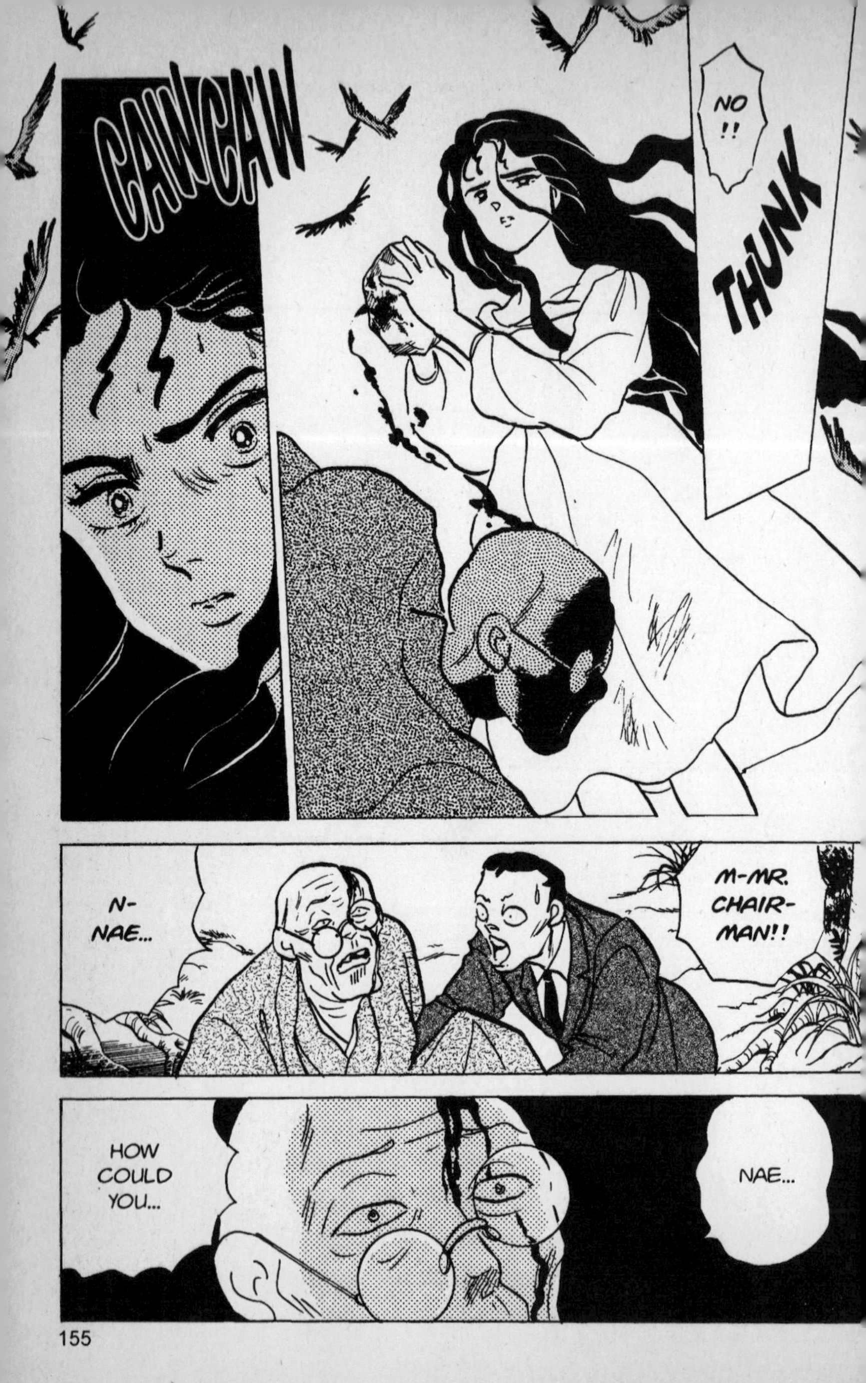
NO !!
THUNK
CAWCAW
M-MR. CHAIR-MAN!!
N-NAE...
NAE...
HOW COULD YOU...

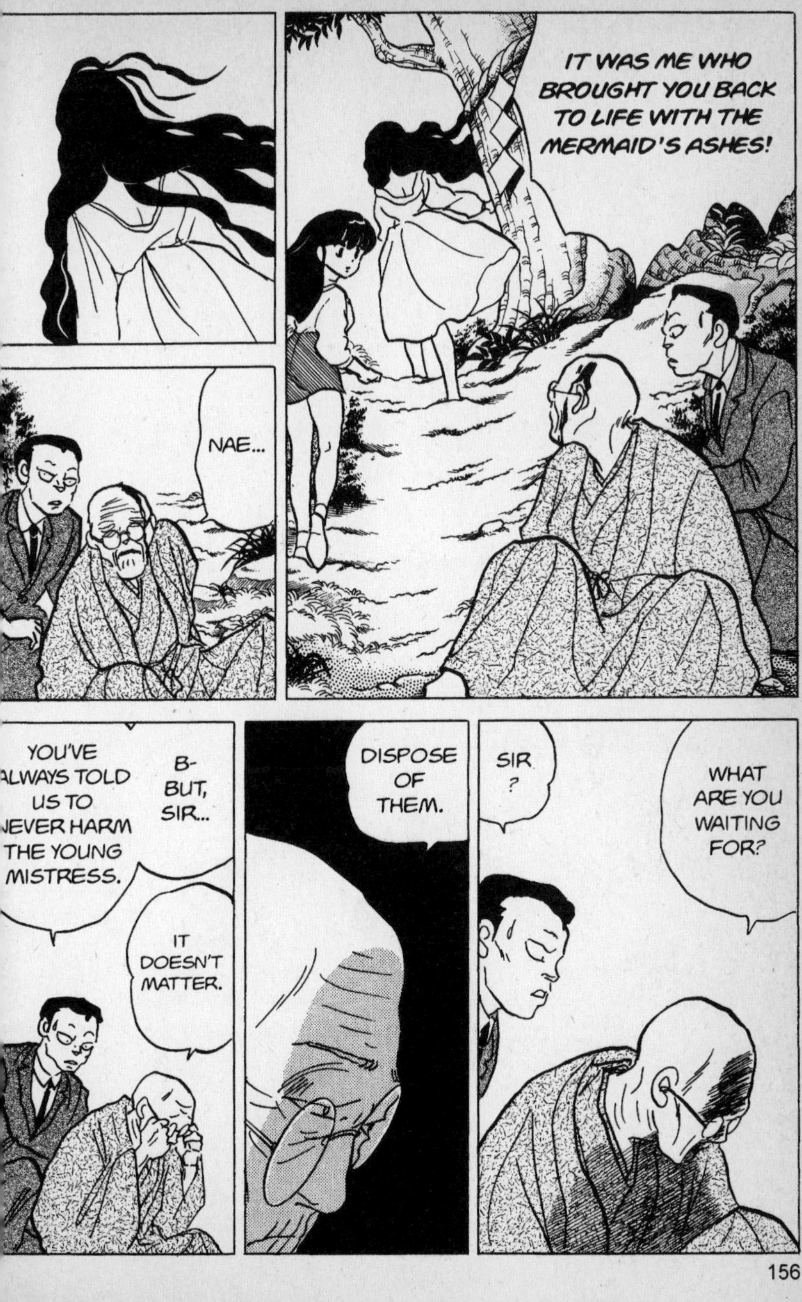
IT WAS ME WHO BROUGHT YOU BACK TO LIFE WITH THE MERMAID'S ASHES!
NAE...
WHAT ARE YOU WAITING FOR?
SIR ?
DISPOSE OF THEM.
B- BUT, SIR...
YOU'VE ALWAYS TOLD US TO NEVER HARM THE YOUNG MISTRESS.
IT DOESN'T MATTER.

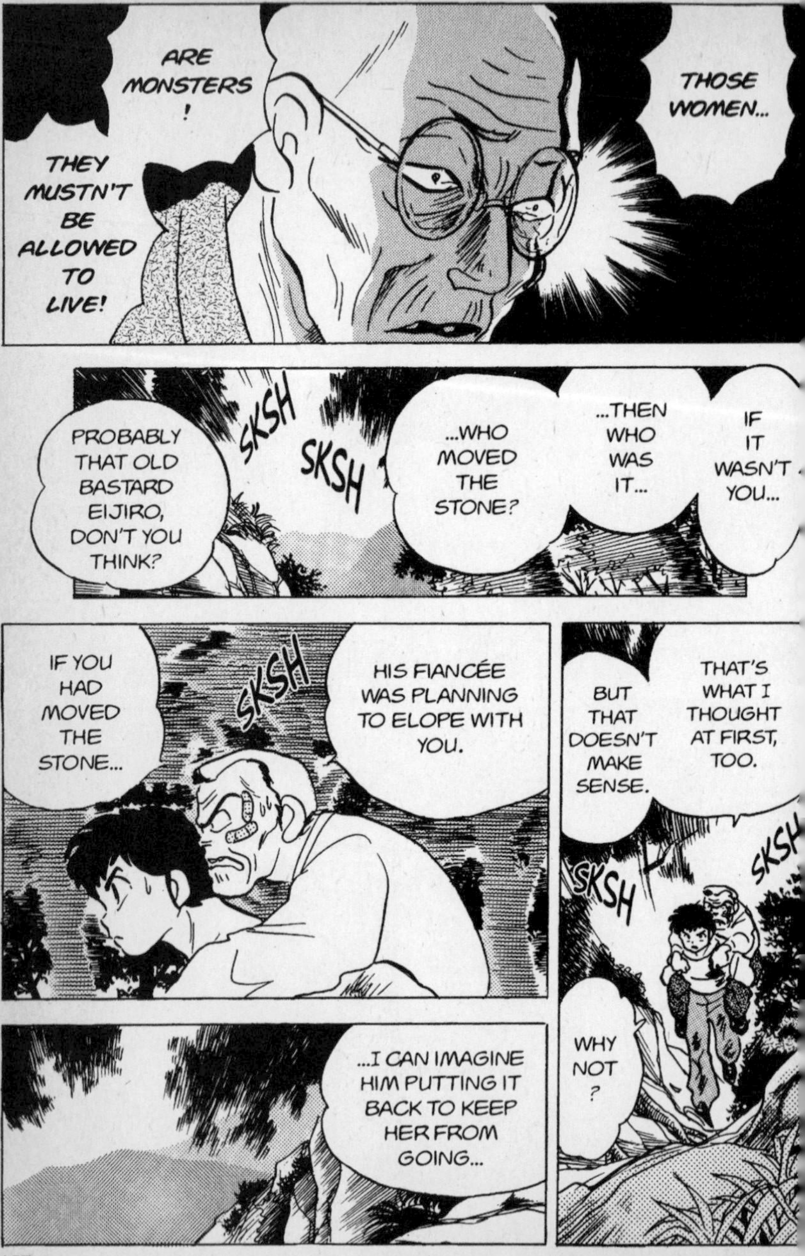
THOSE WOMEN...
ARE MONSTERS !
THEY MUSTN'T BE ALLOWED TO LIVE!
IF IT WASN'T YOU...
...THEN WHO WAS IT...
...WHO MOVED THE STONE?
SKSH
SKSH
PROBABLY THAT OLD BASTARD EIJIRO, DON'T YOU THINK?
THAT'S WHAT I THOUGHT AT FIRST, TOO.
BUT THAT DOESN'T MAKE SENSE.
SKSH
SKSH
WHY NOT ?
HIS FIANCÉE WAS PLANNING TO ELOPE WITH YOU.
SKSH
IF YOU HAD MOVED THE STONE...
...I CAN IMAGINE HIM PUTTING IT BACK TO KEEP HER FROM GOING...

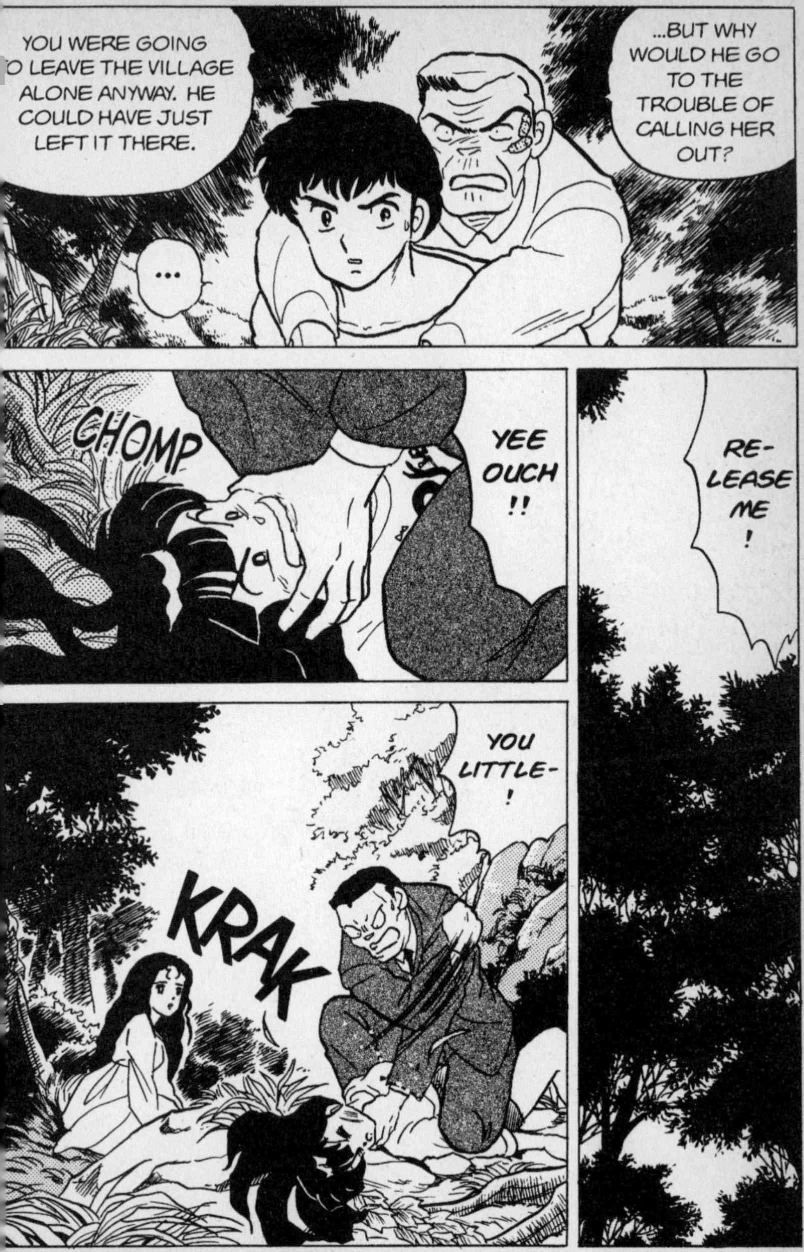
...BUT WHY WOULD HE GO TO THE TROUBLE OF CALLING HER OUT?
YOU WERE GOING TO LEAVE THE VILLAGE ALONE ANYWAY. HE COULD HAVE JUST LEFT IT THERE.
...
RE-LEASE ME!
YEE OUCH!!
CHOMP
YOU LITTLE-!
KRAK

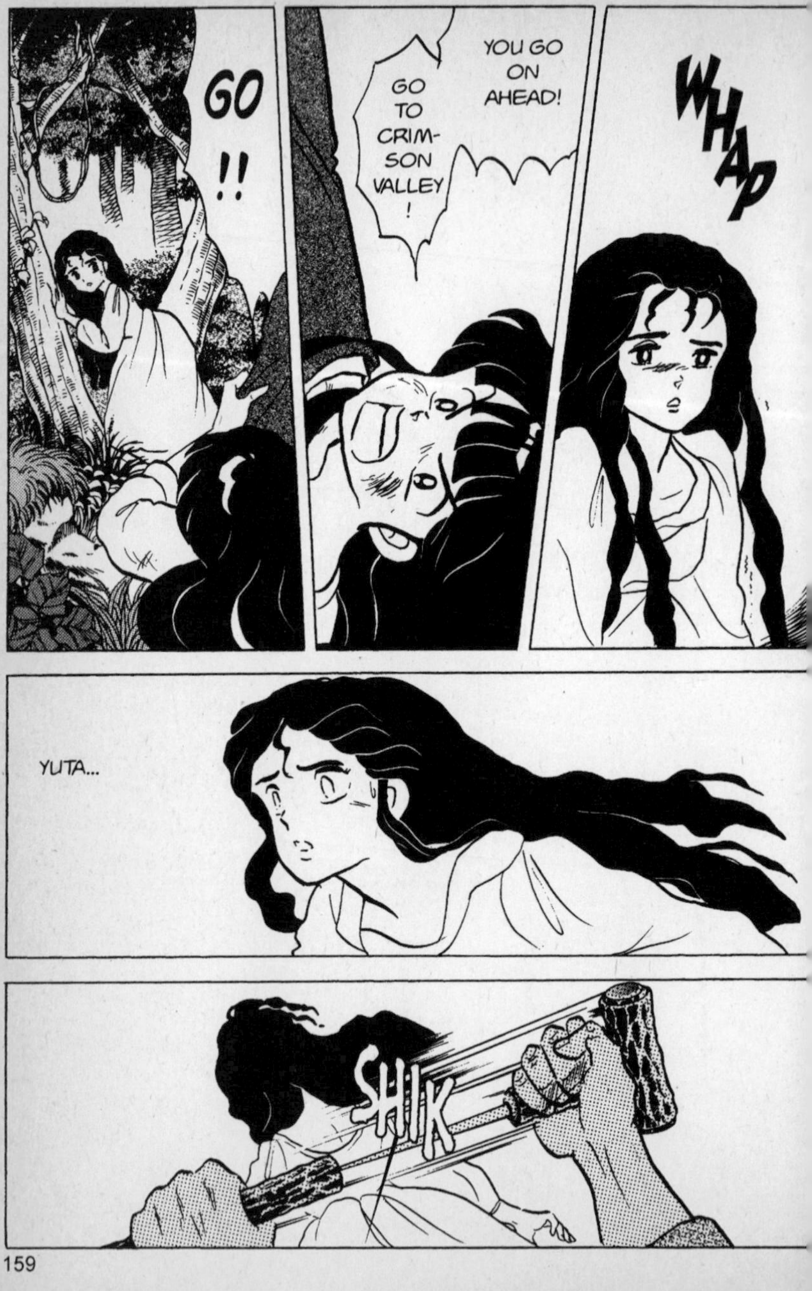
WHAP
YOU GO ON AHEAD!
GO TO CRIMSON VALLEY!
GO!!
YUTA...
SHIK

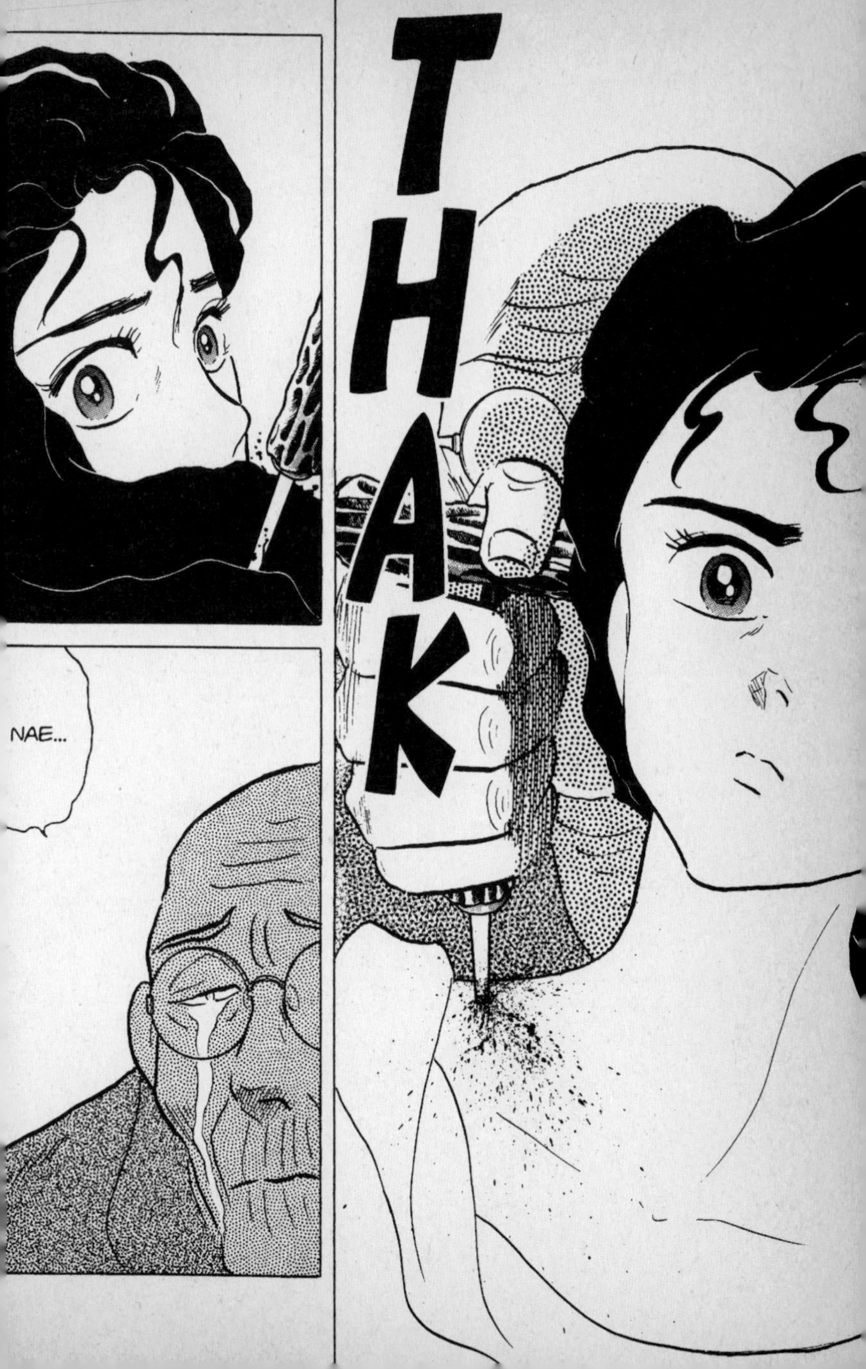
THAK
NAE...

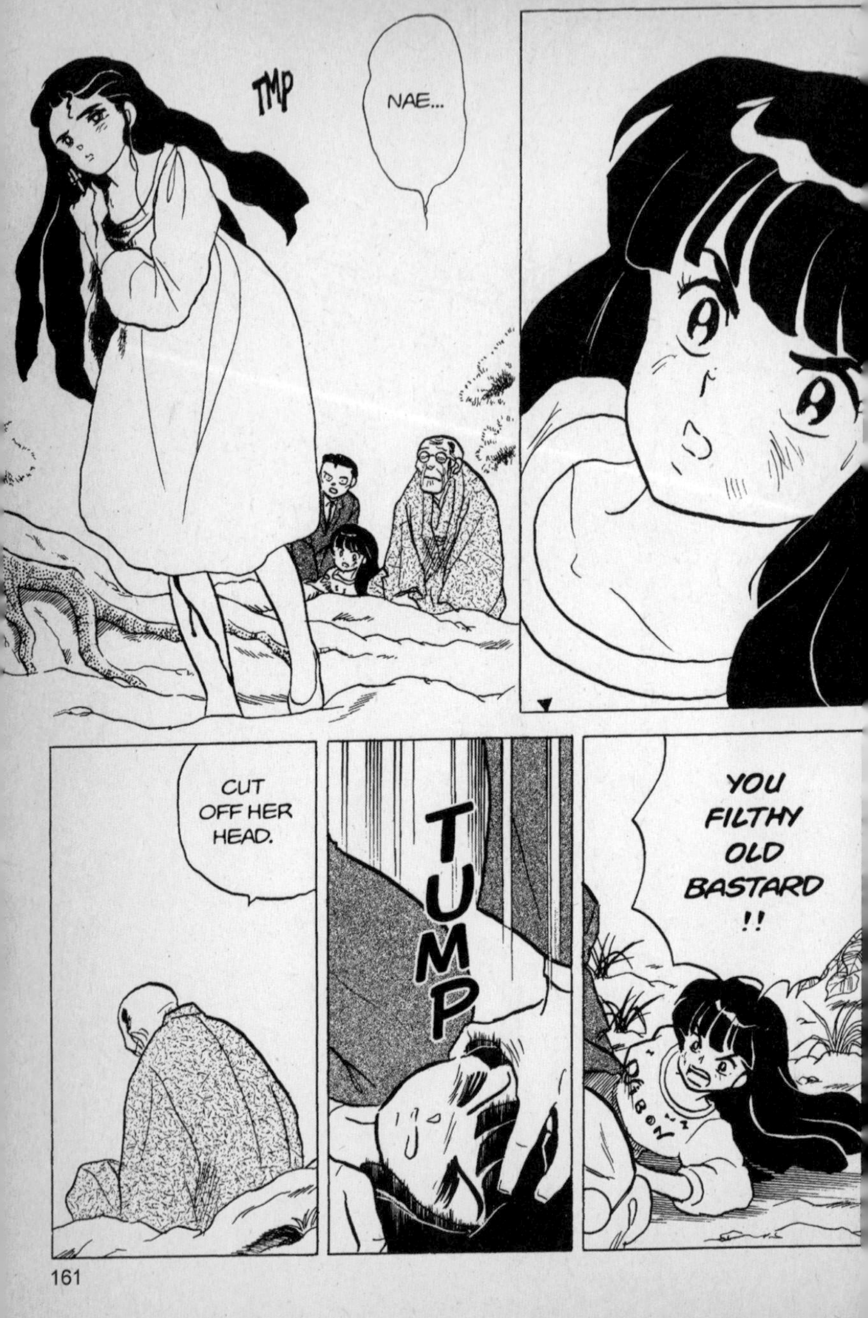
NAE...
TMP
YOU FILTHY OLD BASTARD !!
TUMP
CUT OFF HER HEAD.

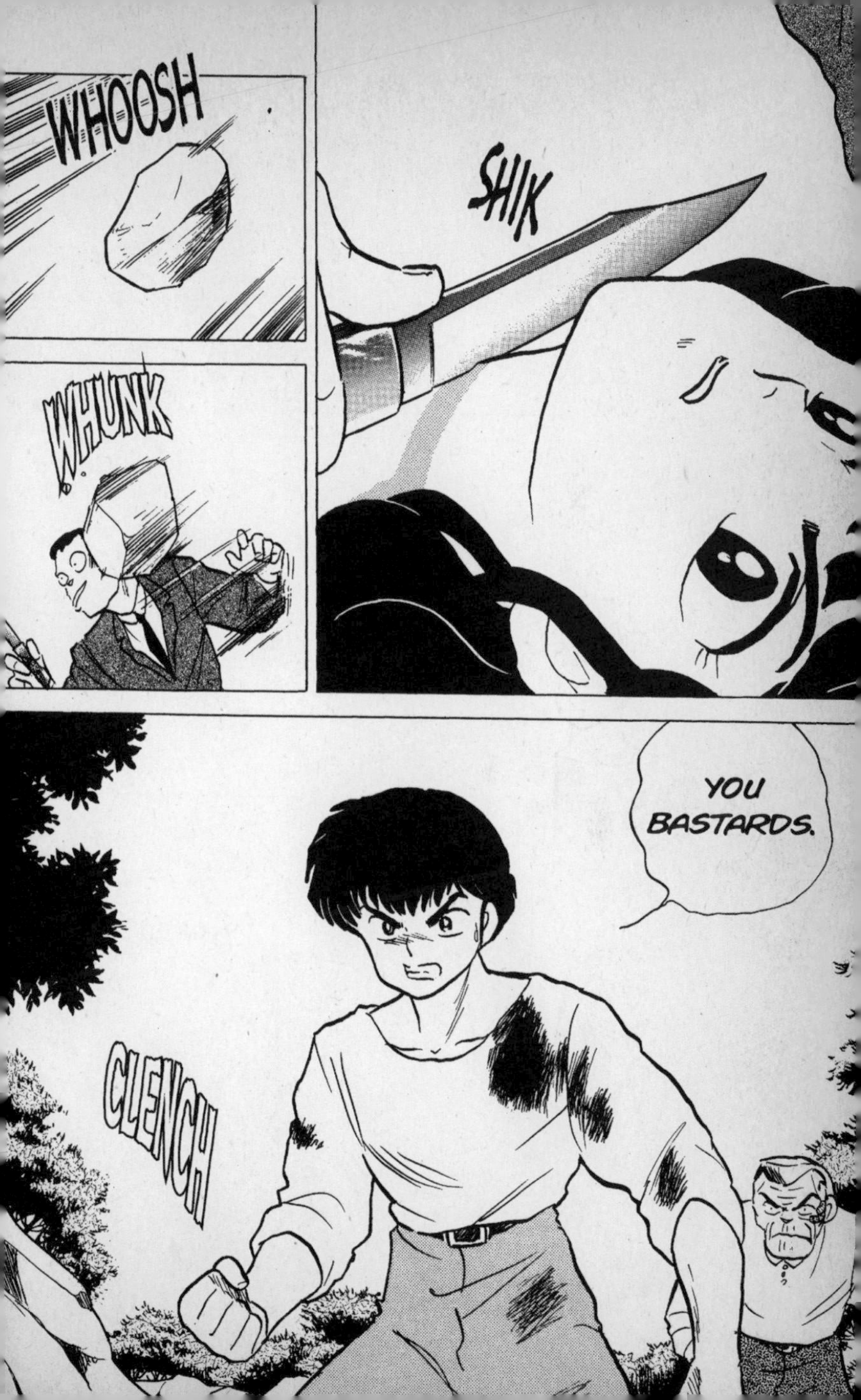
SHIK
WHOOSH
WHUNK
YOU BASTARDS.
CLENCH

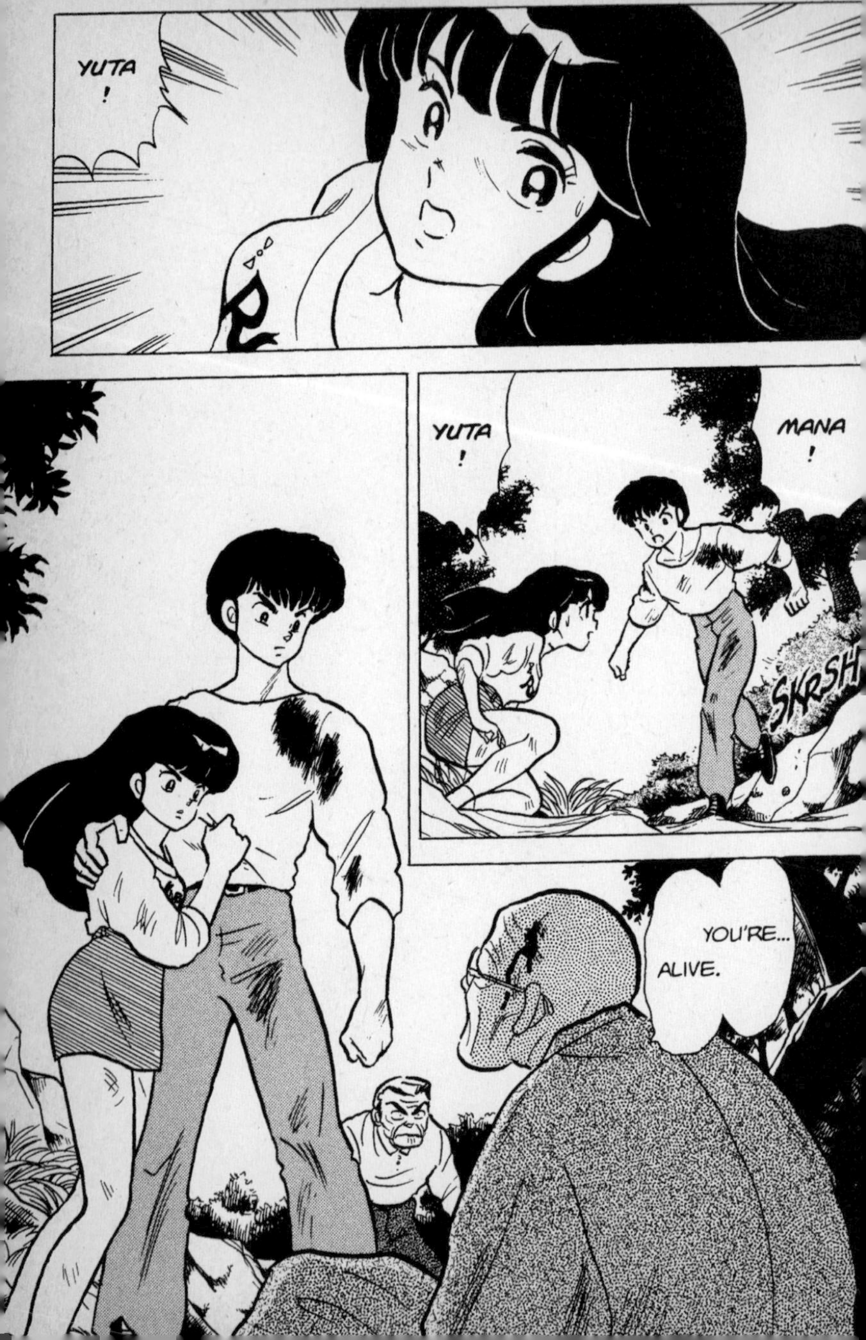
YUTA!
MANA!
YUTA!
SKRSH
YOU'RE...
ALIVE.

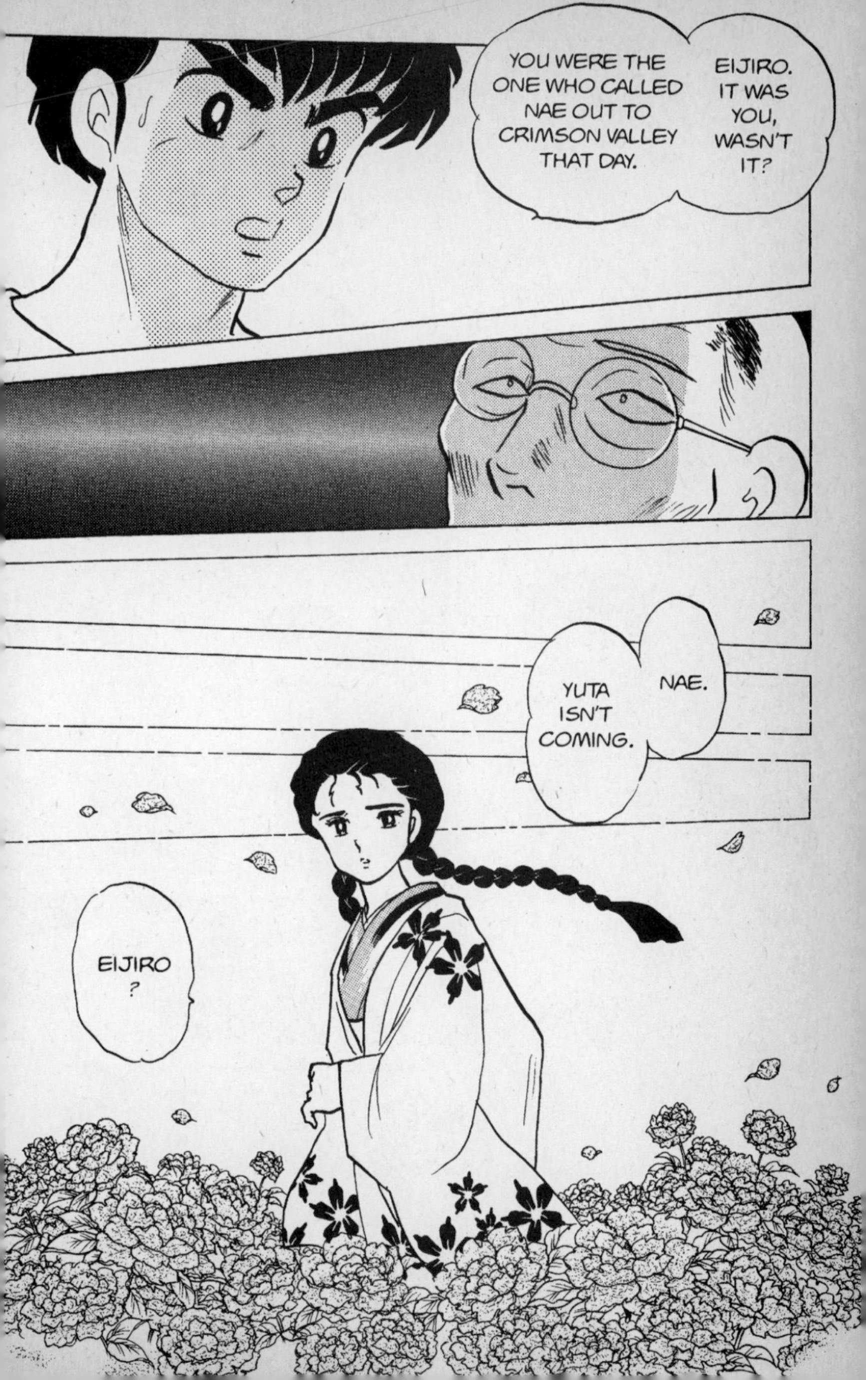
EIJIRO. IT WAS YOU, WASN'T IT?
YOU WERE THE ONE WHO CALLED NAE OUT TO CRIMSON VALLEY THAT DAY.
NAE.
YUTA ISN'T COMING.
EIJIRO?

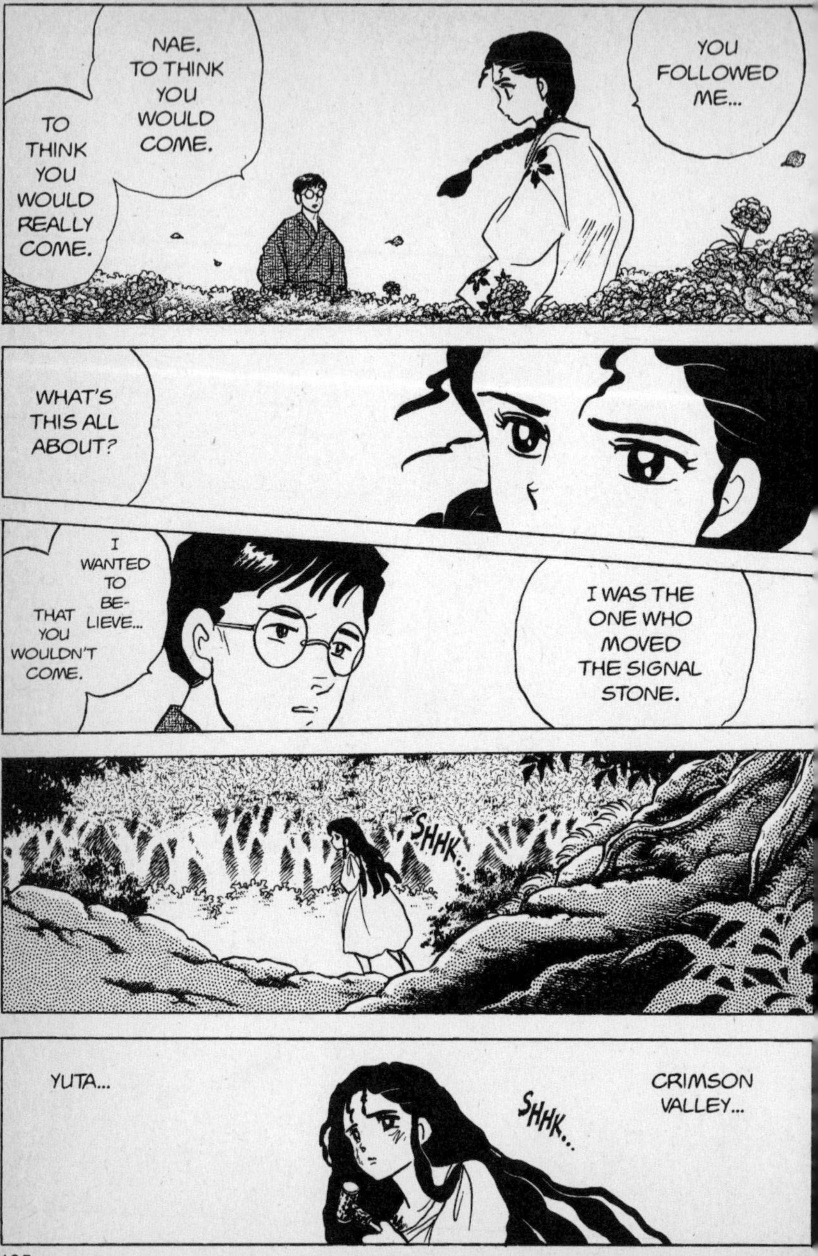
YOU FOLLOWED ME...
NAE. TO THINK YOU WOULD COME.
TO THINK YOU WOULD REALLY COME.
WHAT'S THIS ALL ABOUT?
I WAS THE ONE WHO MOVED THE SIGNAL STONE.
I WANTED TO BE-LIEVE...
THAT YOU WOULDN'T COME.
SHHK...
CRIMSON VALLEY...
SHHK...
YUTA...

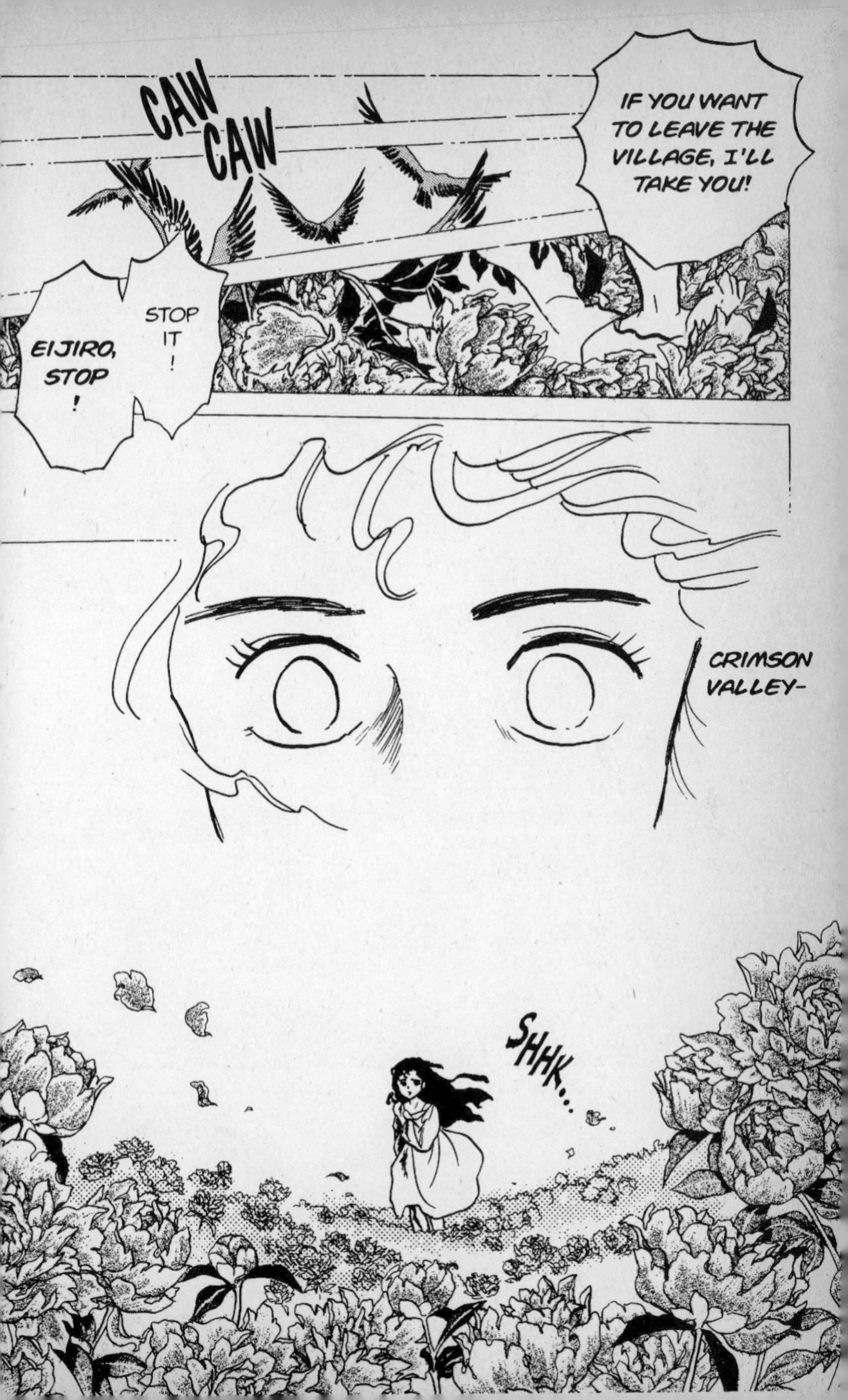
IF YOU WANT TO LEAVE THE VILLAGE, I'LL TAKE YOU!
CAW CAW
STOP IT!
EIJIRO, STOP!
CRIMSON VALLEY-
SHHK...

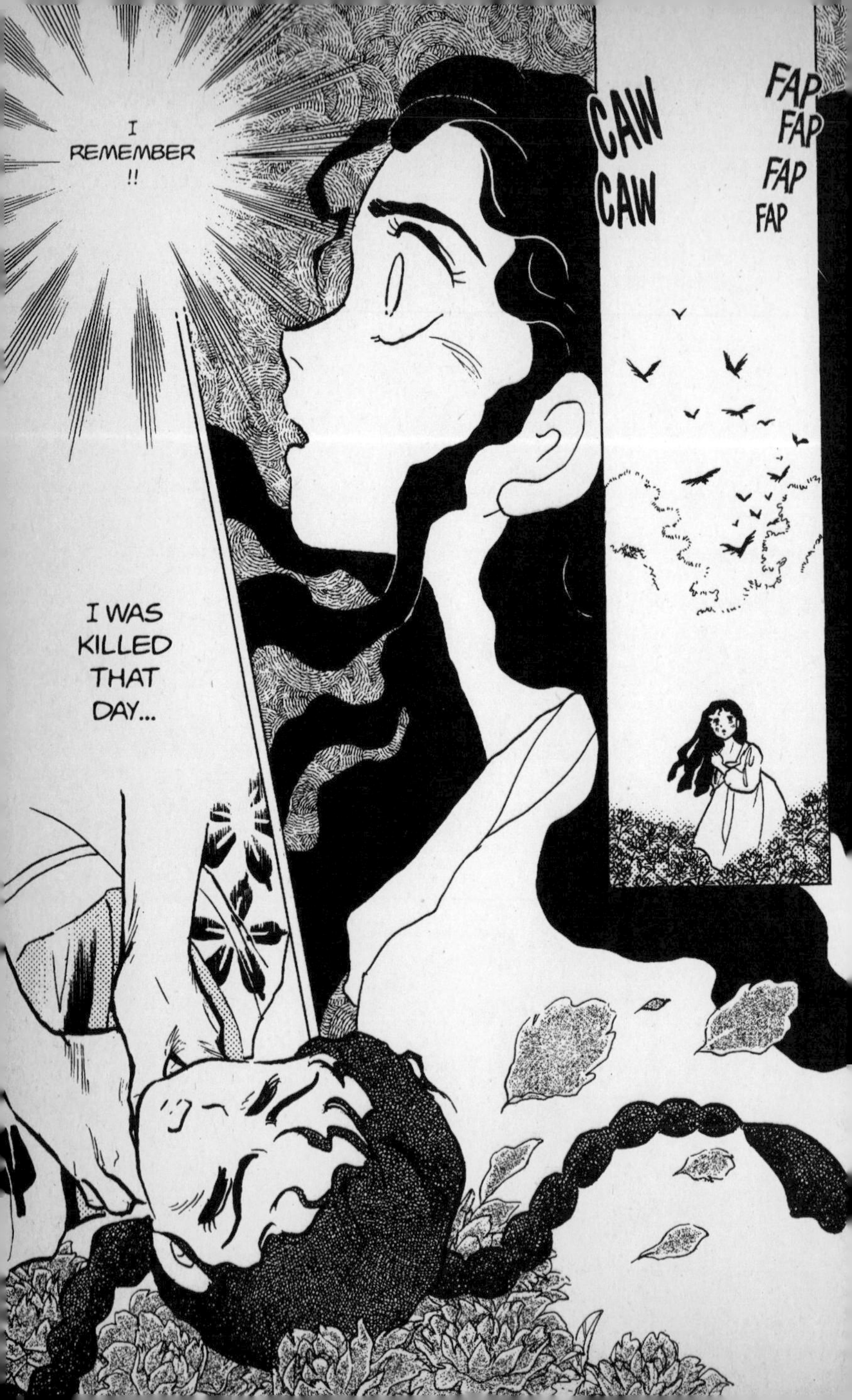
FAP FAP FAP FAP
CAW CAW
I REMEMBER !!
I WAS KILLED THAT DAY...

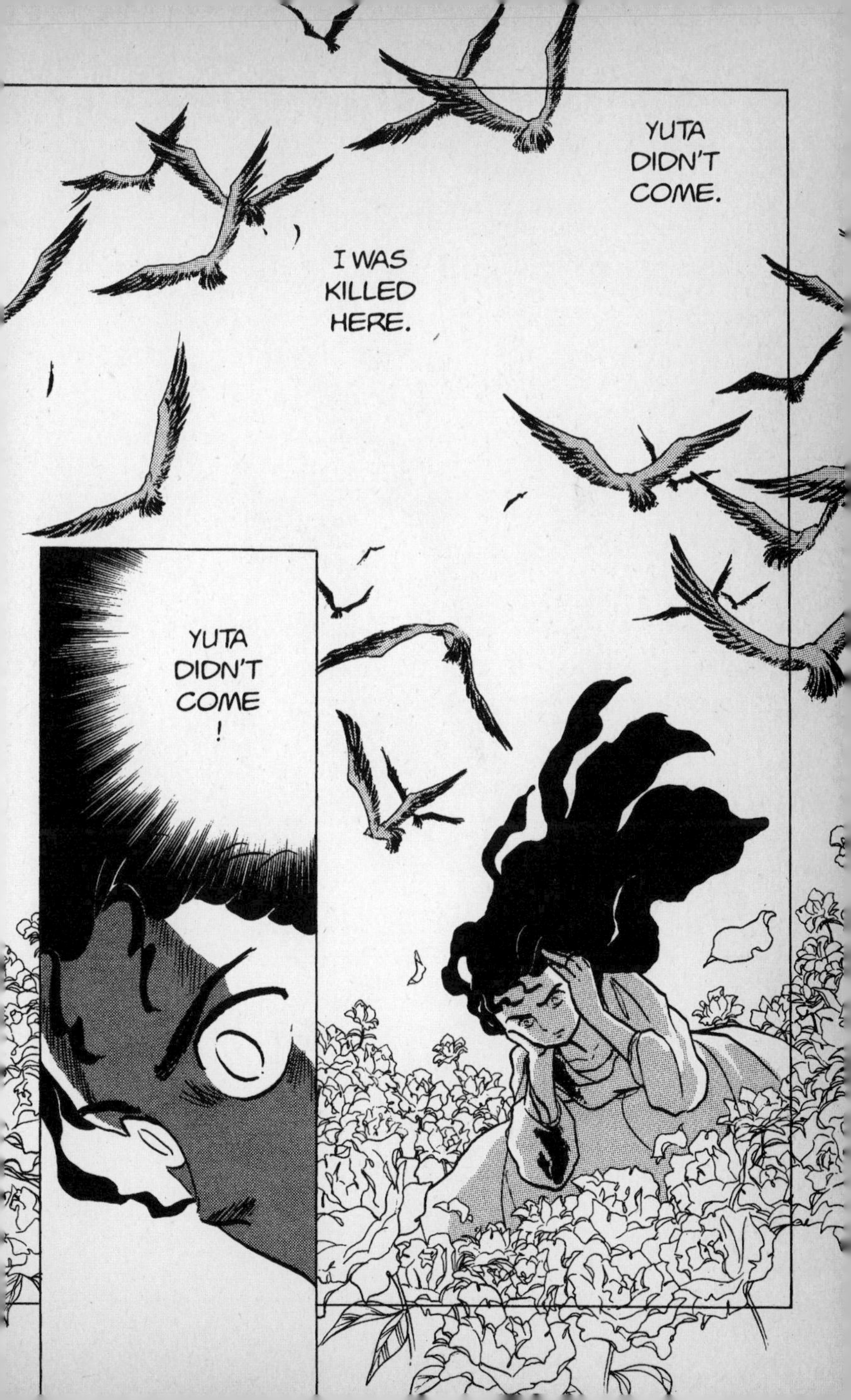
YUTA DIDN'T COME.
I WAS KILLED HERE.
YUTA DIDN'T COME !

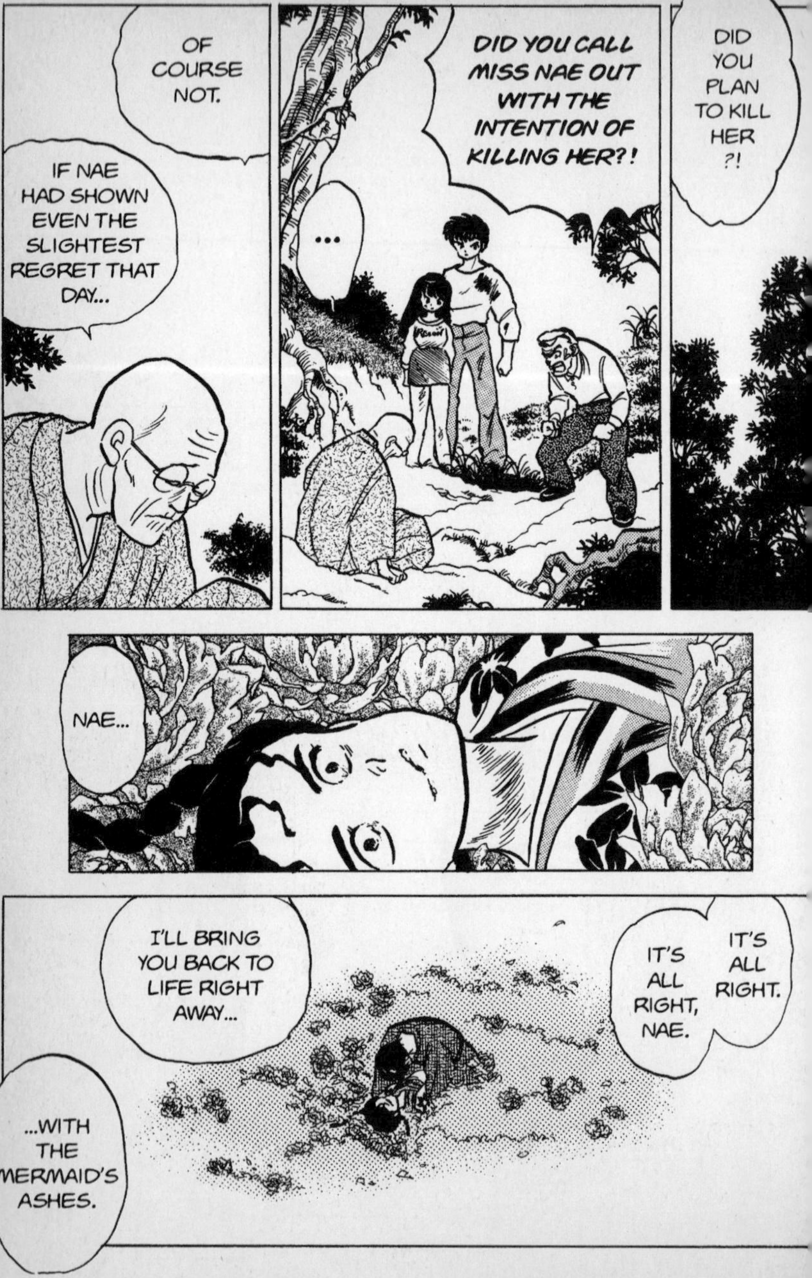
DID YOU PLAN TO KILL HER ?!
DID YOU CALL MISS NAE OUT WITH THE INTENTION OF KILLING HER?!
...
OF COURSE NOT.
IF NAE HAD SHOWN EVEN THE SLIGHTEST REGRET THAT DAY...
NAE...
IT'S ALL RIGHT.
IT'S ALL RIGHT, NAE.
I'LL BRING YOU BACK TO LIFE RIGHT AWAY...
...WITH THE MERMAID'S ASHES.

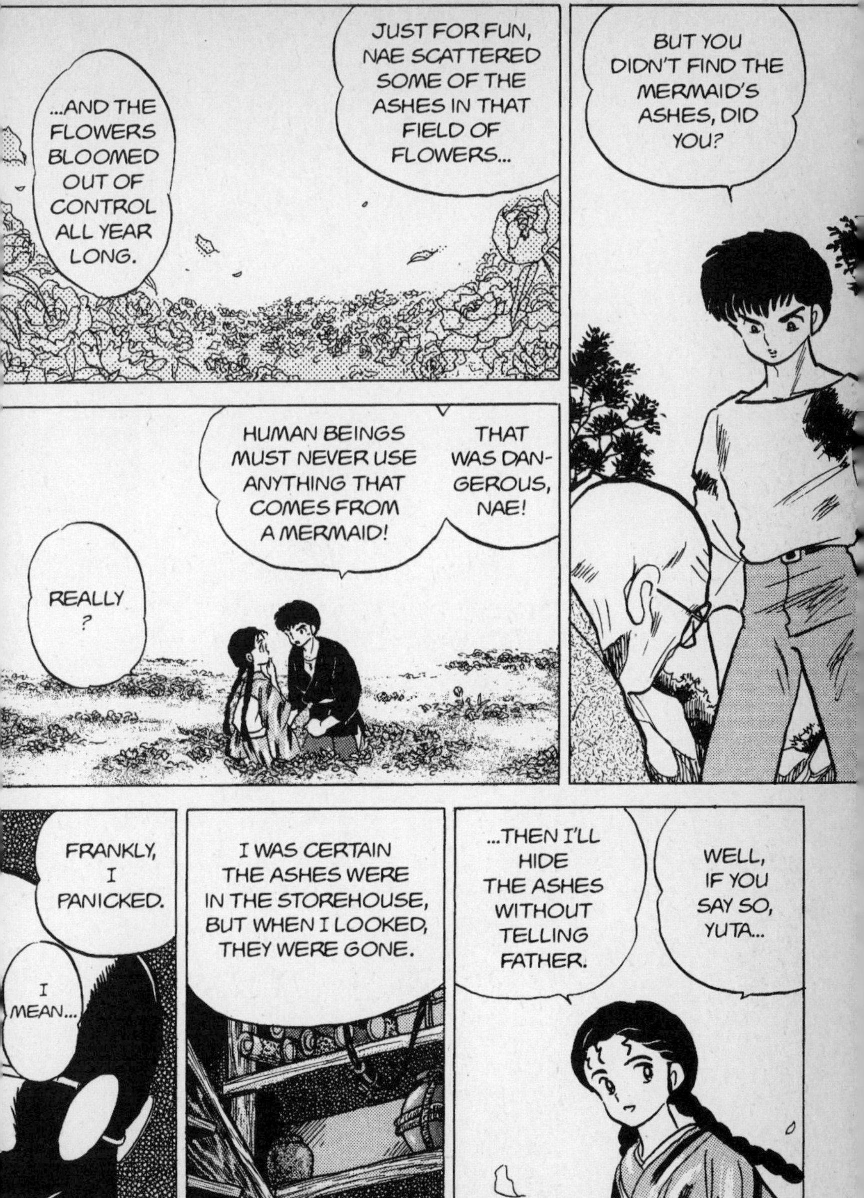
BUT YOU DIDN'T FIND THE MERMAID'S ASHES, DID YOU?
JUST FOR FUN, NAE SCATTERED SOME OF THE ASHES IN THAT FIELD OF FLOWERS...
...AND THE FLOWERS BLOOMED OUT OF CONTROL ALL YEAR LONG.
THAT WAS DAN-GEROUS, NAE!
HUMAN BEINGS MUST NEVER USE ANYTHING THAT COMES FROM A MERMAID!
REALLY?
WELL, IF YOU SAY SO, YUTA...
...THEN I'LL HIDE THE ASHES WITHOUT TELLING FATHER.
I WAS CERTAIN THE ASHES WERE IN THE STOREHOUSE, BUT WHEN I LOOKED, THEY WERE GONE.
FRANKLY, I PANICKED.
I MEAN...

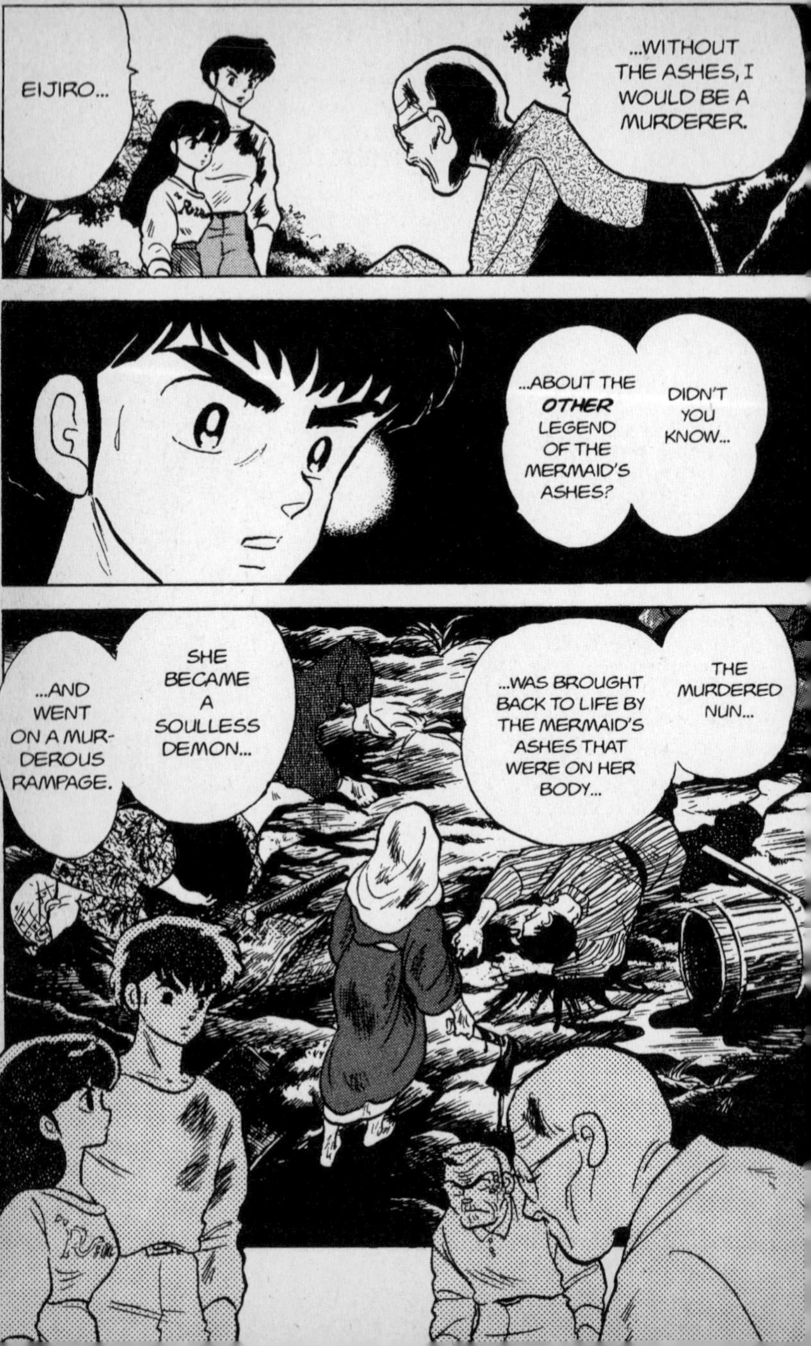
...WITHOUT THE ASHES, I WOULD BE A MURDERER.
EIJIRO...
DIDN'T YOU KNOW...
...ABOUT THE *OTHER* LEGEND OF THE MERMAID'S ASHES?
THE MURDERED NUN...
...WAS BROUGHT BACK TO LIFE BY THE MERMAID'S ASHES THAT WERE ON HER BODY...
SHE BECAME A SOULLESS DEMON...
...AND WENT ON A MUR-DEROUS RAMPAGE.

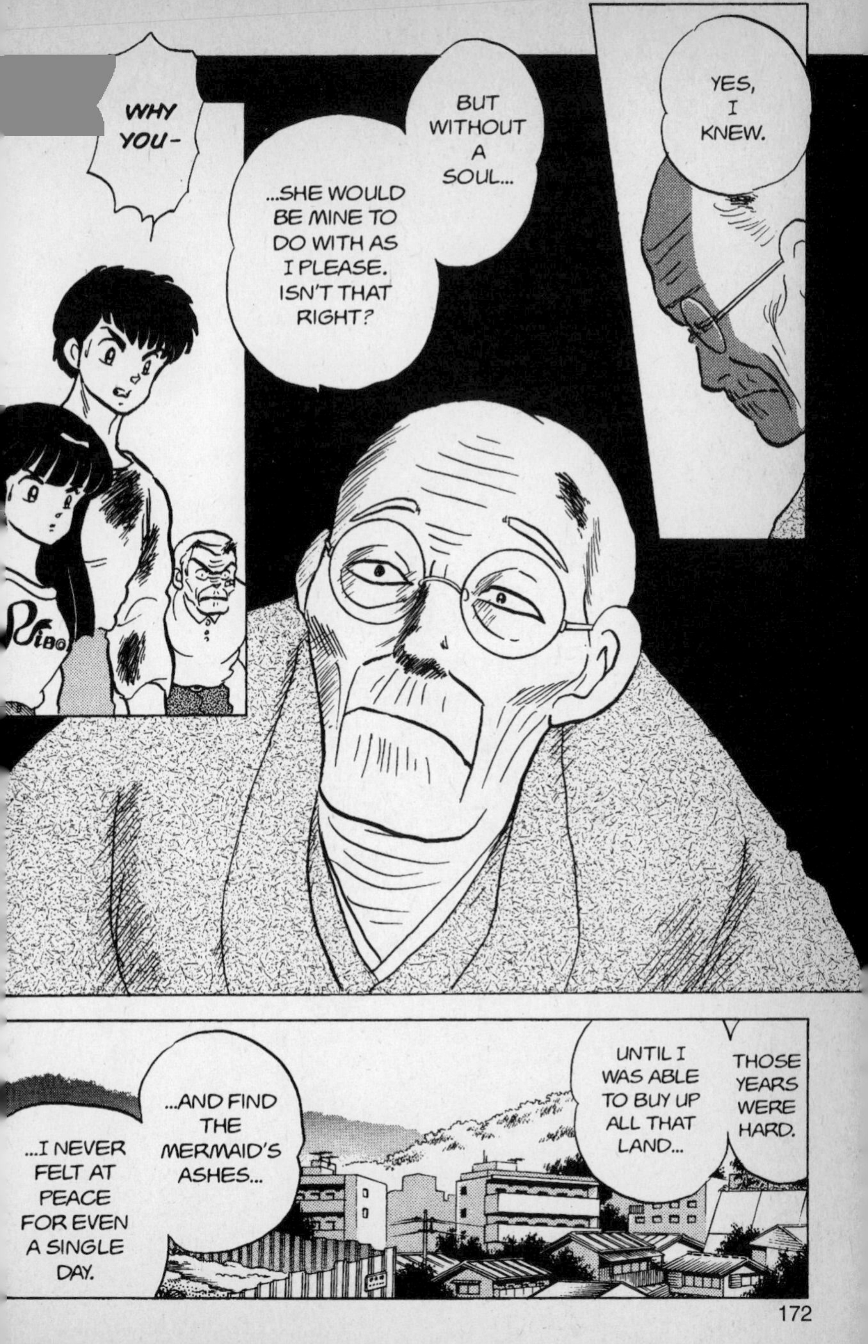
YES, I KNEW.
BUT WITHOUT A SOUL...
...SHE WOULD BE MINE TO DO WITH AS I PLEASE. ISN'T THAT RIGHT?
WHY YOU-
THOSE YEARS WERE HARD.
UNTIL I WAS ABLE TO BUY UP ALL THAT LAND...
...AND FIND THE MERMAID'S ASHES...
...I NEVER FELT AT PEACE FOR EVEN A SINGLE DAY.

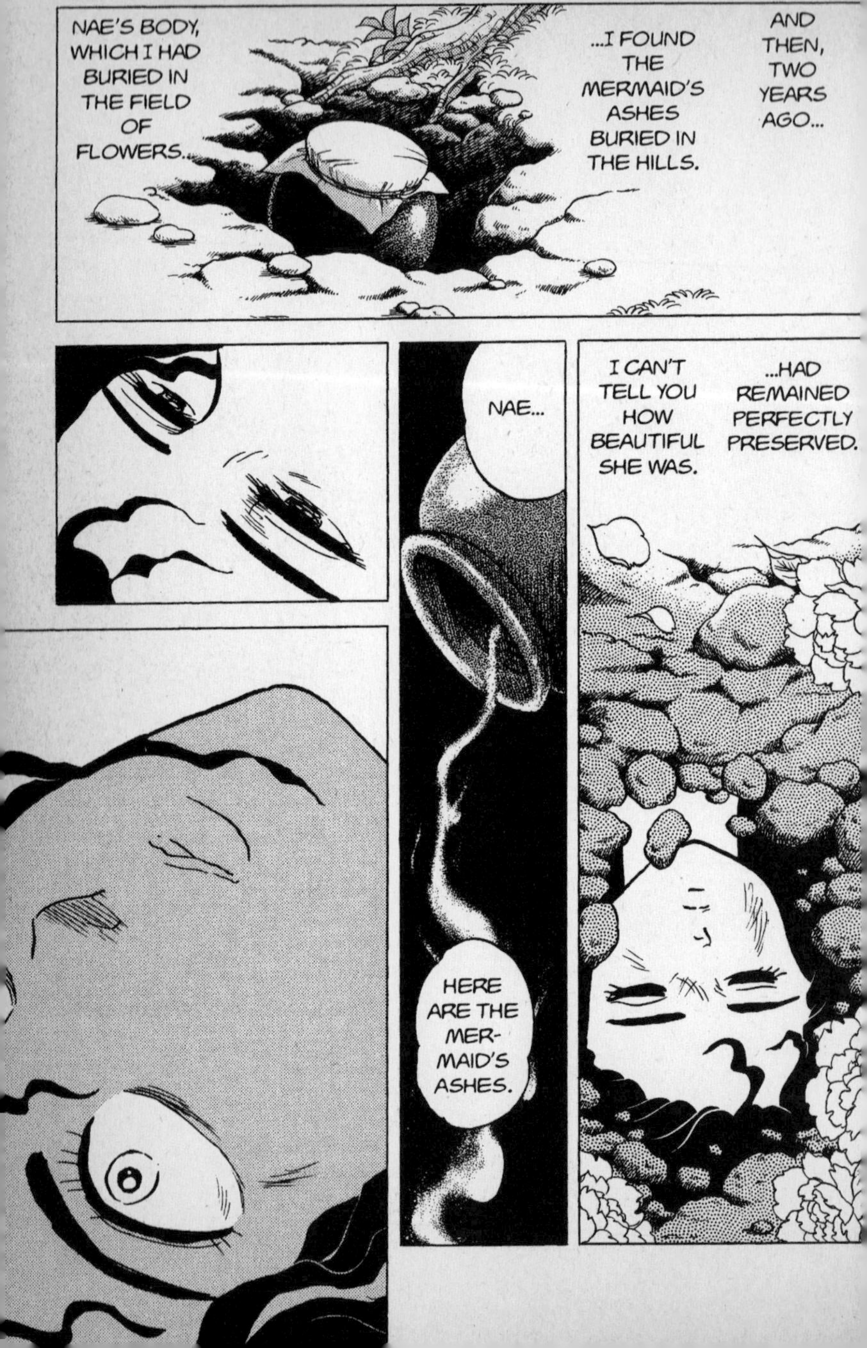
AND THEN, TWO YEARS AGO...
...I FOUND THE MERMAID'S ASHES BURIED IN THE HILLS.
NAE'S BODY, WHICH I HAD BURIED IN THE FIELD OF FLOWERS...
...HAD REMAINED PERFECTLY PRESERVED.
I CAN'T TELL YOU HOW BEAUTIFUL SHE WAS.
NAE...
HERE ARE THE MER-MAID'S ASHES.

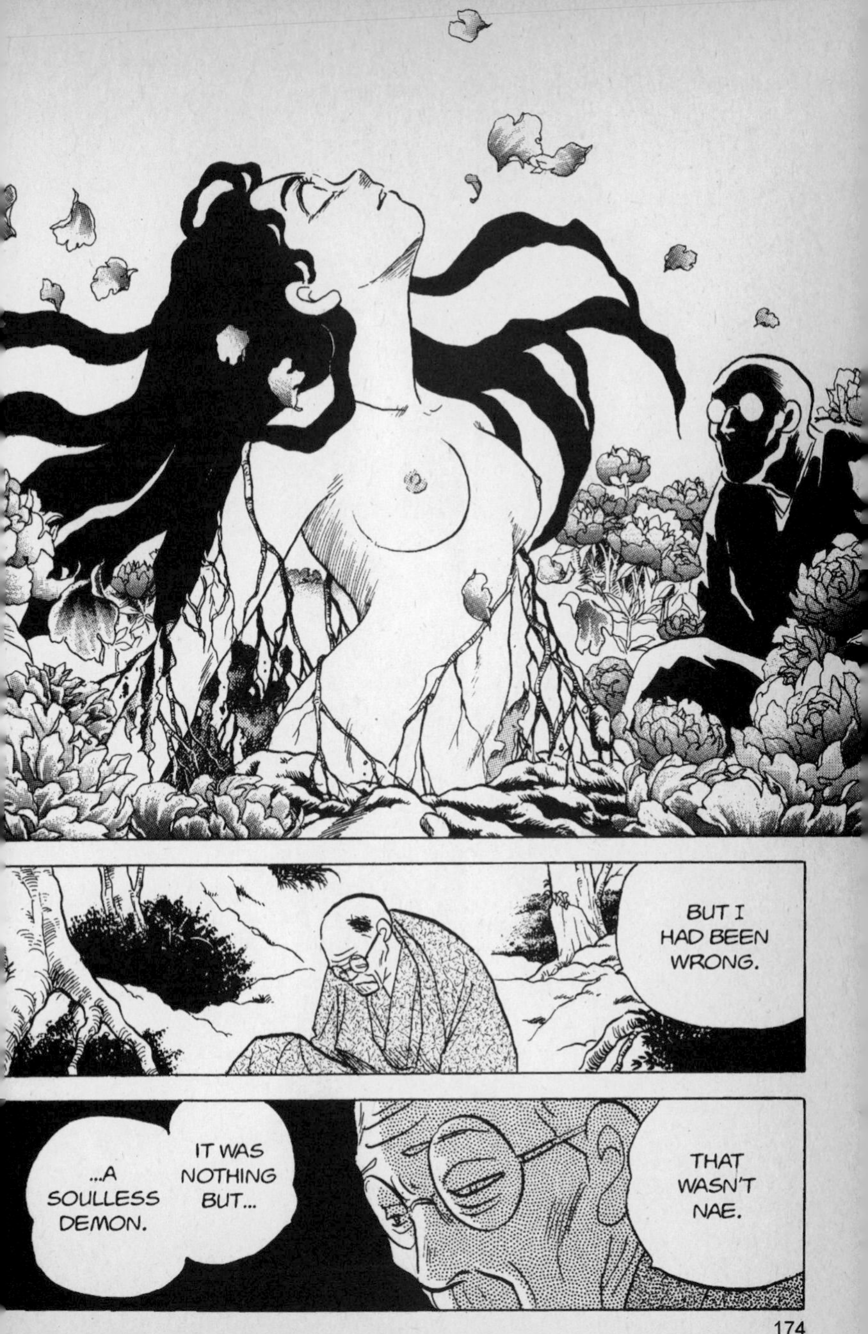
BUT I HAD BEEN WRONG.
THAT WASN'T NAE.
IT WAS NOTHING BUT...
...A SOULLESS DEMON.

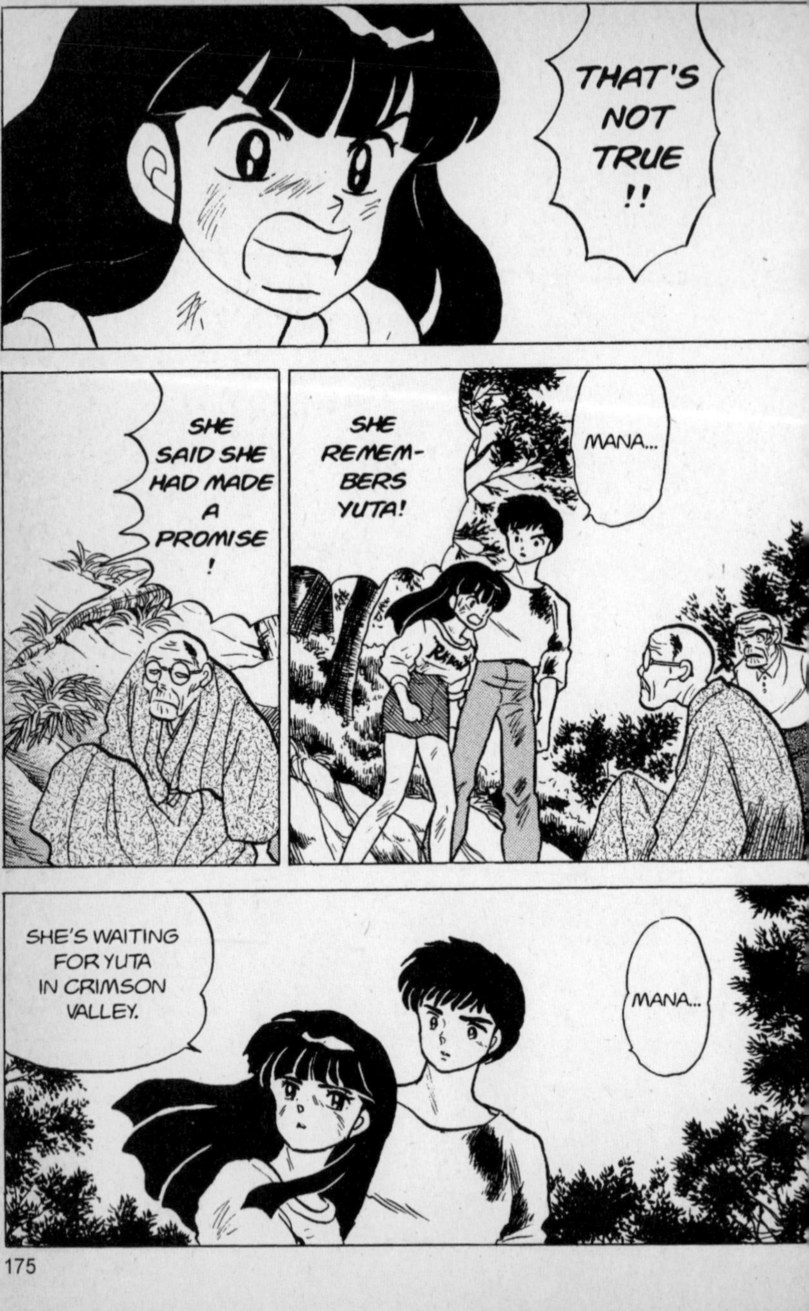
THAT'S NOT TRUE!!
MANA...
SHE REMEM-BERS YUTA!
SHE SAID SHE HAD MADE A PROMISE!
MANA...
SHE'S WAITING FOR YUTA IN CRIMSON VALLEY.

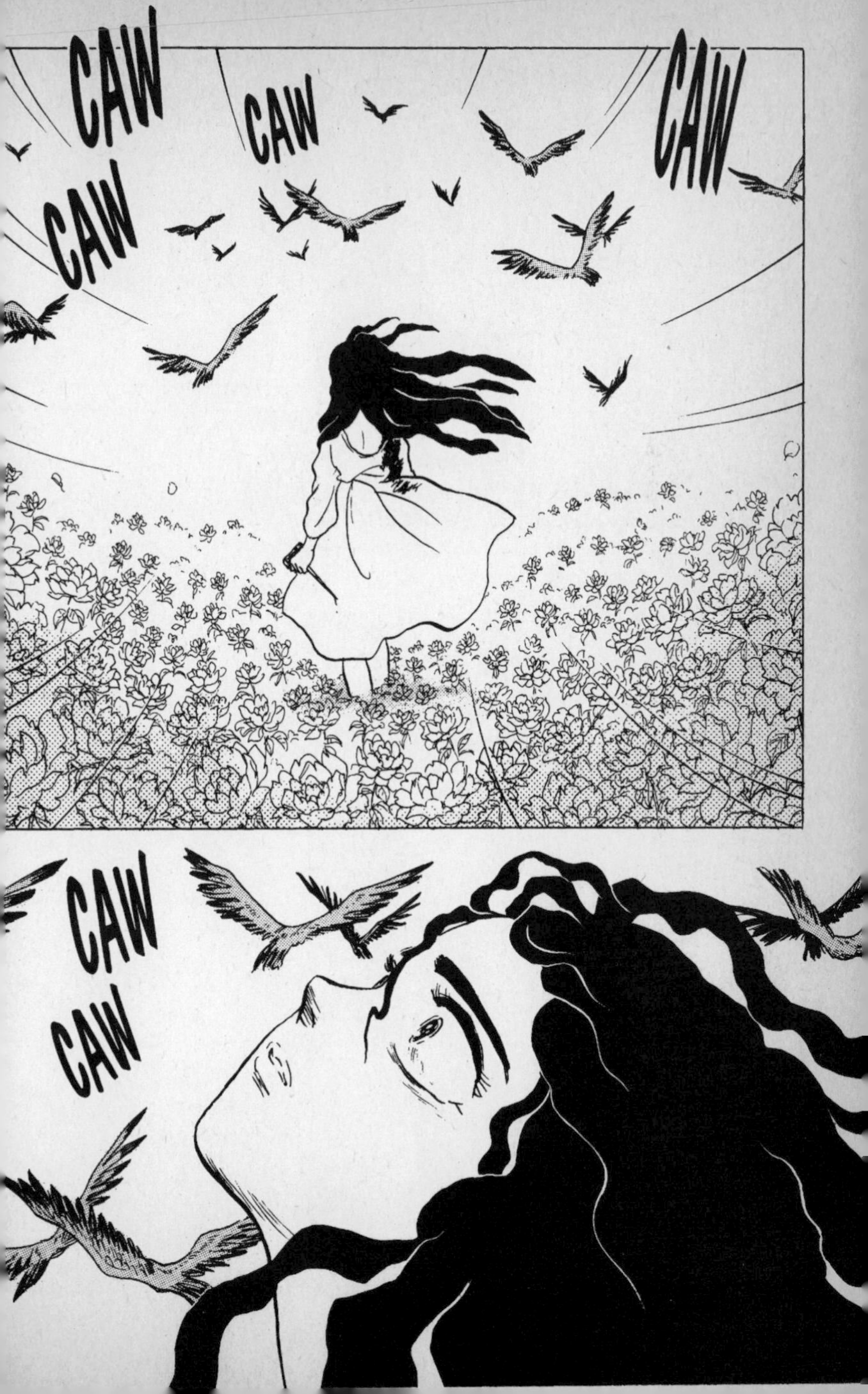
CAW
CAW
CAW
CAW
CAW
CAW

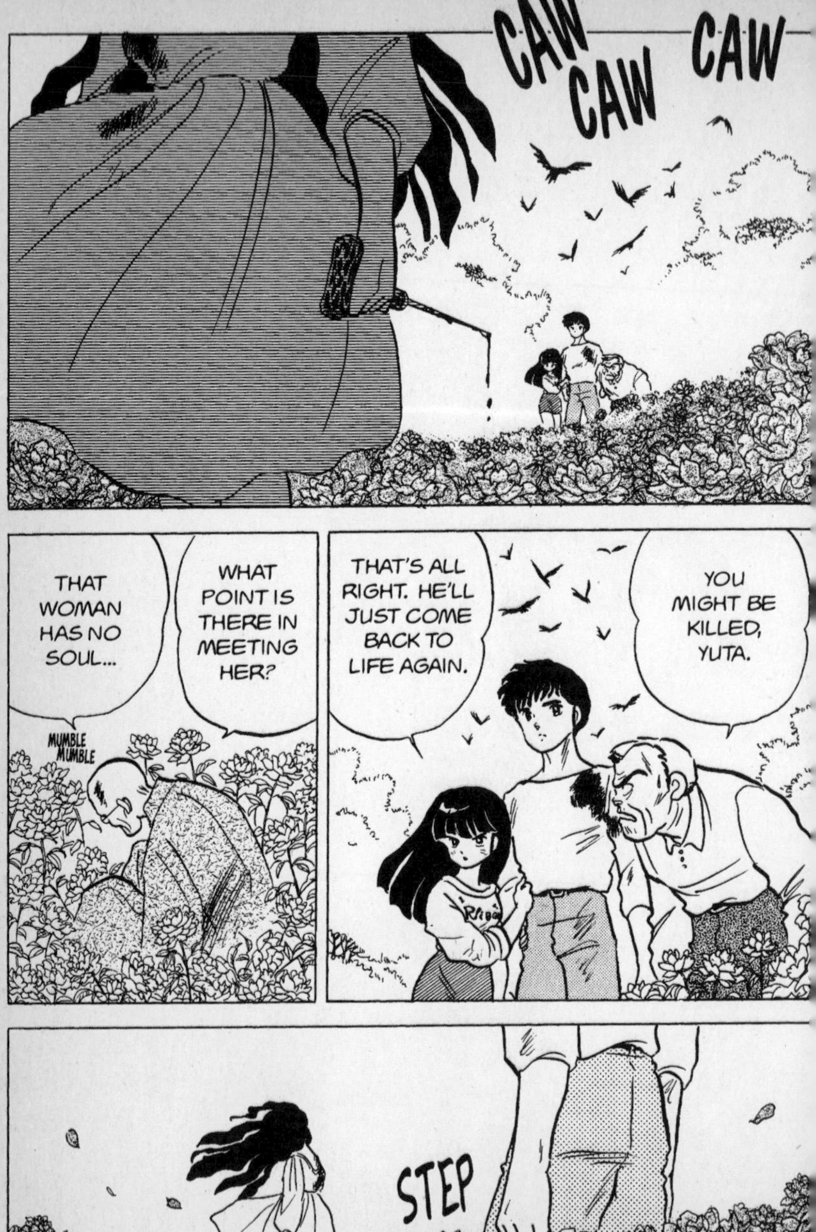
CAW
CAW
CAW
YOU MIGHT BE KILLED, YUTA.
THAT'S ALL RIGHT. HE'LL JUST COME BACK TO LIFE AGAIN.
WHAT POINT IS THERE IN MEETING HER?
THAT WOMAN HAS NO SOUL...
MUMBLE MUMBLE
STEP

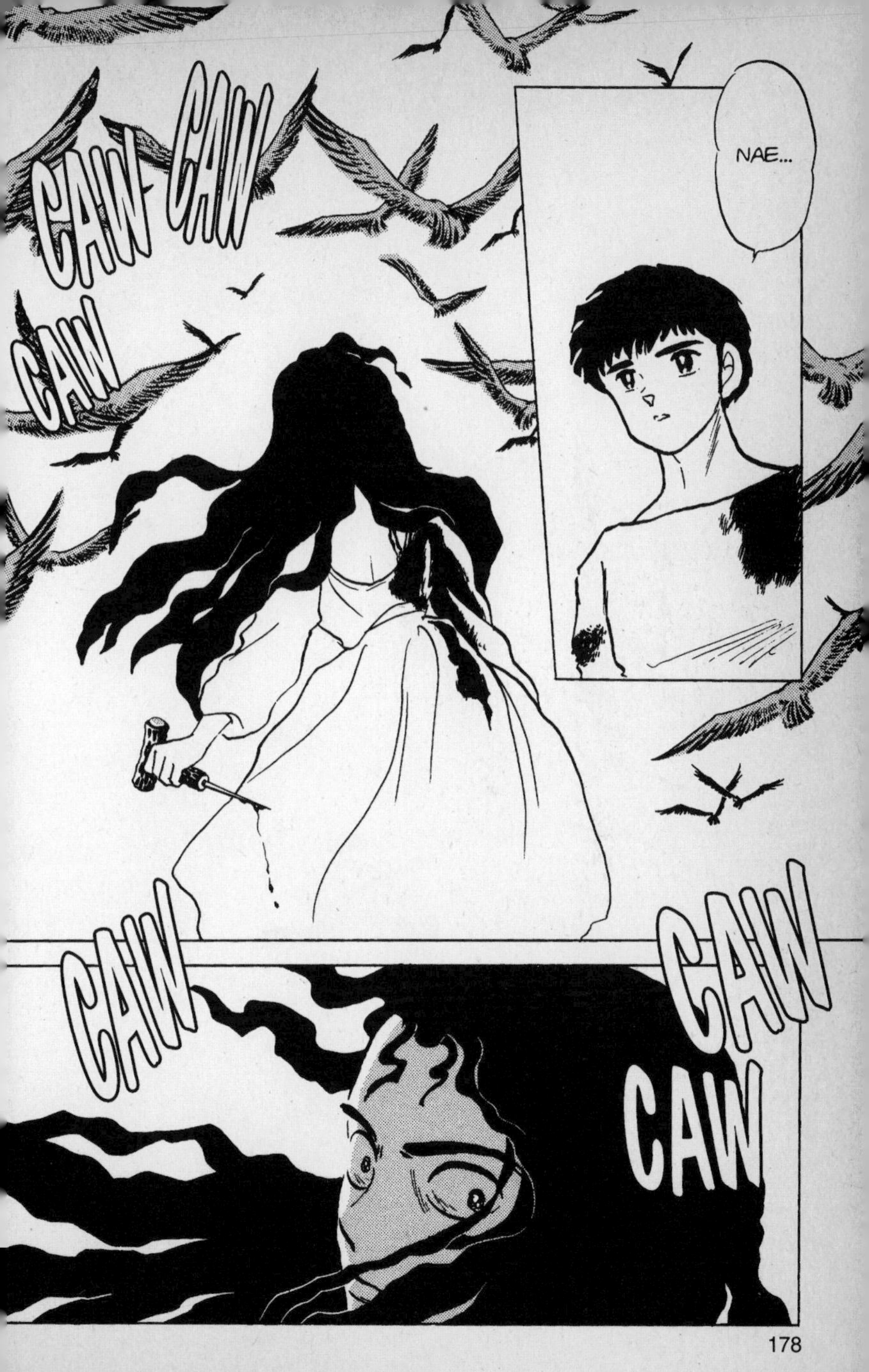
NAE...
CAW CAW
CAW
CAW
CAW
CAW CAW
CAW

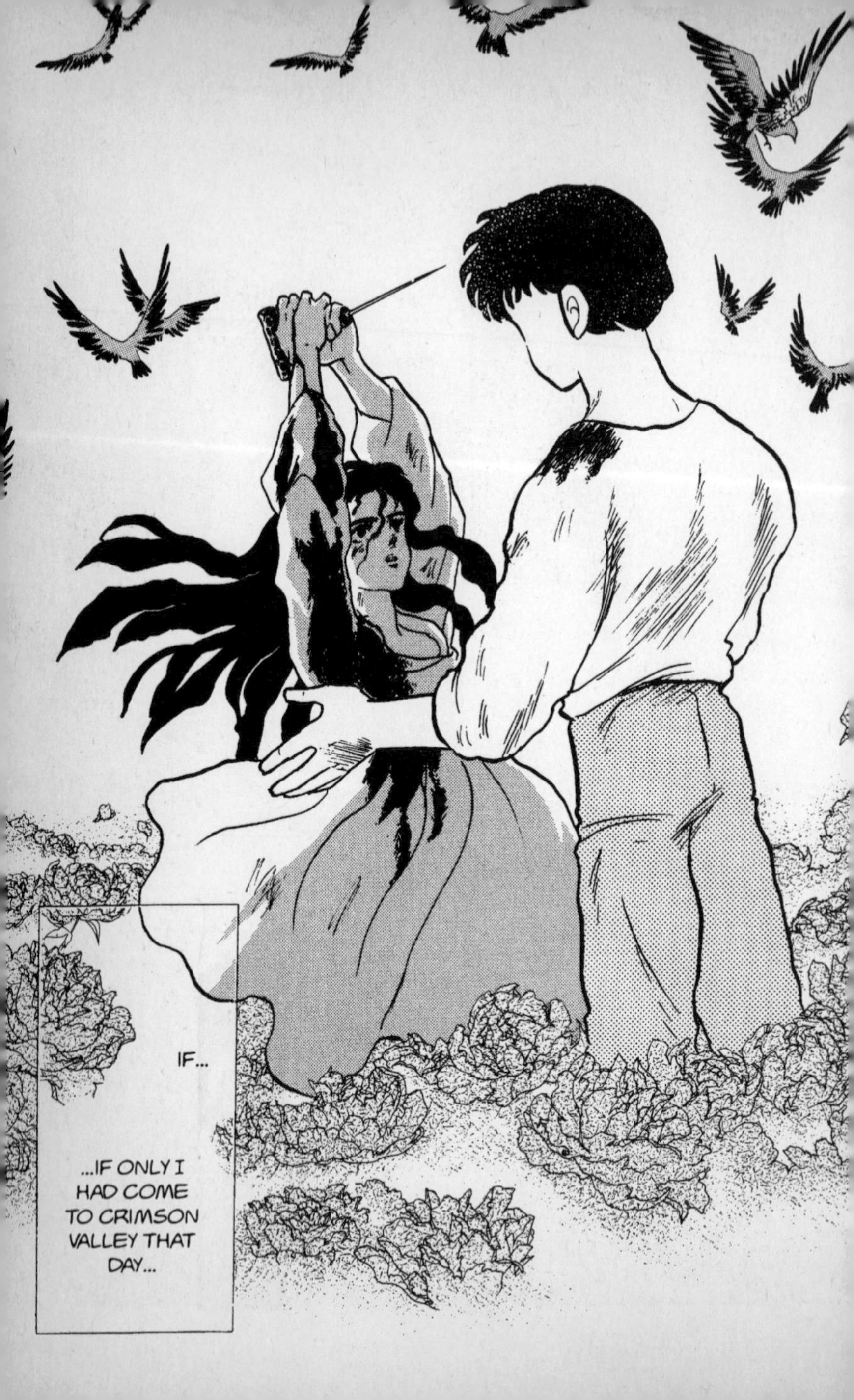
IF...
...IF ONLY I HAD COME TO CRIMSON VALLEY THAT DAY...

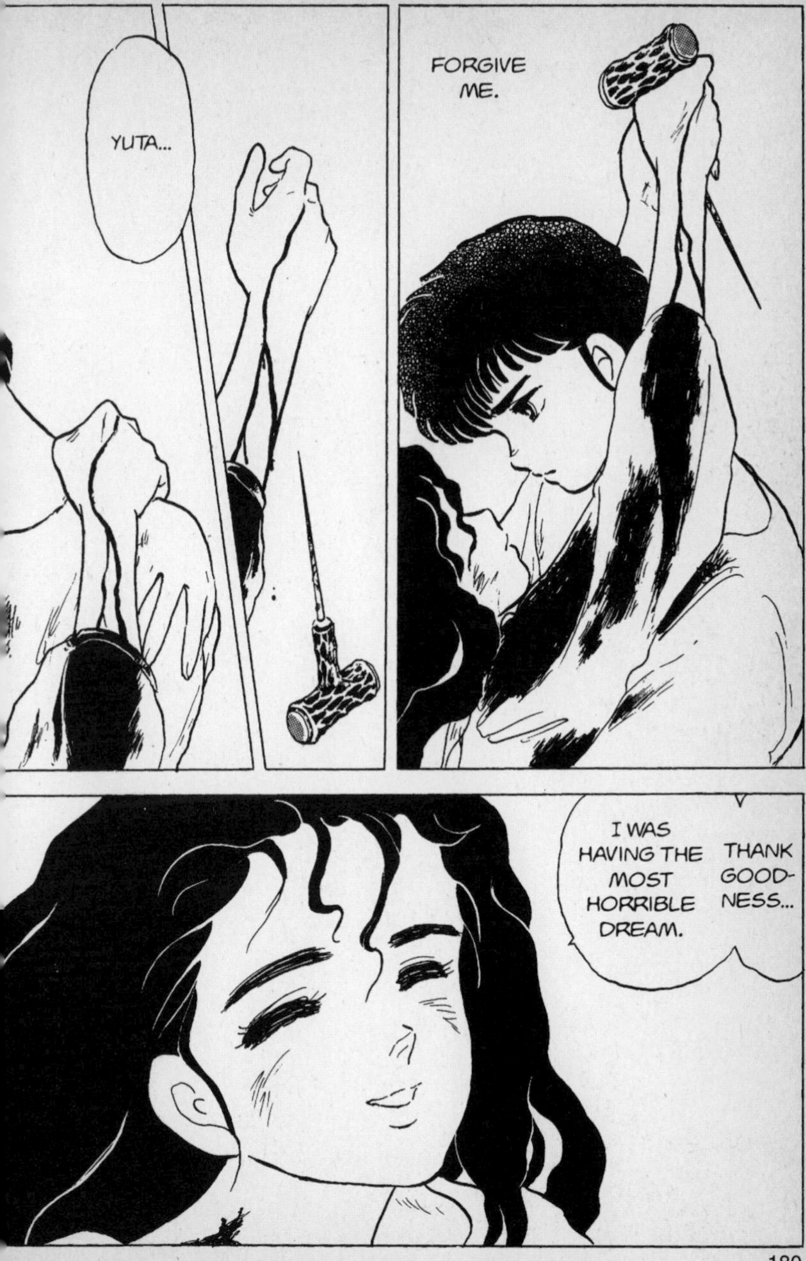
FORGIVE ME.
YUTA...
THANK GOODNESS...
I WAS HAVING THE MOST HORRIBLE DREAM.

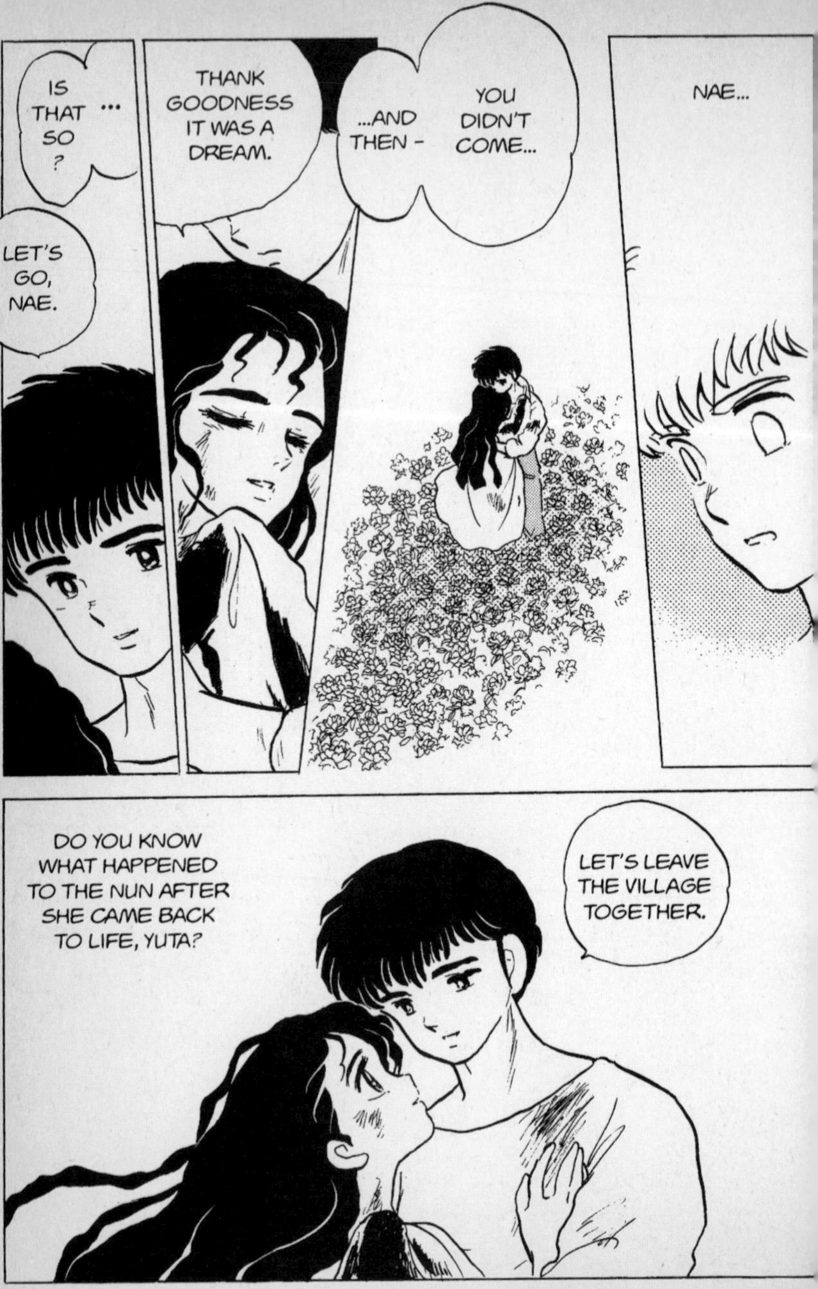
NAE...
...AND THEN - YOU DIDN'T COME...
THANK GOODNESS IT WAS A DREAM.
IS THAT SO ...?
LET'S GO, NAE.
LET'S LEAVE THE VILLAGE TOGETHER.
DO YOU KNOW WHAT HAPPENED TO THE NUN AFTER SHE CAME BACK TO LIFE, YUTA?

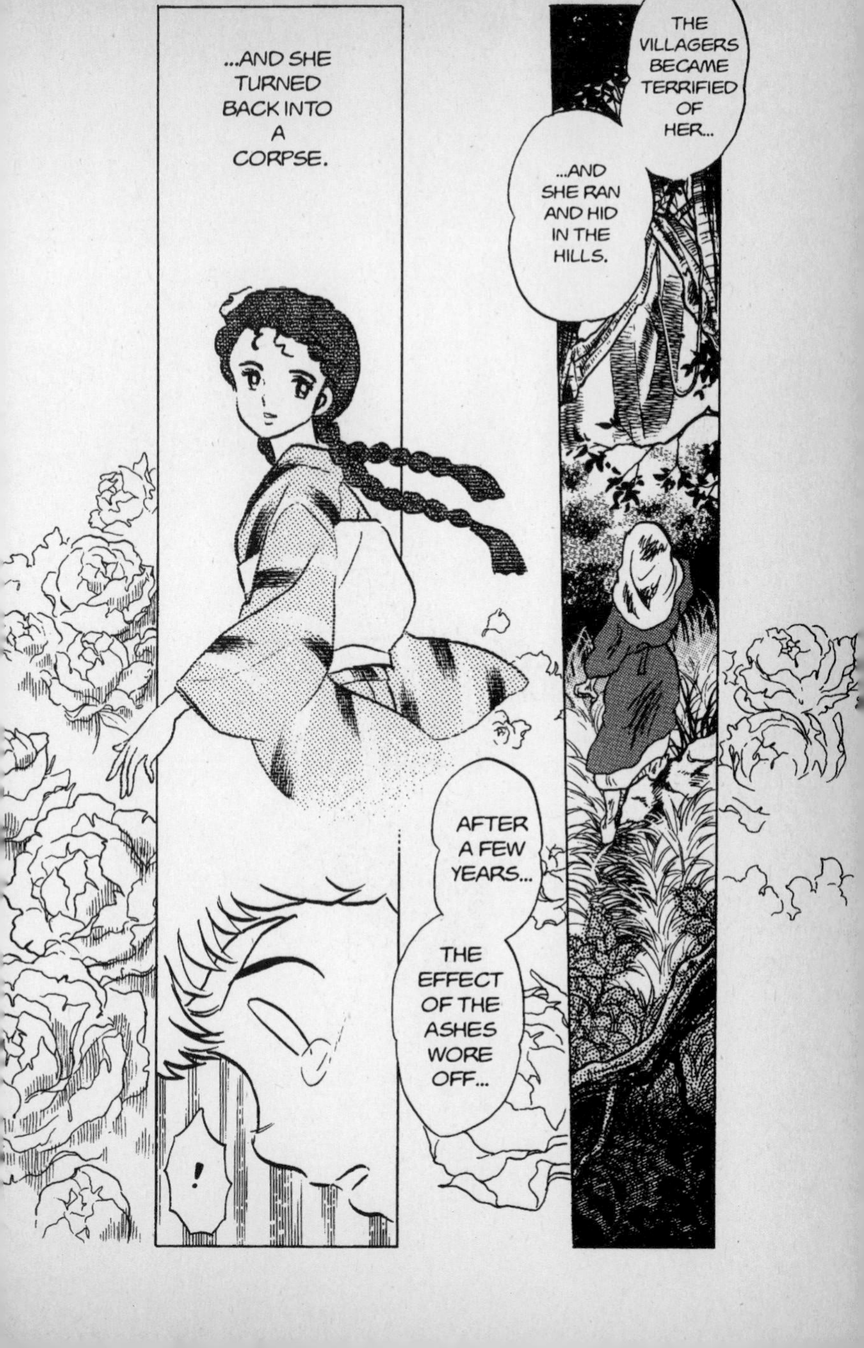
THE VILLAGERS BECAME TERRIFIED OF HER...
...AND SHE RAN AND HID IN THE HILLS.
AFTER A FEW YEARS...
THE EFFECT OF THE ASHES WORE OFF...
...AND SHE TURNED BACK INTO A CORPSE.
!

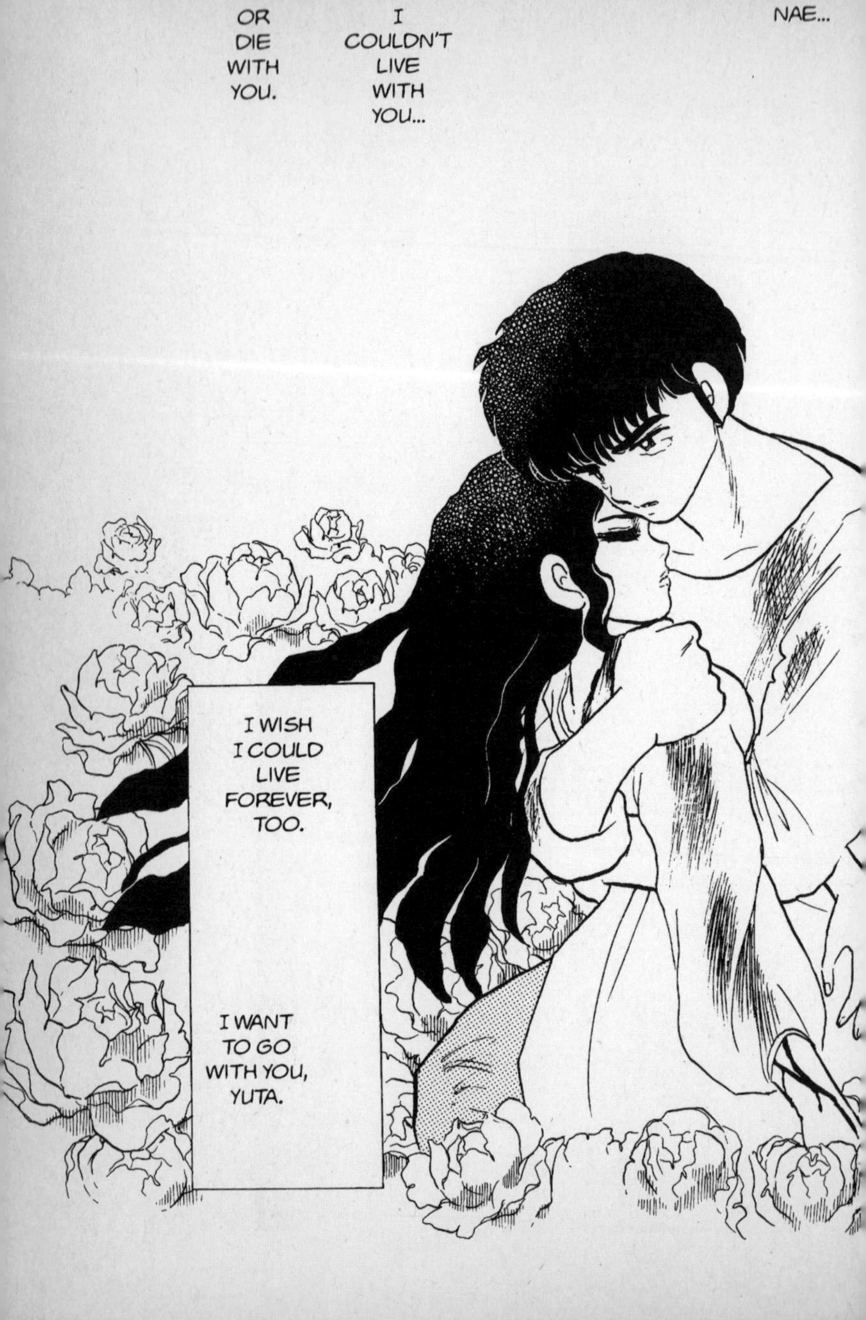
NAE...
I COULDN'T LIVE WITH YOU...
OR DIE WITH YOU.
I WISH I COULD LIVE FOREVER, TOO.
I WANT TO GO WITH YOU, YUTA.

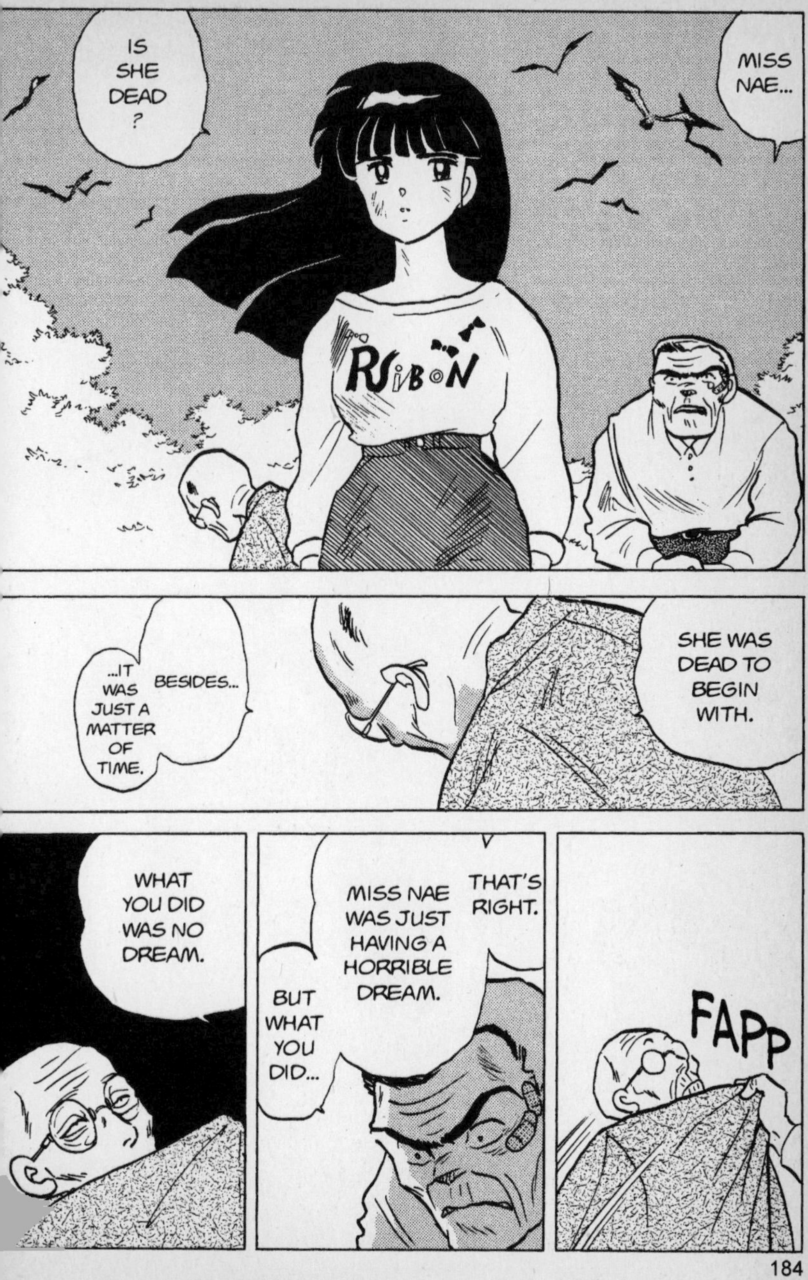
MISS NAE...
IS SHE DEAD?
SHE WAS DEAD TO BEGIN WITH.
BESIDES...
...IT WAS JUST A MATTER OF TIME.
FAPP
THAT'S RIGHT.
MISS NAE WAS JUST HAVING A HORRIBLE DREAM.
BUT WHAT YOU DID...
WHAT YOU DID WAS NO DREAM.

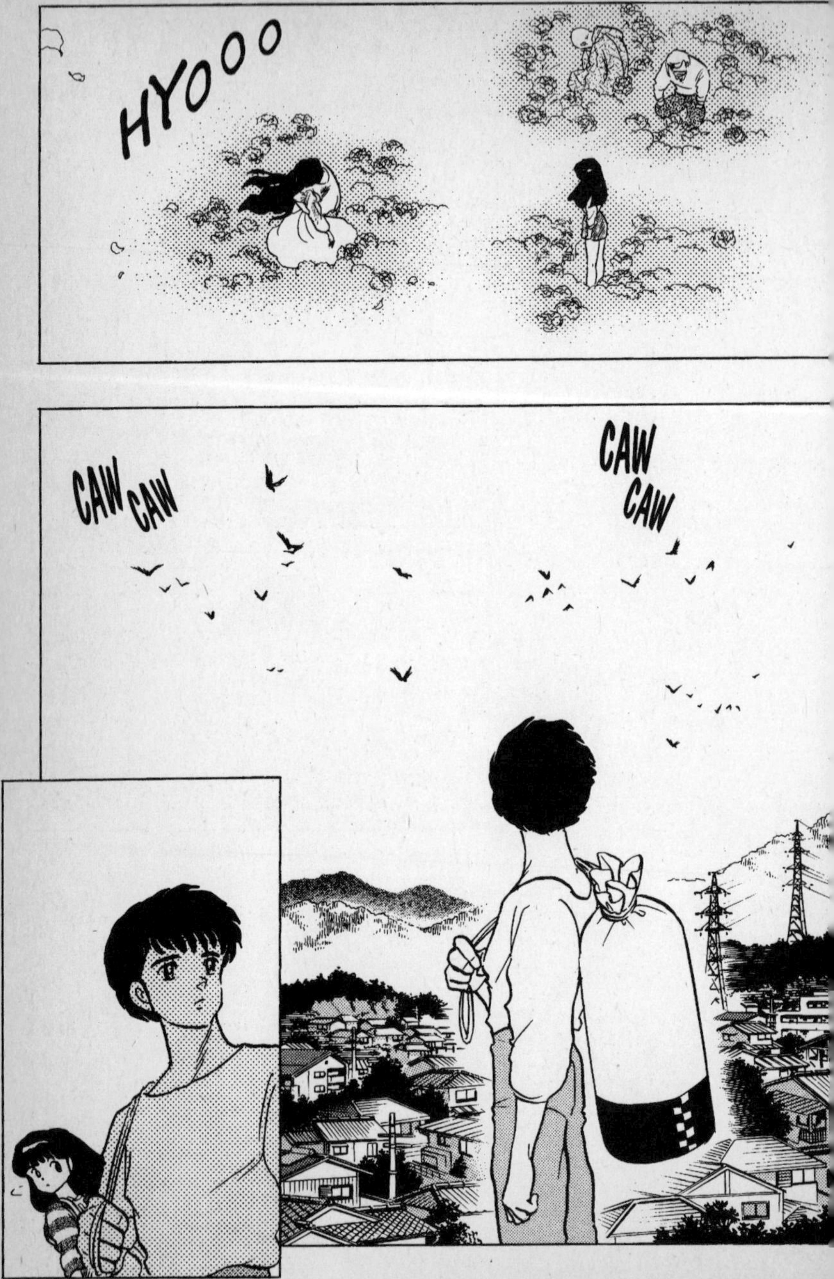
HYOOO
CAW CAW
CAW CAW

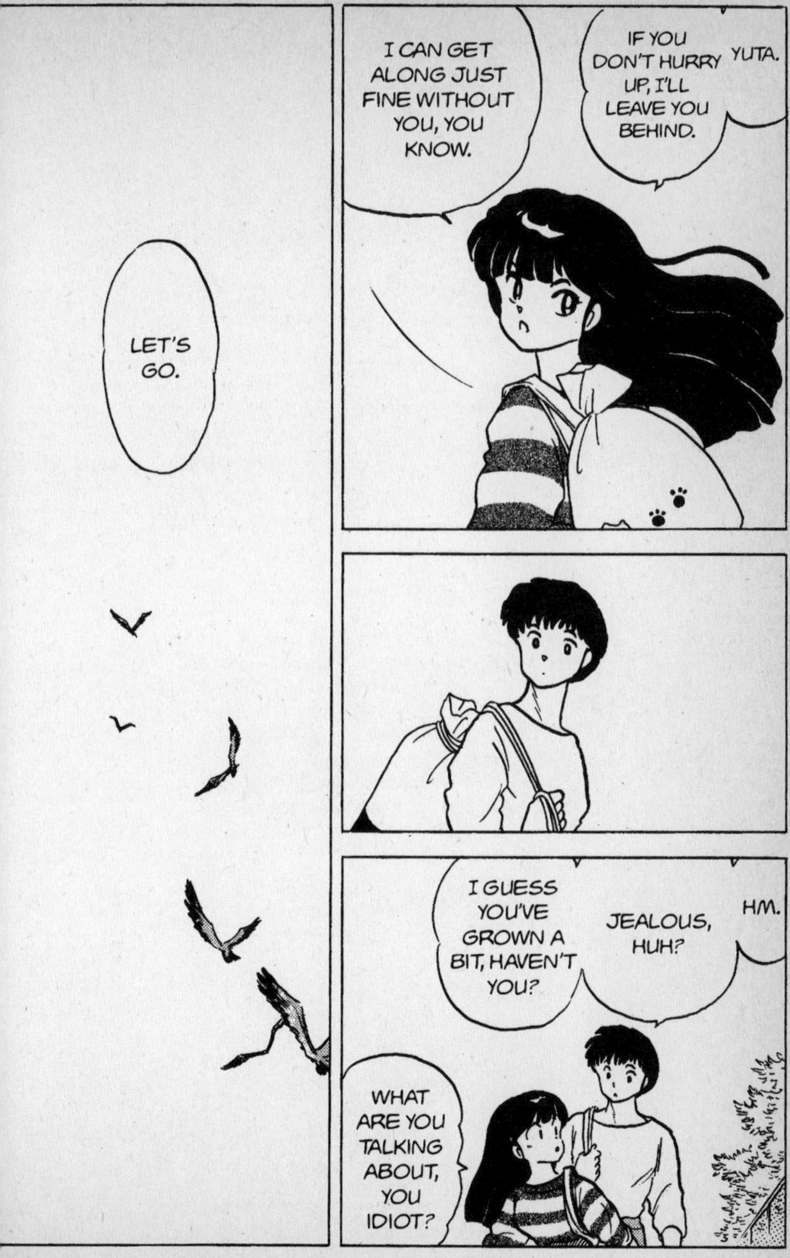
YUTA.
IF YOU DON'T HURRY UP, I'LL LEAVE YOU BEHIND.
I CAN GET ALONG JUST FINE WITHOUT YOU, YOU KNOW.
HM.
JEALOUS, HUH?
I GUESS YOU'VE GROWN A BIT, HAVEN'T YOU?
WHAT ARE YOU TALKING ABOUT, YOU IDIOT?
LET'S GO.

MERMAID SAGA
Vol. 2
Action Edition

Story & Art by Rumiko Takahashi

Translation/Matt Thorn
Touch-up & Lettering/Wayne Truman
Design/Hidemi Sahara
Editors 1st Edition/Satoru Fujii & Trish Ledoux
Editor Action Edition/Megan Bates

Managing Editor/Annette Roman
Editor-in-Chief/Alvin Lu
Director of Production/Noboru Watanabe
Sr. Director Licensing & Acquisitions/Rika Inouye
V.P. of Marketing/Liza Coppola
V.P. of Sales/Joe Morici
Executive Vice President/Hyoe Narita
Publisher/Seiji Horibuchi

Printed in the U.S.A.

Published by VIZ, LLC
P.O. Box 77010
San Francisco, CA 94107

Action Edition
10 9 8 7 6 5 4 3 2 1
First printing August 2004
First English edition 1994 & 1995

www.viz.com

RATED T+ FOR OLDER TEENS

PARENTAL ADVISORY
MERMAID SAGA is rated T+ for Teen Plus. It contains nudity and fantasy violence and is recommended for ages 16 and up.

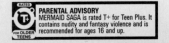

About the Author

Rumiko Takahashi, born in 1957 in Niigata, Japan, is the acclaimed creator and artist of **Mermaid Saga, Inu-Yasha, Ranma 1/2, Maison Ikkoku and Lum * Urusei Yatsura**.

While she attended the prestigious Nihon Joseidai (Japan Women's University), Takahashi began studying comics at Gekiga Sonjuku, a famous school for manga artists run by Kazuo Koike, author of **Crying Freeman** and **Lone Wolf and Cub**. In 1978, Takahashi won a prize in Shogakukan's annual New Comic Artist Contest, and her boy-meets-alien comedy, **Lum * Urusei Yatsura**, began appearing in the weekly manga magazine **Shônen Sunday**.

Takahashi's success and critical acclaim continues to grow, with popular titles including **Ranma 1/2** and **InuYasha**. Many of her graphic novel series have been animated, and are widely available in several languages.

If you like *Mermaid Saga*, VIZ recommends you try:

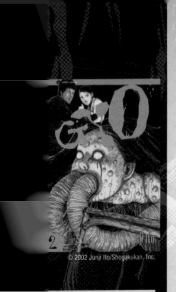

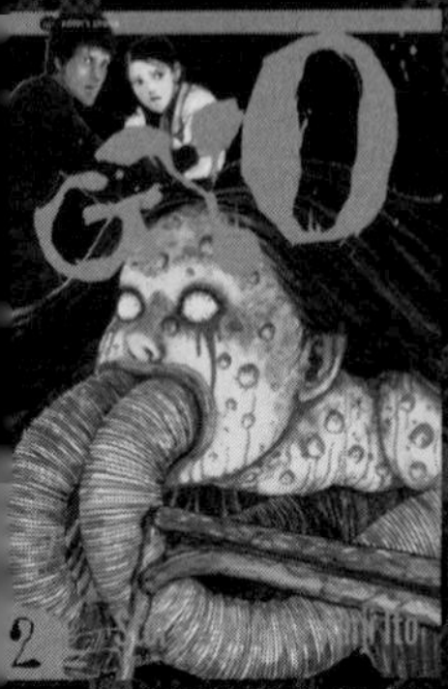
GYO
2
© 2002 Junji Ito/Shogakukan, Inc.

GYO

From the mind of Eisner-nominated artist Junji Ito comes GYO, a mind-searing horror master-work in which horribly mutated fish and sea creatures invade, en masse, a seaside town... Young couple Tadashi and Kaori are on vacation in Okinawa, but their vacation deteriorates as a strange, legged fish appears on the scene. So begins the intrepid couple's spiral into the horror of the sea.

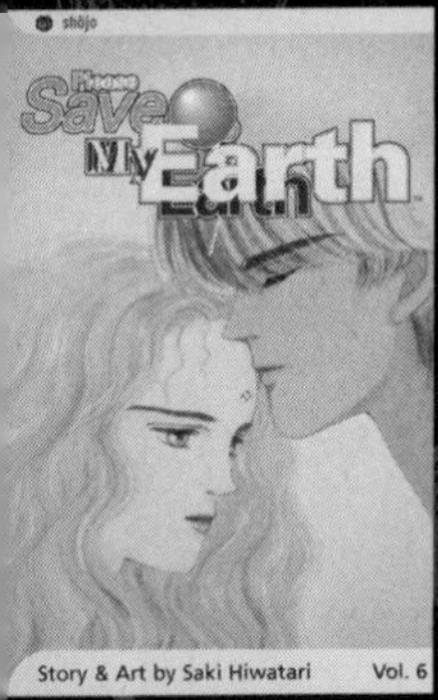
shōjo
Please Save My Earth
Story & Art by Saki Hiwatari
Vol. 6
© Saki Hiwatari 1988/HAKUSENSHA, Inc.

PLEASE SAVE MY EARTH

Saki Hiwatari's tale of love, loss and reincarnation is part science fiction, part fantasy. Seven scientists from a distant planet realize they've been reborn on Earth as teenagers when they discover they're all having the same dreams.

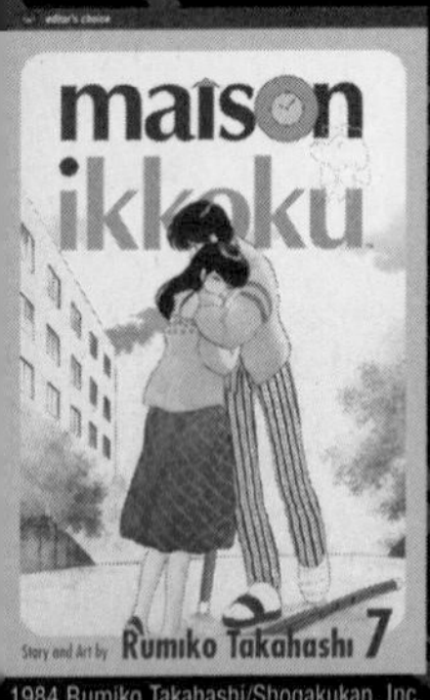
maison ikkoku
Story and Art by Rumiko Takahashi
7
1984 Rumiko Takahashi/Shogakukan, Inc.

MAISON IKKOKU

This sweetly comedic Rumiko Takahashi favorite is billed as "the story of a boy, a girl, and the drunken roomates who live to interfere..." Bashful college student Yusaku is madly in love with Kyoko, the widowed manager of his apartment building, Maison Ikkoku. However, the other Maison Ikkoku residents—a motley crew of volatile personalities—can't resist meddling in their affairs.

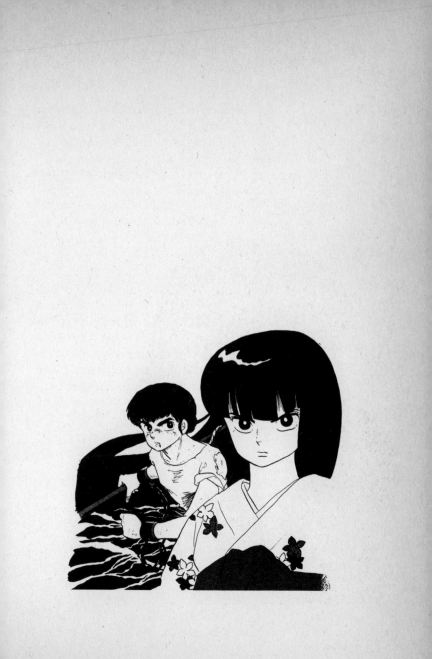

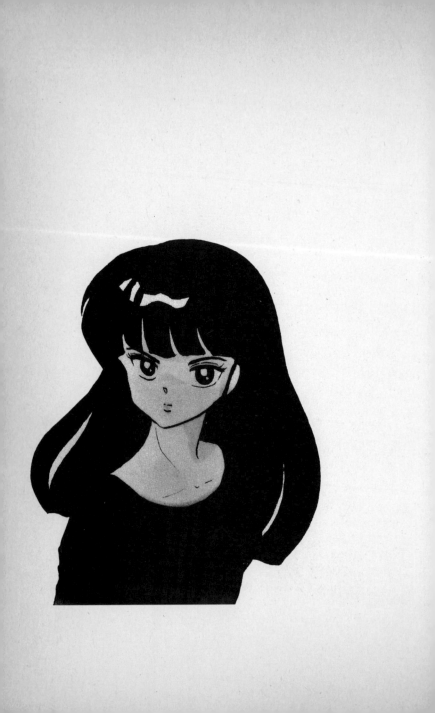

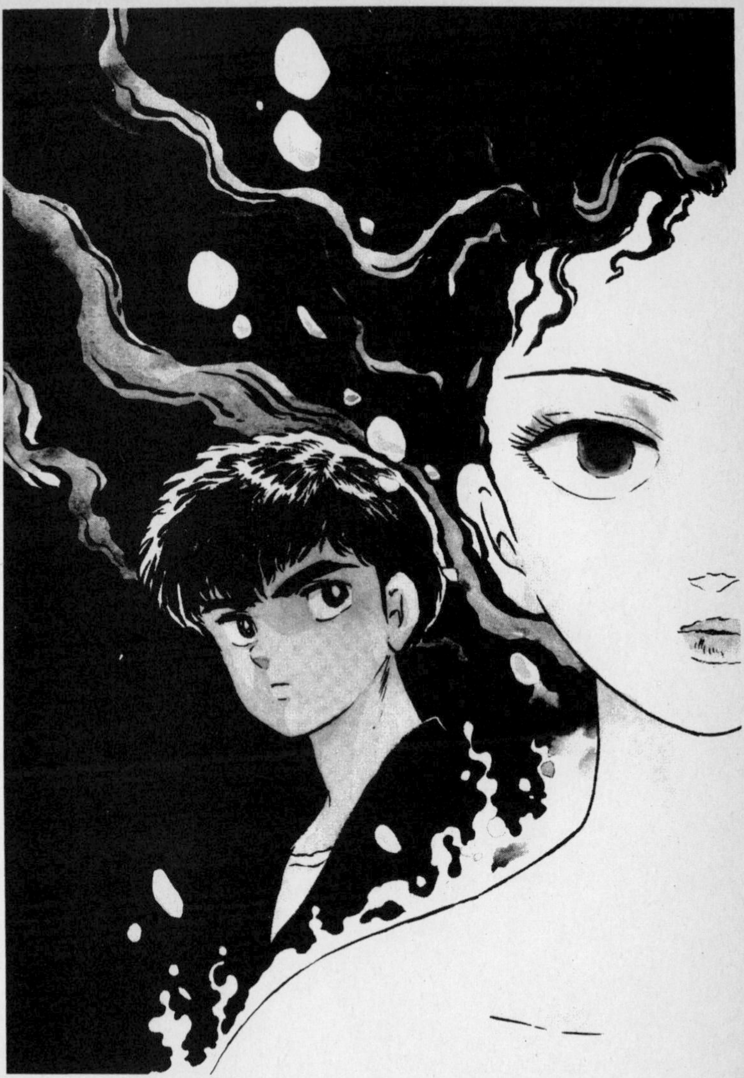

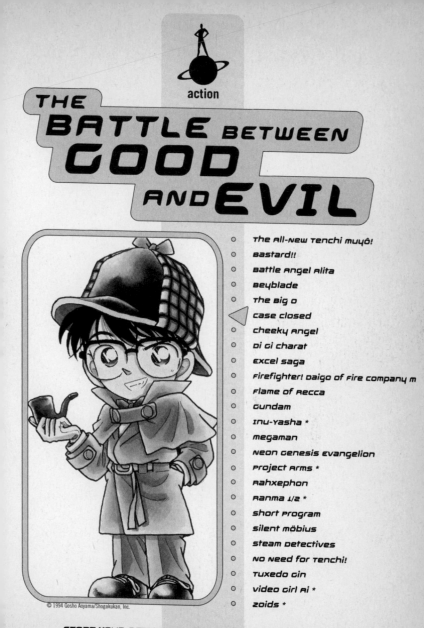
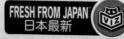

"Takahashi's best gift might be that of characterization...it's no wonder these stories are so universally loved."
—*Courtesy of Amazon.com. All rights reserved.*

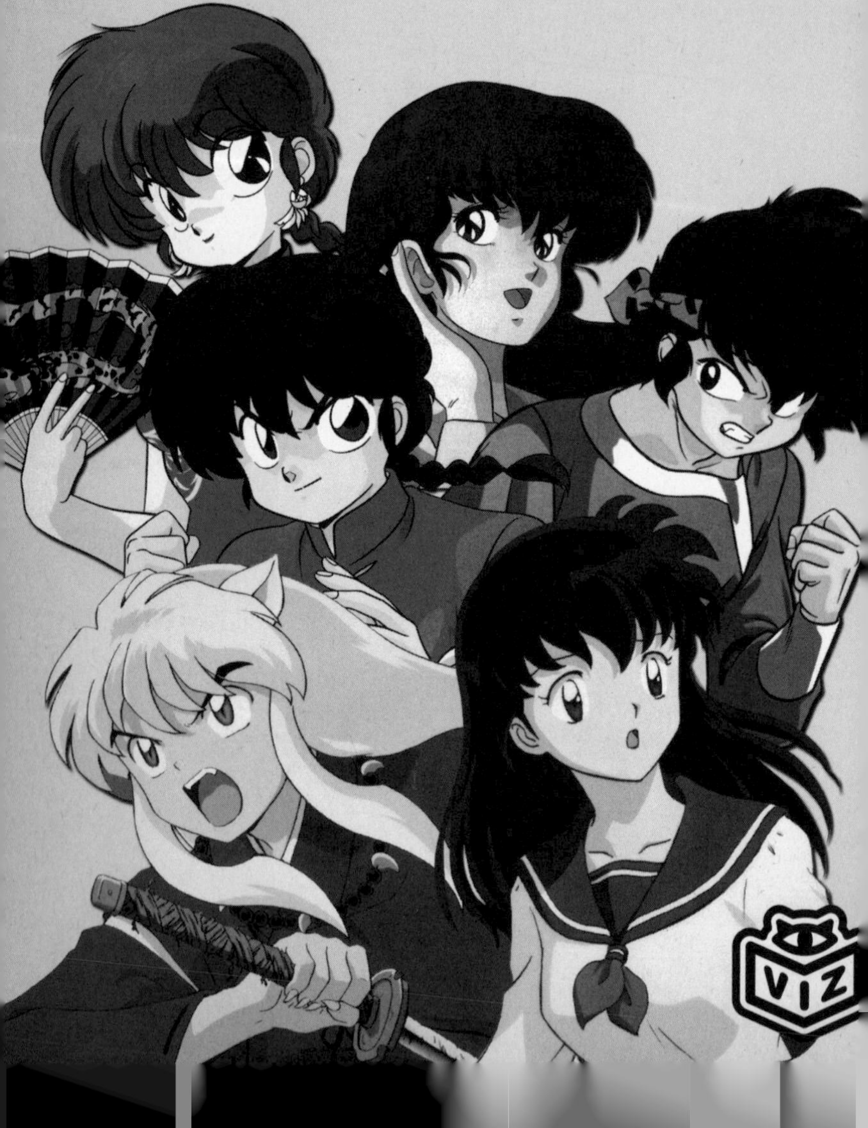
VIZ

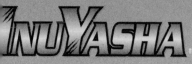
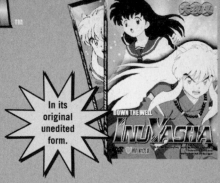
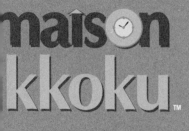
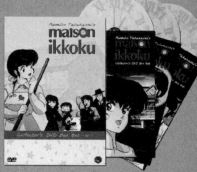
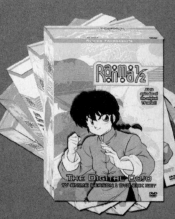

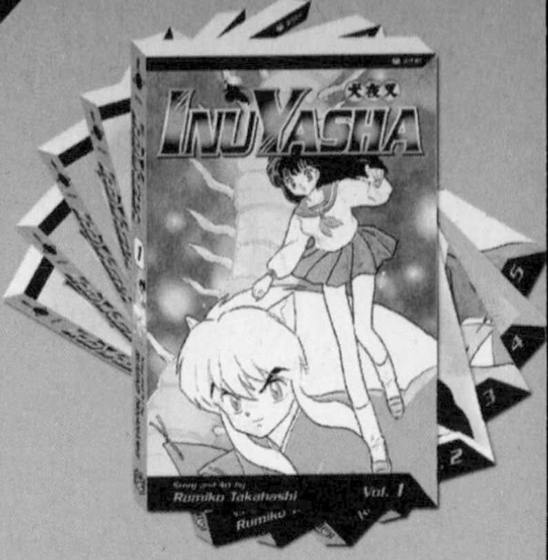

InuYasha
Rumiko Takahashi
Vol. 1

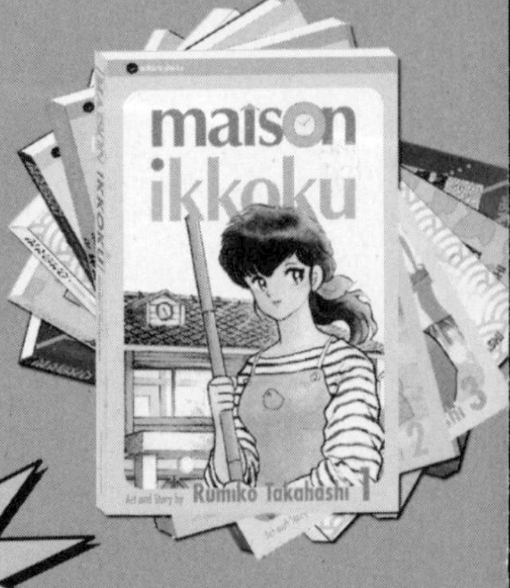

maison ikkoku
Art and Story by Rumiko Takahashi 1

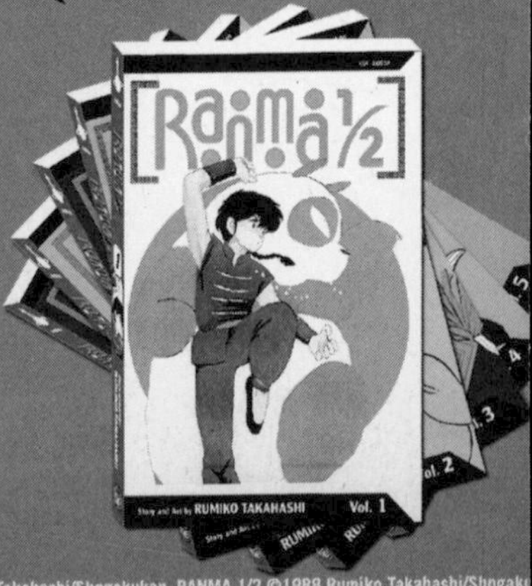

Ranma 1/2
Story and Art by RUMIKO TAKAHASHI
Vol. 1

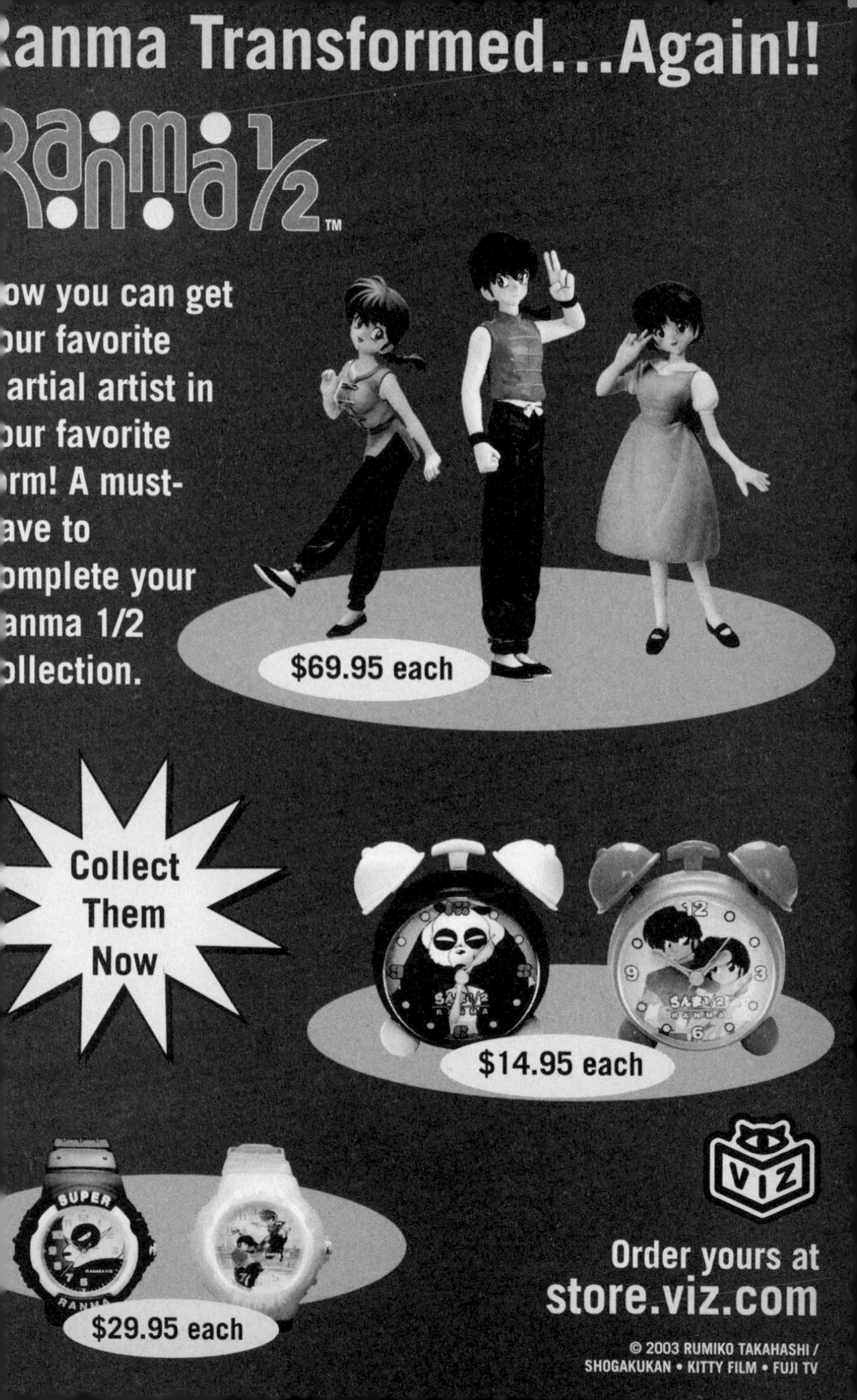

anma Transformed...Again!!
anma 1/2™
ow you can get
our favorite
artial artist in
our favorite
rm! A must-
ave to
omplete your
anma 1/2
ollection.
$69.95 each
Collect Them Now
$14.95 each
SUPER
$29.95 each
VIZ
Order yours at
store.viz.com
© 2003 RUMIKO TAKAHASHI / SHOGAKUKAN • KITTY FILM • FUJI TV

COMPLETE OUR SURVEY AND LET US KNOW WHAT YOU THINK!

☐ Please do NOT send me information about VIZ products, news and events, special offers, or other information.

☐ Please do NOT send me information from VIZ's trusted business partners.

Name: _____

Address: _____

City: _____ **State:** _____ **Zip:** _____

E-mail: _____

☐ **Male** ☐ **Female** **Date of Birth** (mm/dd/yyyy): ___ / ___ / ___ (Under 13? Parental consent required)

What race/ethnicity do you consider yourself? (please check one)

☐ Asian/Pacific Islander ☐ Black/African American ☐ Hispanic/Latino

☐ Native American/Alaskan Native ☐ White/Caucasian ☐ Other: _____

What VIZ product did you purchase? (check all that apply and indicate title purchased)

☐ DVD/VHS _____

☐ Graphic Novel _____

☐ Magazines _____

☐ Merchandise _____

Reason for purchase: (check all that apply)

☐ Special offer ☐ Favorite title ☐ Gift

☐ Recommendation ☐ Other _____

Where did you make your purchase? (please check one)

☐ Comic store ☐ Bookstore ☐ Mass/Grocery Store

☐ Newsstand ☐ Video/Video Game Store ☐ Other: _____

☐ Online (site: _____)

What other VIZ properties have you purchased/own? _____

_____

How many anime and/or manga titles have you purchased in the last year? How many were VIZ titles? (please check one from each column)

ANIME
- [ ] None
- [ ] 1-4
- [ ] 5-10
- [ ] 11+

MANGA
- [ ] None
- [ ] 1-4
- [ ] 5-10
- [ ] 11+

- [ ] 11+

I find the pricing of VIZ products to be: (please check one)

- [ ] Cheap
- [ ] Reasonable
- [ ] Expensive

What genre of manga and anime would you like to see from VIZ? (please check two)

- [ ] Adventure
- [ ] Comic Strip
- [ ] Science Fiction
- [ ] Fighting
- [ ] Horror
- [ ] Romance
- [ ] Fantasy
- [ ] Sports

What do you think of VIZ's new look?

- [ ] Love It
- [ ] It's OK
- [ ] Hate It
- [ ] Didn't Notice
- [ ] No Opinion

Which do you prefer? (please check one)

- [ ] Reading right-to-left
- [ ] Reading left-to-right

Which do you prefer? (please check one)

- [ ] Sound effects in English
- [ ] Sound effects in Japanese with English captions
- [ ] Sound effects in Japanese only with a glossary at the back

THANK YOU! Please send the completed form to:

NJW Research
42 Catharine St.
Poughkeepsie, NY

Santa Fe Springs City Library
11700 Telegraph Road
Santa Fe Springs, CA 90670

All information provided will be used for internal purposes only. We promise not to sell or otherwise divulge your information.